God's Other Book

God's Other Book

The Qurʾān Between History and Ideology

———

Mohammad Salama

UNIVERSITY OF CALIFORNIA PRESS

University of California Press
Oakland, California

Suggested citation: Salama, M. *God's Other Book: The Qurʾān Between History and Ideology*. Oakland: University of California Press, 2024.
DOI: https://doi.org/10.1525/luminos.202

Cataloging-in-Publication Data is on file at the Library of Congress.

ISBN 978–0–520–39184–0 (pbk.)
ISBN 978–0–520–39185–7 (ebook)

32 31 30 29 28 27 26 25 24
10 9 8 7 6 5 4 3 2 1

To Salma, Malachi, Aliya, and Noah

CONTENTS

ACKNOWLEDGMENTS

I would like to express my sincerest gratitude to the University of California Press, especially to Eric Schmidt, whose thoughtful direction, patience, and support have been instrumental. I am honored and fortunate that he gave me the opportunity to work with him. Eric exemplifies the true spirit of a visionary editor. UCP is lucky to have him. I am also grateful to Jyoti Arvey, whose guidance during the manuscript production process led to a smooth and reassuring publication. I am extremely grateful to Cindy Fulton, Senior Production Editor, and Paige MacKay, Senior Publishing Editor, for their exceptional guidance and meticulous attention to detail during the production and typesetting phases of this book.

Because I see this study as a corrective to the 1977 book *Hagarism*, the most ideologically pernicious study against the Qurʾān and Islam in recent memory, I initially offered the book to Cambridge University Press. While Cambridge warned me that some scholars would not be receptive of my ideas, and even cautioned that I would need to line up readers who would be open to my challenge to the status quo regarding the historiography of Islam, my argument was nevertheless clarified through my early interactions with Beatrice Rehl. I would like to thank her for her efforts. It was likewise fruitful for me to think with the comment by the member of the Cambridge Press Syndicate who said that the contrast I underscored regarding scholarship on the Qurʾān between Muslim and Euro-American scholars is "wholly unfair to the latter."

I am deeply grateful to scholars who have offered fruitful and stimulating feedback during the years it has taken me to complete this book. Asad Ahmed read early sections of this manuscript and provided invaluable insights, which pushed me to improve my argument and polish my thoughts. Devin Stewart read this work thoughtfully and provided enriching comments as well as important references.

I am immensely grateful to Devin for our correspondence, which made me discover our mutual love for Egyptian slang. Geert Jan (Gerard) van Gelder has offered me the most generous and attentive commentary on translation and transliteration of pre-Islamic poetry and the Qurʾān that I could have ever imagined. Words fail to express my indebtedness to him. John Turner read this manuscript in its entirety and offered rich comments that honed and enhanced my argument where I most needed direction and clarity. Likewise, I received insightful comments from Walid Saleh, Peter Gran, Maria Dakake, Stefan Sperl, Hany Rashwan, Christopher Livanos, Martin Winkler, Nathaniel Greenberg, Sayed Elsisi, and Dustin Cowell.

I would be remiss not to pay tribute to the accumulative thought across historical eras and geographical boundaries that gave substance to this study—specifically, to Egypt, the birthplace of my intellectual thinking, and to my teachers and professors of Arabic who instilled in me an unfathomable passion for pre-Islamic poetry and the literary aesthetics of the Qurʾān; to the University of Wisconsin-Madison, where I studied comparative literature and taught Arabic as a PhD candidate; to UC Berkeley, where I gave lectures on Arabic literature on numerous occasions, leaving me with wonderful memories of the exceptional kindness of my hosts; to San Francisco State University, where I taught numerous courses on modern and classical Arabic and Qurʾānic studies to many insightful students; to George Mason University, where I continue to teach and interact with outstanding students. My deep gratitude goes to Dr. Ann Ardis, professor of English and dean of the College of Humanities and Social Sciences (CHSS) at George Mason University, for her unfailing encouragement and generous research support to complete this study.

I have been immensely fortunate to have Benjamin Davis read and reread this manuscript. His sharp insight and intellectual generosity have made the argument of this book both sharper and easier to follow. I am grateful to colleagues, friends, and thought partners all over these places! Among the many to whom I owe a substantial debt of gratitude, let me mention only a few: Suzanne Stetkevych, Hanadi al-Samman, Alexander Key, Yasmeen Hanoosh, Abd al-Rahman Abd al-Salam, Aladdin Mahmoud, as well as the late and dearly missed Jaroslav Stetkevych. His absence is felt acutely.

I am thankful to the anonymous reviewers who spent time and intellectual effort reading this manuscript and helped me push my argument even further. I am also grateful to Gabriel Bartlett, who worked diligently to check the style and diacritical consistency throughout the manuscript. His timeliness and efficiency in meeting the submission deadline were remarkable.

My children, Salma, Malachi, Aliya, and Noah have been *the* source of inspiration behind this study. I am always reminded that leaving the world a better place is predicated on an old saying: "We don't inherit the earth from our ancestors; we borrow it from our children." May their world be more peaceful, more inclusive, and more tolerant than our own.

A NOTE ON TRANSLATION AND TRANSLITERATION

This book follows a specialized diacritical system for Arabic for all scholarly purposes. I use the standard Western spelling of terms that have entered the English language, such as "Islam" and "Arab." I also use anglicized country names. I use the noun "Qur'ān" instead of "Qur'an" and the adjective "Qur'ānic" instead of "Quranic" or "Qur'anic." The Prophet's name is transcribed as "Muḥammad" in the nominal form, "Muḥammadan" in the adjectival form, and is referred to either by his first name or as "the Prophet." I use the standard Library of Congress transliteration system for all other Arabic terms, with a few exceptions. In Arabic words such as ʿĀ'isha, the (ʿ) symbolizes the Arabic letter (ع) [ʿayn], while the (') symbolizes the glottal Arabic (ء أ إ و ئ) [*hamza*]. I do not use hamza (') in cases where the initial glottalization is obvious, e.g. "Aḥmad" or "Umayyad." An accented (á) symbolizes the form of *ism maqṣūr* written with *yá* (ى) or *alif maqṣūra* at the end of an Arabic word, as in "الأعشى" (al-Aʿshá). I kept the final long -*ā* written with *alif*, as in *dunyā* or *ʿaṣā* ("stick"), which is also a form of *ism maqṣūr* written with an *alif qāʾima* (a term used to distinguish -*ā* from -*á*, called *alif mamdūda*). This is an important distinction because many Arabists seem to think that only the form written with *yá* is called *alif maqṣūra*.

The definitive (ال) is fully transcribed as (Al-/al-) regardless of whether the following letters are *ḥurūf shamsiyya* or *ḥurūf qamariyya*. In genitive *iḍāfa* constructions, the pronounced (ة) is transcribed as a -*t*- between two nouns. Quotations from the Qur'ān, pre-Islamic Arabic poetry, and Arab-Muslim sources are kept in their original and translated into English between brackets within the sentence, or as block quotations as deemed necessary. Arabic words that have entered the English language (e.g., *Kaaba, qibla*) retain their English spelling. When it was necessary to transliterate a full case ending, in cases of *tanwīn* تَنوين, or nunation, the sign

"

(*-ūn*) indicating the nominative case, (*-ān*) indicating the accusative case, and (*-īn*) indicating the genitive case are all superscripted. Dagger alif, which is also known as symbolic alif, small alif, superscript alif, or historical alif, and which many or may not appear in Arabic script as a short vertical stroke on top of a consonant, is symbolized as a long /*ā*/ sound. For example: (هذا) [*hādhā*] or (الرَّحْمَـٰنِ) [*al-Raḥmān*]. The (ᵒ) at the end of a transcribed Arabic word such as the possessive pronoun in كتابه [his book] refers to Arabic words ending in an (h) (ᵒ) and not in a (ة), as commonly practiced. The final (ة) is not transcribed, as in سورة [*sūra*].

Throughout this study, I translate الله as God. All translations, or rather approximations, of verses from the Qurʾān into English are my own. These approximations are for context and explicatory matters only and are therefore not to constitute a basis for further scholarly investigations without consulting the original Arabic text of the Qurʾān, which may include myriad meanings beyond what I am able to capture in English. Unless otherwise noted, all other translations of pre-Islamic Arabic poetry and Arab-Muslim sources, as well of French and German sources, are my own.

Introduction

Primum Non Nocere

Today, as the concept of religion is receiving less attention in the secular academic world, Euro-American scholarship on the origins of Islam is experiencing an unusual surge. If postmodernity has finished the incomplete project of modernity by secularizing the public sphere, academia included, then what do we make of this renewed obsession with Islam's "origins"? Is there a connection between the academic rise of Qurʾānic studies starting in the 1960s, and, say, the decolonization of Arab/Muslim states, the rise of the Egyptian Muslim Brotherhood (1928–), the Iranian Islamic Revolution of 1979, the Salman Rushdie affair of the 1980s, or the events of 9/11? Did the accumulative ideological shaping of Islam as a threat to the West authorize Western historians of Islam to explain away the "problem" of Islam from exclusive and parochial perspectives? The position of Islam and, in particular, of Qurʾānic studies in the Western academy over the last five decades surely lends some credibility to these questions.

Addressing the status of contemporary Euro-American scholarship on the Qurʾān, Angelika Neuwirth comments that "apparently what is lacking is the hermeneutic corrective accumulated in the inner-Arabic linguistic-stylistic tradition."[1] This timely acknowledgement draws pointed attention to a yet-to-be addressed lacuna in approaching and understanding the Qurʾān. "At present," asserts Neuwirth, "historical Western research is only breathing with one lung, so to speak. The second lung, the *Arabicity and poeticity of the Qurʾān*, has not yet been utilized."[2] If the academic body of Qurʾānic studies wishes to remain healthy and to breathe fresh air, to dwell on the metaphor, it is high time to address this gap or, if I may put it this way, to heal this wound.

Engaging the Arabicity of the Qurʾān in Western research, however, is a task easier said than done. Neuwirth herself is deeply aware that her own work "demands an initial approach oriented to Biblical scholarship, if only to warrant an equal treatment for the Qurʾān and to 'synchronize' the three scriptures, to set their respective perceptions on the same level."[3] In other words, engaging this "hermeneutic corrective" with a focus on the Arabic language and the literary significations of the Qurʾān remains a desideratum that may have to wait until the most urgent task of repositioning Islam on equal footing with Judaism and Christianity is achieved. This repositioning is predicated, Neuwirth stresses, on the crooked line of first engaging with biblical scholarship in order to offer a fresh "European reading" and "a hope that her recent book [*Der Koran als Text der Spätantike. Ein europäischer Zugang* (published in an English translation by Oxford in 2019 as *The Qurʾan as a Text of Late Antiquity: A Shared Heritage*)] will make Western readers aware of the Qurʾān's close connection to an epoch that has been reclaimed for European identity."[4]

I examine the histories of the development of the new framing of the Qurʾān in what is called late antiquity in a separate chapter. For now, it is worth noting that late antiquity means different things for different scholars. Some employ late antiquity to revive Hagarism, which was an extreme and dangerous manipulation of historical sources. Proponents of such radical revisionism want to throw out all Arabic and Islamic sources as unreliable and to rely only on outside sources. There are two major problems with this approach. First, insiders often have better information than outsiders; secondly, the alternative scenarios they present are based on minimal evidence and are often just unscholarly. Others use late antiquity to revive Biblicism, a trend in Qurʾānic studies scholarship that sees the Qurʾān with biblical eyes and emphasizes the connections between the Qurʾān and Christianity in particular as a way of shedding light on some passages of the Qurʾān.

But so far, Neuwirth's approach to late antiquity has been the most involved. Her study is part of a series of recent attempts to explore the category of late antiquity as an "epistemic space" that *includes* Islam. The idea is to prompt Western readership to see for itself that the Qurʾān is part of the same late antique discourse that envelops the Jewish and Christian traditions commonly assumed to be an exclusive European heritage. But Neuwirth also admits that her work "is primarily an engagement with historically oriented Western research."[5] Hers is a project written with multiple goals in mind: it supports the notion that the Qurʾān must be understood in relationship to ancient Arabic poetry[6] in order to open a productive conversation between Muslim and Western scholarship on the Qurʾān, a conversation that has been deeply polarized and fractious.[7] It furthermore seeks to educate Western audiences, teaching them that the "Europeanness" of the Qurʾān is not a fantasy but a remarkable shared history that can be appreciated if only scholars apply a more inclusive epistemic space regarding late antique times.[8] Neuwirth is quite successful in achieving the last of these sundry and ambitious goals. In her over five hundred-page volume, she dedicates a pithy chapter (chapter 12, "The Qur'ān and Poetry") to what she refers to as the Arabic "poeticity" of the Qur'ān. This is a promising endeavor, even though the formidable task of engaging with biblical criticism has exhausted the bulk of her study.

Neuwirth also hoped her book could have something "to say to Muslim readers."[9] Who are these readers? With over two billion Muslims in the world today—concentrated mostly in twenty-three Asian and African countries (to count only the ones where Islam is a state religion) and including a sizable population spread across the Americas, Australia, and Europe—Muslim readers cannot be seen to constitute a monolithic whole. If by "Muslim readers" Neuwirth is referring to more specialized readers and practitioners of orthodox Islam, or traditional scholars of the Sunni and Shia persuasions, then her effort has had a limited effect, largely because her book stays within an accumulated body of Western scholarship, which, Neuwirth would admit, follows a historical-critical method familiar with an extensive hermeneutic tradition of biblical criticism. The constitutive tenets of Neuwirth's study thus remain faithful to the "first lung," so to speak, at least as that lung is outlined in the book's original German title, *Ein europäischer Zugang* (A European approach). Even the exhaustive list of the works consulted in this enormous undertaking makes scant references to Arab-Muslim scholars and texts (e.g., al-Jāḥiẓ, al-Jurjānī, Khalafallah), references that remain inconsequential in the heavy-handed thirty-eight-page bibliography of biblical scholarship. In its totality, then, Neuwirth's book subjects the Qur'ān simply to Western scholars who talk about other Western scholars, Western thought, and Western texts.

I speak more about the Qur'ān's literary signification and Arabicity in the book's later chapters, but a central goal of this study is also to offer an academic contextualization of late antiquity as a contested period in history. This important contextualization is absent from Neuwirth's study, understandably, because she not only thinks of late antiquity as an epistemologically enriching space; she is also positing "a radical turn of perspective," one that will entail "repos[ing] the question of the historical anchoring of the Qur'an in time and place."[10] This drastic shift will necessarily mean (and it is hard not to see the Eurocentrism here) that Muslim readers will cease to read the Qur'ān in hagiographic terms—that is, as part of the life of the prophet, which has always been the case in the Islamic tradition since the seventh century. Instead, situating the Qur'ān "*historically* [emphasis hers] as a document of 'community formation' within a sectarian milieu', a landscape of debate, of arguments fought out between diverse groups, Christians, Jews, and pagans alike"[11] will give it a European stamp, lend it an authentic "voice," and make it "recognizable as a European legacy."[12]

But if the Qur'ān did not offer itself as a linguistic rival to the seventh-century Meccan society, with all its orators and poets, then what do we make of the entire corpus of *Jāhilī* poetry and of *āyāt al-taḥaddī* (challenge verses in the Qur'ān, such as 10:38, 11:13, 52:34)? What do we make of prophetic hagiography, not necessarily the *Sīra*, but the biographical references to Muḥammad in the Qurʾān? What do we do with *asbāb al-nuzūl* (promptings of revelations) and the *iʿjāz* tradition? What do we do the work of al-Jāḥiẓ? What do we make of the inner-Islamic exegesis, when just a terse reading of postclassical scholars like al-Khaṭṭābī, al-Rummānī, al-Bāqillānī, and al-Jurjānī would show how the *balāgha* (rhetorical eloquence/ distinctiveness) of the Qurʾān is not merely a ninth-century theological invention but a culmination of literary thought and a theorization of a stylistic mode that offered itself to a culture deeply immersed in its own poetic achievements? In this very context, the Qurʾān presents itself as serving a dualistic function to this very culture. First, it acts in a manner that lends itself to ordinary human self-perception both linguistically, within the familiar tradition of Quraysh's finely tuned dialect of classical Arabic, especially in its earlier phases, and anthropologically, within the defined sociocultural framework of the seventh-century Arabian Peninsula. Many verses in the Qurʾān (e.g., 44:58, 26:195) emphasize the clarity of its Arabic as well as the accessibility of its content. Secondly, the Qurʾān does not shy away from underscoring and celebrating its rhetorical distinctiveness, of claiming itself both as unparalleled and as inimitable by its own community. Yet, whereas this textual dualism takes place *within* a determined linguistic and cultural milieu, ignoring this all-assertive dialectical mode and its rhetorical power is bound to continue reducing the cognitive perception of the Qurʾān text to a banal historical generality and, consequently, to a lack of common ground not only with Muslim readers but also with global scholarship on Islam, including linguists, philologists, rhetoricians, as well as literary and cultural critics.

If Muslim readers, or more specifically European Muslim readers, were to infer something from Neuwirth's book, it would be that a scholar of Qurʾānic studies has surgically identified a malady in Western Europe's approach to the Qurʾān. To cure this malady, she offers a treatment, via self-critique, of an accumulated heritage of historical biases bent on othering and excluding Islam. Neuwirth's treatment comes from history, an offering of an alternative history, or rather, a different viewing of European history as a space for confronting one's own prejudices and repositioning the place of Islam in Europe. Late antiquity comes to Neuwirth's mind as a perfect remedy: a remedial transitional space that bridges the quintessentially European (the founding legacy of Western Europe) with the quintessentially Qurʾānic (the founding text of Islam), all the while prioritizing a way of reading that is at once remediating and perpetuating our forgetting. Nothing could put an end to old acrimonies or wipe away chronic hostilities better than realizing that Islam and the West have more in common than anyone could have ever thought. In this "shared heritage," the entangled histories of Mediterranean studies (long before modernity/globalization) would happily link Europe to Africa to Asia, and Judaism to Christianity to Islam, and the "gehört der Islam zu Deutschland/Europa?" (does Islam belong to Germany/Europe?) debate will finally be laid to rest. What does such a remedy defer and forget as it selectively heals and remembers? What histories, told by whom, are lost in such a narrative cut?

As much as it is a remedy and an offering, late antiquity is also a scapegoat and a sacrifice. The political unconscious of the return to late antiquity reveals a deep layer of scholarly concern. There is a desire for a new discourse and a need for stopping the persistent othering of Islam—even and especially the insidious othering that occurs through hierarchy-maintaining forms of inclusion—that is often practiced by a systematic network active on numerous sociopolitical levels, including the very field of Qurʾānic studies.[13] This othering was as true in precolonial and colonial metanarratives of the European nation-states as it is true today, and it is particularly evident in the burgeoning of publication industries and a revitalized academic press market focused on Islam in the aftermath of 9/11 in what Manuel Castells aptly identifies as the "new geopolitics" of the "informationalism" concomitant with "the rise of the network society."[14] Many Euro-American scholars of the Qurʾān will admit that both the literary interpretations of the Qurʾān have been silenced in their field and the less inclusive scholarship on Islam has been put into place and practiced uncritically for decades. Muslim readers would be eager to learn why this is the case—why ancient Arabic culture, Arabic sources in general, the Qurʾān and its literary significations continue to be entombed and marginalized, even after the argument against the authenticity of pre-Islamic literature was laid to rest years ago. As a postcolonial Muslim reader myself, I would even ask harder questions about what always gets sacrificed in the relationship between self and other. Such questions matter because the unchallenged and impressionable tone of approaches to the Qurʾān *as* a text of late antiquity may itself not have the same intent, and indeed may obscure the fact that the concept of the political at work in most Western narratives of historical "formations" or "reformations" of other cultures has always been contingent on the authority of a dominant theory of knowledge.

The scope of Euro-American revisionism may offer no space for the local and the indigenous. In addition, Arab-Muslim texts—those of exegetes, biographers, and historians—have received little to no value in addressing their own tradition, often dismissed as too "faith-based" to gain admission into the skeptical mind of the Western historian. But rather than question the futility of searching for historical origins in all religions, we run the risk of dissolving indigenous histories into global melting pots in order to nurse the fragile sensibilities of an idea of Europe and of a "Europeanness" that refuses to respond to the other unless that response proceeds through colossal epistemological oversight, which, if corrected, would allow Europe to see that the other was never really an "other" after all, and that Europe, when it comes to Islam, has always been an ever-expanded and gratified self.

This is precisely the moment when the staging of history, of late antiquity in this instance, could turn into a dialectic: on the one hand, it would seek to course-correct and expand the horizons of Europe's perception of Islam, thus fixing the one operating lung of Qurʾānic studies; on the other, it would continue, albeit unwittingly, to submerge the other in the very act of acknowledging its absence. In the case of Islam, the other is not just a scripture, but a language, a culture, a skin color, a heritage, and a literature. Even if we were to assume that this *Denkraum* was always already there, obfuscated by nationalist and separatist inventions of history, could this historical *Aufklärung* restore the second lung to Qurʾānic studies? If Islam were no longer the other of Europe, then what would become of it? What would happen to the other after the disappearance of its otherness? What would be the fate of its accumulated excisions and erasures, its "negative theology," and its silenced traditions? What would the Muslim readers expect if the study of the Qurʾān were to reemerge as an empirical boomerang in Western historical literature? If a deeper look into the thicket of late antiquity would reveal a "European Qurʾān," so to speak, how would this new identity reimagine the Qurʾān's Arabicity, with all its variegated fabrics of aesthetic weight and literary merit?

A point that might be obvious for the critically minded scholar of the Qurʾān is still worth emphasizing: historians have an academic responsibility to let the chips of their research fall where they may, even if the findings are to the displeasure of Muslim readers. Some Muslims readers may tend to accept uncritically certain versions of their sacred past, but this is not binding for historians who must follow a well-defined method and arrive at conclusions supported by evidence, be it tangible or conceptual. The issue is not the findings, but the very *method* employed in reaching those findings. The challenge in repositioning the Western academy's hardened epistemological lines indeed lies in the fact that scholarship on the Qurʾān in the West is often conducted by dedicated and well-trained scholars who may not see or even understand the need for a "second lung" outside a dominant brand of scholarship. They follow the footsteps of their mentors and advisors in applying sophisticated historical methodologies to continue to examine the same issues that have shaped the field for the last hundred years: debunking Muslims sources; finding alternative theories to the genesis of Islam in lieu of traditional Muslim accounts; rewriting Islam's early history; revising the life of Muḥammad; reshuffling the history of the compilation of the Qurʾān; rearranging chronological order of *suwar* (chapters of the Qurʾān); relocating the Qurʾān's *a ʾjamī* (non-Arabic) vocabulary; and, most famously, analyzing the Qurʾān with biblical lens.

Two methods I want to problematize briefly are "source studies" and the historical-critical method. Recent scholarship that underscores the Arabicity of the Qurʾān continues to be sidelined if not effectively colonized by the Western academy's obsession with extra-peninsular "source studies."[15] Source studies proceed through locating non-Arabic influential texts outside the Qurʾān's first community or positing, à la Gerald Hawting, that the Qurʾān was addressing an imaginary community. One example of this method is Bronwen Neil's seminal article on John of Damascus and Theophanes the Confessor as the earliest known non-Muslim "historians" of Islam. In this article, Neil cautions against what she calls "the dyothelite and iconophile biases" of Syriac authors.[16] Neil admits that historians are fortunate to have in *De haeresibus* and the *Chronographia* two exceptional witnesses to early Greek understandings of Islam. But she pulls no punches in underscoring the completely different genres and perspectives of these two texts. "The differences between them," concludes Neil, "should alert us to the dangers of characterizing early Islam on the basis of evidence provided by Greek Christians, even if they were near contemporaries of the events they sought to understand and represent."[17] The second example comes from two twenty-first century edited volumes on the Qur'ān: Jane Dammen McAuliffe's *The Cambridge Companion to the Qur'ān* and Andrew Rippin's *The Blackwell Companion to the Qur'an*.[18] None of these studies of the Qur'ān makes the slightest reference to the internal dynamics of the Qur'ān's literary language or to pre-Islamic poetry as a significant prehistory to the text.[19]

A further example of a work that effectively deconstructs the historical-critical method is Herbert Schneidau's book on the Bible and Western tradition. The last chapter of Schneidau's book deconstructs the structural dilemmas involved in twentieth-century historical positivism: "It congratulates itself on being liberated from theologization, while its very notions of 'reality' and 'truth' are, fairly obviously, covert theologization."[20] Yet from a disciplinary point of view, these issues in the field of Qur'ānic studies are not, as I explain in this work, simply extraneous or mythological details that it is a historian's privilege to ignore or to dismiss but rather fundamental limitations that return to take their toll on a methodology that has been sacralized for far too long. This methodology merely suspends the literary and linguistic ontology of the Qur'ān text for the sake of extrapeninsular and European epistemological postulates, while reinforcing the old self/other dichotomy that was at the root of the fallacies of classical orientalism. What is perhaps only now becoming clear, at least as we deduce it from Neuwirth's call, is that it is high time we confronted the intellectual harm that has resulted from the willful entombment of the other and replaced it with a new philosophy of inclusivity. But instead of thawing the other in the self, I would make a call for renewed responsible thought, which would celebrate the authentic heritages of alien traditions.

Additionally, there is a grave problem of reductionism in studying the heritage of Islam, a reductionism exercised on language and resources. This explains the one-lunged approach to Qur'ānic studies and the dearth of a dialogue between the two camps. How can Muslim readers be asked to engage in a historical method that consistently dehumanizes them and marginalizes the Qur'ān's preformative tradition and local language, while expecting them to learn the "language" of this method's historical-critical reading? If Muslim readers were to adopt this imposed "language" in approaching their own scripture, then the West, once again, is dictating the rules of the game, owning the terrain, and imposing its own norms and values on that dialogue. Having a sense of conviction in writing historical research matters, but it is just as important that this writing come from an ethical position of fairness to the other. Writing with the conviction that the results of historical-critical research on Islam are not influenced by ideologies or political worldviews, and assuming that one's findings come from a place of objective investigation will never resolve the divide in the East-West academic approaches to the Qur'ān.

I am suggesting that religion does not yield itself to a closed off historical totality. No historical method can strip it off its linguistic, rhetorical, traditional, and conceptual referents. The only true history is a history that perpetually questions itself. What we now have instead, and what the field of Qur'ānic studies needs to overcome, is a type of knowledge entitled by hegemonic political and historical discourses to lay claim to what is an "original" and what is a "false" source of Islam's history. If the field cannot overcome this epistemology, it will descend into a Hades of academic troopers too preoccupied with their own telescopic approaches to history to see the blind spots. Ideology is exactly the belief that we are using the right critical tools to debunk a historical myth and engage in a criticism of a myth, unaware that our own "historical methods," so to speak, have their own mythical history, a history that darkly and deeply exposes the fallacy of its own criticism—that is, the myth of guarding a fundamentalist "strategic" truth and perpetuating a deep state of epistemological sovereignty over the other.

One objective of this book is to rethink the current methodology in the production of scholarship on the Qur'ān in the Euro-American academy. It also makes a call for situating the future of Qur'ānic studies within a functional code of knowledge. Such a future will necessitate relinquishing the tools of the historical-critical method that have accompanied the field since the nineteenth century. Historical positivism does not operate from scientifically verified facts, but rather from a scientism—namely, a postulate that there is a clear and straightforward access to the past against which we must measure our thought. This is not to say that historical positivism has not corrected certain methodological errors. But it tends to assume that only the thinking and the scholarship of a certain strand of historians has somehow been usefully guided by the application of this standard, while Muslim scholarship and Arab-Muslim sources are dismissed as tainted with "faith" and superstition.

In order for a "second lung" to function at all, it would need the support of other systems—different scholarly tools, different academic training, and different linguistic and critical approaches to the Qur'ān. How, then, should one understand the place of the Qur'ān in history? The answer to this question is not vague: by engaging fully with the text itself, examining its historical eventfulness, analyzing its literary, phonological and syntactical codes, and probing its pre-formative native literature, namely, the enormous tradition of pre-Islamic poetry. One does not expect here a full rounded analysis of, say, *Masā'il Nāfi' ibn al-Azraq* (Questions of Nāfi' ibn al-Azraq),[21] or *Lughāt al-Qabā'il al-Wārida fī al-Qur'ān* (Tribal dialects in the Qur'ān),[22] or even *Sirr Ṣinā'-t- al-I'rāb* (Genesis of [Arabic] phonemes).[23] The idea is to examine the largely unstudied local environment of the Qur'ān and explore possible correlations between its Meccan and Medinan themes as well as the social habits and manners of pre-Islamic Arabs. Despite the obvious historical, geographical, and linguistic correspondences between the Qur'ān and pre-Islamic Arabic literature, this aspect is hardly ever approached in Euro-American scholarship on the Qur'ān.

A critically engaged exegesis of pre-Islamic poetry would reveal that pre-Qur'ānic Arabs were nomadic communities with their own sets of beliefs.[24] Even though the belief in a certain "earthly" eternity was common among them, they may have not necessarily envisioned a life after death in the manner, say, in which the Qur'ān portrays it, which is also radically different from the manner in which both Judaism and Christianity depict the hereafter. Pre-Islamic Arabs had communal vices that ranged from *tijāra-t-al-raqīq* (slave trade) to *ẓulm* (social inequities/injustices) to *shuḥḥ* (avarice) to *ʿunṣuriyya* (racialism/racism), vices that were normalized and accepted among pre-Islamic Arabs but that the Qur'ān, with its strong penchant for social justice, vehemently criticizes. But pre-Islamic poetry also celebrates virtues that include *muruwwa* (chivalry, virtue), *fakhr* (pride, mostly tribal), *ḥamāsa* (warrior spirit of heroism) *shajāʿa* (courage/gallantry), *karam* (generosity/benevolence), *ḥaqq al-ḍayf* (right of guest/hospitality), *ḥaqq al-jār* (right of neighbor), and *wafāʾ* (loyalty/fulfilment of promise), traits that Islam was soon to overturn and integrate into more wholistic and socially cohesive values. It does not take long to see these habits represented in pre-Islamic poetry and interpellated in the Qur'ān. Nor does it take long to see how the Qur'ān enters into focused dialogues with this community, both in the Meccan and Medinan periods, valorizing social justice, acknowledging the literary and poetic sensibility of pagan Arabs, but also critiquing and distinguishing itself from it. In verse after verse, the Qur'ān confirms the spiritual tendencies of pre-Islamic Arabs, confronts their polytheistic propensities, and offers a monotheistic alternative to a folk tradition with an enormous appetite for divinity. This dialogic tension, which is clearly articulated in the Qur'ān, is crucial for explaining the tectonic shift in ideals and the revolutionary transformation of social relationships in the first Muslim community as it moved from a society loyal to tribal and blood solidarity to an *umma* regulated by an overpowering oral authority.

To understand the Qur'ān's oral authority, which for secular criticism remains one of history's most compelling linguistic invitations, not only is it necessary to learn of its rhetorical power but it is also important to dwell on its thematic consistency. For how can one really assess a text that emphatically challenges its own community to bring forth something like it in content and in form when one does not know how that language works or what it looks like? And how can one begin to evaluate—much less enjoy—the masterpieces of ancient Arabic literature and the overshadowing *balāgha* of the Qur'ān without having the basic understanding of its composite language and central themes? Reliance on the written and translated words of the Qur'ān certainly has its use, but it must not be the only way of approaching the text. Certainly there is a distinction between a scholarly demand of studying a text in its original language and methodological nativism. No graduate student would be allowed to write a dissertation on Hegel's *Phenomenology of Spirit* without possessing a reading knowledge of German, and no such dissertation would pass its defense without some knowledge of Protestantism and the broader social/religious context from which Hegel's book emerged. Further, it is no secret that even the most celebrated and "enlightened" European translations of the Qur'ān—including that of the seventeenth-century orientalist Ludovico Marracci (d. 1700), in which he relied on major *tafsīr* (explication) sources like *Itqān*–continue to cause confusion and misunderstanding about the Qur'ān and its message.[25] Even a competent, integral, and content-oriented modern translation like that of Marmaduke Pickthall (d. 1930) will always irretrievably fail to capture the full significations of the original text. This does not mean that the Qur'ān is not "translatable." It certainly is. But the constitutive orality of the text—the intricate relationship between its parts and the beauty of its language," whose sound, to use Annemarie Schimmel's words, "defines the space in which the Muslim lives" and "moves people even when they don't understand the word"—demands a level of engagement from a scholar fully conscious of the text's literary power and rhetorical eloquence.[26]

To be clear, this book is not a vote for resurrecting the late dogma of *iʿjāz al-Qurʾān*, which is yet to be taken seriously in Western scholarship anyway. Nor is it a vote for denigrating varied theoretical positions on the Qur'ān, or for exceptionalism, for that matter. One must not conflate the linguistically unique with the theologically exceptional. The Qur'ān specifically states that Muḥammad is one among many prophets who preceded him,[27] and that his call for monotheism is not at all exceptional, rather an iteration of a long chain of historical pleas for the one God, enjoined to Noah, Abraham, Moses, and Jesus.[28] If anything, Euro-American scholarship has telescoped various historical revisions into the genesis of the Qur'ān, which can only accentuate a more profound perpetuity of "Western exceptionalism" in probing Islam's past. This is pertinent to the literary argument because my intention is also to give the simplest academic explanation of how a seventh-century Arabian audience would have understood the language of the Qur'ān as it was directly addressed to them, a basic matter that was complicated, diverted, and redirected by the field of Qur'ānic studies.

As I explain in this study, late antiquity promises an overhaul of traditional approaches to the Christian West and a free hybridity of religiocultural exchanges. It nurses Syriac Christianity and embraces Judaism, Manicheanism, Zoroastrianism, Neoplatonism, and Islam as collective participants in a powerful overflow of the God idea. For all these reasons, it could be exciting because it offers European readers something new. But for the same reasons, it could also be eclipsing because Muslim readers may fear that it may offer them nothing new, especially if it "includes" Islamic heritage as an ancillary to Europe's own grand and expansive historical narrative, an "inclusion" already undergirded by a discourse that serves to control the history of the other. In balance, the epistemic space of late antiquity promises to bring equity among the three Abrahamic religions, treating Islam on equal footing with Judaism and Christianity. This indeed is a welcome turn, no doubt, especially when it has been rare in current Euro-American scholarship to read the Qur'ān as authentic rather than as a derivative byproduct. But what guarantees the Muslim readers, whom Neuwirth genuinely hopes to include, that positioning the Qur'ān within Europe's own narratives of historiography is not yet another variation on the old theme of erasing their own heritage? It is no secret that the field of Qur'ānic studies is confronting an enormous academic divide, which has certainly been anticipated since the 1970s, but which has until today become almost irremediable. Neuwirth has tried to start a conversation between those opposing poles, but her argument for the Arabicity of the Qur'ān, though acknowledged, has still fallen flat.

Such well-intended postulates are also faithful to the exigencies and dictates of a long-standing historical tradition that interpreted the Qur'ān (mostly in translation) from the perspective of Western canonical exegesis. It is not surprising that many eminent Western scholars of the Qur'ān today hail from the tradition of biblical criticism. There is nothing wrong with applying the tools of one's academic training in a certain religious tradition to another, especially if this other intentionally draws on and makes reference to it—in fact, I am deeply in favor of such methodological crossings when they proceed through a reflexive attention to the histories and hierarchies in which they are always already situated. However, one must not stop there. While such scholarship is itself faithful in projecting a European comparative understanding of the Qur'ān, the production of such understanding has yet to connect with, and not just passingly acknowledge, what *Islamic* linguistic and rhetorical scholarship of the Qur'ān has established about it over the last fourteen centuries. This connection, in my view, is an indispensable condition for securing a minimal understanding of the Qur'ān text and its rich tradition. At this juncture in our global history, a literary and rhetorical reading of the text of the Qur'ān—one that goes outside all canonized readings—would shed light on long-neglected corners in Qur'ānic studies, precisely because this reading will pay attention to what the Qur'ān has to say linguistically, figuratively, and rhetorically, but also socially, politically, and culturally, about itself and the organic environment in which it emerged.

This book is thus written in the same spirit of bridging the East-West polarity in Qur'ānic studies. It argues that the field of Qur'ānic studies in the West may have reached a saturation juncture of academic reification and historical self-adoration, to a point that makes it difficult to repudiate its tools for the sake of a precarious and uncharted alternative. It further argues that the historical-critical method did not simply trap the academic potential of Qur'ānic studies in a dark corner but became itself entangled in its own compulsion toward exclusivism and hegemony. In the same vein, this book calls for, and exercises, a literary and linguistic approach to the text of the Qur'ān as a material reality and as an occurrence that must be treated dialectically—the Qur'ān as an oral text that can be celebrated just as much as it has been met with silence, apprehension, and anxiety. To a great extent, the Qur'ān actually celebrates and performs a comparative theology *extraordinaire* and in no way simply eschews the monotheistic ethos outside its geographical contours. This rich spirit of comparativity that I expound in this book has even allowed classical Muslim philosophers to find affinities and inspiration in European thought, which is at any rate hard to define when we think that, for instance, the *Corpus Aristotelicum* owes most of its survival and recovery to classical and medieval Arab-Muslim authors and translators. In turn, this book celebrates those intellectual crossings and complications while raising questions about power and how power preconditions historical inquiry.

The primary goal of this book is to respond to a history, or rather, to a Eurocentric method of approaching the history of the Qur'ān. Usually these responses tend to offer a history of their own, a counterhistory, so to speak. While there is some history in this book, readers will soon discover that my intellectual input shifts with intentionality from the historical to the linguistic and from the applications of methods to the investigation of language and the intricacies of reading. The goal is to be aware how often scholarship is governed by a received version of critical history rather than by a reading of the work itself. Therefore, I start this study by inviting the reader to see through the processes and assumptions of the historical-critical method whereby the modern contemporary study of the Qur'ān emerged in Euro-American academia. Given the new wave of scholarship on the Qur'ān as a late antique text, I am aware that my critique would raise eyebrows in the midst of the pervasive idea that to read the Qur'ān in its late antique context is to contextualize it, situate it, and absorb it into a more enlightening global narrative. My contention is that until today such an absorption remains inadequate to both the content and the form of the Qur'ān. Not only does it reduce the sociolinguistic and literary relations on which the Qur'ān is based to that of a mere search for mutual affinities and parallelisms in the vast span of late antique times, but it taxonomizes the text by pulling it into a formative historicity that serves a metanarrative of domination. A practical approach is to read the Qur'ān's text internally, through a kind of lens that is now posited for studies of the Global South and interruptions afforded by critical theory, not necessarily a critical theory whose anchor is internal to the tradition.

In the first few chapters, I expose how the post–World War II period led to the formation of an academic network on Islam that was responding to its own historical moment. I compare American and European approaches, placing both in a broader context of geopolitics. Next, I interrogate the purposes for which the scholarly concept of late antiquity has been posited, how Qurʾānic studies has been made to fit within its mold, and how—given this framework—approaches to the Qurʾān in modern and contemporary scholarship are more a reflection of the framework and less that of the Qurʾān's local historical environment. The remaining chapters engage more directly with placing the Qurʾān in its own social and literary contexts, focusing primarily on the linguistic and literary connections and disconnections between pre-Islamic poetry and the Qurʾān, as well as the Qurʾān's distinct aesthetic and rhetorical modes. The point is not to go through the body of pre-Islamic poetry and the Qurʾān with a fine-tooth comb to track reiterations of the former in the latter, since other scholars have already explored this venue and arrived at varied conclusions.[29] It is, rather, to hold them in the linguistic and tropological tensions of what remains an intricate discursive relationship between them. While pre-Qurʾānic Arabic literature offers an understanding of the literary tropes and figural language of the Qurʾān, it also includes rich sociopolitical and cultural associations inherent to that very tradition, some of which, like wine drinking, hunting, tribal wars, slavery, and the status of women, appear in the Qurʾān as well as in pre-Islamic poetry. There is a dire need for vigorous studies that situate the Qurʾān within this neglected local code of knowledge.

The challenge these studies would pose for current Euro-American scholarship of the Qurʾān is that it will be a novel and, dare I say, risky departure from the safe methodical and systemic tacklings to which the text has been subjected for decades. It is highly risky, to be sure, for junior scholars deeply tied to the academic field and the market demands of Qurʾānic studies in Euro-American academic institutions to simply dehegemonize themselves and opt out of the channeled course of scholarly expectations, because such desertion of the canon will mean the flight from "the field," the loss of a job or a grant, a rejection of a publication, or even worse, a denial of a dissertation. I cite a concrete example of this ostracization in chapter 1. I believe it is honest to say that this departure is feared because it destabilizes what has become a comfortable Euro-Americanization of Qurʾānic studies in Western universities. Yet, such a liberation of Qurʾānic studies is precisely the place where new scholarship can be a transformative departure from the reified monopolies of standardization.

I am arguing, then, that Islam's core book has become the other of Euro-American scholarship in the field of Qurʾānic studies. To refuse a robust engagement with this foundational text—and worse, to train students without sufficient proficiency in classical Arabic or regional intellectual history to study the Qurʾān in depth—is a sleight of hand that also dispenses with the field's need to recognize the Qurʾān as a living text. The irony is that for a field whose central text is perhaps the most widely circulated book in the Global South today, Qurʾānic studies has yet to take up the basic insights of postcolonial theory. What remains most urgently needed is a profound decolonization of the academic studies of Islam in the West. I begin this undertaking in this book. I will go so far as to argue that decolonial and critical theory must never discount religion, especially that of postcolonial states. In fact, religion lies at the heart of contemporary decolonial debates. And to the question "Is critique secular?" the answer is a categorical "No." Critique is never just secular, and religion is always critique.

1

———

Remapping Qurʾānic Studies

Histories and Methods

It is an illustration of the rule, and not an exception to it, that Cambridge University rejected Wilfred Cantwell Smith's PhD dissertation because of its inclusive treatment of Muslims in India and its Marxist critique of the British Raj.[1] Smith, the most influential scholar of Islam and comparative religion of the last century, was an unyielding critic of intellectual colonialism. In approaching the intricate history of Islam, he did not subscribe to historical revisionism or, for that matter, to any other so-called method.[2] He did not see Islam as an alien object that scholars needed an authorized method to approach. Rather, he studied Islam as an intimate subject, as a fresh source for religious thought. For Smith, a combination of critique and comparison was the only way to avoid flying too close to the sun via intellectual hubris. "Interdisciplinary studies," he maintained, "are the ladder to get out of the hole into which the true scholar never falls."[3]

Like national borders, disciplinary boundaries are not always a thing so much as a series of practices for managing difference. There is not always a gate, but there is much gatekeeping. To start with, Smith calls attention to the politics of a renewed *ʿaṣabiyya*, a group solidarity or mode of turf protection that characterizes the network of Euro-American scholarship on Islam today. We only know of Smith's case because he persevered after what must have been a soul-crushing rejection of his thesis. He went on to become one of the most distinguished professors of Islam and comparative religion in the world—assuming numerous academic posts but spending most of his career at Harvard (1964–73, 1978–84)—until he died in 2000. The records of Smith's case notwithstanding, we cannot be sure of how many other junior scholars of Islam have dared to think differently and have, throughout the years, been denied their degrees or, more likely, been told to change topics or methods at Cambridge, Oxford, or the University of London's

School of Oriental and African Studies (SOAS), as well as at other bastions of scholarship on Islam. To understand the case of Cambridge's rejection of Smith's path-breaking scholarship, we have to understand the institutional landscape, historical and contemporary, of the field in which Smith wrote.

The academic field of Qur'ānic studies in the West was born at a peculiar moment in European history. The attempt to fill a knowledge gap of Islam grew out of a global turning point and a cultural crisis. Regardless of Europe's ideological predispositions toward Islam—many European scholars demonstrated a familiarity with the Qur'ān that was much more sophisticated than that of scholars in the United States, where the needs for public diplomacy and civilizational change loomed large after the fog of two world wars, of decolonization, and of a nascent world order. The need to understand foreign cultures, especially cultures unknown to study in the United States, became increasingly urgent. Europe, which was already undergoing its own set of cultural and intellectual crises, was the obvious supplier of what was needed. At that time in the United States, only a few departments had ancient Near East civilization programs. The most prominent were Columbia, Chicago, Yale, and Princeton. Although Princeton established the Department of Oriental Arabic and Literatures as early as 1927, and launched its first program in Arabic and Islamic studies under the heroic efforts of its pioneer historian, Philip Hatti (1886–1979), it still needed a specialized scholar in Islam and particularly in the Qur'ān to complement its strong Bible studies program.[4]

In the 1940s and 1950s, prominent American universities began to invite European secular academics to give lectures or to teach in the field of Islamic studies in the United States. When the first official conference on Islam took place at the University of Chicago in 1942, it had the title "The Near East: Problems and Prospects." Ever since that conference, up to and including the present, the word "problem" has become the cognate word for Islam in US politics and academia.[5] This despite moderates such as H. A. R. Gibb, who wrote at a time when many scholars did not see a "problem" with the colonization of Muslim nations and the resultant rise of militant dictatorships. Indeed, there was "a common conviction," Gibb wrote, "that these problems stem only partially from external causes, but mainly from factors within Middle Eastern society itself," and "it is not only by careful study that the West can help," he went on.[6] "If the Middle Eastern countries must work out their own solutions," Gibb concluded, "the Western countries alone can relieve the psychological tensions which complicate their task."[7]

But the West would continue to study Islam and the Islamicate world by way of problematization.[8] The opening of new positions in Near Eastern studies, and the continuing migration of European scholars to the United States, marked a palpable shift in academic centers of power by the 1950s. Established European professors were appointed to open programs and spearheaded new projects in the then-infant fields of Arabic and Islamic studies. Before Gibb moved from Oxford to accept his new position as the James Richard Jewett Professor of Arabic at Harvard in 1955, the United States had no academic infrastructure for studying Islam or the Middle East; nor was Europe deeply invested in its knowledge of the pre-Islamic Arabian Peninsula or classical Arabic. The question of "deep" knowledge haunts Qur'ānic studies to the present day, perhaps precisely to the extent that Islam remains a "problem" to think through.

In considering the history of European-informed scholarship on the Qur'ān, one cannot emphasize enough the significance of Theodor Nöldeke's 1860's doctoral dissertation, "Geschichte des Qorān," and its lasting impact on shaping Western scholarship on the origins of the Qur'ān over the last century and until today. Nöldeke's work was important enough to merit the republication, between 1909 and 1938, of a second enlarged edition in three coedited volumes by his successors Friedrich Schwally, Gotthelf Bergsträßer, and Otto Pretzl. Nöldeke's work thus became the cornerstone for writing a positivist history of the Qur'ān and critiquing, with others, both the authenticity and reliability of the immense archive of Muslim sources. More importantly, at least until the early 1970s and before the rise of the overtly "censorious" historical thought of John Wansbrough and Patricia Crone, as I explain below, Nöldeke's work still established the intellectual framework for all academic research on the origins of Islam, at times extending and at times challenging existing research on the text of the Qur'ān (Blachère) or the life of the Prophet (Guillaume, Watt).[9]

What must be historically recorded is that the few decades following World War II were the time when the humanities in Europe, especially in Germany, engulfed in post-Auschwitz guilt, sought to make amends to its criminal othering and persecution of Jews. But if anything, the *Historikerstreit* (historians' dispute of the 1980s) has exposed Germany's moral failure to heed the historical lessons of the Holocaust and learn to interrogate its own categorical prejudice against the other. It is in the name of the historical-critical method, which I discuss in detail in the following chapter, that Germany "othered" and divided human beings into two categories: Aryans (the Germanic people), whom it considered "genetically superior"; and the "inferior races," which included Jews, Slavs, Roma, Sinti, as well as Africans, Arabs, Turks, and Asians who hailed from Muslim lands.[10]

The first wave of European scholars of Arabic and Islam appointed in the United States included senior orientalists such as Gustav von Grunebaum at Chicago (1942), then UCLA (1957), George Lenczowski at Berkeley (1952), and Gibb at Harvard (1955). This wave constituted a strong bedrock and powerful network of Euro-American scholarship on Islam in America and triggered a tradition of subsequent waves. In this new European exodus to America, well-established universities such as Oxford, Cambridge, and SOAS continued to be the "safe" exportation hub of orientalists in American institutions. Joseph Schacht (who taught Islamic law at Oxford from 1946 to 1954) assumed a position at Columbia University from 1957 to 1969; Bernard Lewis joined Princeton in 1974. In 1986, Lewis's student, Michael Cook, was appointed Cleveland E. Dodge Professor of Near Eastern Studies at

Princeton. In 1997, another student of Lewis, Patricia Crone, was appointed to the Princeton's Institute of Advanced Studies as the Andrew W. Mellon Professor of Islamic History. Both Cook and Crone were students of John Wansbrough, the Harvard-educated revisionist, whose unflattering argument against the sources of Islam is even further misrepresented and taken out context in their work.[11]

To be fair, Wansbrough came into Qur'ānic studies with a strong background and training in biblical criticism. In early twentieth-century Europe, biblical criticism underwent a seismic bifurcation, with clashing views on Christian historiography. These clashes resulted in some scholars turning attention away from biographers and historiographers to genres and communities. Academic endeavor to restore the Bible's scriptural significance began at the hands of Karl Barth (1886–1968), whose systemic theology allowed for a shifting of emphasis from the historical Jesus towards the message of the New Testament.[12] Rudolf Bultmann (1884–1976) followed Barth's footprints in critiquing liberal theology and espousing an existential interpretation of the New Testament. Bultmann's work—which left a tremendous impact on Wansbrough's approach to theological history in general,[13] and guided his understanding of the Qur'ān text in particular—deemphasizes, if it does not blatantly dismiss, historical analysis of the life of Jesus and of the New Testament because of the belief that earliest Christian literature exhibited little to no interest in specific locations or geographies.[14]

This reorientation of the theological discourse toward the "thatness" instead of the "whatness" of Jesus allowed Wansbrough to embrace a similar approach toward the Qur'ān—namely, what matters is that the Qur'ān exists, not what is written about it or what happened throughout or after the life of Muḥammad. And just as the Bible is not a book of history, so too the Qur'ān, Wansbrough contends,[15] (perhaps following a hint from Bultmann's critique of Christian historiography and his focus on kerygma)[16] is not a book of history but rather a book of "scriptural authority."[17] Wansbrough makes this point clear in his preface:

> All such efforts at historical reconstruction (*wie es eigentlich gewesen*) tend to be reductive, and here one senses the specter of that (possibly very real) dichotomy in early Christian history: Jerusalem *Urgemeinde* opposed to Hellenistic kerygma (Bultmann). The basic problem associated with that opposition, whether social or doctrinal, seems in retrospect to reflect disputes upon eschatology, much as the development of Rabbinic Judaism has been defined as reaction to or residue from extreme expressions of eschatological belief/activity.[18]

Wansbrough thus comes from a tradition that considers it demeaning and pointless to study the Bible and, by extension, the Qur'ān as books of history. Like Bultmann, Wansbrough is suspicious of tradition in general precisely because "it is quite impossible to ignore the presence of *Nachdichtung* in traditionist literary forms" and because "tradition implies, and actively involves, historicization."[19] In other words, the writing of history to Wansbrough is the writing of literature about literature. "History, like poetry," he maintains, "is mimetic and produces as many necessary truths as it contains fortuitous facts (Lessing)."[20] Wansbrough argues that historiographies surrounding the Qur'ān and the first Muslim community starting roughly from 800 AD became too easily acceptable in the Islamic tradition. He questions therefore *asbāb al-nuzūl, tafsīr,* and *sīra* literatures as belated compositions that are "pressed into the service of salvation history."[21] His training in biblical criticism drives him to conclude that the so-called source "histories" of all religion, including Islam, are constructed ex post facto and projected as views formed amid intense polemics and ideological wars.

In other words, to Wansbrough, while the Qur'ān itself exists as a tangible material and a textual reality, a history of Islam proper does not really exist; nor could a historical approach to Islam prove or disprove anything. And since the writing of history is itself the writing of literature about literature, the only textual reality is literature itself, where religion has the potential of reaching high forms of literary representation. Wansbrough calls this literary representation "mythopoeic"—that is, "artistic reimagining of mythological narratives."[22] Wansbrough derives this definition from Bultmann, who defines myth as "an expression of man's conviction that the origin and purpose of the world in which he lives are to be sought not within it but beyond it—that is beyond the world of known and tangible reality, a realm that is perpetually dominated and menaced by those mysterious powers which are its source and energy. Myth is also an expression of man's awareness that he is not the lord of his own being."[23] Even though he argues that Islam evolved gradually from sectarian forms of Judaism over a period of 150 years in the aftermath of the Arab conquest around the middle of the seventh century,[24] Wansbrough still considers it a unique expression of the same literary mythopoeic monotheism that informs both the Torah and the Gospels. Yet much of what has been written on Wansbrough ignores or fails to understand or consider such formative precepts of his own intellectual thought. The fact that Wansbrough himself makes so few concessions to his readers and uses technical language accessible only to very few scholars familiar with his methodology is largely to blame for this misunderstanding.

Bultmannian as it is, and deep in its quasi-Biblical dehistoricization of the origins of Islam as a solution to the question of origins of Islam, Wansbrough's comparative venture into the Qur'ān is neither useful nor precise. It is true that Western scholarship on the hagiography of Muḥammad has learned not to trust *sīra* or *ḥadīth* literatures, as did some highly regarded classical Muslim scholars. But historically, there is more material available for learning about Muḥammad than former prophets. "The evidence about Jesus," argues Marshall Hodgson, "is almost exclusively contained in the four Gospels and in a letter by Paul. The more they are analyzed, the less dependable the Gospels prove to be . . . As to the personal spirituality of Jesus we have only the thinnest evidence."[25] To be fair, I do not agree with Hodgson's argument against the historicity of Jesus. It is neither fair nor productive to argue that there is "enough evidence to allow scholarship . . . to be based on academic principles" in one (Islam) but not the other (Christianity)." After all, there is a decent scholarly consensus that Jesus existed and was executed. And the authentic letters of Paul are at least a very early second-hand source of information. In the case of Muḥammad, there are also several sources about his life, in which the Qur'ān itself is a direct and primary evidence. These sources range from Muslim to non-Muslim material from the sixth to seventh centuries AD, enough evidence to allow scholarship on Muḥammad to be based on objective academic principles.[26]

Although not a proponent of the German School per se, Wansbrough argues that the Qur'ān and the biography of Muḥammad are material, or rather "literature," controversially and belatedly constructed ex post facto (over the span of three centuries) and formed against a background of other sectarian groups— namely, the rabbinic Judaism of Iraq. This is a mistake superimposed on an old orientalist error. The mistake is the intellectual hubris of snubbing the Qur'ān as a cultural text symbolic of the social, political, and literary significations of its *own* time and place. And the old error is the unyielding reification of the conceptual gap between the self and the other, in which the self paralyzes and distorts the thinking of the other about its own time and place, as boldly as it alienates it from its own logos.

And so it was, at a time of intellectual turmoil in post-Vietnam War America, the study of the Qur'ān made an uneasy debut in the academic halls of US universities, with scholars and ideas mostly imported from Europe, and with Western academics entrusted with launching and leading programs that would set the course on how to ideologically approach, define, and teach Islam. US academe, in turn, divided Islamic studies, and the Middle East, into subdisciplines that included anthropology, economics, history, and sociology.[27] Each of these narrow professional settings approached Islam and, by default, the Qur'ān as an object of analysis from its own specialized standpoint, creating in the process its own disciplinary turfs and boundaries. After more than fifty years, the field of Qur'ānic studies split into a diversity of experimental and methodological projects that not only gave rise to chaos,[28] but also rendered the Qur'ān text irredeemably othered and locked into a web of subdisciplinary specializations, a free-floating object that has almost nothing to do with the cognate Arabic text of the Qur'ān Muslim and informed non-Muslim readers the world over are familiar with, not to speak of the interactive, multifaceted lived reality of the historical or contemporary Muslim world. One cannot, then, emphasize enough that the epistemological framework and ideological dispositions of this Euro-American network of Islamic studies has been engendered with specific "problems" in mind. A strong sense of affiliation and unanimity grew among the adherents of this institutional network to a point that it became intolerant of disagreement, criticism, or alternative approaches. That is, Qur'ānic studies remains characterized by *ʿaṣabiyya*.

The theoretical bedrock and empirical ramifications of this new ʿaṣabiyya are not only perversely visible—we see them manifested in scores of publications on the origins of Islam—but utterly lacking a *theologia civilis*, or what Emmanuel Levinas once described as an imperative ethico-religious relationship to the other.[29] At stake here is the positionality of the history of Islam, in topographical and thematic terms. This is not to point blame at the ʿaṣabiyya well-established scholarship on the Qur'ān. After all, this type of scholarship prepares and trains scholars to disengage not only from faith-based Arabic sources but from direct textual and analytical readings of the Qur'ān text in its original Arabic, therefore siding with what is academically "right." Yet that which is academically "right" is also a parochial right, informed by its virtue as overbearing partiality toward Eurocentric ascendency and the establishment of epistemological hegemony. In that provincial sense of the right, non-faith-based sources basically translate into non-Muslim sources, a presupposition that manifests a gross trivialization of the sources of "faith" in these so called "non-faith" sources of the "self" versus the unreliable accounts voiced by the other. Erasing the other in the name of "method" is not a discourse of objectivity, but a sugar-coated subjectivity predicated on silencing this other, a realization Muslim readers have to reckon with when they cannot recognize themselves or their own scripture and tradition in the very scholarship that should be in conversation with them. Even if the main goal has always been academically grounded in the sense that it would lead to some rational and scientific understanding of the past, or a "shared heritage," one would never commit the mistake of conflating (selected) history with that sought-after understanding. There is no such thing as an "objective" source or a traceable true history of religious language, precisely because it is largely iconic, a point that William Montgomery Watt underscored decades ago.[30]

Since the middle of the nineteenth century, the rise of colonialism, which fed off the frantic energies of Europe's industrial modernity, led not only to the emergence of theories of racial supremacy but also to militant thought and combative ideology against everything the colonies stood for—the peoples, the lands, the cultures, and the traditions. This ideological militarization soon became the *modus operandum* of European scholarship on the history of Islam. But to view the demonization of Islam solely as a Eurocentric phenomenon only truncates our understanding of the ways in which this ideology we witness in the Euro-American academy is deeply indebted to European colonialism and, with it, to the underpinnings of racial and cultural superiority, resulting in a consistent stream of "high culture" scholarship that has methodically "researched" Islam—for the entirety of the twentieth century—as oppositional to the West and as a threat to modernity, globalization, and world peace.

For centuries, the presence of the Qur'ān in Europe and, by extension, in the United States, given the above history of prestigious US universities, has been reduced to an ardent revisionism of its origins, aided by flawed and truncated translations shelved with caution in large European or American libraries and accompanied by Christian apologetic commentaries. Robust European academic interest in the study of Islam's past did not take place before the 1833, the year Abraham Geiger published *Was hat Mohammed aus dem Judenthume aufgenommen?*[31] This epoch coincided with the age of colonialism in Europe and the mad "Scramble for Africa."[32] To say the least, these times were not conducive to dispassionate and unbiased scholarship on Arabs, or on Islam and its origins. This was also a philosophical epoch from which emerged the foundations of "high theory," which justified even slavery in a complex Hegelian dialectic. The usurpation of innocent people's lands and resources was a military and economic competition among European states. It is not a coincidence that the height of European colonialism in the Muslim world was coterminous with Germany becoming a hub for scholarship on the Qur'ān in the nineteenth century. Although the 1919's Treaty of Versailles forced Germany to give up its colonies, German academics still benefited from a perverse culture of imperialism.[33] German scholarship on the Qur'ān profited from European colonization of African and Asian countries through uninhibited acquisition of manuscripts and accessible roaming of Arab-Muslim lands. Culturally and philosophically, Germany harbored a troubled xenophobia against Turkey, an anxious fascination with Muslim culture, and an academic obsession with rearranging Islam's past.[34]

When a postcolonial self-critique of Western imperialism began to take shape in the second half of the twentieth century,[35] the one field that escaped the scythe of this long-overdue deconstructive turn in European thought was that of Qur'ānic studies, especially in Germany. Even Edward Said's *Orientalism*, with its enormously broad critique of eighteenth- and nineteenth-century European scholarship on the "Orient" (mainly French and British), failed to include it, a failing for which Said reproached himself.[36] We see scholastic humility exercised in many humanistic fields, but it remains rare in Euro-American scholarship in the field of Islamic and Qur'ānic studies. In fact, the opposite holds. Qur'ānic studies is the only field that has attracted some scholars who loathe their subject matter more than any other area of knowledge I have come to know, save Holocaust studies.

It therefore matters significantly to interrogate the current push for repositioning the origins of Islam and to radically historicize its intellectual premises. Even though the Qur'ān rightly insists that it is not poetry, pre-Islamic poetry and prose were the only literary genres germane to its emergence, and they remain the only resources for understanding its meaning and significations. Over the last four decades, only a handful of scholars of classical Arabic routinely entertained the literary and rhetorical dynamics of the Qur'ān in relationship to pre-Islamic Arabic poetry.[37] But outside this circle of Arabists, the field of Qur'ānic studies in the West has continued the positivist historical turn advanced in *Hagarism*. Yet to claim that the Qur'ān is a "product" or an "intertext" of late antiquity would not only resurrect Wansbrough's radical method; it would continue to authorize the die-hard approach to the text according to an imperative of sovereignty. A self-critical sovereignty is still a sovereignty. The movement from Cronian othering to Neuwirthian "spacing" and inclusivity, while redeeming, continues to perpetuate the shallowing of the Qur'ān's Arabic cultural and literary tradition.

There are certainly valid historical reasons as to why a robust dialogue with the Arabicity of the Qur'ān has rarely been engaged or deemed worthy of study in the West: the sorrowful lack of proficiency in classical Arabic is one; the uncomfortable anti-trinitarian tone of the Qur'ān is another; the post-Enlightenment fascination with history as a "scientific" discipline capable of objective and non-ideological findings about the past is a third; add to this the public and academic demonization of Islam as Europe's archenemy for centuries. It is not an understatement to say that the normative illusion of the historical-critical method has long enjoyed the benefit of allowing Western readers to measure the complexity of a properly positivist assessment of the Qur'ān against those of Muslim interpretive methods—the semantic, the semiotic, the syntactic, the phonological, the ethical, the aesthetic, and so on. The latter are mostly written in Arabic or non-European languages and are often dubbed apologetic or subacademic. The enduring academic authority of the historical-critical method derives not only from a deep commitment to and continuous refinement of old ideas of the "self," but also from the loyal *'aṣabiyya* of a complex academic superstructure. In the spirit of this "trusted" academic tradition, a direct and text-based rhetorical engagement with the Qur'ān would come across as a distraction—one that disrupts such apparently objective and highly refined academic practice. While this *'aṣabiyya* may not necessarily be premeditated, there is an undeniable scholarly inertia when it comes to Arabic sources. Not only do scholars fail to achieve the competency to read original Arabic sources but, unsurprisingly, they tend to go for the low-hanging fruit, the stories of Jesus, Mary, Joseph, the seven sleepers, and so on that are familiar in biblical texts, and latch onto them as a way of explaining this challenging text.

Devin Stewart is right to argue that "specialists in various subfields in Islamic Studies have biases that make it difficult for them to write objectively and insightfully about other subfields."[38] But he is also keenly aware that "a great deal of scholarship in the academy is shoddy work," a shoddiness caused for the large part by linguistic incompetency. It is no surprise that Stewart starts his "Theses for the Improvement of Islamic Studies" with the clarion call: "For God's sake, learn Arabic."[39] Stewart's twenty-seven well-conceived theses are worth posting on doors of every graduate seminar in Islamic studies. I too would argue for the priority of superior proficiency in classical Arabic as a prerequisite, given the Qur'ān's semantic and rhetorical richness. I contend that only the language of the Qur'ān offers a theoretically sound and intellectually compelling solution to the disarray of the field of Qur'ānic studies discussed above. Even though, to Stewart's point, "fundamental ideological differences will remain, no matter how much historical detail is added to the picture,"[40] solid proficiency in Arabic will still make it difficult for these ideologies to hold, since only the text of the Qur'ān gives us in its own language a fair account of the essential history of its sociocultural and stylistic setting, which, like the transplant of a second lung, will bring it to life and allow it to *speak for* itself but also *to* alien cultures that have systematically silenced it.

Yet the call for improving Islamic studies, and in particular for proficiency in Arabic, still raises the important question of whether certain scholars of the Qur'ān have failed to do so or if the issue is far graver than the problem of mere linguistic proficiency would indicate. In other words, inasmuch as there is a correlation between Western scholars learning Arabic and the quality of their work, the harsh reality is that linguistic competency alone, no matter how refined, is not going to stop a scholar from operating within a colonial mentality. Decolonized understanding of the Qur'ān can only be achieved if one views the other as belonging to a category different from one's own, to be sure, but a category that is not necessarily combative or threatening,[41] and only if more attention is paid to the text at hand, to what it says, not what it refuses to say, nor what one wants it to say—not by way of the convoluted past of late antiquity, or the nitpickings of biblical criticism, or even the moot debates about the Qur'ān's origins. These methods may still claim their academic usefulness and relevance, but only if they are reframed and retold from within an ethic of comparativity, one that does not "embrace" the other as an extension of the self but that listens to and includes the other as an equal participant in the immense and unfinished project of humanism.

There is no question that the Qur'ān is a dialectical text: it offers both a continuity of Abrahamic monotheism and a rupture breaking through rituals and practices not only of the peninsular society in which it emerged but also of the world of late antiquity. While it continues perennial themes, ideas, and narratives of monotheism known to the world of late antiquity, and even of classical antiquity *writ large*, the Qur'ān still shattered fundamental understandings of that very monotheism and disrupted the multiple and complex milieus that constituted late and classical antiquity. Understandably, the choice between continuity and rupture is critical because it is also a choice of deciding beginnings and endings. This choice cannot simply be justified by historical evidence or late antiquity "material," so to speak, because it is in the nature of the choice to organize and select its own evidence and material. We have seen time and time again how critical choices themselves can be reconstructed as facts that generate their own causalities. This book is a result of this very tension, which confirms not only the temporality of historical thought in Euro-American approaches to the Qur'ān but also contemporary trends to colonial guilt and self-critique without changing scholarly habits, such as the committed learning of Arabic, that would demonstrate genuine epistemological respect for a subject. It is, in fact, "natural" for the Euro-American academy to be where it is now. Islam has for more than a millennium been perceived as radically oppositional to the West. This is precisely the perception that informs Neuwirth's argument for a remedy that allows the field to look forward only if it first looked backward. But how far backward in the expanse of late antiquity can one look? Since medieval times, Muslims have emerged as the strangers from another space, οἱ Σαρακηνοί, or desert-dwelling camel riders who spoke an unintelligible language and followed deviant practices, and whose seemingly human appearances belied malevolent traits and inferior levels of intelligence. And if Islam were the hackneyed other of Western history, then the Qur'ān would effortlessly assume the status of its archetype.

The point is not so much that the Qur'ān is a cause of "anxiety" because it is problematic. Rather, it is framed as problematic because it became normalized as the other, the alien, and the unfamiliar in public discourses. And while the late antiquity thesis of embracing the Qur'ān as quintessentially European is a much more progressive approach than the dismissive one adopted, say, in *Hagarism*, one must at the very least raise questions about whether this new paradigm has truly overcome the positivistic and revisionist tendencies of Crone's and Cook's studies, or whether in the process of overemphasizing foreign influences or "intertexts" of late antique times on the Qur'ān, it has, directly or inadvertently, uprooted the text's native context.

In the end, the purpose of offering a genealogy of Euro-American scholarship on the Qur'ān is not to provide a critique of the Euro-American academy per se. Rather, the goal is to de-universalize the academy's claims to historical certitude and highlight it for the whole world to see. The Qur'ān is not a fixed entity; nor is it for that reason a mobile object whose geographical contours and themes could be stretched for political correctness. The Qur'ān, in the words of Wilfred Cantwell Smith, is a "subject"[42]—that is, a living source of engagement that continues to lend insight and discernment outside the forbidding field of Euro-American Qur'ānic studies.

2

What Is Late Antiquity and What Does the Qur'ān Have to Do With It?

The 1972 discovery of the most important document regarding the Qur'ān history at the Great Mosque of Ṣanʿāʾ proved beyond dispute that the text was transmitted semi-orally before 650 AD, thus silencing all faulty orientalist speculations about its historical time and location. This transmission took place, as Behnam Sadeghi and Mohsen Goudarzi effectively demonstrate, "most likely via hearers who wrote down a text that was directed by the Prophet."[1] Yet, Euro-American scholarship, which has largely focused on reconstructing the Qur'ān's textual and contextual history outside its cognate sources, has been slow in recovering from this shock. In the *medias res* of the chaos in the field of Qur'ānic studies today, two main interrelated strategies of exclusion stand out: opposition and avoidance. The first, initiated by John Wansbrough in the 1970s, has typically been an approach in which a scholar extends an act of unwarranted intellectual generosity in order to prove how a certain historical period, or an Arabic or Islamic source, is "problematic" and thus unreliable for objective scholarship on Islam.[2] The second approach avoids reference to Arabic and Islamic sources altogether under the pretext of perpetuating a non-Arabic origin (mostly Syriac) or historical repositioning of the Qur'ān as a rearticulation of the biblical tradition, a "cross-section" of late antique times, or both. It follows, at least by implication for these approaches, that any peninsular Arabic sources about the literary traditions and social habits of pre-Islamic Arabs, or about the customs and practices of Arabs and early Muslims immediately before and during the life of the Prophet, or even in the early decades of Islam, do not apply.[3]

In opposition to these exclusivist trends, a new school that ties the Qur'ān to late antique times has emerged with the prospect of "including" the Qur'ān and breaking away with the methodological foibles of exclusivist scholarship. This "inclusion" entails an annexation of the Qurʾān into the same domain that constituted biblical history. Regardless of the Qurʾān's origins, which this school seeks to resituate, late antiquarians maintain that the text should be integrated as part of the biblical tradition and studied on equal footing with the Torah and the Christian Bible.[4] For centuries, this school maintains, the Qurʾān established itself as a *textus receptus*—a received text, a commanding sealed corpus, committed to memory, informed by and informing cultural traditions of the Islamic world and beyond. Since the findings of Sadeghi and Goudarzi were published more than a decade ago, it is possible that this new school materialized as a response to the discovery of the Ṣanʿāʾ palimpsest (Ṣanʿāʾ1), a critical reassessment of the field's exclusivism, or perhaps a modification and redirection of its force. After all, Patricia Crone and Michael Cook in *Hagarism*, for instance, did ask credible questions, but they manufactured misguided answers. By the mid-1990s, numerous essays and books carrying the names "Islam" and "late antiquity" in the same title began to be published. Both Princeton University Press and Princeton's Darwin Press embraced the initiative quite enthusiastically.[5]

As I argued earlier, the most prominent claims on the Qurʾān as a late antique text to this point come from Angelika Neuwirth, whose work provides the most elaborate model of late antiquarian approaches to the Qurʾān known in the Western academy.[6] Now that Wansbrough's and Crone's hypotheses regarding the belated accumulation of the Qurʾān have become *passé*, Neuwirth's approach comes across as a break with the parochial theologocentrism of her Euro-American predecessors. She positions the Qurʾān as part of the shared cultures that produced Jewish and Christian texts in the larger framework of late antiquity. She emphasizes that her approach to late antiquity treats it not as a historical period but as a "an epistemic space" in which polytheists, Jews, and Christians approached their variegated antiquities with inventive exegetical interpretations.[7] In this larger context, Neuwirth advances the Qurʾān as a response to, or, more precisely, as a commentary on the rampant debates regarding divinity that were typical of late antiquity. To Neuwirth, the Qurʾān draws on rhetorical devices characteristic of Hellenistic culture that engage with and offer fresh theological premises for the *textus receptus* of late antiquity, which include Halakhic and Haggadic traditions of Judaism, as well as the writings of the early church fathers, while claiming its own place amid established Jewish and Christian traditions.[8]

More importantly, Neuwirth seeks to carve an epistemological space for the Qurʾān between two opposing poles: a traditional Muslim and non-Muslim approach that reads the Qurʾān as a primordially Arabic text through the lens of the Prophet's biography; and an archeological Western approach that focuses on "source texts" and relies heavily on the historical-critical method to uphold the perception of the Qurʾān's "secondarity"—namely, its unoriginality and its substantial dependence on a biblical and postbiblical tradition. A major difference between the traditional and the archeological approach to the Qurʾān is that the former approaches the Qur'ān as a radical break with the past and a correction to the course of Abrahamic monotheism,[9] whereas the latter seeks to establish direct connections with and continuities between the contents of the Qur'ān and the biblical intertexts that served as prerequisites for the Qur'ān's *raison d'être*. In this context, it is important to emphasize that Neuwirth's project of connecting Qur'ānic content and form with the debates of late antiquity texts seeks to dispense not with the historical-critical method, which Neuwirth clearly adopts and defends, but with the "traditional" applications of this method that, according to Neuwirth, "rarely contended . . . with illuminating the Qur'an historically."[10]

In this act of historical reillumination of the Qur'ān, proponents of the late antiquity thesis seek to find ties and connections between epistemes of text-based, oral, ascetic, and sermon-centered cultures that became mutually influential from the first to the seventh century AD. Further, they attempt to explore the rise of Islam within this much broader historical background by integrating it into the philosophical, artistic, and legislative framework of that period. The task is colossal: for "late antiquity" as a concept to make sense in the context of Islamic studies *writ large*, it must be defined as referring to the interactions between Judaism, Christianity, and paganism (including Neoplatonism)[11] in the first six centuries AD. In the East, this Judeo-Christian-pagan compound, with its intense debate over the nature of human and divine realms and how they relate to each other stretches geographically from Egypt, Syria, Anatolia, and Mesopotamia in the north to Ethiopia and southern Arabia in the south. The moment a late antique *Denkraum à la* Neuwirth is adopted, Mecca and the Arab dominions would no longer be at the periphery, but squarely in the middle. After all, Mecca was a center where the trade routes of this Afro-Asian dominion converged—to Yemen, to Syria and across the Red Sea to Ethiopia. It is possible that thick epistemological dialogues and debates would take place and travel alongside traders. If Ethiopia and southern Arabia are not integrated into this proposed space, the subsumption of the Qur'ān under the rubric "late antiquity" would fail to make sense not only historically and geographically but also epistemologically. Indeed, how do we explain the geographical references to these regions in the Qur'ān, or, for that reason, the *sīra* narrative of Muḥammad's advocacy for Christian Ethiopia as a refuge and haven for persecuted Muslim migrants?

This question invites the inference that "late antiquity" is more than the sum of its Neuwirthian parts. In the history of Qur'ānic studies in the West, the term "late antiquity" constitutes a relatively new European approach, situating the origins of Islam within a larger geographical-historical context of the cultures of the Near East, including Jewish, Christian, pagan, and syncretic traditions, that preceded it. This approach is both bold and creative. While benign in that it eschews flagrant claims that the Qur'ān is derivative or plagiarized, it still challenges Muslim historical narratives of the genesis of Islam, which present it as a break with existing *Jāhilī* (pre-Islamic) tradition in sixth- and seventh-century Mecca. Proponents of late antiquity contend that such periodization is informative and enlightening precisely because it avoids the accusations of direct textual plagiarism from Jewish or Christian texts advanced by old orientalists and their contemporary devotees. These proponents propose instead a study of the Qur'ān as a key text that draws on narratives and figures from the biblical tradition in an intriguing and vigorous manner. Neuwirth's venture, considered the first full-fledged study to connect the Qur'ān to this larger context, was welcomed with applause and commendation. Praised by *Deutschlandradio Kultur* as a book that will "re-organize all the myths and misunderstandings that have crept into interpretations of the Koran over the course of the centuries on the part of Muslims," and commended by Andrew Rippin as "unrivalled by any other work that has appeared for probably the past 100 years, in its overall scope, analytical depth, unified vision and intellectual rigor," Neuwirth's argument that the Qur'ān is a product of so-called late antiquity is thus positioned to make an impact on studies of the Qur'ān. But what exactly is, or was, "late antiquity"? And what does the Qur'ān have to do with it?

Traditionally, the term "late antiquity" comes out of classical studies and it refers to the end of the classical period. "Late antiquity," as a term, has therefore only made sense historically within the confines of the Roman Empire and as the later epochs of the Greek-and Latin-speaking world. For centuries of active historical scholarship, "late antiquity" has thus been understood and researched as a temporal marker referring to a limited geography. The Roman Empire used Greek administratively in the East in a very small part of the extreme north of the Arabic-speaking world. Since "late antiquity" does not make sense outside this context, and since most of the Arabic-speaking world has historically been marked outside the Roman Empire, while in tangential relationship with it, it is useful to understand precisely how Islam became included within the thicket of "late antiquity." As the liberation philosopher Enrique Dussel puts it, "Chronology has its geopolitics."[12] It is therefore fair, for the sake of Neuwirth's "Muslim readers," to pose a few questions. If the historical investigations of "continuity" versus "discontinuity" in the genesis of Islam have to submit to a new recharting of the contours of such history, how can we assess the validity of Neuwirth's remapping of this space beyond the existing structures of Eurocentric historiographic boundaries? Is the historical past, especially that of Western Europe's most "contested" religion, considered a progression toward an ostensible goal? Or is it, rather, a recounting of an intelligible totality? To ask the question more directly, if the history of Islam's origin is a matter of compulsive scholarship that constitutes itself in relationship to ongoing debates, documents, and historical contexts of Europe's understanding of "late antiquity," what makes the judgment of such theoretical history veritable? What makes it relative or constructed? And for whom?

Before addressing the relationship between the Qur'ān and late antiquity more fully, I would first like to take a detour and examine the origins of "late antiquity"—that is, the origins of the term in Western historical discourses. One must acknowledge that any serious probing of origins in general should situate this old-age conundrum of continuity and discontinuity more squarely. "What is found at the historical beginning of things," Michel Foucault reminds us, "is not the inviolable identity of their origin; it is the dissension of other things. It is disparity."[13] In this disparity, one must always be reminded that the notion of historical (dis)continuity of the Qur'ān derives its momentum and meaning not from late antiquity per se, but from present discourses and ideologies.[14] Historical revisionism, as we have seen, has an unflattering history of tempting the historian to identify an object and to fabricate the context. The history of Islam in the West has always been imbricated in Europe's own historical development and cultural heritage—at least since the seventh century—an involvement whose multiple variegations continue to demand further examination.[15] As Mark Bevir has put it, "Historians cannot access the past and secure facts apart from the context of their present concepts and theories. The past only ever appears in our present beliefs; it is never given at a distance."[16] These protracted and complex projections onto the past have spilled over and permeated intellectual discourses in Europe about biblical history since the eighteenth century, and about Islam since the nineteenth. Regardless of their philosophical underpinnings, most of these methods have, in the process, succumbed to the pressure of a present cultural moment, often trusting a thin linearity when it comes to views of a "real" history of Islam—that is, of the idea of being able to determine, decidedly, what Islam really is, or how it really was, or where and what it emerged from.

As a representative of a historical period that "includes" Islam, the term "late antiquity" was coined only fifty years ago, as it was first used by Peter Brown in the title of his influential book *The World of Late Antiquity: AD 150–750*. Since Brown's book became the founding text of subsequent research in the category of "late antiquity and the Qur'ān," it is incumbent on us to provide a prehistory of his thesis. Brown's book is written primarily as a reaction to a dominant scholarly consensus regarding the decline and fall of the Roman Empire and the collapse of Hellenism, going against the grain of established thought and classical authors, including manuscripts by Latin thinkers chronicling the fall of the Roman Empire (such as Sallust, Livy, and Tacitus), and continuing all the way up to the mid-twentieth-century scholarships of Idris Bell, Ward-Perkins, and Will Durant.[17] The collapse of the Roman Empire could be summarized in the words of Will Durant's important 1944 book, *Caesar and Christ:* "A great civilization is not conquered from without until it has destroyed itself within. The essential causes of Rome's decline lay in her people, her morals, her class struggle, her failing trade, her bureaucratic despotism, her stifling taxes, her consuming wars."[18] Brown's thesis is based on offering a contrarian hypothesis to Durant's statement—namely, that Rome never actually fell but rather transmuted into something else, something better than its original elf. Brown's Rome is not an empire of "decline and fall," as most historians have credibly argued, but one of "change and continuity."[19]

Yet, as though to complicate Brown's ambitious thesis, Theodor Mommsen, many years before, called Islam "der Henker des Hellenismus"—that is, "the executioner of Hellenism."[20] Before Brown published his study, H. Idris Bell, the eminent papyrologist of Oxford and a scholar of Roman Egypt, traced the decline of Rome and the decay of Hellenism in his well-known book of 1948, *Egypt From Alexander The Great to the Arab Conquest: A Study in the Diffusion and Decay of Hellenism*. In this important study, Bell provides a fascinating, evidence-based account of both how antiquity *ended* and how Islam irrefutably ushered in the beginning of new era. Bell's account concludes with the following statement:

> The story of Hellenistic Egypt was at an end, and the country whose gaze has been turned by the victories of Alexander from the East and the past to the West and the future, had returned to the Oriental world of which it had formed a part. But the world, whether Eastern or Western, was very different from that which Alexander knew. The oracle of Ammon was silent. The great temples of Egypt were abandoned or turned into Coptic monasteries. In the Christian churches and monasteries of Europe and Asia men debated subtle points of a theology constructed by Greek thought out of the teaching and life and death of a Jewish prophet, and already from the minaret of many a mosque in Arabia and in the neighbouring lands sounded the cry of the Muezzin, *Allahu akbar; la illah illa' lllah*, "God is great, there is no god but God."[21]

Contrary to Bell's account and, before that, to Durant's, Brown's thesis on the continuity of "late antiquity" appears rosy and extrapolative. While his book focuses on cultural and religious transformations, it does not explain how the Qur'ān is a late antique text. Furthermore, it neither addresses socioeconomic changes nor does it provide evidence to substantiate claims for cultural continuities. To crown it all, the book does not address the seismic shifts in religious discourses from paganism to Judaism to Christianity to Islam, not to mention the political violence, religious dissensions, or economic hardships that permeated antiquity. In short, Brown's book speaks to none of the convoluted circumstances, the socioeconomic factors, the state finance, the aristocratic identities, the peasant societies, the legal and military affairs, the rural settlement, or the harsh taxation systems that led to the fall of the Roman Empire, issues that Chris Wickham brilliantly and patiently examines and documents in his important evidentiary work, *Framing the Early Middle Ages: Europe and the Mediterranean, 400–800*.[22]

In this context, it is useful to draw attention to the famous "Pirennean controversy" of 1922.[23] This was when Henri Pirenne, the Belgian historian of the Middle Ages, made the forceful claim, which had gone uncontested for fifty years, that the event of Islam brought an end to antiquity. This argument did little to help the relationship between Islam and the West; if anything, it worsened it. I bring up this argument here to better contextualize Brown's call for a continuity thesis. It is crucial to point out that a decade before Brown embarked on his continuity thesis of late antiquity, Henri Pirenne had argued with clear evidence that it was not the Germanic invasion but Islam and the Arab conquest that were responsible for a break in continuity in Mediterranean civilization.[24] And so for decades in Euro-American scholarship, Islam was seen, à la Theodor Mommsen, as the executioner of Hellenism but also, at the same time, as the archenemy of Christianity. To be sure, throughout much of the twentieth century, there was a widespread lack of opposition in Western European thought to the collapse, disintegration, or diffusion of the classical ancient world order. The debate was rather about how this collapse happened, whether it took place from within the empire or whether there were external forces, such as a causal relationship between the expansion of Islam and the downfall of the traditional order in Western Europe. In fact, one of the main forces behind this decline was believed to be the general maritime insecurity prevailing in the Mediterranean because of the ceaseless warfare involving Byzantine and Muslim fleets. In support of Pirenne's thesis, Eliyahu Ashtor, another prominent contemporary historian of the Middle Ages, introduced evidence pointing to the rapid decadence of Syrian and Egyptian coastal towns in the wake of Arab victory.[25] A third well-known historian of the period, Andrew Ehrenkreutz, concludes that it is high time Pirennean polemicists admitted to the probability that the roots of Rome's decline "may be found in the progressive and constructive economic policy of the Arab conquers."[26]

What Brown's book does in relationship to this prehistory of discontinuity is offer a radically alternative narrative of how the Mediterranean world was transformed from classical paganism to a medieval Christian civilization during the period from 150 AD to 750 AD. It does not do anything else. In fact, to Brown, Europe entered medievalism when Christianity moved from the peasant cottages to courts and palaces around 700 AD. But this is also the same time Islam came to establish itself as a religion in the eastern Mediterranean and North Africa, a new wave that has created a cultural discontinuity, or, as Brown himself admits, "a division" between East and West, a division that still exists to this day.

Despite their differing viewpoints on this crucial era in European history, both Bell and Durant agree with Brown that Islam is not part of antiquity or late antiquity as much as it is a marker of its end. Oddly enough, for Brown—who does not believe in endings and who views early Byzantines, Sasanians, and Umayyads as constituting a single historical phase—Islam is the sign of the expiration of late antiquity, or what he calls "the most rapid crisis in the religious history of the Late Antique period."[27] To add to the confusion, Brown still acknowledges that Muḥammad's Mecca shielded itself from Near Eastern cultures as well as Western civilization:

> Yet for its foreign contacts, Mecca kept out of the maelstrom of Near Eastern Civilization. Its elder statesmen pursued a canny policy of neutrality. Its inhabitants held aloof from Christians, Jews and Persians. They were still held back by the fully developed style of life which they shared with the nomadic Bedouins. They were as proud

of it as they were of the resources of their own language—a language formed by epic poetry, and ideally suited to a tribal environment; it was a style of life hallowed by custom and by the lack of any viable alternative for that harsh land.[28]

In his brief reference to Islam, Brown remarks that when Muḥammad died in 632 AD, he had transformed the whole Arabian Peninsula into a land of peace and that Islam emerged with a message of unity to make all the hearts of the people of the peninsula one, perhaps in reference to the Qurʾānic verse: "And He brought their hearts together" (Q.8:63).[29] Brown is right. The ethical value of the Qurʾān made Muslims on par with God-fearing Jews and Christians and provided the illiterate Arab tribesman with a unique foundation for a literary culture that would soon rival existing monotheistic traditions. Yet, the focus in the concluding chapter of Brown's book is neither the message of Muḥammad nor its Qurʾānic principles, but rather the rapid rise of dynasties and the swift expansion of Islamic civilization into Mesopotamian Asia and the shores of the Mediterranean that created, in his view, "a division between East and West, which has been blurred throughout the Late Antique period by the confrontation of Byzantium and Persia along the Fertile Crescent."[30]

The deficiencies of Brown's integration of Islam into late antiquity are blatantly obvious to both trained classicists and informed readers. Brown's thesis has been sharply criticized for its heavy illustrations that occupy more than one hundred pages of a pithy 203-page text and for its sketchy summary of six hundred years of complex history.[31] Nothing is more damning than Brown's careless redrawing of the ecclesiastical map of late antiquity. Alexander Murray, for instance, finds Brown's mapping of the "world" of late antiquity to be quite disturbing. "On the end-map Constantinople is exactly in the middle. Even Mesopotamia is far from the eastern edge, which is taken by Kabul." Not only this, but "China is mentioned seven times in the index," contends Murry, while "the West gets correspondingly lighter emphasis."[32] These playful geographical shifts are deliberate enough to create alterations in abstract notions and currents of intellectual thought. Constantinople, while self-styled as the Eastern Roman Empire, was not substantively Rome. Its sociopolitical and historical conditions were shaped quite differently, as were those of Egypt and Syria, for that matter, yet Brown decidedly throws a larger blanket for late antiquity that not only decenters Rome and Hippo, but goes all the way to encompass the Fertile Crescent, Mesopotamia, and Iran, the "Castle of the Near East." Changing the geographical mapping of late antiquity is bound, in turn, to change its chronology and to cause seismic shifts in the weight of historical events. This is a hugely erroneous yet astutely imaginative undertaking: for how else could he show that the end of the Roman Empire in the West was barely an event at all, or even an "end" to begin with? Worse still, Brown never explains what counts as Mediterranean or why his version of the Mediterranean is somehow broken into two seas (excluding northern Spain, northern Italy, and Gaul). He does not tell us why Africa is included in the "eastern Mediterranean" in this peculiar division[33] or why Italy belongs to what he calls "a different world" south of the Apennines than the world to which it belongs in the north.[34] Nor does he explain why there could not have been a better time in world history for Christianity to thrive at the shores of the Mediterranean with a "radical communal appeal,"[35] whereas Islam has been met with the opposite results.[36]

In the confused logic of Brown's late antiquity, Islam cannot be a continuity of something that has already been there, in Rome and Hippo, and at the same time function as a rupture and a rapid discontinuity. This contradiction proves that Brown's argument is largely defective. But this is not new. Revisionist histories depend to a large degree on the intellectual climate and the ideological context in which they are produced. If humanism, the key word of the educated milieus of 1970s academic circles in America, could bring together Roman traditions and Christianity as an optimistic harmonious continuity of the idea of the West, so be it. It is obvious from Brown's contradictory thesis that it certainly could not do the same for Islam. So once again, the Arab conquest and the drastic urban change in Asia Minor that came with it, which were seen as the absolute non-West, are now begrudgingly admitted into the sphere of the West through the crafty act of stretching the historiographical boundaries of late antiquity.

While it is hard to know for how long the Brownian paradigm of late antiquity will continue to structuralize the field Qur'ānic studies, one could make an educated guess. It is likely to remain in vogue as long as it is allowed to do so, despite the fact that Brown's "smooth" theory of continuity is excessively overdone, especially when it comes to Islam's origins. Averil Cameron has forcefully pointed out that late antiquity is itself a muddled "Anglo-centric phenomenon."[37] I would argue that for the Muslim readers invoked in Neuwirth's study, this phenomenon, in addition to being "muddled," is terrifying enough to raise the red flag of Eurocentrism.

All this is to affirm the arbitrary nature of Brown's theory and the unquestionable fact that *The World of Late Antiquity* is written within the framework of a historical debate and a particular method of rethinking history that has little to do with the Qur'ān or the rise of Islam. Yet, in its integrative authority to "include" Islam, this "method" has dialectically managed to bury the peninsular prehistory and early history of Islam in the icy tomb of "otherness." One could only conclude that Brown's *World of Late Antiquity* is at best a colonial fantasy, an imaginary conquest of the past, and another variation on the familiar theme of violating the boundaries and intellectual heritages of alien cultures and traditions. It is a crossing gone too far, but it is also a crossing that is all too familiar, one that has long established itself in Western historical scholarship on the origins of Islam. Thanks to Brown, the thesis that Islam is part of *The World of Late Antiquity* has inadvertently given a new life to a decaying discipline, one that has been struggling to survive after it has long outlived its pertinence.

Thanks to Brown's thesis, it did not take long for a renewed evaluation of the emergence of Islam within the continuous shifts in Europe's Late Antique paradigms. Michael Cook's and Patricia Crone's *Hagarism* was, in fact, the first of many such attempts. When the *Hagarism* thesis received scathing criticism in the late 1970s, many scholars argued that the history of Islam's origins had been deliberately and unfairly distorted in comparison, say, to historical revisionisms of similar religious traditions like Judaism and Christianity. *Hagarism* consists of three parts: "Whence Islam?," "Whither Antiquity?," and "The Collision." Cook and Crone go on to argue that Muslim sources treating the genesis of their religion and Muḥammad's faith are unreliable, concocted ex post facto, include only theological material, and have little to no historical value. This argument, the reader finds out, is the rationale behind their writing of *Hagarism*. In order to set historical records straight, Cook and Crone decided "to step outside the Islamic tradition altogether and start again."[38] The first part, "Whence Islam?," is at best sugarcoated and could have been titled "F— All Arab/Muslim Sources."

The logic is simple: Why trust Muslims to say anything meaningful about their own faith, or even take anything they say at face value? On logical grounds, the argument makes sense. Generally accepted narratives of Islam's origins did not rely on contemporary documents but on sources compiled by Muslims years after Islam. Cook and Crone justify their argument by citing the usual suspects (Geiger, Goldziher, Schacht, Noth), who find problems with Islam's origins. But the alternative they offer is not less problematic. Cook and Crone sought to reconstruct Islam's origins from Greek and Syriac sources contemporary with Muḥammad. According to their findings, invaders from the Arabian Peninsula sought to reclaim Syro-Palestine early in the seventh century based on the pretext that the Arabs, as children of Abraham though his concubine Hagar, who begat his son Ismael, had an ancestral right to Palestine and the holy city of Jerusalem, and that Mecca, their native holy city, was just a temporary asylum. They also concluded that Muḥammad had lived longer than Muslim sources recount, until the beginning of the conquest of Syria, directly succeeded by 'Omar, because there was no Caliph Abū Bakr.

Furthermore, Cook and Crone surmised that Islam was a theopolitical movement and that Muḥammad was influenced by the Jews whom the Byzantines expelled from Edessa and who joined forces with the Arabs to reclaim the Holy Land. This, in addition to a "discovery" that Petra, not Mecca, was the original center for Mohammad's movement. With their "discoveries," Cook and Crone opened up a Pandora's box of world antiquity, demanding that all scholars of early Islam not only jettison those "false" Arabic Islamic sources but also arm themselves for a fierce battle of historical verification. And now, thanks to Cook and Crone, history—Eurocentric history, that is—is wearing its neat laboratory coat and ready to debunk the grand Muslim conspiracy theory of historical falsifications. The new historians of early Islam must now be versed in the Armenian, Coptic, Greek,

Pahlavi, Samaritan, and Syriac languages and must search every corner of late antiquity to find the "true" origins of Islam in whichever form they can be found, including coins, papyri, relics, monuments, inscriptions, and any kind of evidence available in sermons, liturgies, theological manuscripts, or literary works. In the lack of genuine proficiency in the very language of the Qur'ān, the ironic question remains: Who can claim to master this late antique past with all its languages? And what do these languages have to say "objectively" about Islam?

In Part Two, "Whither Antiquity," they use the word "antiquity" for the first time to refer to Islam's origins, a claim that neither Gibbon nor Brown, the polar opposites of those advancing the late antiquity thesis and who have their own problems with Islam, could have dreamt up. In this chapter, Crone and Cook ask a direct question: How does the cultural confrontation between primitive Arabs and highly civilized Byzantium and other civilizations in the Near East of the seventh and eighth centuries lead to the emergence of Muslim civilization? Crone and Cook fail to substantiate both their generalized claim about how cultural traditions emerge and their flimsy hypothesis that Islam emerged out of a certain hybridization of complex cultural materials. Part Three, "The Collision," is an extension of Part Two. The main goal of this part is to disprove that the *Jāhilī* period as recorded in pre-Islamic Arabic poetry is a genuine and authentic background of Islam. Crone and Cook seek to situate Islam's origins in the larger historical framework of late antiquity. Oddly enough, they easily accept non-Muslim sources without any of the scrutiny they use to dismiss the entire corpus of Arabic-Islamic sources. Why, we might ask, should seventh-century Greek and Syriac writers, who viewed Islam as the anti-Christ, be regarded as better informed about the so-called facts and as more credible sources for recounting them than Muslim sources?

My point is that Cook and Crone's hypothesis is not an anomaly that will disappear with an apology and a retraction. Rather, it is a symptom of a deeper malady. *Hagarism* was applauded by some historians not because it was based on concrete evidence. In fact, the opposite holds. It was admired because it created a historical plot *appealing* to the extreme ideological imagination of the Euro-American academy in the 1970s. The book constructed the most scandalous narrative on the origins of Islam to date, one that offers the strongest testimony of the fanciful premises of the historical-critical method in charting the history of the other. And although Crone and Cook belatedly withdrew their thesis, and Crone herself, in her subsequent publications, seems to have distanced herself from the extremism of *Hagarism*, the legacy of this work continues to reverberate across the field of Qur'ānic studies. Might there also be a dialectical benefit?

In a three-decade-belated review of the book, Fred Donner remarks that in *Hagarism* there are "important lessons on method" that need to be "absorbed" and that it compelled "historians of Islamic origins to behave truly as historians, and subject their sources to rigorous criticism."[39] Even though *Hagarism* includes a central thesis that is dreadfully flawed, as well as supporting evidence that is not only insufficient but also appallingly inconsistent, Donner still praises the book as "positive, valuable, and long overdue in a field that was so hidebound that it often resisted looking at the real evidence."[40] There may after all be a silver lining to *Hagarism* in that it makes the task of historians more difficult and holds them accountable to ethical and impartial academic thought. And speaking of impartiality, the systematic delegitimization of Muslim voices for the sake of objective research in the post-*Hagarism* Western academy continues to invite difficult questions. What kinds of methodologies, research tools, or modes of scholarship are given access to prestigious (and widely circulated) publications on Islam in the West? What brand of scholars are allowed to speak with authority on the Qur'ān? What are the prerequisites of scholarship on the Qur'ān, and what scholarly venues and disciplinary or interdisciplinary settings are capable of assimilating, consolidating, or interpreting the Qur'ān and its variegated discourses for a Western audience? If an entire discourse of scholarship on the Qur'ān remains the prisoner of *'aṣabiyya*, of ripping the other of its right to speak and understand itself, it will be virtually impossible to know how such scholarship could ever become aware of its own deficiencies, let alone critique its protracted apparatus through which we have learned to see a completely different "reality" of Islam's past than the one broadly acceptable outside of this elite machinery.

But most importantly, if Crone and Cook have aborted their attempt to reimagine Islam's past, then why has Brown's continuity thesis remained "applicable" to the field of Qur'ānic studies after this (successful) failure of *Hagarism*? Is it because it still carries hope for a more sanguine alternative in a field that has denigrated the subject of its study for centuries? Or is it because the futile insistence on the objectivity of extrapeninsular sources, as opposed to Muslim sources, now seems antediluvian, so to speak, with an overextended continuity thesis that will most definitely signal the death knell of Qur'ānic studies in the West? Could it be because *Hagarism* never really died but continued to be "positive, valuable, and long overdue," to echo Donner's eccentric praise of the book? Does *Hagarism* continue to act like an iceberg informing Euro-American historical thought on the origins of Islam? It is hard to find satisfying answers to these questions. What we know for a fact is that by the time Brown's *The World of Late Antiquity* was published, the old orientalist model that thrived on historical revisionism in mining the sources of the Qur'ān had fallen out of fashion, and for a good reason. In addition, dehistoricized theological approaches of Biblicism left the educated reader confused and hungry for more historical equity and balanced context. In short, it was becoming pronouncedly clear, especially for a global readership of Islam and world history, that denying the immediate context in which Islam evolved any agency to speak for itself simply belies historical facts and benefits only a few zealots for the cause of the historical-critical method. It was becoming even clearer that orientalist approaches were based on strawman assumptions that monotheistic religions before Islam were in some way more developed and more established than an imposing new religion was.

Cryptic and sketchy in its musings on the place of Islam in late antiquity, Brown's book was controversial enough to draw the attention of the Euro-American field of Qur'ānic studies, which immediately espoused the thesis, as we have seen in the case Crone and Cook, in a manner that seeks to view the Qur'ān's origins with "fresh" eyes, so to speak.[41] To be fair, Brown's thesis still has something to offer the embattled field of Qur'ānic studies: a model that promises to be both more historically grounded and more epistemologically nuanced—at least in its appearance—than the good old orientalist approach, with its blatant biases and adverse stereotypes. Even though Brown does not say that Islam is part of late antiquity, he nonetheless believes in continuities. His colonial remapping includes Islam in the complex world of late antique social formations. This "outlet" is all the field of Qur'ānic studies in the West has been looking for. It gives it a ticket out of the prison house of binary oppositions, one in which it trapped itself for at least two centuries. Brown's flexible continuity thesis for the unmastered past of late antiquity has now paradoxically become the new "mastered" present of Qur'ānic studies. Brown's continuity thesis dissolved the barriers and shifted the debate about antiquity from clear partitions between chronological periods toward more subtle expositions of relationships and interactions among various communities of faith, thus opening the door for a new approach and for renewed investigations of the origins of Islam at a deciding historical moment in the field of Qur'ānic studies. The Brownian shift in the historical thought of the Euro-American academy led to the discovery of late antiquity as a new horizon for engaging with Islam's origins.

Such renewed interest alone makes Neuwirth's annexation of Islam into European Late Antiquity both urgent and timely. After all, this is the claim Hegel made almost two hundred years ago, when he included Islam in the medieval Germanic fourth stage of world history: "[T]he old age of the *Geist* in its complete ripeness, in which *Geist* returns to unity with itself, but as *Geist*."[42] In Hegel, Islam becomes the West in the unique Hegelian sense of the West—the self-consciousness of *Geist*. Hegel even calls Islam "the enlightenment of the oriental world."[43] In the Brownian paradigm of late antiquity, this Hegelian "enlightenment" that is Islam may no longer be just of the oriental world, or even *in* the oriental world as Hegel thought, but may render the peninsular geography of early Islam peripheral, by opening the possibility for expanding boundaries and overturning the traditional categories of the late Roman Empire. This, and the claims of detecting traces of Hellenistic culture within the Arabic language, is all Neuwirth and late antiquarians would need in order to make the Qur'ān an integral part of the religious history of the West.[44] This "integration" is already yielding important reconsiderations for European Muslims who would no longer be perceived as the "others" of the West, at least not historically or epistemologically. Dialectically, however, it would also mean that the Qur'ān would risk losing its Arabicity and, to echo Neuwirth, it would risk losing the intimate discursive codes within which the text operated and gained its status as the most revolutionary literary event of the Arabic language par excellence.

THE QUR'ĀN AND THE LATE ANTIQUARIANS: A CONTINUITY THESIS?

The relationship between the Qur'ān and late antiquity has thus gone through two extreme changes in the twentieth century. From the start of the century, passing through the "Pirennean Controversy" of the 1920s, up until 1971, Islam was studied as the kiss of death for late antiquity, a line of separation and division, and a boundary between a familiar self and an unfriendly, distant other—a line emphatically drawn in the sand between the so-called "culture" and "anarchy" of two worlds. In the immediate aftermath of Brown's *The World of Late Antiquity*, the infinite distance that once separated the two worlds disappeared, the boundaries were blurred, and the closer the "ein europäischer Zugang" came to this boundary, the more confidently it would want to assert itself, to interpret, to interrogate, to define, and to claim Islam, not as an entity of affection, or as an amicable or friendly extension of the self, but as an entity of ownership and custodial authority, so to speak. To be sure, there is nothing new about the attempts to include Islam as part of the long late antiquity, except that perhaps earlier attempts like that of Crone and Cook were more hostile. What is new, however, is the categorical claim that the Qur'ān—and by extension Islam—is now, at least conceptually, *part of* Europe, constituted via Europe, and has for long been wrongly mistreated as the other of Europe. In other words, long late antiquity can now afford to claim Islam back to its European self, so to speak.

In this context, Hugh Kennedy's short entry on "Islam" in the volume on *Late Antiquity: A Guide to the Postclassical World*, edited by Brown, among others, serves as an example of the late antiquity thesis of continuity. Like Brown, Kennedy builds an argument against the grain, in defiance of "great monuments of scholarship, like A. H. M. Jones's *Later Roman Empire* and the *New Cambridge Ancient History*," two works that "take it as axiomatic that the coming of Islam in the early seventh-century marked a change so complete that there was no advantage in pursuing the topics that had been discussed into the new era."[45] Inspired in part by, and perhaps written as a prelude to, Sidney Griffith's study of the Christian Arabic tradition of the ninth century, Kennedy's article does not deal with the Qur'ān's commentary on Christianity per se, or with Muḥammad's interactions with the Christian communities of his close surroundings or beyond (e.g., Abyssinia) but rather with what he characterizes is a "gradual and multifaceted" transition of the world of antiquity into the dynasties of early Islam, especially Muslim Syria.[46] "Early Islamic society," writes Kennedy, "built on and developed in the Late Antique legacy."[47] However, Kennedy does not explain how this happened or provide supporting evidence for this vague "gradual transition." Given its focused bibliography, as well as its adoption of the Cronian method of dismissing Muslim sources, Kennedy's article does not cite any examples from the Qur'ān or the Islamic tradition or include a single Arabic reference on Islam from that period. The article lacks both interest in and awareness of the classical texts of its main thesis. Further, it does not reference medieval Arab-Islamic scholarship on the topic and fails to explain how the Qur'ān "built on" the late antique legacy. The result is a hollowed "continuity thesis" of late antiquity into seventh-century Arabia that has little to no support, especially when there is compelling evidence in medieval Europe and Islam that chronicles the drastic changes and discontinuities in official languages and major transformations in identity politics,[48] social conditions, education,[49] military development,[50] and religious practices.[51]

A much more sophisticated and rigorous examination of Islam in late antiquity is to be found in Aaron Hughes's article "Religion without Religion: Integrating Islamic Origins into Religious Studies." In this provocative article, Hughes welcomes the study of Islam's origins under the umbrella of late antiquity. Sickened by the vicious orientalism the field has sunk into, Hughes makes a reasonable plea for Islam to be studied on equal footing with Judaism and Christianity, urging that such inclusion should be left to the specialists in the field of religious studies in order to avoid setbacks, pitfalls, or lapses into the historical errors and generalizations of older orientalism. "Instead of seeing the birth of Islam as a unidirectional and transformative force that enters world history in the early seventh century," contends Hughes in a Spinozan spirit, "we must be attentive to it as a point of arrival or the culmination—and not merely the sum—of an interlocking set of political, social, intellectual, and religious trends of the Hellenistic and Late Antique periods . . . The origins of Islam, then, are no different from the origins of other Western monotheisms: they are clouded in mystery, and are about human ingenuity and worldmaking in the midst of rapid change."[52] In the footnote to his statement, Hughes emphasizes that Ernest Renan was categorically wrong when he argued that "Islam was born in the full light of history."[53]

Hughes's insightful and sanguine plea for inclusivity in treating Islam as an expression of late antique times is reasonable and timely, especially in light of increasing interest in the Abrahamic tradition and its connection to the period.[54] It is not every day that a Western scholar connects Islam to human ingenuity in the same sentence. But where would Hughes's sympathetic and inclusive vision of historical equity fit within Brown's paradoxical paradigm? This is an important question because Brown, who happens to be the very originator of the late antiquity thesis on the Qur'ān, sees Islam not only as a break but also as an event that brought an end to late antiquity. Brown did not perceive the arrival of Islam in Egypt with the Muslim army of 'Amr ibn al-'Āṣ in 640/642 AD as a token of inclusivity, let alone continuity or culmination of anything. He neither saw Islam as a smooth transition nor took the Muslim "conquest" with a grain of salt, as he did, say, the Mediterranean's conversion to Christianity. A historian who contradicts himself usually says two things, and both of them should matter. Brown refuses to see Islam's invasion of Egypt as anything more than a conquest—a rupture and an abrupt discontinuity in the traditional sense of the term. This cold reception makes one wonder: How many other historians of this long late antiquity are going to play down the idea of rupture, emphasize endurance over change, and see Islam as a product rather than as a revisionary event, however equivocal that might be? And why do scholars have to take sides and choose between the two?

The forced continuity with which Brown includes Islam at the transmuting point of late antiquity is celebrated in Neuwirth's work.[55] Despite Cook and Crone's speculative venture into Islam's past, or perhaps because of it, Neuwirth continues to probe the *terra incognita* of Brown's continuity thesis, but to her credit, she does so from a different position. In an earlier essay on the same topic, Neuwirth acknowledges that "the task of positioning the Qurʾān in Late Antiquity still waits to be accomplished."[56] Staying true to her words, and ultimately espousing Brown's continuity thesis, which is supportive of and central to her project, Neuwirth gives her book the perfect subtitle of "Ein europäischer Zugang" (A European approach). In the singular form, "Zugang" connotes access or admission. In that sense, to translate the title as a "European access" to Islam would not be too far-fetched. Connotatively, "Zugang" implies a viewpoint (like *Perspektive*) and a movement (like *Herangehensweise/Annäherung*), as well as an option or a possibility (*Eingang zu/Tor zu/*access to). In the context of Neuwirth's argument, the rich connotations of a European perspective on Islam (from a remote place and without movement) and a European movement/going to/approaching (Annäherung zu) Islam, seem quite telling.[57] In other words, the idea is to see the Qurʾān as neither a hypocritical mimesis nor an illegitimate son of biblical origins, but as a genuine inheritor and an active participant in the very legacy of Abrahamic monotheism of late antiquity. To Neuwirth, long late antiquity has afforded this apologetic admission of Islam into Europe by way of the Roman Empire. "Read together with the writings of Late Antique rhetoricians, the church fathers, and the rabbis, all of whom are commonly claimed as part of the European legacy," writes Neuwirth, "the Qurʾān actually becomes a text that is familiar to us—or it would be, if our own intellectual preconceptions did not skew our perceptions."[58]

So far, so good. But if a historian of Islam begins by interrogating the origins of the Qurʾān, examining not the present-day text Muslims read the world over, but rather the formative process of the Qurʾān, such a historian might at least consider situating the text within the discursive codes of its original language and the symbolic representations of this text as a document of its own time that is intimately in dialogue with its intended audience. One does not need a Bakhtinian theory to see that the Qurʾān is radically dialogical and in constant conversations with the seventh-century Meccan and Medinan communities, communities with deep pride in their tribal codes and the poetic exploits of their language, for which regular poetry contexts were held. While the Qurʾān includes an obvious "intratextuality" that invites comparative inquiry with biblical studies, these intertextualities are commentative and interpretive rather than constitutive, which makes it hard to agree with Neuwirth that this relationship "justifies the urgency of a serious analysis of the structure of the text that is to be informed by biblical studies."[59] The Qurʾān is not just a transcript of an ongoing debate or a cultural translation of this particular "space" of interaction. In fact, most of the dialogical interactions with the Qurʾān's intended audience concern matters germane to the seventh-century Meccan and Medinan communities, including piety, social laws and ethics, aesthetics, and other social matters such as marriage, divorce, adultery, enactments related to children, inheritance, murder, commercial contracts, debts, usuary, food, wine, games, and so on. It is true, to some extent, that the Qurʾān enters into a "dialogue" with other religions—although it is hard to understand this dialogue in pure philosophical terms, given that dialogues are mutual inquiries based on the principle of sharing ideas *at the same time and place* to arrive at a better understanding of that which needs to be understood. In addition to its biblical references, there is a far much larger and more dominant "intertextuality" in the Qurʾān that is best understood in the text's intent to form a just community of believers through a highly emphasized linguistic prophetic discourse known to and practiced by that very community.

This is the case whether one seeks to examine the moment when the Arabic language of the Qurʾān differentiates itself from the conventional ritualistic poetry or prose of pagan Arabia, or whether the investigation is of larger sociohistorical contexts outside the Arabian Peninsula that may or may not have influenced its religious cultures, including the long late antiquity of Europe (via Rome and Hippo) and the eastern Mediterranean. Although Neuwirth dedicates a fraction of her book to the relationship between the Qurʾān and the Arabic language, in particular to pre-Islamic poetry, she acknowledges the obvious illogicality that "while the relationship of the Qurʾān to the neighboring monotheistic traditions across various language barriers has been a central critical interest since the beginnings of Qurʾān research, *the highly developed and extensively transmitted literature in the Qurʾan's own language, ancient Arabic poetry, has rarely been contextualized with the Qurʾan.*"[60] This is a sobering acknowledgement. If the Arabic tradition of the Qurʾān were indeed part of late antiquity, as Neuwirth claims, what would be a better place for the European reader than a study of the Arabicity of the Qurʾān? Neuwirth's peripheral treatment of the Qurʾān's Arabic language and of ancient Arabic poetry in her own book reveals a methodological inconsistency.

Neuwirth is a committed practitioner of the historical-critical approach to the Qurʾān, to which she has dedicated her book,[61] and which she continues to defend even though she acknowledges that it is "an approach that is being questioned from various perspectives in recent times."[62] It is not hard to see why the historical-critical method has outlived its use.[63] It is no secret that this method has informed the German School's framework of inquiry into the origins of Islam since the Heidelberg orientalist Gustav Weil's work, *Mohammed der Prophet, sein Leben und seine Lehre* in 1843.[64] This practice is clearly enveloped in the historical-critical method or what is also known as "high criticism" or "historical criticism," a historical approach originally adopted in studying the Hebrew Bible (Old Testament) and the New Testament. This approach draws on numerous fields, including history, geography, anthropology, archaeology, and antique literature in order to reconstruct the historical setting within which biblical texts were produced.

Today, new approaches in reception theory and synchronic Bible readings argue for reintegrating the Bible into its internal liturgical and theological tradition instead of into "external" contexts. These approaches have effectively displaced the now defunct historical-critical method. Nevertheless, Neuwirth somehow insists that the Qur'ān does not qualify for this luxury and must continue to be studied in light of the historical-critical method. Her reasoning is that "Qur'ān research, unlike this new direction of biblical studies, is not faced with the task of reconnecting the Qur'ān to its traditional exegetical context."[65] Why not? And why is it acceptable for a historical method specifically designed to deconstruct the Bible, a method that has now not only outlived its value but has also proved to have significant shortcomings, to continue to be the arbiter of a text it was never meant to interrogate?[66] Speaking of "Qur'ān research" and the assignments of its tasks, why is it so difficult to see that the biblical bias in this very research ultimately discloses not the meaning of the Qur'ān but how the canon of Qur'ānic studies is shaped in Euro-American academia?

Neuwirth is fully aware that there are mainly two opposite camps when it comes to the study of the Qur'ān: the biblical and the Arabian. Neuwirth's argument for the historical-critical method as the only valid approach for including the Qur'ān under the rubric "late antiquity" is based on an unsubstantiated assumption that the contents and imagery[67] of the early, middle, and late Meccan sūras have strong affinities with biblical psalms, or what she calls "psalmic piety,"[68] while maintaining "poetic" local features present in pre-Islamic poetry, whatever that means. Neuwirth bases her assumption on what she surmises in the Meccan sūras to be a representation of Muslims as the rightful inheritors of the Banī Isrā'il (Israelites), especially in reference to Jerusalem.[69] In other words, the presumption that the Qur'ān appropriates the biblical tradition and reshapes it according to its own existing Arabic "poetic" codes becomes Neuwirth's justification for the application of the historical-critical method. I argue in the following chapter that this deduction is drawn too sharply, given the dense complexity of the relationship between ancient Arabic poetry and the Qur'ān, which has sorely remained understudied in the Western academy. "Almost perversely," emphasizes Thomas Bauer, "Qur'anic scholars (in the West) do not show much enthusiasm about the existence of this literature."[70] But this is how Neuwirth interprets the Qur'ān's earliest sūras—namely, as a reproduction, or rather, a "reinterpretation" of the biblical landscape into Arabia, which, in her scheme, would necessitate an annexation of late antique elaborations on scriptural traditions.[71] In other words, Neuwirth softly resurrects Crone's old orientalist thesis that there was a prominent Jewish community in the Hijaz able to influence the literary evolution of the Qur'ān and the permeation of foundational narratives such as Abraham's "anachronistic" erection of the *Kaaba* in the spirit of constructing Mecca as a new *qibla* in lieu of *al-Masjid al-Aqṣá* of Jerusalem.[72]

All this is to say that Neuwirth's "new" integration of the Qur'ān under "late antiquity" is not a new approach, but a sympathetic restoration of an older method, one that singles out verses and sūras to support a particular theoretical position and to advance an entire epistemology. She dismisses Gustav von Grunebaum's argument for the "Arabicity" of the Qur'ān and considers it both "problematic" and "impaired" for the latter to contend that "from an Arabic standpoint, the teaching of Muhammad [signifies] unmistakable progress towards greater religious and intellectual maturity," and that the Arabs were the intended "receivers of the teachings of Muhammad."[73] She argues that von Grunebaum's logic is flawed because it excises the Arabs, "thus removing them by essentialist logic from the wider circles of listeners educated in Late Antique lore and establishing a firm polarity between the Jews and Christians (who appear only later as theological opponents) on the one hand and the putative pure 'Arabs' on the other."[74] It is hard to see a flaw in von Grunebaum's logic other than that it does not fit Neuwirth's categorical construct. In fact, the Qur'ān supports von Grunebaum's argument in repeatedly asserting that that text's geographical positionality is coterminous with its Arabicity as a mode of intelligibility, and underscoring that its local intelligibility does not necessarily trump the universal appeal of its message:

وَكَذَٰلِكَ أَوْحَيْنَا إِلَيْكَ قُرْآنًا عَرَبِيًّا لِّتُنذِرَ أُمَّ الْقُرَىٰ وَمَنْ حَوْلَهَا

And so We have revealed to you an Arabic Qur'ān, so you may warn the Mother of villages and everyone around it. (42:7)[75]

Not only this. Neuwirth has decided, through a misreading of James Montgomery[76] and an uncritical adoption of Michael Zwettler's Eurocentrist theory on the oral composition of classical Arabic poetry,[77] that the discourse of pre-Islamic Arabic poetry also falls under the blanket of late antiquity.[78] Even though she belaboringly insists that late antiquity is an epistemic space not to be misunderstood as a political chronological period, it is hard to deny the fact that the term has a definitive historical framework, which extends from early Roman imperial times and describes the time of transition from classical antiquity to the Middle Ages in Europe. Sooner or later, one has to come to terms with the fact that the comfort of the historical-critical method has consisted in lending a starry-eyed totalization that gives the impression that an intricate web of themes, styles, ideas, and events has in its overall totality come together over an accumulation of centuries to offer a holistic understanding of a certain period or epoch in history. Such an understanding is diagnostically essentialist, in the sense in which we have seen Hegel condemn the totalizing operations of historicism. Not only Hegel, but Spinoza, who is often credited as the first philosopher to have launched the field of historical criticism of the Bible, sounds a grim warning about its limitations and difficulties, speaking of "the method's capacity to guide us towards a full and certain knowledge of the sacred books" when most of it "is unknown to us."[79]

There is a notable difference between the approach of Western historians to the Qur'ān and that of philologists and literary critics, a gap Neuwirth has sought to bridge. On balance, European historians are growing more frequently ambivalent toward the stretched theories regarding Islam's origins that they inherited from the last generation of revisionist historians—for example, Cook and Crone's thesis on Islam as Jewish sect[80] or Christoph Luxenberg's unscholarly obsession with its Christian borrowings.[81] Many well-informed historians tend to use or propose historical theories of Islam's past with caution and inclusivity.[82] By contrast, literary critics are bound to consider the Qur'ān in relation to an existing body of literature, mostly pre-Islamic Arabic literature, which, according to al-Jāḥiẓ, emerged between 150 and 200 years prior to Islam and continued well into the early years of Qur'ānic revelation. For these reasons, discussions between historians and *littérateurs* often arrive at an insuperable impasse. One must tread carefully, then, on the *terra incognita* of late antiquity's "conversations" with the Qur'ān, lest these conversations carry an unconscious bias or a latent continuity thesis of Cook and Crone's kind. For what else could Cook and Crone's venture be other than a dangerous scheme to disperse the Qur'ān in the labyrinths of late antiquity and dilute its origins in a melting pot of cultural forces within an allegedly Hellenized Middle East?

A suitable example of a study attentive to these literary/historical interconnections between the humanities and the social sciences can be found in Holger Zellentin's recently edited volume, *The Qur'ān's Reformation of Judaism and Christianity*. Zellentin begins the volume with the acknowledgment that it is high time the West moved away from treating the Qur'ān as the scripture of a minority and toward a more inclusive treatment of it as part of Europe's legacy. According to Zellentin, this movement is historical in every sense, stemming from the West's realization that it needs to reposition itself toward the Qur'ān from within its own historical context. "We have come to recognize that the Scripture of Islam should be understood not only as the foundational document of the Islamic community," argues Zellentin, "but also in dialogue with the world of Late Antiquity, whose transition into the Middle Ages was expedited by the rise of the Islamic community itself."[83] This invitation to redirect the course of Qur'ānic studies more inwardly toward Europe feels like a fresh reset button in a field that has systematically been hostile to Islam. Authors cited in Zellentin's volume, especially Walid Saleh and Angelika Neuwirth, are aware of this history and know that they are writing against a grain so selective in its pursuit of the origins of Islam.

Still, while Zellentin's volume does not shy away from engaging with the sources of the Qurʾān's origins, it does so in a manner that appears more nuanced, more benign, and more equitable than former dismissive "Western" approaches. "In contrast to the comparatist efforts of the religious polemicists of past and present," contends Zellentin, "many contemporary scholars have largely digested the lessons of postcolonialism in as far as they tend not seek to establish the superiority of anyone tradition over the other."[84] Zellentin invokes Dominick LaCapra's seminal article on the topic of rethinking intellectual history. LaCapra is a distinct scholar who bridges intellectual history and literary representations, and is thus an appropriate choice to cement Zellentin's repositioning of the West's historical attitude toward Islam with an epiphany of sorts, an overdue realization that "the Qurʾan's value as a canonical text . . . resists common assumptions, and allows for an especially compelling conversation with Islamic Scripture."[85] It makes sense for Zellentin to invoke LaCapra in calling for confronting one's own ideological biases and repairing the damage caused by older orientalism—perhaps in an implicit reference to Crone and Wansbrough—when he acknowledges the unpleasant past of Western scholarship on the Qurʾān.

Elsewhere, Zellentin emphasizes the need to embrace the Qurʾān as a primary text and "a key source reference for Arabian culture."[86] However, there is a stark contradiction in his argument. On the one hand, Zellentin wants to exonerate the Qurʾān from the "derivation spell" cast upon it by the older orientalists and to honor its historical value "regardless of it religious significance," namely, as a document with "a wealth of information about its intended audience" and which "allows for a genuine glimpse into Late Antique Arabia."[87] On the other hand, Zellentin treats "Late Antique Arabia" as an indisputable historical given and falls back to an essentialist theory of "influence," recasting the Qurʾān as a text that belongs "to the category of monotheism and its history from the Hebrew Bible, throughout Late Antique Judaism and Christianity,"[88] thus risking, yet again, silencing the Qurʾān's Arabicity, its informative pre-Islamic poetic corpus, and its sociolinguistic specificity.

The invocation of LaCapra could not have been more timely, for all the reasons Zellentin mentions. In fact, LaCapra touches a sore nerve in intellectual history, one that, dialectically enough, interrogates the validity of the very project of late antiquity that Zellentin represents. "The belief in pure interpretation," contends LaCapra, "is itself a bid for absolute transcendence that denies both the finite nature of understanding and the need to confront critically what Freud discussed in terms of "transference."[89] What this means for late antiquity as a new venture for investigating the Qurʾān is that it finds itself in danger of projecting itself onto the other. When it comes to the relationship between the Qurʾān and late antiquity, the Euro-American academy's excessive denigration of the genesis of the text to external, non-Arab origins is based on an unmistakable case of "attribution bias"—namely, an alarming self-identification with these origins.[90] Usually, this is not necessarily harmful. But variations on the Brownian theme of a continuous and unending late Antiquity have to come face to face with the fact that while the Qur'ān comments on and invites comparison with Judaism and Christianity, there remains no clear-cut historical evidence to support the hypothesis that it is "shaped" by external forces outside Muḥammad's Meccan society, linguistically, philologically, or socially.

Nor can the field articulate a clear delineation or a trace for any of the themes of late antiquity in the Qur'ān that are *not* already germane to its immediate context in the Arabian Peninsula; even notions such as asceticism, revelation, miracles, and prophecies had already existed in the collective consciousness of the Arabian Peninsula before Islam. If anything, just a cursory reading of pre-Islamic Poetry would situate the Qur'ān thematically and linguistically at the heart of the seventh-century Arabian Peninsula. The linguistic organicity, the communal dialogue, and the social context of the Qur'ān's revelation all play a substantial part in this relationship. There is a sharp irony between the confirmed state of the field's indiscernibility when it comes to the distinction between what is "native" and what is "foreign," or what Zellentin characterizes as "the ultimate unknowability of much of pre-Islamic Arabic culture and religion," and the degree of certitude and inevitability with which he embeds the Qur'ān into the fabric of late antiquity. Here, again, LaCapra is useful. "Historiography would be an exercise in narcissistic infatuation," maintains LaCapra, "if it amounted to a willful projection of present concerns upon the past. The notion of 'creative misreading' is itself mis-leading when it legitimates one-sided, subjectivist aggression that ignores the ways in which texts may actually challenge the interpreter and lead him to change his mind."[91]

Treating the Qur'ān as a text of late antiquity is enveloped in postcolonial guilt. The unending late antiquity tsunami of Peter Brown and its ramifications threaten to drown something linguistically organic to its people. The problem here is not that the Qur'ān includes a universal message or narrates stories from the Old Testament, or even continues themes of codes from late antique times. It does. But notions of piety, social justice, and high moral codes do not necessarily have to come from Europe to receive a stamp of originality. It is almost as if LaCapra predicted the late antiquity thesis, and in particular Peter Brown's fanciful version, on Islam when he wrote that historiography "is not an autonomous hermeneutic undertaking that moves on the level of pure meaning to establish a 'fusion of horizons' assuring *authoritative continuity with the past.*"[92] If anything, the issue of late antiquity, which promises to bring some unity of theory and practice, serves instead to dramatize the ambivalence and uncertainty of the Euro-American academy's position regarding Islam's origins. In this well-intended attempt to locate a privileged space within the self to include the other, we risk defaulting back into the trap of "revisionism," the return of a historical boomerang thought to have been vanquished after the onslaught of *Hagarism.*

This risk brings back the urgent question of a proper approach to the study of the Qurʾān in the West. This question is owing as much to the collapse of one's own inclinations and presuppositions as it is to any conscious and learned awareness of the textual weight of the Qurʾān in the world outside the narrow prisms of scholarly and academic *ʿaṣabiyya*. One may, therefore, as a practitioner of the larger field of the humanities, acknowledge the crucial need to liberate the Qurʾānic text from the cancerous growth of ideologies, both Eastern and Western, that have beset it since the seventh century. I use the word "text" here deliberately—not in the reductive way that may be meant to resurrect old debates on the text-ness of the Qurʾān, which a scholar like Naṣr Ḥāmid Abū Zayd had to endure, but precisely in order *not* to reduce the Qurʾān to one governable discipline or "method" over the other. The idea is to turn one's attention to the presence of the Qurʾān, its message, its rhetorical power, not solely and rigidly to how it came to be, but to what it is and what it does. One is compelled to ask: How long can scholarship on Islam in the West afford to lapse into a collective "defense mechanism" of "transference," to echo LaCapra, and how long before it starts to transcend the obsession with searching for its image in alien texts?

It has become increasingly evident that "interpretive findings" of late antiquity, no matter how stretched or hyperbolic they might be, have become the *modus operandi* of recent and current publications on the Qurʾān. Forcefully armed with Brown's "continuity thesis," the negative authority of Crone's *Hagarism*, and Garth Fowden's notion of "maturation,"[93] late antiquarians have one clear goal: to restore the Qurʾān, scripturally and prophetically, to what one might venture to call "operation millennium." In this operation millennium, the thousand-year span between Aristotle and Muḥammad is a fair game, despite the fact that Muḥammad lived in a remote place, far outside the fringes of Aristotle's sphere of influence, and may have not heard of him. This is not to say that the work and ideas of Aristotle did not travel far or did not leave indelible impacts on Islam's cultures and civilization. Yet, there is in the late antiquarian theses regarding the Qurʾān a troublesome assertion of historical totalization. The comparatist in me would normally embrace all forms and themes of textual affinities across time and space, and the influence of Aristotle and the peripatetic school is undoubtedly far-reaching in Islamic philosophy, but I will argue that the imperatives here carry with them pernicious consequences.

Let me illustrate this paradox with an example from Edward Gibbon's *History of the Decline and Fall of the Roman Empire*. In chapter 33 of this multivolume work, Gibbon discusses Q.18 (*Sūra-t- al-Kahf*, the Chapter of the Cave); he refers to the story of the Seven Sleepers of Ephesus. Gibbon argues that this "insipid legend" must have traveled from late antique Christianity to the land of Islam. To Gibbon, the story of the seven sleepers was originally a narrative about the emergence of Christianity as a victorious religion in the aftermath of a dark era of persecution. In other words, the story of the seven sleepers accurately enough preceded Islam and may have well been narrated and circulated by Syriac bishops prior to Islam. There is nothing new about this. The Qurʾān refers to parts of this narrative in the Chapter of the Cave, named after the place in which the sleepers stayed. The story of the sleepers, however, constitutes only seventeen verses (Q.18: 9–26) of the sūra's 110 verses. Because the Qurʾān incorporates the narrative of the sleepers of the Cave, Gibbon assumes that Muḥammad must have stolen the tale "when he drove his camels to the fairs of Syria" and recast it "as a divine revelation into the Qurʾan." Furthermore, relying exclusively on Marracci's polemical translation and commentary on the Qurʾān, Gibbon concludes, sarcastically, that "Mahomet has not shown much taste or ingenuity," even when "he has invented the dog (Al Rakim) of the Seven Sleepers; the respect of the sun, who altered his course twice a day that he might not shine into the cavern; and the care of God himself, who preserved their bodies from putrefaction by turning them to the right and left."[94] What Gibbon's thesis leaves out is a system of allegorical interpretation whereby the story of the sleepers, whose account comes as a verification test for Muḥammad's prophethood,[95] is radically transformed in its Qurʾānic context to respond to local communal interrogations and redirect the story from the quibble of historical details to the ultimate moral lessons that need to be drawn from it. Moreover, Gibbon omits the need for a serious interrogation of the veracity and cohesion of that "first millennium," which he employs uncritically as a period in the history of monotheism. This is how Gibbon drags Muḥammad into the declining world of the Roman Empire. This is also how he declares Islam as the end of late antiquity—by mocking Muḥammad's character and presenting his prophethood as a debt to Syriac Christianity.

But given the rowdy orientalism of Gibbon's age, one would not have expected him to write favorably about the Qurʾān. It is, rather, the recycling of Gibbon in modern scholarship that is alarming. In writing *Before and after Muhammad*, Garth Fowden states that he has "come to a better appreciation of Edward Gibbon,"[96] not because of his unapologetic Eurocentrism, his firm belief that European civilization is the pinnacle of human achievement, or because of his unflinching support of the "discontinuity thesis" on the fall of the Roman Empire, which Fowden rejects, but because Fowden sees Gibbon as "setting an agenda that today seems more valid than ever."[97] Gibbon, who flagrantly accuses Muḥammad of plagiarism, has an "agenda" that inspires Fowden to write a history that includes Islam in a European millennium, the longest periodization the human mind could ever conceive. Is it likely that Fowden did not know or simply ignored this troubling aspect of Gibbon's scholarship? It is precisely in learning to confront the monstrosity of one's own tradition that the hope of dismantling this machinery of systematic othering and bringing it face to face with what it cannot grasp without succumbing to the larger of metanarrative of Euro-American ʿaṣabiyya lies.

When Michel Foucault spoke of "periodization" and when Frederic Jameson cautioned critics to "always historicize," they did not have in mind any period longer than a hundred years, let alone a thousand years. Yet Fowden's work has inspired many. It is probably the driving force behind Aziz al-Azmeh's long-winded study on the topic; it also features prominently in Neuwirth's thesis on late antiquity. This is how Europe is making amends and reimagining its relationship to Islam. This is how the Euro-American academy overcomes its long-guarded western-Mediterranean and Byzantine turfs and jumps well beyond its boundaries to intellectually colonize the Qurʾān in an unending stretch of a grand narrative that spans a millennium: a wild subordination of history to a cosmetic surgery and a decadent feast for the Eurocentric historians of the Qurʾān. To be fair, incorporating Islam under "late antiquity" remains a colossal task and a difficult argument to make or even accept in contemporary Europe, precisely because it entails an extension in the teleology of Abrahamic monotheism,[98] with the hopeful presumption that Islam would still be treated as equal to and not as derivative from both Judaism and Christianity. This will in turn entail a different reading of the Qurʾān as a complement to and a commentary on both Judaism and Christianity. In the other direction, this incorporation will necessitate a radical retooling of Christian theology, which will have to accept Islam, and not Christianity, as the latest update of Abrahamic monotheism. This development is bound to "turn traditional patristics on its head," to use Averil Cameron's fitting words, "by making Islam, not Christianity, the end point."[99]

But my point in citing these examples is to emphasize an important fact: the appeal of late antiquity as framework for research has already opened a portal between two kinds of academics: the "new" historians who see late antiquity as a *fait accompli* periodization that opens up boundaries and geographies to include Islam; and the *Hagarism*-infused historian who is uninterested in the traditional Muslim argument that the Qurʾān ushers in a new age and insists instead that the text is an iconoclastic myriad of repetitive modes recast from previous religious and cultural traditions.[100] While the latter brand of historians are free to locate sources for the Qurʾān wherever they please, they have no qualms in boasting that the practical advantage of studying Islam as "a child of Late Antiquity," is that "it widens the scope of their [late antiquarians] field to include a new geographical region, a new religious phenomenon and a greater span of time."[101]

Stewart warns against exactly such a maddened rush into what he characterizes as a "quantum leap" in present publications on the Qurʾān, leading to a state of "confusion" and "a feverish activity" that "has produced no grand consensus" in a field that continues to appear "chaotic, even to insiders."[102] Cameron also calls this trend "the explosion of Late Antiquity" and cautions that scholars will eventually have to face "the challenge to be aware and to try to take account of the immensely complex context with which we are now presented."[103] In this vein, a question that was asked before must be asked again: Does the late antiquity thesis run the risk of participating in a different uprooting of Islam? Is it a radical departure from the crass orientalism that still haunts the field, or is it a return under a different name, of another metanarrative, another constructed historical category designed to control the event of Islam, its Arabicity and sociolinguistic particularity? Even at this point, it is hopeful to imagine that a productive and decisive position in the field of Qur'ānic studies is still possible, one that, while admitting the messiness and complexity of history, and while grateful to the efforts and methodical approaches of their predecessors, is unafraid to leave behind the carved gods of Eurocentrism and embrace fresh approaches outside the façades of the "objective" method and the convenient metanarratives of authenticity and epigonality. Today, the chaos and disarray in this field warrant an urgent intervention and an ethical response to what Emmanuel Levinas not so long ago characterized as "the face of the other."

There is no denying that until today, and despite its fundamental drawbacks, the historical-critical study of scripture and biblical texts still rules the academy,[104] especially in terms of what gets transmitted to nonspecialists. Scholars who are not operating within an explicitly theological Jewish or Christian perspective often have almost the same attitude toward the Bible as Western scholars have toward the Qur'ān. *Almost!* They do not come at it with the same Eurocentrism and colonialist mentality. So, it is *almost* as if Western scholarship on the Qur'ān sometimes takes the same condescension toward the biblical text and amplifies it with all of the colonialist and postcolonialist hostility and appropriation. It is *almost* a form of intersectionality, except that, in the case of Islam, it is a combination of derision toward religion and derision toward a culture.

While the ghost of "continuity," as I have argued elsewhere,[105] never fades away but lurks like a receding telos, such a telos may take many different faces and could even mutate within fluctuating contexts and epistemologies. Appropriations of history for the service of the present are neither new nor appropriate, but as "old as Babylon and [as] evil as Hell," to borrow Edward Abbey's words. In fact, Nietzsche, who once expressed a desire to live among Muslims in order to deconstruct better Europe's crisis in values—so that his "eye and judgement for all things European will be sharpened"—summed up these tendencies to appropriate history quite eloquently in the following statement:

> If a man who wants to do something great has need of the past at all, he appropriates it by means of monumental history; he, on the other hand, who likes to persist in the familiar and the revered of old, tends the past as an antiquarian historian; and only he who is oppressed by a present need, and who wants to throw off this burden at any cost, has need of critical history, that is to say, a history that judges and condemns.[106]

This statement plays at the heart of the crisis of current Euro-American scholarship on the Qur'ān. Nietzsche's reference to "critical history" is a history that recognizes the misdeeds of the past and endeavors to liberate people from dominant forms of ideological representations of events. Critical history provides a context in which the historian is irked by a present need to search history maliciously, twisting facts and drawing cryptic conclusions precisely in order to make a partisan statement on that history. It is crucial, therefore, that interpretations of history, especially of histories that belong to cultural and linguistic traditions different from one's own, should include the historian's own cultural, intellectual, and ideological position vis-à-vis the multiple imbrications of these events outside the historian's familiar grounds. If we follow Nietzsche's hint, when the call for reassessing history is in the service of a present need, then the reassessment of that history will always be "critical"—that is, it will serve the immediate fulfillment of a desire, a desire to contest the study of the prehistory of the Qur'ān as a replacement of the study of the Qur'ān itself. The current postmodern direction of the humanities offers a unique opportunity to rethink Qur'ānic studies in a different light. There surely is a way to see approaches to the Qur'ān as something other than an allegory of an epistemological colonization emanating from a strong cultural desire to reappropriate the other. Or, is there still a lingering conviction that texts of alien cultures are innately subordinate to what the Eurocentric former US Secretary of Education William Bennett has referred to as "the great tradition the world has seen . . . the great books and civilization of the West . . . great, texts, great minds, great ideas"?[107] If this is indeed the case, then the study of the Qur'ān in Euro-American academia *demands* a new look at ourselves, not just a look inward, but a Nietzschian look from the outside in, to see if we have become, consciously or not, the very ghostly embodiments of those older ideologies we denounce the most.

3

Intelligence versus Power

Rhetorical Dynamics in Pre-Islamic Poetry and the Qurʾān

Literature begins where history ends. This statement is not necessarily a claim for the supremacy of one discipline over another. Rather, it allows us the opportunity to engage a tradition that includes volumes of Arabic literature prior to the Qurʾān. Examination of this tradition does not necessarily imply that reading ancient Arabic literary texts has to be exclusively literary. Nor does it proclaim that the basis of the difference between the treatment of Western and non-Western texts is only an institutional one in which some texts deserve more aesthetic appreciation than others. By studying the Arabic prehistory of the Qurʾān as well as the Qurʾān in relation to its cognate literature, one is bound to better understand their linguistic and aesthetic specificities. In this chapter I seek to investigate the shared characteristics of pre-Islamic literature and the Qurʾān. In pre-Islamic poetry, as well as the Qurʾān, these specificities are measured through a highly aesthetic language that represents deeply held communal values. The link between aesthetics and ethics will be the subject of a separate chapter, but it is worth introducing the connection here as I begin to contextualize the sociolinguistic dynamics between pre-Islamic poetry and the Qurʾān. The basic argument of this chapter is that if one is seeking to understand the context in which the Qurʾān came forth, how could one not study contemporaneous and pre-Islamic Arabic poetry? The question of the relationship between pre-Islamic poetry and the Qurʾān still feels fraught to many given the complexity of the topic. In this chapter, while I argue for a connection between the two, lexically, syntactically, and imagistically, I do so while cautioning against derivativeness, precisely because of the discursive distinction of each. While the idea that the Qurʾān is "the most beautiful of speech" may fall flat to non-Arabic speakers and even appear to be merely self-flattery to non-Muslims, who rarely take this claim seriously, it is important to note that the power of the Qur'ān does not consist solely in that speech.

To begin with, the Qur'ān consists of the same language that constitutes the very source of its value, the same language ancient Arab poets used to express their emotions, describe their surroundings, exalt their tribes, and lampoon their enemies. The nexus between pre-Islamic poetry and the Qur'ān received heated critical attention in the last century, which witnessed the emergence of a now long-retracted presumption that pre-Islamic poetry did not precede the Qur'ān but appeared after it. The English orientalist David Samuel Margoliouth (1858–1940) was the first to propose the hypothesis in 1925, followed by the Egyptian intellectual Ṭāhā Ḥusayn in 1926, who was exposed to Margoliouth's work during his graduate studies in Europe. But the argument that poems of pre-Islamic Arab peninsula were forgeries of later times has long been defeated to the point that is now absurd to hold on to such a notion.[1] In the last century, Theodor Nöldeke confirmed that Arabs lived in the Arabian Peninsula and composed poetry at least several centuries before the advent of Islam. Nöldeke treated pre-Islamic poems as authentic relics of the pre-Islamic past and referenced them in his research.[2] Even Margoliouth rescinded his own "inauthenticity thesis" years later.[3]

In a similar yet less sophisticated fashion, Ḥusayn, who harbored immense fascination with *fin du siècle* orientalist scholarship on the Qur'ān, read Margoliouth's postulate and applied it uncritically to his own work in the mid-1920s. To a fault, Ḥusayn admired theories of historical determinism without understanding that such theories are already based on false postulates, especially the postulate that pre-Islamic poetry may not have been produced in the historical era in which it is supposedly set. Here is Ḥusayn's thesis:

> The first thing in this study that you will find shocking is that I have come to doubt the value of pre-Islamic poetry as a verifiable historical document and persist in my doubts, or say my doubts persist. I started to research, examine, read, and think until I concluded with near certitude that the larger majority of what we call pre-Islamic poetry has nothing to do with pre-Islamic times. Those poems were counterfeited in the aftermath of Islam. Those poems are more Islamic than they are pre-Islamic, representing the lives, attitudes and dispositions of Muslim communities more than any other time prior to it. I have almost no doubt that what is left of pre-Islamic poetry is an insignificant sum which does not amount to much and which cannot be deemed reliable in portraying a correct and complete picture of the pre-Islamic era.[4]

Ḥusayn's rationale is based on a Margoliouth-inspired conclusion that "it is inconceivable that Judaism and Christianity, two great religions of pre-Islamic Arabia, would exist and spread among the Arabs without any major references to them in pre-Islamic poetry."[5] While it is not accurate to assume that there was no monotheistic poetry in pre-Islamic Arabia,[6] it is likely that much of this poetry may not have survived the fierce and mundane competitions of Sūq ʿUkāẓ poetry contests, where poets had to be absolutely original and where the emphasis was primarily on worldly and secular themes. Additionally, Judaism and Christianity were minority religions in a predominantly polytheistic society. Composing poetry in devotion to Judaism or Christianity in these notable *mufākharāt* (contests) may have looked like bringing a sword to a gun fight. Even a brief reading demonstrates how the agency of pre-Islamic poetry in the Meccan community was almost exclusively secular, celebrating tribal and ancestral supremacy, worldly gains, power, pride, sexual exploits, and other godless themes.[7]

Repulsed by Margoliouth's postulates, A. J. Arberry condemns them as an act of sophistry: "the sophistry—I hesitate to say dishonesty—of certain Professor Margoliouth's arguments is only too apparent, quite unworthy of a man who was undoubtedly one of the greatest erudites of his generation."[8] In a similar fashion, H. A. R. Gibb dismisses Margoliouth's thesis, and subsequently Ḥusayn's, on the account of its improbability. "It would be as impossible to 'reconstruct' the poetry of *Jahiliyya* from the poetry of the Umayyad period," contends Gibb, "as it would be to 'reconstruct' Elizabethan from Caroline drama."[9] Since then, few scholars have engaged pre-Islamic poetry more methodically. Jaroslav Stetkevych's magisterial work, *Muhammad and the Golden Bough: Reconstructing Arabian Myth*, studies the rich relationship between the Qurʾān and the tradition of ancient Arabic. Stetkevych reconstructs the story of the destruction of Thamūd, the ancient Arab tribe of North Arabia mentioned repeatedly in the Qurʾān. He connects the narrative and the non-Qurʾānic story of the Prophet Muḥammad's discovery of a golden bough at the site the people of Thamūd thought had been demolished by an act of divine wrath.

This textual interviewing of ancient Arabic tradition shows the extent to which the relationship between the Qurʾān and pre-Islamic narratives opens up new and much needed horizons for critical, philological, and mythological insights into the intricate connections between the literary and the social in the fabrics of pre- and post-Qurʾānic Arab communities.[10] In this context, Suzanne Stetkevych brings fresh structuralist analysis and meaningfulness to the understanding of the pre-Islamic Arabic *qaṣīda*, especially its major motifs and their relationship to the Qurʾān. In her path-breaking work, *The Mute Immortals Speak: Pre-Islamic Poetry and the Poetics of Ritual*, S. Stetkevych investigates local elements that carry Arabic poetics to superior aesthetic horizons. For example, the she-camel, who plays an essential role in the motif of *raḥīl* (passage, departure) in pre-Islamic Arabic poetry, is, for S. Stetkevych, "the preeminent symbol of culture, the 'staff of life.' The she-camel provided not only transport for men and goods but also hair for tents and food in the form of meat, milk, and blood (drunk from a slit vein in times of dearth)."[11] Moreover, camels were the barometer of wealth, measuring the value of human life, blood price or bride price, and so on. S. Stetkevych, who has successfully redefined our understanding of the pre-Islamic ode, brilliantly links the social value of camels, with their germane and innately rich symbolism of "fecundity and prosperity, a sign of divine blessing," to the narrative of the prophet Ṣāliḥ and the she-camel in the Qurʾān, as a proof of his prophecy, thus deepening the innate ties between the text and context of the Qurʾān, on the one hand, and the indigenous social prehistory of the Arabian Peninsula, on the other.[12]

Outside this small circle of literary Arabists, however, the relationship between pre-Islamic literature and the Qurʾān continues to be a neglected topic.[13] An obvious and important reason for this negligence is *linguistic incompetence*, a term that can serve to remind us of the inherent difficulty of the Arabic language. Both native and nonnative learners of Arabic know that it takes decades, if not one's entire life, to master classical Arabic, the only veritable access to any reliable scholarship on the Qurʾān in its original language. When we speak of the Arabic language of the Qurʾān, we also speak of the way in which its grammatologies, phonology, homophonies, ambiguities, polysemes, synonymies, antinomies, denotations, connotations, and associations work within the text: in short, a whole material galaxy of this immaterial space we call *Arabic*. And this is just one component. While meaningfully high in significations, the Arabic words of the Qurʾān do not alone make basic units of meaning. Arabic syntax and sentences do. But again, they do not do so in or for themselves; rather, as ʿAbd al-Qāhir al-Jurjānī (d.1078/1081) emphasizes, they do so as *naẓm*—namely, as elements in a more complex signifying system, whose multiple mechanisms, including binary oppositions and figurations, come together to organize *relationally* that cluster of themes we call *ma ʿná* (meaning/signification).[14]

The linguistic difficulty of Arabic might explain why the push to situate the Qurʾān within the historical context of late antiquity has remained peculiarly dismissive of ancient Arabic literature. It simply does not make sense to dismiss a corpus that lends deep and direct insight into understanding the Qurʾān, not just aesthetically or sociolinguistically, but also thematically. This dismissal is ironic given the fact that close readings of antique literary texts have consistently been applied to the Hebrew Bible. Popular publication venues, such as the series *Texte aus der Umwelt des Alten Testaments* (Texts from the World of the Old Testament) are dedicated exactly for that purpose. "Given the degree to which Western scholars value a critical historical approach," writes Bauer, "it seems odd that so much of contemporary research into the history of the Qurʾān seems to be able to get by without any real or serious critical consideration of the texts contemporary with it."[15] In exposing the inexplicable neglect of ancient Arabic literature as a primary source for studying the Qurʾān, Bauer maintains that understanding pre-Islamic Arabic poetry not only leads to more responsible and nuanced translations of the Qurʾān into European languages, but is bound to correct methodological approaches toward the Qurʾān and its formative tradition.[16]

The practice of excluding ancient Arabic literature or Arabic sources in general still remains a sore source of discomfort for the field, especially when it is no longer disputable that the tradition of Arabic poetry has its roots in the pre-Islamic era and has to a large extent accurately survived in the available written Muslim sources.[17] In an essay on "The Nature of Arab Unity Before Islam," von Grunebaum relies on pre-Islamic literary works to make an important distinction between pre-Islamic *'Arab al-Shamāl* (Northern Arabs) and *al-Badw* (Bedouin), one in which "the Northern Arabs constituted a *Kulturnation* rather than a *Staatsnation*."[18] These two terms, which von Grunebaum borrows from Friedrich Meinecke's early examinations of nationalism in Germany,[19] in reality differentiate between two forms of European nation-states. It is difficult to agree that pre-Islamic Bedouins were a *Staatsnation avant la lettre*, even though some South Arabian communities, such as the Ghassanid and the Lakhmid principalities, which were sometimes referred to as 'Arab al-Furs wa-'Arab al-Yūnān (Arabs of Persia and Arabs of Greece), grew as dependencies of larger non-Arab political structures surrounding them. If we agree with this anachronistic adoption of the term "nations" to describe pre-Islamic tribal communities, or even see these communities as microcosmic variations on Meinecke's categories, then von Grunebaum may be drawing a meaningful analogy in classifying pre-Islamic urban settlements like Mecca, al-Ṭā'if, and Yathrib as a *Kulturnation*. A "cultural nation," in the sense von Grunebaum applies the term, characterizes elusive large communities with a social structure unaffected by political shifts and unidentifiable by one single individual tribe or a specific political unit, though still subscribing to "a concept of the ideal Arab."[20] This ideal Arab, and its adjective "Arabic," argues von Grunebaum, is traceable to the Qur'ān and pre-Islamic prose, but not articulated much in pre-Islamic Arabic poetry.[21]

Von Grunebaum's keen interest in classical Arabic stems from his preoccupation with universal facts, and in particular with how pre-Islamic poetry offers its vocabulary and textual content "a description of the mental structure, or in other ways, psychological truth" of pre-Islamic Arabs.[22]

The reference to poetry is a key discovery in von Grunebaum's argument that has allowed him to make a strong case for preventing a misunderstanding that pre-Islamic Arabs constituted a holistic "Arabic" unity.[23] When pre-Islamic Northern Arabs distinguished themselves from the Southern Arabs,[24] they did so in terms of differences in habitat, language varieties, and social and religious practices. "The notorious antagonism between the Northern and Southern Arabs, Qays and Kalb, Muḍar and Qaḥṭān," argues von Grunebaum, "occurred within the 'Northern' area of pre-Islamic history and cultural integration."[25]

In a more focused study of pre-Islamic Arabic poetry as a document of early Christian figurations of creation, Kirill Dmitriev discovers in a poem by the Christian pre-Islamic poet 'Adī Ibn Zayd al-'Ibādī significant affinities with the Qur'ān text.[26] Dmitriev concludes that despite the lexical affinities between 'Adī ibn Zayd's poem and the Qur'ān, "the Qur'ān is very selective in its adoption of biblical tradition" and "unlike the Bible, the Qur'ānic stories of creation and paradise are not comprehensive chronological reports, but are evoked in a number of separate passages with clear hermeneutical implications."[27] What is remarkable for our purposes in Dmitriev's argument is not the affirmation that the Qur'ān has a "striking admonitory intention"[28] or that it is "less concerned with the narration of history than with presenting its ethically relevant message,"[29] but the Qur'ān's conscious communicative tone. "The Qur'ānic message," emphasizes Dmitriev, "does not unfold in a silent vacuum . . . it does not explain something absolutely new to its audience but tries instead to draw out the moral of something already known."[30] This heightened dialogical attentiveness to its intended listeners makes it indispensable, even for proponents of the historical-critical method, to understand the Qur'ān without studying pre-Islamic Arabic poetry.[31]

Yet despite all this, classical Arabic literature has remained peripheral to Western historians of the Qur'ān, even Western historians of the Bible. It could well be argued that the historians of the Qur'ān are not the same as the historians of the Bible, but what is at stake is the determining forces of historical categories when it comes to the inclusion or exclusion of literature. As we have seen from the examples above, the field of Arabic literature does not have a "problem" with the classical sources of Arabic literature. On the contrary, classical Arabic literature, which includes the pre-Islamic, is a cornerstone in the foundation of Arabic *belles lettres*. Since the early decade of the twentieth century, classical Arabic literature has received pointed attention from scholars of Arabic all over the world, in the Arabic speaking world (especially in Egypt, Lebanon, and Iraq), in Europe, and in the Americas. Even today, classical Arabic poetry is approached in terms of its biographical, historical, socioeconomic, phonological, semantic, aesthetic, and psychoanalytical significations. Our engagement with it thus comes from a strong position of responsibility toward it, and more so toward its future status in world history and literature, in order to create a space for de-othering pre-Islamic Arabic literature so it can transform what we understand or what we think we understand about its history and our own.

When it comes to the relationship between pre-Islamic Arabic literature and the Qur'ān, the literary and linguistic manifestations of these texts not only furnish the ground for understanding the Qur'ān, but they are what makes this understanding possible. Pre-Islamic Arabic literature is not an oral emblem or an enclosed hermetic space. True, all poems are governed by a structure of musicality, meter, and rhyme scheme, but they also differ in style, tone, manner, emphasis, argument, and signature. Above all, they are unique in that they respond to a particular situation—to celebrations, calamities, or even other poems. In so doing, they call for other responses and intimately remind us of what is literary about the practice we call literature.

To understand this level of rhetoric in the pre-Islamic Arabic literary tradition, one must see that the logic of *balāgha* rests on the harmony between the multiple possibilities that an utterance in-classical Arabic could afford to offer and the distinct articulations of this utterance, say, in the Qur'ān. And this is just on the semantic level of lexicons, which, in this case, unravels the depths of morphological signification in the language of pre-Islamic poetry *vis-a-vis* the language of the Qur'ān. In this context, Bauer is right. The language of the Qur'ān must establish itself as unique and distinct from the language of poetry. "Any attempt to make the language more like that of contemporary poetic expression," writes Bauer convincingly, "would have blurred the differences between poetic and prophetic speech."[32] However, it is difficult to accept Bauer's statement that "the Quran is the complete antithesis of contemporary poetry."[33] It is true that a balance has to be established between the two discourses. One must emphasize, however, that the distinction between the aesthetics of poetry and that of the Qur'ān is by no means antithetical. It is much more complex and much more intricate than mere antithesis and therefore entails patient linguistic exegesis to reflect on the two discourses and to carefully explain the juxtaposition.

I argue that the Qur'ān is an opening after the tropological discourse of pre-Islamic poetry had already triumphantly tested the limits of the rhetorical brilliance of the Arabic language. I further argue that the language of the Qur'ān creates a portal that opens a passage from one level of rhetoric to another, or even a pushing of rhetorical language to a completely different horizon. It would therefore be hard to embrace views that position both pre-Islamic poetry and the Qur'ān as one wholistic discourse. Richard Serrano, for instance, argues that the Qur'ān and poetry "are two sides of a single intertextured Qur'āno-Arabic discourse."[34] Linguistically and rhetorically, this is a difficult case to make as such; it is an even more difficult case to make for pre-Islamic poetry. But, to Serrano's point, both the Qur'ān and poetry lexically draw on a sociolinguistic and literary heritage of *Ayyām al-ʿArab* (chronicles of the Arabs), which explains why there is a certain continuity of the pre-Arabic poetic tradition well into the Umayyad and even ʿAbbasid dynasties, as well as a substantial reliance of postclassical *tafsīr* and commentary on the latter in order to explain the former.

Despite its obvious doctrinal biases, we learn to learn from the tradition of *Iʿjāz al-Qurʾān*. While it is undeniable that the tradition of *Iʿjāz al-Qurʾān* carries inherent doctrinal biases, it is important to acknowledge that we can still glean valuable insights from it. Moreover, when we shift our focus to postclassical Arabic literary *Iʿjāz* theorists and critics, we find that they have a wealth of knowledge and perspectives to enrich the field of literary aesthetics. Postclassical Arabic literary theorists and critics have much to offer the field of literary aesthetics. At their hands, Arabic literary criticism became one of the earliest world traditions to establish a sophisticated system of tropes and literary terms to highlight the affinities between poetry, prose, and the Qur'ān. This is how Abū al-Ḥasan al-Rummānī (909–94), one of the earliest scholars to categorize and theorize aesthetic imagery, arrives at the conclusion that the Qur'ān is *nāqiḍ lil-ʿāda* (that which interrupts/contradicts existing norms).[35] The linguistic and rhetorical relationship between pre-Islamic Arabic poetry and the Qur'ān is exactly that: a relationship of interruption. I define this relationship or rather juxtaposition as a passage from rhetorical intelligence to rhetorical power. Let me explain this further: intelligence and power are not antithetical to each other. There is a power of intelligence, since intelligence has its own power. But there is also power that is not commanded by intelligence, so they are not polar opposites, nor should they exclude one another. Nor is this relationship even "a negation of poetry" as Bauer claims,[36] since neither is a progression or a regression from the other. While there are clear thematic divergences, the relationship is simply one of transformation, which can be explained by juxtaposing some examples of the use of the term *layl* (night) in both pre-Islamic Arabic and the Qur'ān. The night is indeed a perversive motif in classical Arabic.[37] It would be easy to find hundreds of poetic passages describing *layl* in pre-Islamic poetry as well as manifold references to it in the Qur'ān. In comparing the function of the night in *Jāhilī* poetry and the Qur'ān, I would therefore limit myself to a few illuminating examples from Imru' al-Qays and al-Nābigha al-Dhubyānī.

In pre-Islamic classical Arabic, ليل denotes "night" or "evening." The classical lexicographer Ibn Manẓūr defines ليل as follows:

الليل عقيب النهار، ومبدؤه من غروب الشمس . . . ، الليل ضد النهار، والليل ظلام والنهار ضياء . . . ،

والليل اسم لكل ليلة . . . ، وليلة ليلاء وليلى طويلة، شديدة، صعبة، قيل هي أشد ليالي الشهر ظلمةً . . . ،

وليلٌ أليلُ ولائل ومليّل . . . أرادوا به الكثرة"[38]

The night is that which immediately follows daytime. It begins at sunset . . . the night is the opposite of the day. The night is darkness and the day is light. The night is the name for every *layla, laylā', laylá* (evening, night). These names refer to long and harsh nights, said to be the darkest night in a month . . . adjectives like *layl mulayyil, lā 'il,* or *alīl* are meant to indicate plenitude of night.

In pre-Islamic poetic parlance, significations of *layl* turn the term into a fierce competition in aesthetic virtuosity among poets. Regardless of the authenticity of feelings, the aesthetic of the night is lodged in the form of the ode, even though that form shields itself against the monotony of symmetry through prosodic meters. In this metered contest, two poets, Imru' al-Qays (d. 500) and al-Nābigha al-Dhubyānī (d. 604), stand out at the top of this aesthetic ladder. Imru' al-Qays's celebrated lines of *layl* are perhaps some of the earliest and most pioneering examples of pathetic fallacy known to world literature.[39] In this fallacy of natural subjectivity, *layl* participates in a complex simile. The poet sees the night as waves of a sea that have accumulated a darkness:

عَليّ بأنواعِ الهُمومِ لِيَبْتَلي	وَلَيلٍ كَمَوجِ البَحرِ أرخى سُدولَهُ
وأردفَ أعجازًا وناء بِكَلْكَلِ	فَقُلتُ له لمّا تمطّى بصُلْبِه
بصبح وما الإصباحُ منك بأمثل	ألا أيها الليل الطويلُ ألا انجلي
بكل مغار الفتل شدت بيذبل[40]	فيا لكَ من ليلْ كأنَّ نجومهُ

A night like waves of the sea laid its drapes on me/with sorts of sorrow to test me.
I said to it, when it stretched its spine/ stressed its buttocks, and pressed its chest,

"O lingering night, dissipate/with a morning, a morning which won't be any better
O what a night whose stars are hauled/with all tight ropes to mount Yadhbul."

Imru' al-Qays paints a portrait of his personal affliction, one in which the night becomes the objective correlative of a general mood of despondency. In this complex image, the night resembles the accumulated waves of the sea that keep flowing darkness mixed with sadness in his direction. The night is as motionless as a picture with painted waves on a painted ocean. The stars are tied to rocks in an image of reverse anchorage where they act like ships on a sea. The implication is that the night is long and not going anywhere. The poet/persona is no longer able to speak directly about his sadness and has thus cast it onto the elements—speaking his pain through nature, through a painfully unending night. The poem's pathetic fallacy is itself an element of intention. In Imru' al-Qays's ode, meaning is constituted by the relation to the night as the most effective means for the aesthetic articulation of suffering.

Al-Nābigha must have known of al-Qays's ode and must have marveled at this unrivaled depiction of the night. Poets who come after other poets have achieved the highest degree of rhetorical brilliance are always haunted by this after-ness. Afraid of being derivative in contests of originality, they possess a vaulting desire to equal or surpass the previous work. Al-Nābigha lived affluently at the court of the Lakhmid Arab kings of al-Ḥīra. Known for his poetic genius (from which the Arabic word *nābigha* derives), he was pursued by many kings in order that he commemorate their heroic exploits in his poetry, an assignment not unfamiliar to most classical Arabic poets of pre-Islam and classical Islam. Soon, al-Nābigha got himself caught between the Scylla and Charybdis of two rival kings, 'Amr ibn al-Ḥārith, king of the Ghassanids, and al-Nu'mān, king of the Lakhmids. When al-Nābigha's tribe lost a battle to the Ghassanids, he rushed to compose a "night" poem in praise of 'Amr ibn al-Ḥārith and his soldiers in order to seek refuge in Shām and prevent more bloodshed:

كِليني لِـهَمٍّ يـا أُمَيْمَـةُ نَاصبِ   وليل أقاسيه بَطِيء الكـواكبِ

تطاوَلَ حتى قلتُ ليس بمُنْقضٍ   وليسَ الذي يرعى النجومَ بآيب

بصَدْرٍ أراح الليل عازبَ هَمَّه   تضاعف فيه الحزنُ من كل جانب

....

وَثِقتُ لَهُ بِالنَصرِ إذ قيلَ قَد غَزَت   كَتائِبُ مِن غَسّانَ غَيرُ أشائِب

تَقُدَّ السَلوقِيَّ المُضاعَفَ نَسجُهُ   وَتوقِدُ بِالصُفّاحِ نارَ الحُباجِبِ[41]

let me attend to a sadness, Umayma / And suffer a night of slow-moving stars
persisting till I thought it were unending / and the shepherd of the stars is sleepless
A chest, which the night should distance from daily cares / holds a sadness swelling
   from all sides.

. . . .
I was certain he would win once it was said / pure-blooded forces of Ghassan invaded
[their swords] shattered the double layers of their Seleucid armor / and lightened—
   when they stroke their enemy's helmets—the taillights of fireflies.

The antithesis between the gloomy opening of the *qaṣīda* (where the sluggish-
ness of a starry night in the manner of Imru' al-Qays evokes pain in the poet's
heart) and the exciting sword blazes in the Ghassanid-led battlefield scene creates
a powerful dramatic shift. To be sure, the lines on the night at the beginning of the
poem is conventional in *nasīb* and other love poetry and may not necessarily form
a thematic correlation with the battle scene. Still, the semantic associations of the
night in the poem connotes a symbiotic relationship hard to ignore. Poetry often
connotes more than it denotes. The light of the fireflies is only visible at night, and
while the references to lightning bugs is figurative—namely, as a *tashbīh* (simile/
comparison) for the sparks made by the swords, it still creates an antithesis to the
idleness of the starry night at the opening of the poem. Even though there is no
direct reference to the battle taking place at night, the light of the "night" fireflies
suggests a nocturnal warfare. Moreover, the contrast between stasis and movement—that is, the heavy-hearted condition of the poet in a static night versus
the action on the battlefield, not only signifies a palpable praise of the Ghassanid soldiers, but it also suggests an incomparable and superior military quality in
warfare. In a unique hyperbole, we see the flashings of Ghassanid swords—when
they tear trough the chain mail armor and clash with the helmets of their enemy—
flickering across the battlefield like fireflies dancing in the night sky. The implication, and the praise attached to it, is far from vague: al-Nābigha invests in a
remarkably exaggerated figurations of a "night" trope to hail ʿAmr ibn al-Ḥārith
and his squad of Ghassanid soldiers as superior and unrivaled masters of warfare.

Yet, when the poem reached the ears of the Lakhmid king al-Nuʿmān ibn al-
Mundhir, the archenemy of the Ghassanids, who also happened to be a generous
patron for al-Nābigha, it did not take long for the poet to fall out of grace. When
al-Nābigha finally decided to return to al-Ḥīra, he knew he must have offended
King al-Nuʿmān too grievously to warrant a pardon. The only way out, the only
way a poet of al-Nābigha's caliber would know how to dig himself out of this poetic
mishap, was poetry itself. But this time, not only his poetry, but the trope of *layl*
had to be different from itself. What this meant was that the poet had to rival not
only the poetic brilliance of al-Qays but his own poeticity; he had to engineer a
life-saving poem that would dwarf his own hyperbolic trope in his panegyric to
ʿAmr ibn al-Ḥārith and his Ghassanid soldiers. This was one of the rare occasions in the tradition of Arabic poetry where a poet's life hinged on the aesthetic,
indeed on a specific "re-aestheticization" of his own poetic trope of the night. Just
as Odysseus was able to clad himself in lofty words to cover his nakedness when

he washed up onto the island of Skheria and faced King Alkinoos's daughter, Nausicaa, so too did al-Nābigha have to find the right image to win back his life and regain amnesty from a wrathful king. This is when the signification of *layl* reaches a new height. In this "forgive-me-please" poem, al-Nābigha brings back the night trope, uses it against itself, cancels his own image of triumphant Ghassanids and delineates a poetic mood that mixes fear with desire and power with hope and regret. Al-Nābigha's poetry, it seems, is a free art that does not need to defend itself against the rebuke that it causes to others; it simply meets this rebuke with another as it affirms its subsidiary relation to power. Certainly this holds true for the production of all pre-Islamic poetry, where a poet could start a poem that he might or might not complete, allowing it to survive as a fragment, or, as is the case with al-Nābigha, could compose a poem that is blatantly dialectical with another of his own making, either because he is frightened and bored, or because he detests being accused of repetition or lack of originality. Unlike the Qur'ān, pre-Islamic poetry has the power to compliment mortal enemies and harbor its own opposite without losing the value of its aesthetic imagination:

وإنْ خِلتُ أنَّ المنتأى عنك واسعُ   فإنَّك كالليلِ الذي هو مُدرِكي

تمدُّ بها أيدٍ إليكَ نـوازِعُ [42]   خـطاطيفُ حُجنٌ في حبالٍ متينةٍ

> You are like the night that will overtake me / and I thought the distance from you
>   was vast enough
> Curved hooks in strong ropes/ extended by hands drawing toward you.

Interestingly enough, al-Nābigha describes himself as if caught in a deep well, like a bucket to be hauled up. The power dynamic in these poetic lines highlights a deep antithesis between a helpless and chased persona (the poet) and an all-mighty king whose domain is the night, who *is* the night, thus portraying a state of helplessness and inescapability. The sense of fear that overwhelms the poet reflects panic and anxiety, especially in the certainty that the king will eventually capture him. The inevitability evoked in the predicate *mudrikī* sinks deep in pre-Islamic poetry but also in Qur'ānic diction, where the word is associated with dismay, defenselessness, and surrender, as in the moment when the Israelites reached the end of the shore and could see the pharaoh closing in on them with no way out, just before Moses applies his staff to split open the Red Sea:

فَلَمَّا تَرَاءَى الْجَمْعَانِ قَالَ أَصْحَابُ مُوسَىٰ إِنَّا لَمُدْرَكُونَ [43]

> When the two groups could see one another, the companions of Moses said, "We are certainly captured."

Or with "death,"[44] as when the pharaoh becomes certain that the water will overtake him and he is soon to drown:

حَتَّىٰ إِذَآ أَدْرَكَهُ ٱلْغَرَقُ قَالَ ءَامَنتُ أَنَّهُ لَآ إِلَٰهَ إِلَّا ٱلَّذِىٓ ءَامَنَتْ بِهِۦ بَنُوٓاْ إِسْرَٰٓءِيلَ وَأَنَا۠ مِنَ ٱلْمُسْلِمِينَ[45]

When drowning began to overtake him, he said, "I believe that there is no god except the one whom the children of Israel believe in, and I am among the submitters."

In recasting the night trope, the mighty king al-Nuʿmān, who has a reputation for slaying poets in cold blood, is likened to the night that is sure to come and overtake the poet no matter where he might be hiding. This pathetic fallacy points to the ineluctability of capture but also to the supernatural power of the king. It is as if al-Nābighaʾs poetry is in dialogue with itself: if he has previously praised ʿAmr ibn al-Ḥārith and his Ghassanid soldiers as the masters of the night combat, he is now praising king al-Nuʿmān as the night incarnate, the night whose power and dominion are unavoidable. In this well-thought apologetics, *layl* is at once a vehicle for the king's supernatural authority and the poet's vulnerability, enveloped in deep hope that the poem is aesthetically intelligent enough to please the king and merit his pardon.

Layl then as a signifier in pre-Islamic poetry becomes a sign of history, not the progressive or influential "history" in the periodizational or late antiquarian sense, but history in a materialist sense, a textual history—that is, where semantic significations mark an event in language. There is history from the moment poets like al-Qays and al-Nābigha created tropes from words like *layl* and compelled the emergence of a language of *balāgha* out of a language of everyday use. Thanks to pre-Islamic poetry, *layl* will simply never be the same since its denotative continuity is disrupted with a new discourse of rhetorical intelligence. This disruption does not mean that *layl* would not continue to be used to refer to a common "night," but that the tropological "night" in pre-Islamic poetry has now added to our cognition of *layl* a new dimension that, while not negating the performative use of *layl* in everyday language, would still demand to be recognized as the highest achievement in the tropological system of pre-Islamic Arabic aesthetics, an achievement that would make it difficult, if not impossible, to improve on. These figurations are unequaled not because the voice of the poet speaks "the night," but because, through their language, the poems impersonate what is unspeakable in the language of nature.

The aesthetics of *layl* in the Qurʾān carry the same significations we find in Imruʾ al-Qays and al-Nābigha but are also markedly different from their figurations in pre-Islamic poetry. In the Qurʾān, *layl* transforms from a rhetoric of intelligence to a rhetoric of power. It is true that the semantic interconnections between *layl* and *mudrikī* invoked in al-Nābigha continue to retain their same performative functions in the Qurʾān, as in the following example from Qurʾān 36:

لَا ٱلشَّمْسُ يَنۢبَغِى لَهَآ أَن تُدْرِكَ ٱلْقَمَرَ وَلَا ٱلَّيْلُ سَابِقُ ٱلنَّهَارِ ۚ وَكُلٌّ فِى فَلَكٍ يَسْبَحُونَ

Neither it is for the sun to overtake the moon nor is it for the night to surpass the day. Each swims in an orbit of its own. (36:40)

But the Qurʾān comes into its own by distinguishing the significations of its language from that of the preexisting discourse, a discourse that also claims for itself the right to be highly rhetorical. As we see in the examples of al-Qays and al-Nābigha, the rhetoric of pre-Islamic poetry avows a self-affirming mortal human nature. Depictions of mortality in pre-Islamic Arabic poetry, which I address in more detail shortly, demonstrate that the two discourses of poetry and the Qurʾān are separated by an unsurpassable void. At the very moment when the Qurʾān reaches a fulfillment of itself, it lays out a totality of an incommensurable mode of object perception. The reference to *layl* in the Qurʾān confirms this discursive separability.

Take, for instance, the *layl* in Qurʾān 36:40, which indicates the common understanding of the night—namely, as a recurring period of darkness enveloping the earth every twenty-four hours. Yet the Qurʾānic night is also a negative aesthetic, a personification without agency, always passivized, constantly controlled. Or, if there is agency, it is a divine and creationist one. The night in Qurʾān 36:40 is not a projection of sadness, or a scene for military prowess, or even an image of a terrifying king. The Qurʾān *owns* the night. Suddenly, we are witnessing a figurative metamorphosis whereby *layl* transforms into a phenomenon functioning within an orbit that owes its existence to a metaphysical being. In the Qurʾān, *layl* becomes a manifestation of divine order and a sign of a preordained creation that cannot act on its own. What thus marks the discontinuity between pre-Islamic poetry and the Qurʾān is not an "antithesis" between two conceptual understandings of the night. The positionality of the Qurʾānic *layl* does not emerge from a discourse of poetic talent keen on the use of a word to project sadness or fear, or to create a mythical simile of a mighty king. It is, rather, a difference between rhetorical intelligence and rhetorical power. Whereas poetic intelligence functions from within gifted yet anthropologically determined limits, the rhetorical power of Qurʾānic language renounces the overshadowing motive of self-assertion. It conceives of referents like *layl* in a completely different relationship, one that severs all tropological projections with human life. This does not mean that the Qurʾān does not compare humans to elements of nature, but it is always a figuration predicated on deeds. Al-Rummānī identifies this type of comparison in terms of *tashbīh balāgha* (rhetorical simile), where the deeds of unbelievers are likened to a mirage in Qurʾān 24: 39:

فتشبيه البلاغة كتشبيه أعمال الكفار بالسراب . . . فمن ذلك قوله تعالى {والذين كفروا أعمالهم كسراب بقيعة يحسبه الظمآن ماءً حتى إذا جاءَه لم يجده شيئاً}. فهذا بيان قد أخرج مالا تقع عليه الحاسة إلى ما تقع عليه، وقد اجتمعا في بطلان المتوهم مع شدة الحاجة وعظم الفاقة.⁴⁶

An example of a rhetorical simile is when the deeds of unbelievers are likened to a mirage, as when God says, may He be exalted, says: "those who disbelieve, their deeds are like a mirage in a vast desert which a thirsty man would mistake for water but when he reaches it, he will find nothing." This type of rhetorical eloquence likens what is not perceived by the senses to what the senses can indeed perceive, thus bringing the two parts of the simile together to portray the falsehood of the presumption despite the dire need and the great lack.

But it turns out, even though al-Rummānī stops shy of including the following verse, that 24.39 and 24:40 are interlocked in a dual allegorical act of two similes of the wasted deeds of unbelievers. The second simile that follows the mirage simile further intensifies the allegorical relationship between unbelievers and their zero-sum deeds. The trope of deeds thus moves from desert to sea, complementing the trope of a false vision of water (mirage) with another of blindness in a dark night at sea, thus doubling its depiction of unbelievers as having sight without insight and as living in blindness without light:

أَوْ كَظُلُمَاتٍ فِي بَحْرٍ لُّجِّيٍّ يَغْشَاهُ مَوْجٌ مِّن فَوْقِهِ مَوْجٌ مِّن فَوْقِهِ سَحَابٌ ۚ ظُلُمَاتٌ بَعْضُهَا فَوْقَ بَعْضٍ إِذَا أَخْرَجَ يَدَهُ لَمْ يَكَدْ يَرَاهَا ۗ وَمَن لَّمْ يَجْعَلِ اللَّهُ لَهُ نُورًا فَمَا لَهُ مِن نُّورٍ

Or [their deeds are] like layers of darkness in a deep sea, with waves piling on top of waves, topped by dark clouds. Darkness upon darkness! If he stretches out his hand, he can hardly see it. And whoever God does not bless with light shall have no light! (24:40).

Here the night is not mentioned by name but is implied in the atmospheric spirit of the verse. Readers of Imru' al-Qays's poetry would sense a similar piling and accumulation of darkness in this verse, except that the absent night in not likened to the waves of the sea. Instead, the night collaborates with the sea and the clouds to produce a condition of pitch blackness. The darkness [of the night] in Qur'ān 24:40 is juxtaposed to the brightness of the day in the preceding verse (24:39). In other words, the extended rhetorical simile, as al-Rummānī calls it, brings together an optimal degree of visibility that leads to a false form of seeing and an ultimate darkness that makes such seeing impossible. Deep water makes it difficult for the light to penetrate it, thus resulting in darkness. This darkness is not only already enhanced by night but also intensified by accumulated waves and thick clouds. This powerful comparative simile, according to which the deeds of unbelievers are just as misguided as those following illusionary mirages in the desert or vainly trying to make their way through impenetrable darkness in the sea as portrayed in 24:39–40, produces a shattering depiction of loss and blindness. Neither can a desert mirage slake an unbeliever's thirst nor can a condition of pitch blackness allow one to find the light in a sea darkly. The allegorical, inter-versal oscillation between two illusions, the illusion of seeing and the illusion of blindness, is not brought forth to evoke an emotional state of sadness or dejection, but to drive home an eschatological trope that doubly approximates the total failing of the unethical deeds of unbelievers. In other words, there is no pathetic fallacy in the Qur'ān, no room for nature that mimics human emotions. The night does not embody our cares, nor does it incarnate the worst of our fears. This abandonment is itself a radical break, a discontinuity based on the belief that there is something else to the night, something more serious than bemoaning the departure of the beloved's encampment and something worse than being captured or killed by a livid king. This thematic distance from mortal life fundamentally distinguishes the Qur'ān from poetry. Not only this. On the level of form, while both pre-Islamic poetry and the Qur'ān are historically conditioned to manifest an aesthetic inherently oral in nature—another complex and immense issue difficult to get into here—the Qur'ān does not think of itself as poetry; nor is it thought of as poetry by the learned community of its contemporary audience.[47] Nor again is aesthetic appreciation of language limited to the poetic. This is certainly not the case with the Arabic tradition. While some, as the Qur'ān mentions, may have hurriedly called it "poetry" and labeled Muḥammad as a "poet" to play down the text's communal appeal, this labeling was conceived of in contempt and ridicule. Al-Jurjānī reminds us that the contemporary community of Muḥammad knew quite well that he was not a poet and that the Qur'ān was not poetry:

أما دلالة الأقوال فكثيرة منها حديث ابن المغيرة روي أنه جاء حتى أتى قريشاً فقال: إن الناس يجتمعون غداً بالموسم، وقد فشا أمر هذا الرجل في الناس فهم سائلوكم عنه فماذا تردون عليهم؟ فقالوا مجنون يختنق، فقال: يأتونه فيكلمونه فيجدونه صحيحاً عادلا فيكذبونكم! قالوا: نقول هو شاعر. قال: هم العرب، و قد رووا الشعر، وفيهم الشعراء، وقوله ليس يشبه الشعر، فيكذبونكم.[48]

Narrative evidence [of the Qur'ān's inimitability] abounds. Among the stories is the account of Ibn al-Mughīra. It was narrated that he went to the tribe of Quraysh and informed them that there would be a gathering of people at the [pilgrimage] festival the next day, while news of this man [Muḥammad] had spread fast. He told them that people would ask about him, and inquired what they would see when people asked about him. They said, "we would say he is mad and manic." "But they would come and talk to him," he replied, "and when they would judge him to be sound and fair, then they would call you liars." They said, "we would say then that he is a poet." "They are the Arabs," he answered, "they recite poetry and they have poets living among them. Whatever he says does not resemble poetry, and then they would call you liars."

Unlike al-Khaṭṭābī (d. 996/998) and al-Jurjānī, al-Bāqillānī (d. 1013) polarizes the relationship between pre-Islamic poetry and the Qur'ān, rendering the former antithetical to the latter.[49] Over the last one hundred years of literary theory, we have seen radicalism like that of al-Bāqillānī's occur over and again—that is, when a new school of thought delegitimizes the older one, which it thoroughly interrupts. Al-Bāqillānī's mistake is similar in that he tried to open a space for the aesthetics of the Qur'ān in the Arabic canon, but thought to do so at the expense of denigrating pre-Islamic poetry. Criticizing pre-Islamic poetry puts al-Bāqillānī in the same paradoxical situation occupied by his own critique, a position by which radicals take on the presumption that they are somehow against the mundane, whereas it is the concept of the mundane as an aesthetic category and a poetic choice that is thereby under discussion. Still, the flare of religious fanaticism in al-Bāqillānī's criticism of Imru' al-Qays and of pre-Islamic poetry *writ large* is useful for understanding radical theology's strategies of containment. Exposing this logic will at least help deconstruct the concepts that seek to demonize a literary aesthetics without which any appreciation of the Qur'ān's own aesthetics is inconceivable.

It is therefore crucial to emphasize that the Qur'ān does not necessarily trivialize poetry, but it aestheticizes language in a different discourse. When experiencing the reference to *layl* in Imru' al-Qays and al-Nābigha, the audience can sense the pathetic fallacy in the element of nature. But the Qur'ān invites its contemporary audience to engage with the statement, "there is more to life and death than a king chasing a prodigal poet in the desert." Al-Nābigha's plight may merit one's *ta'āṭuf* (empathy) and may instill some sense of *shafaqa* (pity) and *rajā'* (hope), but it does not instill *khawf* (fear) or *rahba* (terror) in the reader's mind or heart. A reader of Imru' al-Qays will marvel at his poetic genius, identify with his sufferings, and sympathize with the loss of his beloved and his kingship. The same reader will see in the Qur'ān a different use of language, a calling for abandonment, a ridicule of self-preservation, and a redefinition of survival. In other words, the Qur'ān asks its audience to be unconditionally pious and to consider that much more is at stake, that one's whole existence hangs in the balance, whereas a loss of *ḥabība* (beloved) or *diyār* (dwelling/encampment) or even fortune and status can always be reconciled somehow. The discourse of power in the Qur'ān is all-encompassing and is also terrifying, whereas the loss of the lover, or the disruption of happiness, evokes sadness and empathy that are a part of our human existence. What distinguishes a rhetoric of power from a rhetoric of intelligence (or poetic talent) is the sense of awe the former instills in its receiver.

There is, to be sure, a noticeable absence of transcendental anxiety in pre-Islamic poetry. Neither infinity nor eternity—in the sense of infinite or endless time after death—seems to bother the poets. In the Qur'ān, however, the entire *rahba*, the unease that accompanies its enveloping awe, arises not necessarily from the failure to stand up to the direct rhetorical *taḥaddī* (challenge) it poses to its audience, or even from the *ṣarfa* or rather *ṣarf al-himam 'an al-mu'āraḍa* (turning their ambitions away, or distracting them, from emulation),[50] but rather from the incapacity of the classical poetic mind, with all its imaginative talent, to tap into a mimetic poetics that rivals the magnitude of this Qur'ānic *rahba*. The closest English equivalent to *rahba* that I could think of is fear, or terror, or something in between, which is reminiscent of what Edmund Burke describes as a state where the pleasurable experience of the "beautiful" comes into stark opposition with the fearful experience of the "sublime," causing pain at the same time that it causes pleasure:

But if the sublime is built on terror, or some passion like it, which has pain for its object, it is previously proper to inquire how any species of delight can be derived from a cause so apparently contrary to it. I say delight, because, as I have often remarked, it is very evidently different in its cause, and in its own nature, from actual and positive pleasure.[51]

Pleasure and fear are the signatures of the Qur'ān, a text that strikes a perfect balance between *wa'd wa wa'īd* (promise and warning). In fact, the Arabic language of pre-Islam instilled a strong sense of poetic imagination, one that prepared the Qur'ān's first audience to grasp the enormity of its figurative power. Take, for instance, a verse from *Sūra-t- al-A'rāf* (7:46), which depicts a futuristic purgatory scene unmatched in any language. In this bone-chilling scene, some unidentified people are standing on *al-A'rāf* (mounts, or a purgatory of sorts) at the boundary between heaven and hell; their eschatological destiny remains undecided. But they are still temporarily able to see both the spaces of heaven and hell (separated by a seal) from a high vintage point, and to view with awe both the pleasures of the people of heaven and the unimaginable torture of the people of hell:

وَبَيْنَهُمَا حِجَابٌ ۚ وَعَلَى الْأَعْرَافِ رِجَالٌ يَعْرِفُونَ كُلًّا بِسِيمَاهُمْ ۚ وَنَادَوْا أَصْحَابَ الْجَنَّةِ أَن سَلَامٌ عَلَيْكُمْ ۚ لَمْ يَدْخُلُوهَا وَهُمْ يَطْمَعُونَ

There is a barrier between them. And on the mounts there are men who recognize the people of both abodes by their appearances. They would call for the people of heaven and say, "Peace be upon you!" They had not entered it [heaven], but they so desperately desire to. (7:46)

Readers of this verse could only ponder on this "imaginative visualization" in all its beauty and terror. Knowledge in the form of recognition heightens the desire for salvation. But the language of the Qur'ān makes the contrast startling. Knowledge or recognition is primarily linguistic and from this world, but the entire scene is eerily eschatological. This knowledge in *ya'rifūn* (they know) is a future in the past, a representation of something that is yet to come, a belated "aha" moment after death. The implication is that knowledge acts as a transit between two worlds, and only through linguistic imagination can such a recognition be made possible: an imagination of a future moment that could still be saved by whoever reads or listens to the verses in the present tense before it is too late. Whereas self-preservation in its pre-Islamic representations is of the order of the real, its concreteness is shattered by the *terrifying* recognition emphasized in the Qur'ān:

وَإِذَا سَمِعُوا مَا أُنزِلَ إِلَى الرَّسُولِ تَرَىٰ أَعْيُنَهُمْ تَفِيضُ مِنَ الدَّمْعِ مِمَّا عَرَفُوا مِنَ الْحَقِّ

When they heard what was revealed to the messenger, you would see their eyes overflowing with tears for recognizing the truth. (5:83)

This is a landmark in the aesthetic transformation from the "before" to the "after" in the language of the Qurʾān. Even though what the Qurʾān presents is purely structural and purely tropological, because it is an act of language after all, its language is so familiar yet so aesthetically defamiliarized that it substitutes for a tangible reality a highly evocative imaginary scene. As we see in this example, salvation must always be imaginary instead of being real, and the knowledge of it, that is, the knowing by way of "seeing" and facially recognizing and distinguishing between the people of hell and the people of heaven, in the end relates solely to a linguistic reality with a careful, yet highly haunting, economy of words. The result is a chiasmus of embedded sentences and pronouns (7:46), an inversed grammatical enmeshment of a verse that oscillates between two spaces and between third- and second-person pronouns, yet still holds a powerful linguistic imaginary that bridges a yet-to-come "real" experience. This linguistic passage to imagination, this link to the afterworld, is what allows the audience of the Qurʾān to conceptualize the dangers and calamities of what is now depicted as a transient world by recognizing, through imagination, that death may not be the end. But this imaginative leap into a metaphysical anagnorisis, so to speak, could not be possible without the linguistic preparedness in the background of the secular poetic world like that of Imruʾ al-Qays and al-Nābigha.

The stylistic visuals of *al-Aʿrāf* setting begin with portraying a *mise en scene* of separation, an impenetrable barrier set between heaven and hell, then move to show the yet to be accounted for, the people lost in between heaven and hell, the ones who have now come to know and *recognize* what the people of heaven and the people of hell look like. The verse ends with the *al-Aʿrāf* people stranded on the mount between heaven and hell, while offering a yearning peace-greeting to the dwellers of heaven, and expressing a deep wish to join them. There is nothing "poetic" here in the pre-Islamic sense of the word, just a fearful and symmetrical aesthetics expressing a most terrifying uncertainty.

Iʿjāz, or the defiantly incapacitating quality of the Qurʾān, thus lends itself to this oscillation between the beautiful and the sublime as a discourse of rhetorical power *aware* of a preexisting discourse of poetic talent. The psychology of *rahba* depicted in Qurʾān 7:46 allows the reader/listener to exquisitely imagine how terrifying it would be to be on the *Aʿrāf*, to witness both pain and pleasure without experiencing either of them, and without knowing his or her own destiny. Evidently, there is always the choice to eschew this interpolating rhetoric altogether and dismiss it as imaginary (8:29). After all, not all the Arabs of Muḥammad's time became Muslims, but all the people who lived around him were Arabs who spoke and understood classical Arabic. For the first Muslim community, an Arabic-speaking community, this *rahba* brings about a sense of self-preservation and produces *in the body* something analogous to what the experience could be. The Qurʾān describes this affect eloquently in 39:23. In this verse the fearful pious would start to shudder and tremble with *rahba* as the language transports them to that terrifying space without actually being there. And for a brief while, in the act of reading or listening, the imagination of terror is replaced with a feeling of real terror, and the trope becomes tangible:

ٱللَّهُ نَزَّلَ أَحْسَنَ ٱلْحَدِيثِ كِتَٰبًا مُّتَشَٰبِهًا مَّثَانِىَ تَقْشَعِرُّ مِنْهُ جُلُودُ ٱلَّذِينَ يَخْشَوْنَ رَبَّهُمْ ثُمَّ تَلِينُ جُلُودُهُمْ وَقُلُوبُهُمْ إِلَىٰ ذِكْرِ ٱللَّهِ

God has revealed the best/the most beautiful of speech—a book of perfect consistency—which causes the skins of those who fear their lord to shudder and then their skin and their hearts will soften for the mention of God. (39.23)

Aḥsan al-ḥadīth (the best/most beautiful of speech) in Qur'ān 39:23 takes us back full circle to that discourse of difference. As I point out in the following chapter, not only is the Qur'ān aware of pre-Islamic poetry, but its relationship to language—as well as to listeners/readers through that very language—is always determined by a competition in expressiveness. *Aḥsan* means best and most beautiful at the same time. It is a comparative that brings an awareness of something else other than the Qur'ān, something that is linguistically "good" and "beautiful," but it is also something that the Qur'ān *has to* transcend and surpass in matchless betterment and beauty, in order to be worthy of asserting itself as God's eternal words. This competition is not just on the level of language, but on the level of scriptures as well. In fact, the Qur'ān intentionally utilizes *prolepsis* in many of its sūras, most notably in 12:3 and 29:48. It is as if the Qur'ān knows that the accusation of plagiarism will be leveled against it, and insists that this is an Arabic revelation to a prophet who previously didn't know *aḥsan al-qaṣaṣ* "the best of stories." One can also see this in 29:48, as I will show in chapter six. It matters for the Qur'ān to outperform both Judaism and Christianity in depicting heaven in terms far more attractive and hell in terms far more graphic than its parent scriptures.[52]

In this declaration of transcendence, the Qur'ān points to the limits of language. Language characterizes the Qur'ān as a discourse of rhetorical power par excellence, one that cannot come second to or fall beneath any other possible rhetorical representations in the Arabic language. The Qur'ān declares that it not only speaks well, but does so better than any other possibilities of speech available in the effable world of classical Arabic. This competitiveness is a defining characteristic of the Qur'ān. In addition to its scriptural implications, the idea of *aḥsan al-ḥadīth*, contrary to the desire for creating a startling rhetorical image, radically distinguishes the Qur'ān from the use of language in the poetic sense. This distinction is what creates a status of absolutely irreducible difference, a difference between a concern with the totality of the world and a concern with a particular human experience and condition. But it is also a difference predicated on a distinction from all preceding poetry and scripture,[53] without which one may never come to know or even appreciate that difference. In other words, if the Qur'ān is rooted in difference, one must safely assume that, especially in the case of poetry, it would demand that its reader face its difference from such discourse through a rigorous practice of linguistic comparison and conceptual philological distinction. This is itself the demand al-Jurjānī would advance in his defense of poetry, leading to the birth of the discipline of rhetoric in the field of Arabic literary criticism.

The literary tradition that preceded the Qurʾān, Ibn Qutayba tells us, was poetry of the loftiest sense. Ibn Qutayba reminds us that the word *ḥasan* was already used to describe the poetic talent of the pre-Islamic poet Ṭarafa ibn al-ʿAbd (543–69), who was renowned for his *shiʿr ḥasan* (good/beautiful poetry). Ṭarafa did not live long, but his poetry left everlasting imprints on searching for meaning in life and articulating a human existential crisis. His ode brings together all the usual themes of pre-Islamic times. It begins with the patterned convention of *al-wuqūf ʿalá al-aṭlāl wa bukāʾ al-diyār*:

تَلوحُ كَباقي الوَشمِ في ظاهِرِ اليَدِ   لِخَولَةَ أطلالٌ بِبُرقَةِ ثَهمَدِ

يَقولونَ لا تَهلِك أسىً وَتَجَلَّدِ[54]   وُقوفًا بِها صَحبي عَلَيَّ مَطِيَّهُم

> There are traces of Khawla on the pebbled lands of Thahmad / They appear like the fading tattoo on the back of a hand.
> There, my friends halted their mounts to look after me / Saying "don't let grief kill you; have some fortitude."

By now, we are familiar with the formulaic structure of the pre-Islamic ode. It starts with a memory of a lost beloved whose departure breaks the poet's heart and prompts his friends to console him. Nonetheless, the patterned aesthetic of the *qaṣīda* excels in matching the meaning to its empirical manifestation. We are meant to feel and sympathize with the poet's dejected condition despite the formulaic nature of the poem. Poetic talent, as well as its rhetoric of intelligence, is, above all, a contract between meaning and comprehending this meaning through the linguistic vehicle that carries it in its totality: the language that speaks loss, nostalgia, anxiety, doubt, love—and speaks them all *beautifully*. Ṭarafa writes poetry about the tribe that excised him, poetry that questions existence and the meaning of life. His poetry is not seeking an answer to resolve a crisis. It is, rather, a poetry that knows the answer and is aware of the impossibility of eternity and the unavoidable tragedy of death. Ṭarafa's ode tells us that death is not something chosen by us; we are thrown into it, that to fear death is to live a life of cowardice. In a strong and uncanny Heideggerian moment *avant la lettre*, Ṭarafa reconciles that death is "freedom towards death,"[55] that *there is* freedom in holding on to the idea that we are best at "being" in embracing "not being," and that to be fully alive we would want to exit from life willingly:

وأنْ أشهدَ اللذاتِ هل أنت مخلدي؟   أَلَا أيُّهَذا الزاجري أحضرَ الوغى

فـدعني أبـادِرُها بما ملكتْ يدي[56]   فـإنْ كنـتَ لا تستطيعُ دفـعَ منيَّتي

Hey you, who blame me for going to war / and indulging in pleasures, can you
 make me live forever?
If you cannot stop my death / then let me advance to it with all that I have.

The Qur'ān addresses the question of eternity and resurrection in many of its verses. Here are a few examples from 6:29 and 45:24, respectively:

وَقَالُوا إِنْ هِيَ إِلَّا حَيَاتُنَا الدُّنْيَا وَمَا نَحْنُ بِمَبْعُوثِينَ

And they said this is the only life we have and we won't be resurrected.

وَقَالُواْ مَا هِيَ إِلَّا حَيَاتُنَا ٱلدُّنْيَا نَمُوتُ وَنَحْيَا وَمَا يُهْلِكُنَا إِلَّا ٱلدَّهْرُ ۚ وَمَا لَهُم بِذَٰلِكَ مِنْ عِلْمٍ ۖ إِنْ هُمْ إِلَّا يَظُنُّونَ

And they said this is the only life we have, we die and we live and only time makes us perish, but they have no knowledge, they are just taking a guess.

These verses suggest that it is only after the linguistic mediation of pre-Islamic poetry that a deeper contextual understanding of the Qur'ān becomes possible. The Qur'ān knows, and Ṭarafa's poem confirms, that it speaks to a community headstrong in its belief that no resurrection awaits the dead and there is nothing beyond this worldly life. Ṭarafa's image thus reignites a classical distinction between pre- and post-Qur'ānic concepts of death and resurrection, which is of value in understanding the dialogical tension in the early Muslim community prevalent in the Qur'ān.[37] After all, Ṭarafa may not be alone. The positioning of the biological subject in an environment to which he remains irrevocably bound is, in Ṭarafa's poetic imagination, opposed to a realm of metaphysical knowledge. There was, to be sure, a certain belief in resurrection in pre-Islamic Arabia, a belief that, as Jawād ʿAlī reminds us, was never positioned as paramount or significant.[58] Semantically, al-mawt (death) implies sukūn (silence) in classical Arabic. To say someone is dead is to say someone has become silent.[59] This understanding should not contradict the widespread motif of "living" after death as ḥadīth/ aḥādīth (story/stories), which Geert Jan van Gelder excellently examines,[60] and which the Qur'ān references as a moral lesson for posterity. Rather, pre-Islamic Arabs believed in the immortality of memory but not the resurrection of the body. Death is thus the silence of the body after al-rūḥ (spirit/soul) has departed it, a phenomenon that bewildered pre-Islamic Arabs—hence the burning question to Muḥammad, "wa yasʾalūnaka ʿani al-rūḥi" (they ask you about the spirit/soul) (17:85). Quoting Shaddād ibn al-Aswad in the aftermath of the Battle of Badr as he mocks the prophet's talk on resurrection, the nineteenth-century Iraqi exegete Maḥmūd Shukrī al-Ālūsī (1802–54) states that pre-Islamic Arabs considered it absurd to believe humans returned from the dead:

من الشِّيزي تزين بالسنام	وماذا بالقَليبِ قليبِ بَدْر
من القَينات والشَرْبِ الكِرام	وماذا بالقَليبِ قليبِ بَدْرٍ

تحيينا السلامة أم بكر   فهل لي بعد قومي من سلام

يحدثنا الرسول بأن سنحيا   وكيف حياةُ أصداءٍ وهامِ[61]

What of the Qalīb, well of Badr / of the platters of Shīzá wood-holding camel-hump fat?
What of the Qalīb, well of Badr / of singing women and noble drinkers?
Umm Bakr bids us a peace greeting / How can I have peace after my people (were killed)?
The messenger tells us we would live / But how can ghosts and wraiths live again?[62]

In crude anthropological terms, pre-Islamic Arabs positioned their own subjectivity against the knowledge of the unknown. They were *le sujet supposé savoir* of their own time, "the subject [who] is supposed to know," who is the bearer and generator of the knowledge of his own existence and who was disinclined to take a step into the abstract. Pre-Islamic Arabs accepted *inkār al-baʿth* (the denial of resurrection) and even mocked folkloric and fairytales that men turn into birds when they die.[63] What Ṭarafa's ode affirms is not that he lacks knowledge of the world and its abstract totality—the Qurʾān provides such a totality and does so in a manner that claims knowledge to itself: "*qāla in labithtum illā qalīlan law anna-kum kuntum taʿlamūn*" (23:114) (He said you had been [on earth] but for a brief time, if only you had knowledge). The Ṭarafian poetic formula, by contrast, articulates a gap between experience and abstraction, a gap that the poet is disinclined to even attempt to bridge. The ironic question Ṭarafa poses is therefore profoundly disheartening yet deeply rhetorical. It seeks no answer. The empirical moment that materializes itself in facing danger and "initiating" an advance toward death is nowhere present in the Qurʾān. And the appearance of figurative language in the Qurʾān, as we have seen it in the extended rhetorical simile of 23:39–40, has to do with a completely different act, the act of juxtaposing the empirical and the conceptual. In the tender tropes of the pre-Islamic *qaṣīda*, there is no place for the conceptual. The poet speaks as one among the tested and experienced few, and poetry is the only theology there is.

Conventional aesthetics would commend the poem for its well-kept archetypal features. What has been lost since that time—and what does not come back in the Qurʾān, at least not explicitly—is the suppressed ethos of the human condition. The total alienation we hear in somber lines such as "*ufridtu ifrāda al-baʿīri al-muʿabbadi*" (I was excised [from my clan] like tainted camel, coated in tar) represents this human condition in which the second person's voice (*anta*) of a nomadic desert community whispers counsel to a persona that feels as discarded as a diseased camel. To Ṭarafa, there is no meaning in a life that is constantly threated by death. As the heart of a poet has fully hardened, the counsel from his fellow man becomes absurd. The double interjection "*alā ayyuhādhā*" (Hey, you) does not have an equivalent in English. Its untranslatability signifies a determined rebellion against conceptual knowledge, a rebellion raised by a poet who defiantly translates his own repression and alienation into the truth claim of an artistic medium. The pre-Islamic ode genre, whose aesthetic structure compels it to observe and celebrate communal values, becomes in Ṭarafa the opposite of itself, an epitome of singularity and human alienation. The poem challenges tribal wisdom because, in representing a state of utter isolation, it eclipses the compliance this conventional wisdom expects from a supposedly conforming member of the tribe. There is an unresolved dialectic in the relationship between form and content in Ṭarafa's poem. Although he cannot abandon the ode's technical and formal conventionality, he still sacrifices its thematic conformity for the sake of a different kind of aesthetic sensibility—that is, the power to own one's own fate.

At other moments, this sensibility bears witness to a hedonistic content through a powerful forcing of pleasure. The nihilistic meaning of life in these lines is enhanced in the very moment of disavowing life. To speak of the issue in a manner reminiscent of Roland Barthes, all art is enveloped in sadness and death. The more Ṭarafa's ode touches the core of the human condition, the more heightened the dejection that emanates from it. Ṭarafa's suppressed feeling of "Oh, if only we do not perish" brings to the fore the most painful and unresolved existential dilemma. Compared to this melancholy, the Qurʾān is a hopeful text, hopeful in the sense that it opens up a heavenly possibility, or rather a realm of eternity and a felicity relegated to a future promise, a reverse image of longing for a pleasure yet to come. But what radiates woefully in Ṭarafa is this vulnerable element of a pragmatic universal truth, a secular revelation of mortality where living in absolute danger and in absolute pleasure looks death in the eye and makes it appear as if life were preying on death, and not vice versa. There is nothing in these lines that does not belong to this world and nothing that could not be taken away from this world at a price less than death.

4

Poetic Paganism
and the Monotheistic Aesthetic

In the previous chapter, I argued thar the Qurʾān is not antithetical to pre-Islamic poetry. Rather, pre-Islamic Arabic is the linguistic native vehicle of the Qurʾān. In this chapter, I further elaborate the argument that a rhetorical literary analysis of the Qurʾān is neither reductionist nor peripheral. The Qurʾān not only includes literary aesthetics, but it also offers a social aesthetic that manifests itself in literary forms, content, contextual settings germane to the historical, political, and socioeconomic values leading up to the first Muslim community. In other words, the Qurʾān is a value-transforming and value-creating text. Rhetorical examination of the Qurʾān involves an investigation of the dialogic tension inherent in the linguistic expressions that represent modes, conflicts, alliances, and oppositions at the literary as well as social and political levels of the Meccan and Medinan societies in seventh-century Arabia.

Interrogation of the Qurʾānʾs content and rhetoric thus has a bearing on the philosophical views as well as the economic structure and social values of seventh-century Arabia. For example, in the early Meccan period (e.g., 83; 102; 104; 107), the Qurʾān explicitly condemns greed, trade fraud, money-mongering, avarice, apathy to the poor, and mockery of the deprived, among other forms of social injustices. Such injustices were the common law of the Meccan society. But the Qurʾān does this using rhetorical language and syntax familiar to its intended audience. The Qurʾān critiques the economic structure of its own society as well as its religious and social habits.[1] These accepted elements of the society created the ways in which people lived and the literature that mirrored their way of life. As we see in the examples of Ṭarafa and al-Nābigha, as well as the Qurʾān, the ideology of pre-Islamic Mecca represents a complex relationship of individuals to the practical conditions of their existence. The Qurʾānʾs historical value as a seventh-century scripture lies not in its relationship to former monotheistic scriptures, although it does refer to biblical narratives and events knowable to the collective consciousness of the time, sometimes in endorsement and sometimes in disagreement. But the very the heart of the Qurʾān is a rhetoric of Arabicity—that is, a rhetoric that adheres to the linguistic rules of the Arabic language and is in intertextual dialogue with its own tradition of ancient Arabic poetry. This rhetoric engenders a critique of what it perceives as false views of the world not only in terms of divinity but also in terms of social relationships between the rich and the poor and the rulers and the ruled. Examining the rhetorical properties in the works of poets like Ṭarafa and al-Nābigha, among many others, allows us to see how their poetry, despite its discursive difference from the Qurʾān, is tied to the rhetorical forms and themes of the Qurʾān. After all, the task of pre-Islamic poets, no matter how agonized or dejected they might be, was primarily aesthetic. They sought to be concrete and imagistic in their poetical works and to make sure that their respective poems would stand tall, that the lines would have no broken meters, and that the imagery would be creative. For example, we have seen how the "rhetoric of death" in Ṭarafa gives perpetuity to a passing life, not by wanting to save it from death, but by wanting to crush it under its wheels. Understating how al-Nābigha had to excel in his own poetic talent to save his life and how Ṭarafa rushed into a fated pattern of mortal heroism is crucial for understanding the Qurʾān. Investigating how pre-Islamic poets depict the malaise of their harshly led lives through a carefully structured and metered ode, a hedonistic aesthetics of sorts, makes the understanding of the relationship between poetry, the community, and the Qurʾān even more compelling.

Likewise, the real and the concrete of the Qurʾān's text is its own language. In fact, the Qurʾān does not have any material reality outside the Arabic language, and more specifically outside the orality of the Arabic language. For the sake of all pre-Qurʾānic poets who took Arabic aesthetics to heights envied by their successors, it is important here not to eschew altogether the historical engagement with the Qurʾān, but rather to slow it down, to take it all the way in, to immerse it in this rhetorical "materiality" of pre-Qurʾānic and Qurʾānic Arabia so thoroughly that when we emerge on the other side, we would have a material history, especially for the literary and cultural historian, that we can debate, and with which we can generally agree. Reading pre-Islamic poets and examining the aesthetic properties of the Arabic language of the Qurʾān does not mean one has to replace one discipline with another or jettison the historian for the literary critic. But instead of suspending the relative autonomy of specialized disciplines, it is crucial for the study of the Qurʾān to arrive at a transformational ethical space where disciplines transcend their specializations and converge on the material ground of the Qurʾān text itself.

Above all, the Qurʾān is an oral text,[2] one that is meant not just to be *read* but to be *heard*, and to be heard *with* others.[3] This fundamental oral/aural anchorage means that the Qurʾān is always already part of a community of readers and listeners—hence its ethical authority, its ability to engage current values and create future values. To be able to hear the Qur'ān properly requires superior proficiency and knowledge not only of classical Arabic, but also and more importantly, of ancient pre-Islamic Arabic.[4] This grim conclusion also means that a great majority of Muslims today are not able to hear the Qur'ān properly, and that only a small number of specialized Arabists, whether Arab or non-Arab, whether Muslim or non-Muslim, will qualify as proper hearers of the Qur'ān. This "proper hearing" models a kind of ethics, especially for the Western historian, where one does not need to feel the need to sacrifice the acoustic encounter with aesthetic orality for the sake of applying a calculated disciplinary methodology to "study" the Qur'ān while bypassing a language and a history that are not his own.

To be sure, there are no parallel texts that have the same aesthetic condition of the Qur'ān as an oral text in the Western canon, nor are there parallel intertextualities like the ones between pre-Islamic poetry and the Qur'ān. The Qur'ān's oral rhythm is of such substantive importance that attempts to examine it under scripted models of European aesthetics is already a doomed project.

The source of the Qur'ān's resistance to such normative scriptural aesthetics is that materialized scripted approaches tend to lead to the dismissal and denigration of the written text meant to transcribe its orality. The Qur'ān itself makes this admonition against the rushed perseveration of it explicitly clear:

وَلَا تَعْجَلْ بِالْقُرْآنِ مِنْ قَبْلِ أَنْ يُقْضَى إِلَيْكَ وَحْيُهُ[5]

لاَ تُحَرِّكْ بِهِ لِسَانَكَ لِتَعْجَلَ بِهِ . إِنَّ عَلَيْنَا جَمْعَهُ وَقُرْآنَهُ . فَإِذَا قَرَأْنَاهُ فاتبع قُرْآنَهُ . ثُمَّ إِنَّ عَلَيْنَا بَيَانَهُ[6]

Do not rush the Qur'ān before its completely delivered to you
Do not move your tongue with it to rush it. It is upon Us to make it whole and
    recitable. So once We have recited it, you must adhere to its recitation. Then it is
    upon Us to make it clear.

In the case of Arabic, and especially the Qur'ān, Euro-American understandings of aesthetics as a theory of the beautiful can be unproductive and limited precisely because the normative characteristics of the concept of beauty remain inadequate to the full content of Arabic aesthetics, especially its orality. Hegel's famous claim that beauty is "the sensuous appearance [or manifestation] of the idea"[7] makes it difficult to locate this appearance or manifestation in ancient languages or even in nature.[8] There is no place for oral aesthetics in Hegel's figure-focused conception of beauty, even though in Western tradition the dialectical relationship between beauty and *phone* (voice) is as old as the *Odyssey*. One should not forget that we are dealing with an oral tradition, not with the *figura*, or the written or scripted system that has become its correlate. Incidentally, this is exactly the argument van Gelder makes for all of classical Arabic poetry in *Sound and Sense*—that is, its oral/aural dimension is too often ignored and neglected.[9] Even the writing of the Qur'ān suggests that it is only after the mediation of *I'jāz* that a certain appreciation of the acoustic becomes possible, but that mediation itself involves orality, as any transcription of the Qur'ān in essence has no existence without voice.

However, this has been the problem Europe has always had with Arabic: its difficulty, its untranslatability, its unassimilability, indeed its "un-aesthetic-ness." But absence of parallelism does not mean that literary tools could not be used to approach the text. Yet, a tool is not a method and there is no one universal or global standard to assess the aesthetics of texts. Take, for instance, the remarks of Thomas Babington Macaulay, who was a member of the British Parliament and a renowned historian in the nineteenth century. Macaulay served on the British Supreme Council for India between 1834 and 1838. In a debate on allocating government funds in the colonies, Macaulay has the following to say about Arabic and Sanskrit languages:

> The whole question seems to me to be, which language is the best worth knowing? I have no knowledge of either Sanskrit or Arabic. I have read translations of the most celebrated Arabic and Sanskrit works. I am quite ready to take the Oriental learning at the valuation of the Orientalists themselves. I have never found one among them who could deny that a single shelf of a good European library was worth the whole native literature of India and Arabia. The intrinsic superiority of the Western literature is, indeed, fully admitted by those members of the Committee who support the Oriental plan of education . . . It is said that the Sanskrit and Arabic are the languages in which the sacred books of a hundred millions of people are written, and that they are, on that account, entitled to peculiar encouragement. Assuredly it is the duty of the British government in India to be not only tolerant, but neutral on all religious questions. But to encourage the study of a literature admitted to be of small intrinsic value only because that literature inculcates the most serious errors on the most important subjects, is a course hardly reconcilable with reason, with morality, or even with that very neutrality which ought, as we all agree, to be sacredly preserved. It is confessed that a language is barren of useful knowledge. We are told to teach it because it is fruitful of monstrous superstitions. We are to teach false history, false astronomy, false medicine, because we find them in company with a false religion.[10]

There is in Macaulay's address a clear Eurocentric antipathy toward Sanskrit and Arabic. But why this resurrection of a nineteenth-century orientalist account now? Because the roots of the anti-aesthetic are deep and far-reaching in historical discourses and, in particular, in the scholarship of the Euro-American academy on the Qur'ān, which is characteristically undergirded by these anti-aesthetic accounts as they have developed since colonial times.[11] This is the same epistemic space that informs Reynold Nicholson's approach to classical Arabic, which resulted in a book that became the core required text for training generations of specialists in the field of Arabic literature in the English-speaking world in the twentieth century. But if Nicholson fails in his assessment of classical Arabic poetry,[12] then one cannot expect him to have any meaningful understanding of the Qur'ān.[13] In *A Literary History of the Arabs*, Nicholson writes:

> European scholars, with the exception of von Hammer, have been far from sharing this enthusiasm [for al-Mutanabbi], as may be seen by referring to what has been said on the subject by Reiske, De Sacy, Bohlen, Brockelmann, and others. No doubt, according to our canons of taste, Mutanabbi stands immeasurably below the famous Pre-Islamic bards, and in a later age must yield the palm to Abu Nuwas and Abu 'l-'Atahiya. Lovers of poetry, as the term is understood in Europe, cannot derive much aesthetic pleasure from his writings, but, on the contrary, will be disgusted by the beauties hardly less than by the faults which Arabian critics attribute to him.[14]

To his credit, Nicholson, perhaps with tongue firmly in cheek, ameliorates his "disgust" by deferring to the judgment of the native speaker when it comes to the assessment of Arabic aesthetics. Nicholson refers to the native speaker of Arabic as the "born oriental" who "is able to appreciate Mutanabbi at his full worth," counseling his camp of European lovers of poetry to "try to realize the oriental point of view and put aside, as far as possible, our preconceptions of what constitutes good poetry and good taste."[15] Not only does the work of many remarkable Western scholars of Arabic and Islam belie Nicholson's prejudiced statement, but Nicholson's framing of aesthetics is itself epistemologically peripheral. He surrenders without reservation to the sensibilities of his European audiences. His book is peppered with comparative aesthetics, a framework in which "the longest of the *muʿallaqāt*, the so-called 'Long Poems,' is considerably shorter than Gray's *Elegy*, and an Arabian Homer or Chaucer must have condescended to prose."[16] Though condescending in tone, this critical exercise is itself enriching, except that Nicholson's comparative thought process is hierarchical rather than deferential, a prisoner of its own norms of poetic aesthetics "as the term is understood in Europe."[17] Clearly some "outlandish" classical Arabic gibberish like that of al-Mutanabbī's poetry would appear "disgusting" through Nicholson's Eurocentric lenses. Al-Mutanabbī (d. 965 AD) lived and composed poetry in the tenth century, that is, three hundred years after the Qur'ān. To pit al-Mutanabbī against "pre-Islamic bards" in an aesthetical context, as does Nicholson, is to pretend that the Qur'ān never happened and to fail to see the change in the socioeconomic conditions in post- Qur'ānic communities and the enormity of the task of composing poetry after the Qur'ān. This "afterness" is crucial for understanding the quantum leap in Arabic aesthetics in the aftermath of the Qur'ān. It opens up further historical and literary inquiries about what it means for a literary genre to "precede" or "follow" a discourse of rhetorical power and whether or not the Qur'ān in the aftermath of pre-Islamic poetry or even poetry in the aftermath of the Qur'ān signifies a sharp severance, or, subliminally, recasts its precursor in further enhancement of the aesthetics of that very tradition.

The examples from Macaulay and Nicholson are not isolated incidents or exceptional oddities but signs of a more serious problem and a confirmation of an irreparably condescending Eurocentric approach toward the aesthetical tradition of the other, an approach that has continued to characterize contemporary Euro-American thought on the status of Arabic in world literature. Both Macaulay's imperialistic hubris and Nicholson's aesthetic bias manufactured, in their own respective categorizations, bizarrely paradoxical views to bear on Arabic (and, in Macaulay's case, Sanskrit) literatures to Euro-American universities: on the one hand, they assume that all Arabic literature must be valued according to a universal code of rational thought, and must be paraphrased, argued with, and quickly situated in a hierarchy based on a European "ideal" of aesthetic judgement. Their views carry within them the deadly epistemological germs of the discourses that shaped them and the discourses they inspired.

For the sake of clarity, let us take a quick detour and offer an example of the Qur'ān's influence on the late classical poet of the 'Abbasid era, Ḥabīb ibn Aws al-Ṭā'ī (known as Abū Tammām). This example will help illustrate the point and shed light on some of the aesthetic complexities involved in the making of classical Arabic poetry *after* the Qur'ān. One of the most celebrated poets of the Arabic language, Abū Tammām (d. 845–46) was a Syrian-born Christian who converted to Islam and reached the pinnacle of his poetic career under the rule of the al-Muʿtaṣim (833–42). An unforeseeable event at the height of Abū Tammām's fame almost cost his career. As he was giving a panegyric in honor of the caliph's son, Prince Aḥmad Ibn al-Muʿtaṣim, the Kufa-born philosopher and polymath Yūsuf Yaʿqūb Ibn Isḥāq al-Kindī, who happened to be among the audience, did not seem to appreciate the "praise similes" he heard in the poem. Abū Tammām began to liken Prince Aḥmad to remarkable figures in Arab-Islamic history:

أَبْلَيْتَ هذا المجدَ أَبْعَدَ غايةٍ   فيه وأكرمَ شيمةٍ ونِحاسٍ

إقدامِ عمرٍو في سماحةِ حاتمٍ   في حِلمٍ أَحْنَفَ في ذكاءِ إياسٍ[18]

You have accomplished this glory at its highest reach / its noblest quality and its purity.
The mettle of ʿAmr, the tolerance of Ḥātim / the equanimity of Aḥnaf and the acumen of Iyās.

At this moment al-Kindī insultingly interrupted him, objecting that "The prince is above those whom you liken him to."[19] Taken aback by the unexpected insult, Abū Tammām remained silent for a moment, but then ventured the following two verses on the spot, which had not been part of his prepared ode:

لا تنكروا ضَرْبي لَه مَنْ دُونَهُ   مثلاً شَرُوداً في النَّدَى والباسِ

فاللهُ قَدْ ضَربَ الأقلَّ لِنُورِه   مثلاً من المِشْكَاةِ والنّبْراسِ[20]

Do not reproach me for citing exemplars / that are less than him, who is matchless
in bounty and mettle.
For God has given less for his own light / an example of the niche and the lantern.

This poetic act of quick wittedness won Abū Tammām the immediate commendation of his audience, including al-Kindī. On this particular occasion, Abū Tammām would not have been able to compose brilliant poetic lines on the spot without committing the language and imagery of the Qurʾān to heart. Al-Kindī was so moved by Abū Tammām's immediate response that he demanded the poet be granted whatever reward he asked for, because, according to al-Kindī, a poet with such an extraordinary aesthetic talent like Abū Tammām's "won't live long . . . he is a man whose intellect is rapidly consuming his body."[21]

Very few poems in the Arabic tradition bring together such great poetic talent with the architectural employment of the Qurʾān. The allegorical complexity of the lines alone makes them one of the most eccentric and impressive improvisations in the history of Arabic literature. This improvisation invites the larger question of the connections between Arabic literature, Qurʾānic authority, and the limits of rhetorical language. In particular, this improvisation invites a deeper interrogation of the relationship between oral tradition and individual talent, as well as the depths, influences, and commanding presence of the Qurʾān in Arabic poetics. If what we call *al-qarīḥa al-shiʿriyya* (poetic talent/afflatus) is the "raw" gift a poet enjoys, in the manner in which such a gift gets "cooked" and molded into poetic expressions and cultural themes, these expressions will always be linked to an unspoken aesthetics of intelligence. Before the Qurʾān, this unspoken aesthetics of intelligence was itself the tradition of the classical Arabic *qaṣīda*, especially its glorious examples in the Golden Odes. After the Qurʾān, Arabic poetry continued to be enhanced, or impeded, by the former's textual authority as a sublime discourse of rhetorical power.

It is impossible to know what could have taken place in Abū Tammām's mind during this moment of awkward silence following al-Kindī's insult, what scores of poetic tropes he could envisaged, or what hundreds of Qurʾānic verses could have run through his mind. Whatever it was, he was able find an escape in these two Qurʾān-inspired lines. He performed three acts of poetic intelligence simultaneously: he evoked the most fitting Qurʾānic verse to the occasion; he employed it in a manner that did not reduce him to a mere imitator; and he managed to mold the freshly composed tropes into *baḥr al-kāmil* (*al-kāmil* metre) of his panegyric, with a poetic talent "as natural as the pattern that was made by the dust on a butterfly's wings," to quote Ernest Hemingway's description of F. Scott Fitzgerald.[22]

If the most accomplished of classical Arabic authors are those whose poetic intelligence is tested to the point of delivering striking lines, *on the spot*, from the looming disgrace of mediocrity, it is safe to argue that intimate oral knowledge of pre-Islamic Arabic and the Qurʾān is a fundamental prerequisite for Arabic poetic genius post-Islam. In this particular case, the spontaneous recall of the Qurʾān not only offers the potential to bring about poetry interconnected with sacred language but also to *transform* it by this interconnection. To be sure, almost every post-Islamic Arab poet either committed the Qurʾān to memory or had a deep familiarity with its verses and imagery. The Qurʾān includes a rhythmic quality and aesthetic beauty in its *sajʿ* (rhyme and rhythmic assonance) that makes it easy to memorize with regular practice. Yet learning the Qurʾān by heart and being sufficiently quick-witted to produce powerful and compelling lines on the spot a la Abū Tammām is almost an impossible task, not to mention putting those lines in sync with the poem's main theme and rhyme scheme. The verse that Abū Tammām beckons in his poem comes from the Qurʾānic chapter *al-Nūr* (The Light), named after the verses that describe the light of God:

اللَّهُ نُورُ السَّمَاوَاتِ وَالأَرْضِ مَثَلُ نُورِهِ كَمِشْكَاةٍ فِيهَا مِصْبَاحٌ الْمِصْبَاحُ فِي زُجَاجَةٍ الزُّجَاجَةُ كَأَنَّهَا كَوْكَبٌ دُرِّيٌّ يُوقَدُ مِنْ شَجَرَةٍ مُبَارَكَةٍ زَيْتُونَةٍ لا شَرْقِيَّةٍ وَلا غَرْبِيَّةٍ يَكَادُ زَيْتُهَا يُضِيءُ وَلَوْ لَمْ تَمْسَسْهُ نَارٌ نُورٌ عَلَى نُورٍ يَهْدِي اللَّهُ لِنُورِهِ مَنْ يَشَاءُ وَيَضْرِبُ اللَّهُ الأَمْثَالَ لِلنَّاسِ وَاللَّهُ بِكُلِّ شَيْءٍ عَلِيمٌ

God is the light of heavens and earth. The example of his light is like a niche inside of which is a lamp, the lamp is in a glass, the glass is as if it were a bright planet lit from a blessed tree, an olive, neither easterly nor western, whose oil almost glows even when untouched by fire. Light upon light. God guides to his light whom he wills. And God gives examples to people. And God knows everything. (24:35)

Abū Tammām must have known that offering what his fellow Muslim audience believed to be the inimitable words of God would silence his detractors. And he chose the perfect example for it: a verse from the Qurʾān that presents an extended simile of God, lesser than himself, to approximate the magnitude of his divine light to humans; a simile of a simile, so to speak, one that could only capture a fracture or a glimpse of divine light, so humans could come to understand, though not completely comprehend, the incomparable light that is divinity itself. The association is clear. If the Qurʾān brings in a reduced simile to approximate the brightness of God's light, then certainly a poet can use archetypal models of Arab bravery, lenience, and charity to approximate the magnificence of Prince Aḥmad. Abū Tammām, who understands the supreme authority of the Qurʾān text, knows that al-Kindī cannot dispute this level of poetic intelligence.

Nor does the poetic intelligence of Abū Tammām stop there. The genius of this particular Qurʾān-inspired moment remains unrivalled. In the "afterness" of the Qurʾān, it would be impossible for an Arab poet to imitate or steal from it without being caught, given the authority and popularity of the text. We see this inspiration represented in many instances of post-Qurʾānic classical Arabic. Little did Nicholson know that al-Mutanabbī in this context would fall under the rubric of the "mature poets" who must enhance their poetic talent in the afterness of the Qurʾān. The Qurʾān has thus been a dialectical presence for all poets who came after it precisely because it cannot be ignored at the same time it cannot be matched. Mainly because of the quality of its *balāgha* as well as the religious authority it has acquired, the gravitational pull of the Qurʾān's aesthetic power makes it comparable to none, enveloping content and form in a manner that could only astound and overwhelm anyone who listens to it. The following lines from one of al-Mutanabbī's poem are an excellent example of this type of dialectical relationship to the Qurʾān. Al-Mutanabbī refers to prophetic figures from the Qurʾān economically and imagistically (because he knows that his listeners know who he is talking about) to express his deep sense of distress, loss, and emotional alienation from the people around him:[23]

ما مُقامي بأرضِ نَحْلَة . . . إلاَّ كَمُقامِ المسيح بينَ اليهودِ

. . . .

أنا في أُمَّةٍ تدارَكَها اللهُ . . . غَريبٌ كَصَالِحٍ في ثَمُودِ[24]

My stay in the land of Naḥla /Is very much like the stay of the messiah among the Jews.
. . . .
I live among a people, may God handle them / as an outsider like Ṣāliḥ among Thamūd.

This pregnant example of Qurʾān-inspired poeticity is meant to show that there is an ethical imperative to rethink the canonicity of the aesthetic in Western scholarship on the Qurʾān, an imperative that should not only be premised on counterbalancing the othering of the text's Arabicity but on exposing the causes of this othering. The insistence on a Eurocentric marginalization of Arabic aesthetics is still widespread in the Euro-American academy. It remains questionable in its attribution bias to the origins of the Qurʾān. To judge from recent publications, the wind of Qurʾānic Studies is not blowing in the direction of the Arabicity and rhetoricity of the Qurʾān. We do not read much about the Qurʾān's literary connection to pre-Islamic poetry or the social aesthetics of the time, but we keep hearing a great deal about the "external" context and influence—that is, late antiquity—to which the Qurʾān's language refers. The emphasis now is not on the structural analysis or the linguistic or verbal status of the Qurʾān, a property that is so easily dismissible, but on the "inter-texts" between the language of the Qurʾān and these grand categories that are said to constitute it. One of the most controversial among these categories coincides with the new approach to late antiquity. This approach does not ask what Arabic words of the Qurʾān mean or even how they mean, but rather what existing late antique epistemic categories the text must have drawn from, thus emboldening the historical-critical discourse to bypass the literary dimensions and aesthetic significations of the Arabic language. In this approach, what we call aesthetics is screened through specific geographical and institutional settings that translate the other into tailored perceptions and judgements.

In what follows, I would like to provide a few further examples of these aesthetic moments that materialize in the Qur'ān's rhetorical power in its dialogic interaction with the social context we see represented in pre-Islamic poetry. The relationship between the world and the text of the Qur'ān is an ever-inclusive category involving religious and cultural practices, economy, politics, law, gender, ethnicity, sex, marriage, divorce, death, inheritance, and so on. This category is enveloped in a specific rhetoric of Arabicity that reflects the totality of how one understands the first Muslim community and interprets the Qur'ān. Even the stories of prophets from centuries past are brought in with such rhetorical authority to teach a moral lesson to the present community—or, as the Qur'ān puts it:

لَقَدْ كَانَ فِى قَصَصِهِمْ عِبْرَةٌ لِّأُوْلِى ٱلْأَلْبَٰبِ ۗ مَا كَانَ حَدِيثًا يُفْتَرَىٰ وَلَٰكِن تَصْدِيقَ ٱلَّذِى بَيْنَ يَدَيْهِ وَتَفْصِيلَ كُلِّ شَىْءٍ وَهُدًى وَرَحْمَةً لِّقَوْمٍ يُؤْمِنُونَ[25]

> In their stories there is a lesson for the mindful ones. This narrative is not a myth, but a validation of previous revelations, an explication of everything, in guidance and mercy for those who believe.

In the Qur'ānic accounts of Moses, for example, one hears a story of resistance to a despotic regime signified by defiance and exodus. In another example, a clear message of gender, ethnicity, morality, and class emerges from the story of Mary (Maryam). Mary is seen as an outsider in her community, with her honor and chastity questionable by her people.[26] Even though the Qur'ān blesses and exonerates Mary, granting her a voice and the status of being the only woman whose name is mentioned in the Qur'ān with a full sūra (*Sūra-t-Maryam* [19]) dedicated to her, her vocal agency practically disappears from its narrative after giving birth to Jesus.[27] Other passing references to Mary in the Qur'ān emphasize her chastity (e.g., 66.12), denounce in the strongest terms the false accusations leveled against her (e.g., 4:156), and present her legacy and that of Jesus as a sign and a miracle from God (23:50). If anything, references to biblical figures and prophets serve to provide a thought space for readers of and listeners to the Qur'ān to reflect on the totality that the text brings forward. But stories of prophets are just one aspect of the Qur'ān. In fact, a considerable part of the Qur'ān highlights tensions between established tribal customs and the nascent allegiances to Muḥammad. The more one reads the Qur'ān, the more it appears deconstructive of the textual authority and customary practices of seventh-century Arabia.

In its communal address, the Qur'ān represents what James Joyce would call "the most commonplace, the deadest among the living,"[28] even nameless victims, such as a female child killed alive (81:8), a blind man seeking learning (80:2), and a poor divorced wife pleading for counsel (58:1). These examples show how the Qur'ān enmeshes itself in the fabric of its constitutive social reality and becomes a historical sign of the socioeconomic conditions in which it appeared. Compared to the language pre-Islamic poets used, especially in its philosophical musings and ecological depictions of nomad life, the language of the Qur'ān oscillates between apocalyptic and quotidian, and it does so in a manner that is not incomprehensible to its contemporary listeners and readers. This audience lived at times that oddly combined tribal solidarity with secular individualism; we see this especially clearly in the environmental depictions of nomadic life we see in pre-Islamic poetry.[29] This is why the move from tribal and blood solidarity to social solidarity is at the core of the Qur'ān's sociolinguistic aesthetics. Pre-Islamic poets gained their distinction through the abandonment of hackneyed language and speech as particular attributes of common language among their own people. But what does this abandonment of hackneyed language and speech consist of, and, more importantly, what does it signify for our understanding of the relationship between pre-Islamic poetry and the Qur'ān?

Precisely because aesthetics is concerned with what Ibn Qutayba describes as *ḥusn al-lafẓ wa jawda-t-al-maʿná* (the beauty of wording/expression in language and the quality of meaning),[30] there are irreducible distinctions and expectations from poetry as art, namely, as a rhymed and perfected expression of human thought and feelings. In Arabic, the contrast of *lafẓ* with *maʿná* is more or less equivalent to that between form and content. Poetry's relationship to its object, sometimes fateful if the poet is directed to lampoon an enemy of the tribe or praise a tribesman, is always determined by the challenges of linguistic expression and always pushed to avoid the triteness we have seen al-Kindī accuse Abū Tammām of. Ibn Qutayba's definition reminds us why from its incipiency, pre-Islamic poetry is concerned with uniqueness, newness, and the possibilities and limits of language. Reflection on its own language has been an integral part of the self-understanding and self-evaluation of pre-Islamic poetry. This reflection characterizes the poetic enterprise as one that cannot be subjected to any of the possible types of redundancies or repetitions that characterize prose or ordinary speech. Composed in a language whose etymological infrastructure makes it quite symmetrical and balanced, pre-Islamic odes owe their existence to the unique system of tri-consonantal roots of Arabic.

For instance, the opening line of 'Antara's ode includes the verb *ghādara*, which I cite below, a verb that means "to leave behind" or "to abandon." The word is derived from the Arabic root Gh/D/R, where Gh sound is only one consonant in Arabic. Many Arabic words and variations on the same root could still be formed, following a specific pattern of analogical derivation, and they would still retain the same or a similar denotation. For instance, *mughādara* means departure; *ghadr* means treachery—that is, departure from loyalty/abandonment of morals; *ghadīr* means "stream," that is, departing or running water, and so on. The ancient Arabic ode runs from fifteen to one hundred lines, consisting of highly rhythmic patterns that follow specific meters. Each poetic verse includes two evenly metered half-lines (hemistichs) and maintains a single meter throughout, with every line ending in the same sound. Highly organized, with a measured thematic and acoustic unity throughout, the ode both accomplishes and exhibits an aesthetics. It is a museum of words, itself a powerful poetical and communal force.

In fact, there is a unique Arabic verb specified for composing poetry: *yuqarriḍ al-shiʿr*. Form I in Arabic verbs is used with the same meaning: *qaraḍa yaqriḍu, qarḍ al-shiʿr*. The basic sense of the root *Q/ R/ Ḍ* is "cutting, gnawing, trimming," and *qarīḍ* means "cut to shape," which is an apt description of composing metrical rhymed verse. In *Asās al-balāgha*, al-Zamakhsharī defines the root *Q/ R/ Ḍ* as follows: *qaraḍa l-shāʿir wa-lahū qarīḍ ḥasan, li-anna al-shiʿr kalām dhū taqāṭīʿ*.[31] The complexity and talent involved in *taqrīḍ al-shiʿr*[32] (i.e., the mental effort of cutting, trimming, and polishing poetry in one's mind) makes it almost impossible to compose a classical ode today. Even the most erudite of Arabic readers might miss the subtleties and brilliant imagery at work in these pre-Islamic odes. The ode of ʿAntara ibn Shaddād, for instance, imperceptibly critiques the reversal of values, slavery, and racial discrimination at the same time that it beautifully contrasts blackness with whiteness, brokenness with wholeness, outsiders with tribe members, and wandering with rootedness. ʿAntara is at once a lover and a warrior, a man of fierce action and beautiful words who uses all elements in his surrounding environment, including sound imagery, animal imagery (e.g., horses, camels, and ostriches), and place symbolism to create new and fresh figures of speech. The goal is for the ode to pass the test of originality and gain fame among contemporaries by making itself rhetorically incomparable.

ʿAntara's ode, which begins with the anguished statement of poetic anxiety revealing his concern that his predecessors left nothing rhetorically startling or new for him to say, reminds us of the fierceness of these poetic contests and the constant strife for uniqueness and originality:

أم هلْ عَرِفْتَ الدارَ بعدَ توَهُّمِ[33]   هلْ غادرَ الشُّعراءُ منْ مُتَرَدَّمِ

> Have the poets left any speech to patch / Or have you recognized the home after much doubt?

It is the search for something new that irks the mind of the pre-Islamic poet, and all artists for that reason. Theodor Adorno describes this quest for newness as a desire for something already there but not yet revealed. "The relation to the new is modeled on a child at the piano," writes Adorno, "searching for a chord never previously heard."[34] Knowing that the chord has always been there, "given in the keyboard," is the best image one could conjure for the composition of poetry. This constant search for the chord of a new poem, then, a chord that never ceases to exist, makes the new, in Adorno's language, "a longing for the new, not the new itself."[35] This is what makes the new worth searching for. There is no alternative for this quest if the goal is to achieve poetic glory. Poets risk losing everything when they borrow from or echo other poets, or when they "patch" metaphors or images that have already been used before. That is why in composing an ode, a poet must be fiercely prepared, committing to memory every possible line of poetry that has been said before and managing, not only to avoid it, but to surpass it in talent and beauty. The fear is always that of derivativeness and banality, of striking a familiar chord and of saying what has been said before, a fear of failing to be original, as Kaʿb ibn Zuhayr warns:

ما أرانا نقول إلاّ معارا   أو معادا من لفظنا مكرورا³⁶

I do not see us say anything but borrowed utterances / Or retold copies of our speech.

It is also a fear of replicating emotions verbatim in the same manner of former poets, as Imruʾ al-Qays concedes:

عوجا على الطلل المحيل لأننا   نبكي الديار كما بكى ابنُ خِذامِ³⁷

Turning towards the year-old ruin because we / / bemoan the homes as did Ibn Khidhām.

In the above example, Imruʾ al-Qays acknowledges the formulaic nature of pre-Islamic poetry, submitting that there is nothing necessarily wrong in crying over deserted ruins like those left by the obscure poet Ibn Khidhām. In fact, the tradition is rife with echoing and borrowing among other forms of "friendly emulation." Yet, if themes and emotions are part and parcel of classical Arabic poetry, it is "how" these emotions are expressed that marks the difference between poets. Such lyrical anxieties and obsession with "newness" in formal expressions prompted many pre-Islamic poets to strive to be the voices of their community. They were the ones who recorded, aesthetically through the art of poetry, the heritages of their respective tribes we have today. They had critical social roles to fill, such as singing the praises of their warriors and chieftains, lampooning their enemies, and supporting their allies. Their poetry spoke of wars and divided tribalisms, and their works explored various subgenres like *hijāʾ* (invective and ridicule), *fakhr* (vaunting or boasting [tribal] pride), *rithāʾ* (elegy), and *ḥamāsa* (zeal, fervor, valor, bravery, fighting spirit, heroism). Their poems thrived on themes of love, longing, and dejection, but also on those of hunting, irreverent masculinities, erotic pauses, self-laudations, tribal vanities, and ancestral pomposity. Like the entire corpus of ancient Arabic literature, the pre-Islamic *qaṣīda* was an offspring of an intrepid way of life, a tribal desert society that settled in with or carried along its own ethos and values wherever it went. Poetry came into life to document and commemorate these values, and by its ceremonial role to allow the pre-Islamic Arabs of those distant epochs to feel love and to confront conflicts and death in a desert geography that was constantly unforgiving.

Challenging indigenous Arab perspectives, Peter Brown has once provocatively called the desert a "myth" and even labeled it as "one of the most abiding creations of late antiquity, a myth of liberating precision."[38] In Brown's view, the desert of late antiquity was "a clear ecological frontier, delimit-[ing] the towering presence of the 'the world' from which the Christians must be set free . . . . a brutally clear boundary, already heavy with immemorial associations."[39] Understandably, Brown is making a reference here to the Desert Fathers and their expressions of sexual renunciation and asceticism in the late Roman (early Christian) world. But the desert of pre-Islamic Arabic and the Qur'ān is the complete opposite. It is neither metropolis nor a town. The desert is the competing and punitive *real* pre-Islamic Arabs had to grapple with. It is the harsh *Ṣaḥrāʾ al-Lubayn*[40] of dried wells that haunts the opening lines of Zuhayr Abī Sulmáʾs elegy, the great flood that devastates Imruʾ al-Qays's world, engulfing everything in its path (*wa Taymāʾa lam yatruk bi-hā jidhʿi nakhlatin*),[41] and the scorching *sarābin biqīʿatin* of the Qurʾān. The desert, as it permeates the space of pre-Islamic poetry and the Qurʾān, is not simply the extra-epistemic space of Brown's late antique times. Beyond being a mere backdrop for divine encounters, like those in the Old Testament with Abraham and Moses or the New Testament's depiction of Jesus being tempted by the devil, it holds a richer, more complex identity. It is neither the "imaginary space" beyond the metropolis nor the nonworldly and uninhabitable vastness that late antiquity imagined it to be. The desert in pre-Islamic Arabic poetry and the Qurʾān is, in every sense, the competing space of the "other." It stands as the space that Western articulations of late antiquity overlooked or covered over. This is a fragment that versions of late Antiquity could not subsume, particularly in Brown's interpretation, which painted the desert as an imaginary place and overlooked its reality as a tangible, inhabited region. Here, real people cultivated profound, human-all-too-human traditions, encompassing not only ideas of transcendence and received divinity but also a tapestry of life experiences and cultural narratives. It's a realm where the human and the divine coalesce, offering a more nuanced and authentic understanding of the desert's role and significance in these ancient texts.

All these characteristics bring to life a landscape and a map that extends from tents and seasonal encampments vulnerable to the caprices of a harsh desert weather, tribal rivalries, and fierce battlefields, with detailed references to the topographies, meteorologies, and social customs of the inhabitants of the Arabian peninsula. Poets portray nomadic ways of life and itinerant travels for sources of water and cultivable lands. The emotional trigger that often characterizes pre-Islamic odes is the nostalgia the poet has for the beloved who moved away with her tribe from her encampment to inhabit a new one in distant lands. Just like the ancient Japanese *haiku*, a deep sense of sadness is often associated with a radical change in seasons in pre-Islamic Arabic poetry. The desert landscape, as well as elements such as rain, thunder, floodings, clouds, the vegetation of the otherwise barren landscape, and even the passage of day and night in the single revolution of the sun all come together to project a mood of dejection and chagrin in the pre-Islamic Arabic قصيدة. The poets describe both domesticated animals such as horses, donkeys, camels, and dogs, and untamed creatures like ostriches, lions, snakes, wolves, hyenas, and birds of prey.

In the same context, we have come to see how pre-Islamic poets engage in deep philosophical questions about the meaning of life. Pre-Islamic Arabia developed a strong resignation to chance, randomness, and acts of fate while harboring a refusal to see a purpose of life, though not necessarily a purpose *in* life. The poetry of Maymūn Ibn Qays al-Aʿshá (570–625) provides perhaps the best verses that depict these musings on chance and life's absurdities when reflecting on his own personal relationship to his beloved, Hurayra:

عُلِّقْتُها عَرَضاً وعُلِّقَت رجلاً   غيري وعُلِّقَ غيرَها الرجلُ

وَعُلِّقَتْهُ فتاةً ما يحاوِلُها   وَمن بني عمِّها ميْتٌ بها وَهلُ

وعُلِّقَتْني أُخَيْرَى ما تُلائمُني   فاجتمعَ الحبُّ حبٌّ كُلُّه تبِلُ

فكلُّنا مغرمٌ يهذي بصاحِبِه   ناءٍ ودانٍ ومخبولٌ ومختبلُ[42]

I fell for her by accident, but she fell for another man / the man fell for another woman.

Another woman fell for the man, but he was not interested / though her cousin was madly in love with her.

A woman fell for me, but she did not suit me / love comes wholesale, love-madness.

Each of us in pain raving about his beloved / distant, close, lovesick, crazed.

Al-Aʿshá 's lines reflect on unrequited love and disintegrated personal relationships, resulting in emotional inference that there could be no meaning to life and that human existence is a painful absurdity. In other words, accident and chance are the basis for human connections, resulting in a corporal community lacking mutual love and emotional balance. We have already seen a glimpse of this in Ṭarafa's ode, whose striking line on the defiance of death offers less of a rhetorical question about "eternity" than an anagnorisis of the futility and randomness of life. This realization is expressed in Ṭarafa's powerful use of the word *manūn* (pl. *manāyā*) in its poignant attributive genitive case of *maniyyatī*, enveloped in a rhetorical question, a question which refuses to say what it is really questioning. The word *maniyyatī* does not exactly translate as "death," but as the random acts of fate that might cause it, the haphazard events or vicissitudes of fortune that bring about a sense of deep anxiety about the uncertainty of it all. Or, as the *mukhaḍram* (a poet whose lifetime straddled the *Jāhiliyya* and the Islamic age) knight/poet Abū Dhuʾayb al-Hudhalī (d. 649) puts it:

فتِلكَ خطوبٌ قد تملَّت شبابَنا   قديماً فتُبلينا المنونُ وما نُبلي

مَنايا يُقَرِّبْن الحُتوف لأهلها   جَهارا، ويستمتعن بالأنَس الجِبِّلِ[43]

These are vicissitudes that have taken our adolescence / Acts of fate that finish us when we can't fight back.

Acts of fate advancing deaths to its people / Openly, and enjoying taking the lives of mortals.

The Qur'ān uses the same root to convey a similar meaning in a negative "death wish" Muḥammad's detractors inflict upon him:

$$\text{أَمْ يَقُولُونَ شَاعِرٌ نَّتَرَبَّصُ بِهِ رَيْبَ ٱلْمَنُونِ}$$

Or they would say: "[He is] a poet; we shall wait and see what fate's uncertainty/ vicissitude does with him." (52:30)

In this Meccan verse, which represents Muḥammad's early call of Islam, the wish (by his detractors) for random acts of death to overtake him before his message prevails is linked to his supposed poethood. The idea, since they are convinced he is a "deluded mortal," is to humiliate him by reducing him to a poet and by waiting out his so-called "prophetic affectations" until death, under whatever circumstances, overtakes him and blasts him into oblivion:

$$\text{إِنْ هَٰذَا إِلَّا قَوْلُ ٱلْبَشَرِ}$$

This is nothing but the saying of mortals. (74:25)

In other words, in the logic of poetic Arabia, poeticity equals secularity and mortality, and if Muḥammad is merely mortal, it must follow that what he is saying would be nothing other than poetry or, at best poetic, and there is nothing divine about it. In all these examples, death is depicted by pre-Islamic Arabs as always a matter of chance: References to *manūn/manāyā* exemplify a preoccupation with death or with a death-anxiety syndrome that brings not just the end of life but a pragmatic philosophy of the world we inhabit. Sixth- and seventh-century Arabia saw death, then, as a matter of fact, a lurking inevitability masked in chance, a game played by those mischievous acts of fate. Ṭarafa knows the game so well that he opted to take the lead and happen upon death instead of waiting for death to happen upon him. Zuhayr ibn Abī Sulmá (520–609) turns *manāyā* into a Russian Roulette *avant la lettre*, a lethal game of chance and a matter of hit and miss:

$$\text{تُمِتْهُ وَمَنْ تُخْطِئْ يُعَمَّرْ فَيَهْرَمِ}^{44} \qquad \text{رَأَيْتُ ٱلْمَنَايَا خَبْطَ عَشْوَاءَ مَن تُصِبْ}$$

I saw the clumsy randomness of the acts of fate, whoever they hit dies / and whoever they miss lives and grows old.

Zuhayr's line relays a form of personification, which, far from being prearranged and methodical, is depicted as an inevitably recurrent event and unmediated by any poetic anesthetization. Death not only comes randomly, irrespective of one's age or status, but it also appears as a performance of luck on a ground of sheer indifference, one that promises no resolution to any of life's unsettling inconsistencies. Zuhyar's metaphor of death is so commanding that it not only showcases the aesthetic superiority of the poetic over the commonplace in this fearful depiction of death as an arbitrary hitman, but it also almost makes it blasphemous to question its authority. The reason for this command is because its claim is a powerful one, precisely because it envisions death as it appears to be: random and indiscriminate in its occurrence. This claim is achieved by a basic logic of observation and deduction that forms the phenomenological ground of the linguistic system that allows for the aesthetic to evolve as a category of the beautiful. Zuhayr's trope brings about a disquieting feeling of the constant proximity of death and of life itself as an exercise in ceaseless peril. However, as is the case with Ṭarafa, Zuhayr's understanding of the perils of death, his imaginative poeticization of its unpredictability, and his use of a figure of speech to personify it, is what allows the listener/reader to cope with this constant threat. The personification of the haphazard and blind blows of death (*khabṭ ʿashwāʾ*), a Beethovenian "fate knocking at the door," so to speak, does not in any way mitigate the empirical moment of undergoing or surviving death. What it does, however, is depict the vulnerability of our collective humanity in the face of death, in the coming into life itself as a material signification of a random *suqūṭ/saqṭ* (loss or fall), as Imruʾ al-Qays puts it exquisitely in the opening line of his ode:

بِسِقطِ اللّوى بينَ الدَّخول فحَوْملِ⁴⁵   قفا نبك من ذِكرى حبيب ومنزل

> Stop, you two, so we could mourn the memory of a beloved and an abode / at the
> tip of the coiled sands between al-Dakhūl and Ḥawmal.

It would be impossible to understand, explicate, interpret, or even translate the Qurʾān without this fundamental context of pre-Islamic poetry. The Qurʾān comes into the world of the seventh-century Arabian Peninsula aware of itself as a metaphysical category of rhetorical power interrogating a phenomenological category of rhetorical intelligence. It is rare to see metaphysics deconstruct phenomenology, but this is the aesthetic pattern that exactly corresponds to the Qurʾān's dialogic critique of pre-Islamic Arabia's poetic philosophy, including that of life and death. It is exemplified in the poetical works that predate the text by a hundred years.⁴⁶ The key to this critique of pre-Islamic reason, which is itself a recurrent motif throughout the Qurʾān,⁴⁷ is the aesthetic mode of delivering "new" and differing news, especially about the predictability and deliberateness of death,⁴⁸ of faith, and of the promise of paradise.⁴⁹ The insistence that there is something worse, or better, that lies beyond corporeal death, and the aesthetic elaboration of this "beyond," radically distinguishes the Qurʾān from poetry and allows it to establish its own authoritative difference. This insistence makes of the Qurʾān, to recall Adorno's piano metaphor, the very utopia of the Arabic language. "What takes itself to be utopian," contends Adorno, "remains the negation of what exists and is obedient to it."⁵⁰ The Qurʾān's continuity of the linguistic pattern we see exemplified in Ṭarafa's ironic question, "*hal anta mukhallidī?*" (can you make me live forever) is indicative of its "obedience" to the rules of classical Arabic already established in pre-Islamic poetry. This continuity also explains the insistence of the Qurʾān, *in the very context of its relationship to the language of poetry in the chapter of the Poets*, that it is revealed *bi-lisānin ʿarabiyyin mubīnin* (in a clear/clarifying Arabic tongue).[51] More importantly, this continuity is indicative of the Qurʾān's awareness of a common audience deeply immersed in understanding the difference between a syntax that allows Ṭarafa to ask his yes-or-no question and a rhetoric that negates the very prospect of expecting an answer to his question. After all, we are dealing with a community and a world, as Walid Saleh reminds us, "in which the reality of death was the only certitude and the only predictable element in human life."[52]

But Saleh's topic is not merely about death and dying; it is resurrection and after-world existence as such. Expectedly, when it comes to notions of death and resurrection in the Qurʾān, there is always the question of the sources. Saleh solves this source problem—which concerns notions of mortality, accountability, and immortality (such as heaven and hell)—by stating that they do not come from one source. Perhaps because he is not working closely with the same historico-philosophical Arabic poetic corpus that preceded the Qurʾān,[53] Saleh chooses to focus on the Qurʾān text[54] and to regard those sources as universally "shattered" (to use a Foucauldian term) in the multiplicity of religio-ideological customs and "collective heritage from late antiquity," while still cautioning that "on its own, this world is coherent and constructed according to the Qurʾān's internal logic."[55] Indeed, Saleh, who predicates his discussion of the Qurʾān's paradise and hell verses on "a summation of late antiquity's world"[56] identifies clear points of departure from traditional societies of late antiquity in the Arabic depiction of mortality as a definition of humanity, which he considers "a gulf that truly separated the pagan Arabs and any society of late antiquity, whether Christian or Jewish."[57] On the level of rhetoric alone, the mockery embedded in Ṭarafa's question about the certainty and predictability of his own death speaks forcefully to Saleh's point. Ṭarafa provides a precise example of using the structure of Arabic grammar to generate a sentence with a double-entendre, one that simultaneously declares and negates its own speech act.[58] This rhetorical mode of questioning only works and *is only identifiable* where there is a familiar and recognizable extratextuality behind the crude linguistic field of classical Arabic. Otherwise, it will be impossible to determine grammatically or rhetorically which of the two meanings is intended in Ṭarafa's lines and, subsequently, in the Qurʾān.

To see how this rhetorical question functions in the Qurʾān, let us consider the following Meccan verses that utilize the same rhetorical mode, but only in deconstructing the dominant pre-Islamic belief in chance and the randomness of death. What we have here is a questioning *of* the rhetorical questioning:

وَقَالُوٓاْ أَءِذَا كُنَّا عِظَٰمًا وَرُفَٰتًا أَءِنَّا لَمَبْعُوثُونَ خَلْقًا جَدِيدًا؟[59]

They said, "If we were to turn into bones and ashes, would we really be resurrected anew?"

وَيَقُولُ ٱلْإِنسَٰنُ أَءِذَا مَا مِتُّ لَسَوْفَ أُخْرَجُ حَيًّا؟ ⁶⁰

A human would ask, "If I were I to die, would I really be raised alive again?"

وَيَقُولُونَ مَتَىٰ هَٰذَا ٱلْوَعْدُ إِن كُنتُمْ صَٰدِقِينَ ⁶¹

They would say, "When would this promise ever come to pass, if you were truthful?"

In these examples we see how the Qurʾān "obeys" to the letter the structure and intentions of its preceding corpus, showing how a well-established syntactic pattern generates a sentence that has at least two meanings. One is not talking here about the realm of metaphor where one meaning is literal and the other figurative, but about a question that is and is not a question at the same time, and, more importantly, about a question that is not suspended or unresolved. In other words, the "disbelievers" in 17:49 are not genuinely asking, questioning, or seeking a confirmation about their resurrection after death. The very sarcasm they display in what al-Jurjānī refers to as *hamza-t-al-taqrīr wa-al-inkār wā-al-tawbīkh* (the interrogative particle for affirmation, negation, and reproach) cancels and mocks the question. The syntactic use of the interrogative particle ء is already indicative of their sarcastic *inkār* mode of disapproval and denial. This is an excellent example of how rhetoric suspends logic in classical Arabic. This rhetorical suspension is not something the Qurʾān invented or imported from late antiquity. When its language concomitantly confirms and denies the power of its own rhetorical mode, the Qurʾān enters into a superior rhetorical dialogue with the very community of its constitutive language:

واعلم أن "الهمزة" فيما ذكرنا تقريرٌ بفعلٍ قد كان، وإنكار له لِمَ كان، وتوبيخ لفاعله عليه. ولها مذهب آخر، وهو أن يكون إنكار الفعل من أصله. ومثاله قوله تعالى (أَفَأَصْفَىٰكُمْ رَبُّكُم بِٱلْبَنِينَ وَٱتَّخَذَ مِنَ ٱلْمَلَٰئِكَةِ إِنَّاً ٕ إِنَّكُمْ لَتَقُولُونَ قَوْلًا عَظِيمًا) وقوله عز وجل (أَصْطَفَى ٱلْبَنَاتِ عَلَى ٱلْبَنِينَ. مَا لَكُمْ كَيْفَ تَحْكُمُونَ). فهذا ردٌّ على المشركين وتكذيب لهم في قولهم ما يؤدى إلى هذا الجهل العظيم. وإذا قُدِّم الاسم في هذا صار الانكار في الفاعل. ومثاله قولك للرجل قد انتحل شعراً: "أأنت قلت هذا الشعر؟ كذبتَ، لست ممن يحسن مثله"، أنكرت أن يكون القائل ولم تنكر الشعر. ⁶²

Know that the hamza in the aforementioned is an affirmation of an action that took place and a denial of it for what it was, and at the same time a reproach for its agent. It has another usage, that is, the denial of the action itself, as in when God, may he be exalted, says, "Has your lord favored you with sons and taken angels as his females? Verily, you are saying something grievous." or when he, in all his magnificence and glory, says, "Has he favored daughters over sons? What is wrong with you and with how you judge?" This is a response to the associators and a denial of what they say, which reflects great ignorance. If the noun/agent precedes the verb in this mode, then the denial is of agency. An example of this is when you say to a man who falsely attributes poetry to himself, "Did you really compose this poetry? You are a liar. This poetry is too good to be composed by you," thus denying his agency as the author of said poetry but not the poetry itself.

In this context, al-Jurjānī positions *both* pre-Islamic poetry and the Qur'ān in a rhetorical and grammatical continuum, with a deep conviction that the language of ancient Arabic constitutes the text of the Qur'ān in the first place. He is aware that the language of the Qur'ān may differ discursively, and in degree, from pre-Islamic poetry, but it is not a difference in kind:

وذاك أنا إذا كنا نعلم أن الجهة التي منها قامت الحجة بالقرآن وظهرت، وبانت وبهرت، هي أن كان على حدٍ من الفصاحة تقصر عنه قوى البشر، ومنتهيا إلى غاية لا يُطمَح إليها بالفكر، وكان محالا أن يعرف كونه كذلك، إلاَّ من عَرَفَ الشعر الذي هو ديوان العرب وعنوان الأدب. . . . وقد استشهد العلماء لغريب القرآن وإعرابه بأبيات فيها الفحش، وفيها ذكر الفعل القبيح، ثم لم يعبهم ذلك. ⁶³

> This is because the position from which the Qur'ān distinguishes and demonstrates its mesmerizing authority comes from a degree of eloquence inimitable by humans and arriving at a telos unthinkable to their minds. It is impossible for anyone to understand the Qur'ān's power unless this person is versed in poetry, the *Dīwān* of the Arabs and the discourse of their literary heritage.

A linguistic utopia, to echo Adorno, is predicated on a dialectic of adherence (or obedience) and negation. The Qur'ān's adherence to the grammar and rhetoric of Arabic for the sake of communicability and clarity of its message, which I address in fuller details in a following chapter, dialectically forces "the negation of what exists," a negation that combines a shock of "newness" and a challenge for imitability, simultaneously. Not only does the Qur'ān establish itself as something new and different from poetry, but, in what is known as *Āyāt al-Taḥaddī* (Verses of Challenge), it emphatically declares itself as forever irreproducible by anyone, poets or nonpoets alike. The confrontational tone in the following verses positions the Qur'ān as an aesthetic manifestation that is simultaneously internal to the linguistic tradition of Arabic and external to the *modus operandi* that produces poetry:

وَإِن كُنتُمْ فِي رَيْبٍ مِّمَّا نَزَّلْنَا عَلَىٰ عَبْدِنَا فَأْتُوا بِسُورَةٍ مِّن مِّثْلِهِ وَادْعُوا شُهَدَاءَكُم مِّن دُونِ اللَّهِ إِن كُنتُمْ صَادِقِينَ⁶⁴

أَمْ يَقُولُونَ افْتَرَاهُ قُلْ فَأْتُوا بِعَشْرِ سُوَرٍ مِّثْلِهِ مُفْتَرَيَاتٍ وَادْعُوا مَنِ اسْتَطَعْتُم مِّن دُونِ اللَّهِ إِن كُنتُمْ صَادِقِينَ⁶⁵

قُل لَّئِنِ اجْتَمَعَتِ الْإِنسُ وَالْجِنُّ عَلَىٰ أَن يَأْتُوا بِمِثْلِ هَٰذَا الْقُرْآنِ لَا يَأْتُونَ بِمِثْلِهِ وَلَوْ كَانَ بَعْضُهُمْ لِبَعْضٍ ظَهِيرًا⁶⁶

> And if you are in doubt of what we have descended unto our servant, then bring
>> forth a sūra like it and call your ungodly witnesses if you were telling the truth.
> Or would they say: "he made it up." Say: "bring forth ten made-up sūras like it, and
>> call out to whom you can other than God if you were telling the truth."
> Say, "if humans and jinn were to collaborate in producing something like this Qur'ān,
>> they would not produce anything like it, even if they backed one another."

Because the Qur'ān cannot rely on any ethos or objective realities expressed in these poems, it has to produce its own system of knowledge, its own supremacy, so to speak. Saleh understands this tension very well. "The Qur'ān speaks to humanity triumphantly," he says, doing so in a tone "based on the presumption that it knows human beings better than they know themselves."[67] This knowability, however, is only achievable through the pretext of pre-Islamic poetry, as al-Jurjānī notes, since the Qur'ān's aesthetic eloquence would be impossible to asses, comprehend, or appreciate "except by those who know poetry, the very *dīwān* of the Arabs and the signature of their literature."[68] These accounts alone would make the valorization of historical categories occur at the expense of aesthetic rigor, or any claim for reducing the Arabicity of the Qur'ān as a self-enclosed totality of epistemic "intertexts," an exercise in dogmatism. Once again, (Arab) aesthetics are not a self-enclosed totality awaiting the defensive Western literary critic, a la Nicholson, to denigrate it in comparison to his own tradition. The nexus between social and linguistic habits of the Arab community, their art, and their oral aesthetics is built into the structure of pre-Islamic poetry and the Qur'ān, not in the dogmatic sense that aesthetics are concerned with matching poetic meters with tribal politics as their main focus, but in the much deeper sense that, here again, the discursive passage from a rhetoric of intelligence (pre-Islamic poetry) to a rhetoric of power (the Qur'ān) must include communal aesthetics as the one and only *prerequisite* for such a passage to take place and be understood in the first place. How Qur'ānic oral aesthetics are articulated is not a simple matter to research, but this is nonetheless a topic that continues to be dismissed in Euro-American scholarship.[69] A truly meaningful reflection on the Qur'ān can therefore only be achieved through the practice of aesthetic thought, accessible exclusively by engaging with the literary figurations and tropes of its formative language. This is because tropes do not just adorn language; they unlock its deepest layers, revealing the profound truths and wisdom embedded within.

5

Adab and the Ethical Authority
of the Qurʾān

"The dialogue of thinking with poetry is long. It has barely begun."[1] This commanding statement by Martin Heidegger invites us to reevaluate the connection between pre-Islamic poetry and the Qurʾān. This connection remains under scrutiny, often through rigid, antiquated norms that have long questioned poetry's historical validity as a source. Returning again to the nature of the comparative itself, and judging from recent scholarly tendencies, we see that there appears to be a compulsive avoidance of "thinking with poetry" in Euro-American scholarship on the Qurʾān.[2] This is not to say that a comparative approach to the Qurʾān bypassing pre-Islamic poetry and focusing on the Bible, or on the broader epistemic space of late antiquity, is untenable. On the contrary, these sources remain a meaningful part of Islamic religious heritage, and such studies undoubtedly have the appeal of connecting epistemological dots, especially by putting scriptures in a larger context and casting a different light on their subject matter. Additionally, as the latest variation on the theme of Abrahamic monotheism, the Qurʾān in many cases, as I exemplify in this chapter, self-evidently invites comparison with the Torah and gospels, and at times even compels these comparisons to take place as a way of understanding and interpreting the scripture. Yet, Heidegger's statement is highly relevant in its application to the current state of affairs in Qurʾānic studies. Pre-Islamic poetry is conditional for understanding the Qurʾān, not only as a syntactic and semantic prerequisite for making sense of the scripture, as al-Jurjānī, for instance, would see it, but also as a literary corpus that invites us to step beyond the conventional framing of this relationship as "antithetical" or of the Qurʾān as a scripture that derives its ethical paradigm from elsewhere and is only interested in eclipsing rather than entering into genuine dialogue with its local context.

This chapter is devoted to reading verses from pre-Islamic poetry and the Qur'ān, noting the dialogue and the numerous ethical negotiations that can be seen clearly thereby. But before I address these communal/ethical dialogues available in pre-Islamic sources, it is important to recall that a fundamental historical/ethical issue in understanding the Qur'ān has lain in the mess of problematizing Islamo-Arabic sources. Many have thus offered either an Islamicist faith-based apologia or an obverse periodization of a sort (a continuity under the rubric of "late antiquity") whose authenticity and reliability are hardly questioned. In this case, the issue of weighing and deciding sources raises two crucial questions. Is the Qur'ān's ethical authority—namely, the human burden of moral responsibility, its critique of social inequalities, its codification of sexuality, its sympathy for the poor and the deprived, its emphasis on sustainable communal justice, and the accompanying complex baggage of accountability, sin, guilt, and conscience that come with all religious discourses—drastically different from its pre-Islamic environment? Or are such ethics indeed an imported and adapted *byproduct* of moral practices and codes in ancient Rome, the biblical tradition, or the classical late antique world more than they are a reflection of the Qur'ān's sociolinguistic structure? The second question has to do with the constitution of ethical authority as such: Where does it come from? How does one learn to trace it objectively to its so-called origins? What verification tools does one need to successfully locate or point from afar to the origins of such ethics?

Answering these questions will offer a valuable lesson for interrogating the theoretical applicability of late antiquity as an "inventory" for ethics in the Qur'ān and for "understanding" Islam in the West today. If "history is what hurts," as Fredric Jameson famously reminds us, then the denial of genuine historical thinking would always be at risk of carrying its own germs of self-critique. Peter Brown himself, in fact, offers a valuable insight into this dilemma. In an essay on the parallels and contrasts between late antiquity and Islam, which he wrote in the aftermath of *The World of Late Antiquity*, Brown acknowledges "quite frankly" that "as a non-Islamicist but a layman, I am concerned not simply to garner a rich crop of acceptable interdisciplinary insights and erudition."[3] To be sure, Brown still holds tightly to the conviction that "Graeco-Roman civilization . . . was a culture that aimed at realizing a single human ideal from which all valid human achievements were held to radiate."[4] Yet, his reconsideration that "the deeper we enter into the common ground between late antique *paideia* and Islamic *adab*, the more *sympathy* we gain for the refusal of men in great classical civilizations to put their faith in any safeguard other than the patient and intimate grooming of the behavior of their elites, and for the faith that such grooming can happen, can be seen to happen, and can be repeated in every generation."[5] Key to Brown's argument is the word "sympathy," which not only suggests the specificity of his approach to the difference between late antiquity and Islam (with a crooked detour through early medieval Christian celibacy); it also explains how self-critique of seemingly unavoidable historical categorizations, if there were to be any, would still fall back in the face of the other:

> Yet, no sooner have we entered with sympathy into this common concern than the difference between Islam and the Graeco-Roman world springs to the eye. Though often brought to bear on men of deep religious belief, Hellenistic and late-antique *paideia* contained no religious code and imposed no religious sanction whatsoever. The sanctions imposed were those brought to bear by purely human significant others in the society. Ultimately, a man was brought to heel by the sense of shame, by reminders of the antithesis of *aischron* and *kalon*, and by the revulsion felt by the refined soul for those unrefined elements of raw human nature that betrayed themselves in breaches of decorum, *aschemosyne*. "My lord, you forget yourself"— *aschemoneis hegemon*—is the ultimate put-down placed in the mouth of a Christian martyr confronting an ill-tempered Roman governor. Late antique *paideia* only brings us half the way to the Islamic product of *adab,* as *adab* is defined by Georges Anawati: "*un vrai code de savoir-vivre ou se melent Jes exigences d'un homme 'bien eleve' mais en meme temps soucieux de bien se comporter 'en presence de Dieu.'*"[6]

While Brown does not go so far as to admit that *any* type of unwritten laws of moral conduct and ethics could be transferrable anywhere in the globe from one generation to the next through inherited ancestral and tribal customs, his "after-thought" statement confirms what we already know about Greek *paideia:* that it is in essence a process of *anamnesis,* where humans are educated into their genuine humanity, at least according to Werner Jaeger, through *mos maiorum*—that is, through the rich wisdom of ancestorial heritage aimed to develop a person into maturity.[7] Not only does *mos maiorum* have a "religious" component to it, but it can on occasion generate resemblances among other cultures. If, according to Brown, late antique *paideia* provides only "half the way" to the Islamic product of *adab,* one wonders not merely about the second half of that way, but about how that "first half" came to be and how *paideia* traveled in Brown's fluid world of late antiquity and found its way to pre-Islamic and then Qur'ānic Arabia. Could an argument be made that because *xenia*—the great concept of Greek hospitality and the guest-host relationship—was first celebrated in Homer's *Odyssey,* must all ethics of human hospitality trickle down from "the rugged land of Ithaca, too cramped for driving horses" to the desert sands of the Arabian peninsula, where ancient Arabs cleverly adapted it into their own *al-karam wa-wājib al-ḍiyāfa* (generosity and moral duty towards guests)? Or would we go even further back and wonder who taught Homer the art of *xenia* in the first place? Abraham?[8] Or is *xenia* itself an innate human virtue that emanates spontaneously in the world under different names? It would seem implicit in Brown's description that what previously passed under the so-called influence or "continuity" of late antiquity is at least a phantasm to the degree that it has no historical evidence to support its precedence over other cultures, especially oral and preliterate communities in general.

A strong ethic of *ḍiyāfa* (hospitality) did indeed permeate pre-Islamic Arabia. Before the Qur'ān, pre-Islamic poets such as 'Amr ibn Kulthūm, Imru' al-Qays, Ṭarafa, Zuhayr, Mālik ibn Ḥarīm al-Hamdānī, and Umayya ibn Abī al-Ṣalt, to refer but to a few examples, composed poetry that thematized clear ethical imperatives in reference to the guest-host relationship, among other virtues such as *al-murū'a, al-shajā'a, al-karam, al-amāna, al-ṣidq, al-wafā'*, and *al-'iffa* (virtue, bravery, generosity, trust, truthfulness, loyalty, and chastity). These poets were the mouthpieces of their clans, boasting tribal virtues in addition to other exploits like honor, pride, love, female beauty, mettle in battles, heroism, camel nomadism, and praise of family and friends as well as mockery of foes and adversaries. Poetic contests were so fierce that even a cursory reading of any of the *Mu'allaqāt* would bring the tension of these ethical rivalries back to life. Many of these ethical tenets survived in the Qur'ān as many were filtered out. Why would Brown then choose to bypass this rich pre-Qur'ānic tradition and offer a reading of the Qur'ān, or Islam for that reason, that is so selective and so ahistorical?

In his defense, Brown derives his argument on *adab* from Georges Anawati's post-Qur'ānic definition, which confines it to a mixed duality of *bien eleve* (good upbringing) and *bien comporter en presence de Dieu* (behaving well in the presence of God) and only to an understanding of *adab* as theogony. Anawati's definition is well taken, but it only addresses a fraction one of the many complex variegations of *adab*, thus truncating the term from its fountain sources as well as its sociolinguistic and ethical associations in polytheistic pre-Islamic Arabia. Pre-Islamic Arabic happens to be the fountainhead of *adab* in the Arabo-Islamic tradition; its absence from Brown's argument makes it impossible to understand his point. In the field of Arabic studies, what we call *adab* is located in a constellation of historical shifts from the era of the pre-Islamic *qaṣīda* until now. The emergence and codification of Arabic *belles lettres* has also resulted in the formation of aesthetic and philological principles across time that eventually separated *adab* and distinguished it from nonliterary forms of human expressions.[9]

Still, Brown's acknowledgment offers us an entry into what has been historically othered and repressed in the study of the Qur'ān in the West. This is an area which shows palpable gaps in broad categorical thinking in surrendering to an *'aṣabiyya* that oftentimes obliges certain historians to "patch" human time and events, to use 'Antara's powerful expression, as they dismiss records of genuine historical thinking as "immaterial" or "unavailable" to them, when in reality such records lie gravely in wait for scholars to dis-inter them. My attempt to de-other native sources, however, is not simply a protestation against the intensely ideological dismissiveness inherent in the study of the Qur'ān, which continues to examine it with Eurocentric eyes.[10] It is rather an invitation to commiserate with a neglected tradition whose dialogue with the Qur'ān is bound to broaden our understanding of early Islam. It is also noteworthy that while the divide between Islam and Hellenism was reconciled in the early centuries of Islam when measured Muslim scholars translated Greek manuscripts into Arabic, the Qur'ān kept a marked ethical distance from Hellenistic thought, one which manifested itself in "a moral turn," as Gustave von Grunebaum puts it "to the concepts of paradise and hell, of reward and punishment, law and freedom."[11]

When Arnold Toynbee arrived at a parallel conclusion that "between the Koran and Hellenism no fusion was possible,"[12] he did not draw his conclusion too sharply but based his findings on what he perceives to be a clear moral and thetic disconnect between the culture of the Qur'ān and Greek-Hellenistic thought.[13] Similarly, Carl Heinrich Becker states that the Qur'ān projects an anti-pagan sentiment unique enough to make it *unhellenistisch* in a predominantly Hellenized era.[14] Even Theodor Nöldeke dismisses the allegation that the Qur'ān could be a product of late antiquity or Hellenism owing to what he considers to be an absence of intellection and abstract thought in its scripture.[15]

Nöldeke's dismissal of the Qur'ān as a product of late antiquity reminds us that in the realm of humanism, the rise of monotheism itself signified a profound shift, dissolving the vast and cosmic internationalism of Hellenistic polytheism. This earlier spiritual landscape allowed for a range of divine beliefs, where choosing to believe in one, many, or none of the gods was less contentious. Monotheism broke through this celestial plurality, redefining the divine and the sacred, leaving an indelible mark on the fabric of spiritual history. Embracing humanism thus compels us to reflect on monotheism's emergence from Akhenaton's devotion to the Sun as the one and only God, marking a pivotal departure from the rich tapestry of polytheism. This transformation itself invites a deeper, nuanced interpretation of the Qur'ān, positioning it within a broader, literary and cultural context. It evokes memories of an era when divine multiplicity was the norm, a time prior to the Abrahamic monotheistic paradigm that pressured scholarship into debates over authenticity and derivation. The Qur'ān, while firmly monotheistic and critical of polytheism, encapsulates a linguistic and aesthetic legacy that transcends its religious orthodoxy. It demands an intellectual appreciation that honors its unique place in the annals of literary heritage, free from the binary of original versus derivative, and without the overtones of secular nostalgia.

Yet Brown's earlier work has managed to trigger a growing influence on the practice of Hellenizing the Qur'ān's context in recent Euro-American scholarship, one which often follows a methodical approach of "inclusion." This "inclusion" is at best dialectical. One the one hand, it embraces an ethos of "incorporating" Islam under banners of late antiquity[16] and Hellenism.[17] Garth Fowden, for instance, argues that Islam is a religion "rooted in Antiquity, even consuming it."[18] On the other hand, this very approach betrays a colossal deficit in Arabicity and fails to capture the Qur'ān's strong ethical negotiations with the established customs of pre-Islamic Arabia. Such a hurried approach to the Qur'ān cannot but arouse an anxiety of otherness. More than the teachings of Plato and Aristotle, more than the wines of immortal Greek gods, and more than the veiled women in the *Didascalia*, it is pre-Islamic poetry (as well as the ethics and aesthetics of its constitutive communities) that is the great absent from these debates. Brown's argument that Hellenistic and late-antique *paideia* was practically irreligious and imposed no theological sanctions is not only informative but crucial for understanding the ethical context of early medieval Christianity, its promotion of clerical celibacy, and to the Qur'ān's commentary on the topic, a point which I address in detail toward the end of this chapter.

For now, suffice it to say that Brown's categorical fixation on connecting the dots between Islam and late antiquity, which has already left absent an entire corpus of literature behind it, is itself a symptom of this imaginative Eurocentric *'aṣabiyya*. This fixation not only leaves gaps in its totalizing vision, but also suffers from theological contradictions and the absence of a fair assessment of a history of the other. It is not without notice to observe the deep affinities between Hellenism, the Bible, and the Qur'ān. Yet, only a thorough and in-depth reading of this corpus of ancient Arabic literature will allow us to begin to grasp the distinctiveness of the Qur'ān's ethical intervention as a different socio-linguistic order than the one already familiar to us in pre-Islamic Arabia. For this reason, it is important to excavate some of the perineal ethics of pre-Islamic Arabia and assess their relevance to the early years of the Qur'ān. Even in Islamicist scholarship, pre-Islamic poetry is often associated with but rarely thanked for the founding of the Qur'ān's ethico-linguistic landscape as well as its exegetical tradition. Al-Jāḥiẓ reminds us that the genre of ancient Arabic poetry started about 150–200 years before the Qur'ān, thus establishing the proper Arabic register that appears in the Qur'ān. Ibn Qutayba too confirms that ancient Arabic poets are the authority when it comes to understanding the Qur'ān and all things Arabic:

يقع الاحتجاج بأشعارهم في الغريب وفي النحو وفي كتاب الله عز وجل وحديث رسول الله

> They [pre-Islamic Arab poets] are the authority for understanding unfamiliar vocabulary, grammar, the Qur'ān and hadith.[19]

Pre-Islamic Arab tribes celebrated poetry as their *dīwān*—that is, the record of their lives, cultural practices, genealogies, and histories. Ibn Sallām al-Jumaḥī (d. 845/6) states that pre-Islamic poetry has *ṣinā'a wa thaqāfa* (a craft and a skill).[20] The sixth-century Arabic literature into which Muḥammad was born consisted thus of remarkable poetical (as well as prosaic) pieces that comprised all the records of the Arabs, which included, to use the language of Ibn Qutayba, "useful events, correct genealogies, fine wisdom on par with philosophers, and knowledge in fields of equinology, astronomy, among others."[21] In addition, Muḥammad s knowledge of pre-Islamic poetry is well documented in Arabic sources.[22]

On balance, the problem with the origin of the word *adab* is that there is no conclusive evidence of its ethical meaning and usage either in pre-Islamic Arabic or in the Qur'ān. It is understandable from the example I cite shortly, according to which the Egyptian critic Shawqī Ḍayf relates *adab* to *ma'duba* (pl. *ma'ādib*)—namely, "a banquet, a communal meal." But this would not be the only time that words of seemingly identical roots come to be speculatively connected. Another plausible theory is that *adab* is formed from a plural *ādāb*, interpreted as *a'dāb* but originally *ad'āb*, the plural form of *da'b*, "custom, manner, habit," in what linguists would traditionally refer to as "a back formation."

Yet this understanding too cannot be proved with concrete evidence. In its very general ethical sense, however, *adab* is akin to, or at least a part of, *murū'a*, a defining pre-Islamic feature of virtue, which M. M. Bravmann carefully traces in the study of the *Jāhilī* background of the Qur'ān, defining the latter as a practice of "ethical duties of several kinds."[23] Furthermore, Bravmann shifts attention to considerations of the important role *murū'a* played "even in Islamic days,"[24] thus acknowledging Ignác Goldziher's influential study of the word and the concept, while debunking his long-standing theory on the categorical contrast between "*Muruwwah* und [and] Din."[25] Thus, when Ḍayf cites examples from pre-Islamic poetry to situate the root of *adab* in the heart of sixth-century Arabia's ethos of *murū'a*, he does so with the understanding that *adab* emerges from a communal invite for sharing food, a remarkable act of *xenia* at the heart of pre-Islamic customs. Food ethics thus manifested itself in bountiful acts of hospitality, originating from offering food, where *al-ādib*—namely, *al-dā'ī ilá al-ṭa'ām* (the food-offering host)[26]—offers a meal to everyone and presents a holistic communal invitation that is unconditional and indiscriminatory, one that is performed at all times, and especially in the harshness of winter, where food is scarce and most needed in the deserts of Arabia. The following lines from Ṭarafa record this earliest association of *adab* with the ethics of hospitality and the guest-host relationship:

لَا تَرَى الآدِبَ فِينَا يَنْتَقِرْ   نَحْنُ فِي المَشْتَاةِ نَدْعُو الجَفَلَى

We, in the winter, invite all / you don't see the *ādib* (host) among us discriminating.

There is in Ṭarafa's line a deep sense of ethical fulfillment in performing communal acts of hospitality, which manifests itself in offering banquets to the stranger, the orphan, and the homeless. Ṭarafa's ethical reference finds its match in the following line from al-Hudhalī:

سَفَكْنا دِماءَ البُدْنِ في تُرْبةِ الحالِ[27]   وكُنّا إذا ما الضيفُ حَلَّ بأرضِنا

When a guest visits our land / we spill the blood of cattle in the muddy sand.

The confirmation and celebration of hospitality ethics confirms that the obligation to offer hospitality to strangers in the Arabian Peninsula before Islam is both tribal and communal, a collective ethic embodied in the insistent spirit of the plural Arabic pronouns that permeate those lines: *naḥnu, nad'ū, fīnā, kunnā, bi 'rḍinā, safaknā* (we; we invite; it is our custom; our land; we spill). Note the conditional case in al-Hudhalī's verse. The particle *idhā* in the verse's first hemistich initiates a conditional clause that is met with the direct and unmediated *safaknā* verb phrase in the main clause of the second hemistich. This structure carries a rhetoric of alacrity and immediacy. The language also makes this instance of hospitality conditional, but conditional only on the appearance of a stranger. In other words, hospitality in pre-Islamic Arabia is not only seasonal, per Ṭarafa's verse, but ongoing. There is no excuse for denying hospitality to anyone; even the untimely arrival of a stranger in town is reason enough to trigger immediate hospitality. In this respect, al-Hudhalī's line is as Abrahamic as it could possibly be. The Qur'ān celebrates

Abraham's hospitality toward his guests with a similar linguistic code of immediacy. In the following verse, the Qur'ānic verb phrase "fa-mā labitha" creates a similar effect of speed and wholeheartedness we see in al-Hudhalī's line:

لَقَدْ جَاءَتْ رُسُلُنَا إِبْرَاهِيمَ بِالْبُشْرَىٰ قَالُوا سَلَامًا قَالَ سَلَامٌ فَمَا لَبِثَ أَن جَاءَ بِعِجْلٍ حَنِيذٍ

When our messengers arrived at Abraham's with the good tidings, they said "peace";
he said "peace," and rushed to bring in a stone-roasted calf. (11:69)

The ethical demeanor of unhesitant swiftness to attend to strangers/guests—without knowing who they are—sinks deep into the tribal and communal values of pre-Islamic Arabia, a feature that makes the reception of Qur'ānic ethics of hospitality seamless and relatable to its receiving community. There is an intimate correlation between these sentiments and the Qur'ān's clarion call for being hospitable to the stranger and the homeless.[28] So, in addition to its early manifestations in Greek mythology, hospitality can in fact be traced back to Abraham's enthusiastic welcome of his visitors in the Old Testament (Genesis 18:1–15) and its corresponding version in the Qur'ān (11:69–70; 15:51–52; 51: 24–27), making the responsibility toward the stranger as quintessentially "Godly" as it is quintessentially human. With the exception of the Amalekites, where the narrative is more contentious, kindness toward strangers is a core value in the Bible's teachings: : "But the stranger that dwelleth with you shall be unto you as one born among you, and thou shalt love him as thyself; for ye were strangers in the land of Egypt."[29]

Hospitality is also a key component of the ethical rhetoric and practice of pre-Islamic Arabia, as a practical application of *adab*, and it seems to conform to features in the Qur'ān. What the Qur'ān does differently, however, is co-opt this preexisting *paideia* into the larger framework of its own eschatological narrative. As a practice, then, hospitality may come down to an offer of food to strangers and impoverished fellows who come to find themselves within one's vicinity, but it is crucial to see it in its Qur'ānic framework as a commendable ethical practice *outside* one's home domain. In other words, the Qur'ān lends hospitality an intratribal and even national mobility, evoked with respect to empathy toward the other, not just as a local tribal act of giving food to those who come to "our" land, but of giving it outside the comfortable and the familiar, and even in circumstances when one could not afford to give it, in fact when one would rather not give:

وَيُطْعِمُونَ ٱلطَّعَامَ عَلَىٰ حُبِّهِ مِسْكِينًا وَيَتِيمًا وَأَسِيرًا. إِنَّمَا نُطْعِمُكُمْ لِوَجْهِ ٱللَّهِ لَا نُرِيدُ مِنكُمْ جَزَاءً وَلَا شُكُورًا. إِنَّا نَخَافُ مِن رَّبِّنَا يَوْمًا عَبُوسًا قَمْطَرِيرًا

They give food *despite their love for it* [my emphasis] to the homeless, the orphan, and the incarcerated. [They say,] "We feed you for the face of God; we do not expect from you return or thanks. We fear from our God a stressful, face-frowning day."

From a historical viewpoint, we might note that feeding one's enemy is an ethical trait that derives from the Bible: "But if your enemy is hungry, feed him, and if he is thirsty, give him a drink."[30] Further, there is much to say about the ethics of feeding the incarcerated. The Qur'ān confirms this biblical ethics not just by making it conditional upon request, but by giving food, without solicitation, to the enemy of God, food that one would rather keep for oneself. According to al-Bayḍāwī, this Qur'ānic verse makes specific reference to prisoners of war, the *usarā' al-kuffār* (captive nonbelievers) who are categorically opposed to monotheistic faith and the idea of God.[31] In today's context, we might think about this ethical call in terms of attending to fellow humans living under siege or kept in the cages of the carceral state—how this attention plays a role in educating the food-giver in the overarching logic of the state, its criminalization of the poor and the disempowered, its reliance on race as a conceptual tool to divide humans, and its refusal of any redistributive policy that would work overall against the hunger of those experiencing homelessness, those lacking kin support, and those locked up.

To return to Brown's point, at the heart of Qur'ānic *adab* there lies a call for disciplining human desire and a high moral order of self-denial. Yet, this *adab* of self-discipline is not completely alien to ancient Arabia, even though an exaggerated sense of personal and tribal glory often predominates pre-Islamic poetry. However, ancient poems of glory and pride must always be read in their historical contexts. While such poems include themes of personal glory, exaggerated pride, tribal honor, panegyrics, and vindictive, they still carry strong overtones of communal *adab*. Take, for instance, 'Amr ibn Kulthūm's long ode, which is often associated with the series of protracted battles known as Ḥarb al-Basūs [(the Basūs War). The war between two tribes in ancient Arabia, which is referenced in the context of this conflict, is one of the most famous pre-Islamic Arabian wars that was purportedly sparked by the killing of a camel belonging to a member of the Bakr tribe by a member of the Taghlib tribe. The Basūs War is said to have lasted for around forty years, starting in the late fifth century and continuing into the early sixth century. 'Amr ibn Kulthūm's ode is said to have contributed to bringing peace between his tribe, Taghlib, and the neighboring tribe of Bakr. In particular, the following lines of the ode composed likely in the early part of the sixth century, describe the gallant deeds of his tribe and portray a genealogy of the glory, nobility, and compassion toward refugees that run through his ancestors:

بِنَقْصٍ فِي خُطُوْبِ الأَوَّلِيْنَا   فَهَلْ حُدِّثْتَ فِي جُشَمٍ بِنْ بَكْرِ

أَبَاحَ لَنَا حُصُوْنَ المَجْدِ دِيْنَا   ورِثْنَا مَجْدَ عَلْقَمَةَ بِنْ سَيْفٍ

زُهَيْراً نِعْمَ ذُخْرُ الذَّاخِرِيْنَا   وَرِثْتُ مُهَلْهِلاً وَالخَيْرَ مِنْهُ

بِهِمْ نِلْنَا تُرَاثَ الأَكْرَمِيْنَا   وَعَتَّاباً وَكُلْثُوْماً جَمِيْعَاً

بِهِ نُحْمَى وَنَحْمِي المُلْتَجِينَا   وَذَا البُرَةِ الذِي حُدِّثْتَ عَنْهُ

فَأيُّ المَجْدِ إلاَّ قَدْ وَلِيْنَا[32]   وَمِنَّا قَبْلَهُ السَّاعِي كُلَيْبًا

Have you been told of any lack in Jusham ibn Bakr / When it comes to great affairs
 with early tribes?

We inherited the glory of ʿAlqama ibn Sayf / Who made lawful to us all forts of
   glory.
I inherited from Muhalhil the goodness of Zuhayr, the best of all the renowned.
And ʿAttāb and Kulthūm as a whole / To them we owe the heritage of the noblest ones.
And Dhū al-Bura of whom you know / Who protects us and make us care for others
   in need.
And from us before him comes Kulayb / What glory have we not attained?

While the ethical code of ʿAmr ibn Kulthūm's ode gives the impression that tribal
pride and glory are the trademarks of his people, a closer look reveals that his celebration of the *adab* of his tribe—namely, the generosity, kindness, and protection
of strangers inherited from his ancestors—is in fact the motor of his pride. Praising high moral standards is a key element of pre-Islamic poetry. Zuhayr's ode, to
give another example, is also dedicated to a celebration of kindness and virtue as
much as it is a criticism of vicious behavior such as cursing, avarice, and the misdirection of charitable deeds:

وَمَنْ يَجْعَلِ المَعْرُوفَ مِنْ دُونِ عِرْضِهِ   يَفِرْهُ، وَمَنْ لَا يَتَّقِ الشَّتْمَ يُشْتَمِ

وَمَنْ يَكُ ذَا فَضْلٍ فَيَبْخَلْ بِفَضْلِهِ   عَلَى قَوْمِهِ يُسْتَغْنَ عَنْهُ وَيُذْمَمِ

وَمَنْ يُوفِ لَا يُذْمَمْ وَمَنْ يُهْدَ قَلْبُهُ   إِلَى مُطْمَئِنِّ البِرِّ لَا يَتَجَمْجَمِ

وَمَنْ يَجْعَلِ المَعْرُوفَ فِي غَيْرِ أَهْلِهِ   يَكُنْ حَمْدُهُ ذَمًّا عَلَيْهِ وَيَنْدَمِ

وَمَهْمَا تَكُنْ عِنْدَ امْرِئٍ مِنْ خَلِيقَةٍ   وَإِنْ خَالَهَا تَخْفَى عَلَى النَّاسِ تُعْلَمِ[33]

He who gives charity to protect honor / will increase his honor, and he who curses
   shall be cursed.
He who is generous but dispossesses his people of his generosity / shall be dismissed
   and reproached.
He who fulfills his promise cannot be reproached / and he whose heart is guided/
   toward benevolence cannot falter.
He who shows charity to those who do not deserve it / his praise shall turn into
   censure and he shall be regretful.
And whatever demeanor a person has / but thinks no one will notice, it shall be
   revealed.

The above lines from Zuhayr indicate that pre-Islamic Arabic poetry represents the
classical corpus of *adab* par excellence. It could be argued that *adab* is the major
articulation of this genre, and that the key forms of communal relationships are
the ones that are weaved around it. In addition, the social and moral code of *adab*
is the chief means of distinguishing between men and tribes in ethical terms. As
it is obvious from the following lines by al-Muthaqqib al-ʿAbdī (553–87), men
who have virtue, who keep their word, who are courteous to their neighbors, who

do not backbite, and who are not hypocrites, are praiseworthy because they follow a high moral code of *adab*, regardless of their social status:

أن تُتِمَّ الوَعْدَ في شَيءٍ نَعَمْ   لا تَقُولَنَّ إذَا ما لم تُرِدْ

وقَبيحٌ قَوْلُ لاَ بَعدَ نَعَمْ   حَسَنٌ قَوْلُ نَعَمْ مِنْ بَعْدِ لاَ

فَبِلا فابْدَأ إذَا خِفْتَ النَّدَمْ   إنَّ لاَ بَعْدَ نَعَمْ فاحِشَةٌ

بِنَجاحِ القَوْلِ، إنَّ الْخُلْفَ ذَمُّ   فإذا قُلْتَ نَعَمْ فاصبِرْ لَها

ومَتَى لاَ يَتَّقِ الذَّمَّ يُذَمْ   واعْلَمَ انَّ الذَّمَّ نَقْصٌ للفَتَى

إنَّ عِرْفانَ الفَتَى اْلحقَّ كَرَمْ   أُكْرِم الجارَ وأرْعَى حَقَّهُ

في لُحُوم النَّاسِ كالسَّبْعِ الضَّرِمْ   لا تَرَاني رَاتِعاً في مَجْلِسٍ

حينَ يَلْقانِي وإنْ غِبْتُ شَتَمْ³⁴   إنَّ شَرَّ النَّاسِ مَن يَكُثِرُ لِي

Do not say, if you do not wish/ to fulfill a promise, "yes."
It is good to say "yes" after saying "no" / But "no" after "yes" is bad.
"No" after "yes" is scandalous / begin with "no" if you fear regret.
If you say "yes," then commit yourself to it / carry it to a successful end, for breaking it will get you vilified.
Know that vilification belittles a man / and he who does not keep his guard will be vilified.
I care for my neighbor and I honor his right/ a man's true gratitude is kindness.
You won't see me cannibalizing people in councils, biting their flesh like a voracious beast.
The most evil of people is he who smiles / when he sees me and backbites me in my absence.

I should clarify that adhering to this moral code of al-ʿAbdī is not an easy matter since it does not entail a Brownian compliance in the theological sense of the word—namely, the way it is clearly outlined as *al- ḥalāl wa al- ḥarām* (the religiously legitimate and the religiously forbidden) in Islam. Rather, it subscribes to a humanist code of an ethical ideal that cultivates its moral obligations from human nature and from being in the world. Yet, at the heart of this pre-Islamic "morality" code still lie earthly riches, even a crazed desire for amassing huge fortunes. Thus, we see Ṭarafa reflecting on his materialistic culture by describing how a woman not only blames him for his poverty, but equates fortune with "eternity":

بغد ولا ما بعده علمُ   وتقول عاذلتي و ليس لها

نَّ المرأ يكرب وجهه العدمُ³⁵   إن الثراء هو الخلود وإ

My blamer would say, having no / knowledge of tomorrow or after:
Wealth is eternity and / a man's misfortune is brought by the lack of it.

Another well-known poet of the pre-Islamic era, Mālik ibn Ḥarīm al-Hamdānī,[36] has a different poetic view from al-ʿAbdī on the wisdom of life. To al-Hamdānī, one is better off becoming wealthy, since life with money and richness can change one's fate for the better. Oddly enough, al-Hamdānī states that lack of wealth leads to lowliness, misery, and corruption: Unlike al-ʿAbdī 's wise man who is rich in morals, al-Hamdānī's wise man is a moneyed man whose fortune is bound to bring him praises even when he is censurable and morally unworthy:

أنبئتُ والأيامُ ذات تجاربٍ   وتُبدي لك الأيامُ ما لستَ تَعلَمُ

بأن ثراءَ المالِ ينفعُ ربَّه   ويُثنى عليه الحمدَ وهو مُذَمَّمُ

وأنَّ قليلَ المالِ للمَرءِ مُفسِدُ   يَحِزُّ كما حَزَّ القطيعُ المُحَرَّمُ

يرىَ درجاتِ المجدَ لا يستطيعُها   ويقعدُ وسْطَ القومِ لا يَتَكَلَّمُ[37]

I learned, and time is the best teacher /—for it reveals to you what you do not know—,
That wealth benefits its owner / and allows him to be praised even when at fault.
And that lack of money degrades / and hurts like a harsh fresh whip.
He [the man without wealth] would see the grades of glory he cannot attain /
    and would sit among people but cannot speak.

Al-Hamdānī is not alone in adopting a prudential view of the importance of being well off. We continue to see in pre-Islamic poetry palpable delineations of a materialistic community that favors affluence and possessions, inhabiting an opportunistic moral code whose greediness engendered taking booty in the manner of the Vikings, an ethical laxity that had become to a large degree a predominant disposition in pre-Islamic Arabia. The following example from Ṭarafa illustrates not only the life of lasciviousness, alcoholism, and insobriety that he led with his cronies, but also a sense of bitterness and indignation owing to his lack of wealth. Like al-Hamdānī, Ṭarafa contends that richness equals societal respect and admiration:

فإن تبغني في حلقة القوم تلقَني   وإن تلتمِسْني في الحوانيت تصطدِ

متى تأتني أصبحك كأساً رويةً   وإنْ كنتَ عنها ذا غِنًى فاغنَ وازْدَد

. . . . . .

ناماي بيضٌ كالنجوم وقينةٌ   تَروحُ عَلينا بَينَ بُردٍ ومَجْسَدِ

. . . . . .

فلو شاءَ رَبي كنتُ قَيْسَ بنَ خالِدٍ   ولو شاءَ ربي كنتُ عَمْرَو بنَ مَرثَدِ

فأصبحتُ ذا مال كثيرٍ وزارني   بنونَ كرامٌ سادةٌ لمسوّدِ[38]

If you are looking for me, find me in the folk's gathering / and if you want to catch
    me, I will be in the taverns

Whenever you visit in the morning, I'll offer a cup of wine full to the brim / and if
you don't need it, do without, and continue so
My drinking mates are white, like the stars, and a singing-girl / comes to us late in a
robe and revealing garment.
If my lord willed it, I could have been Qays ibn Khālid / and if lord willed it, I could
have been ʿAmr ibn Marthad.
And I would have possessed a vast fortune and received visits from / noble sons and
masters of masters.

I should add that the desire for material gain explicitly expressed in these poetical
works is bound to clash with the Qur'ān's antimaterialistic view of the world. The
poetry of pre-Islamic Arabia paints a peculiar picture of material immortalization,
one that the Qur'ān vehemently opposes in its early Meccan sūras and beyond.
From the start, the Qur'ān takes the side of the poor and deprived, expressing
concerns over a type of people who *yadduʿu al-yatīm wa-lā yaḥuḍu ʿalá ṭaʿāmi
al-miskīn* (rebuff the orphan and do not urge the feeding of the homeless),[39] thus
breaching even the most basic tenets of *adab*, which had evidently been in place as
a common custom before the Qur'ān to protect the rights of the poor and the
underprivileged in a predominantly materialistic community. This compassionate
attitude toward the disadvantaged eventually transcribes itself as one of five obligatory commandments of Islam and becomes known as *zakā* (obligatory alms tax).
In an organic, direct response to the excessive celebration of wealth, the rise of a
greedy apathetic tribalism, and the perverse embrace of materialistic values in pre-
Islamic Mecca, some of which we see unabashedly reflected in these poems, the
Qur'ān pulls no punches in drawing on the preexisting ethos of *adab* in denounc-
ing every act of avarice and money-hoarding in the Meccan and Medinan communities of early Islam. It even mocks those who believe that wealth equals eternity.
And this is where the ethical turn reaches its acme: the only eternity of accumu-
lating wealth for wealth's sake and of looking down on fellow humans, retorts the
Qur'ān unequivocally, is going to be hellfire. For instance, sūra 104 is one of
the early Meccan chapters that presents the Qur'ān's harsh response to those who
seek to amass fortune while denigrating their fellow humans:

وَيْلٌ لِّكُلِّ هُمَزَةٍ لُمَزَةٍ ــ الَّذِي جَمَعَ مَالًا وَعَدَّدَهُ ــ يَحْسَبُ أَنَّ مَالَهُ أَخْلَدَهُ ــ كَلَّا لَيُنْبَذَنَّ فِي الْحُطَمَةِ ــ وَمَا أَدْرَاكَ
مَا الْحُطَمَةُ ــ نَارُ اللهِ الْمُوقَدَةُ الَّتِي تَطَّلِعُ عَلَى الْأَفْئِدَةِ ــ إِنَّهَا عَلَيْهِم مُّؤْصَدَةٌ ــ فِي عَمَدٍ مُّمَدَّدَةٍ

Woe to every backstabber and turncoat. Who accumulates wealth and keeps count
of it. He thinks that his wealth will make him eternal. Nay! He shall be thrown into
the *Ḥuṭama*. And what do you know of the *Ḥuṭama*? It is God's lit fire, which sees the
hearts. It is sealed upon them. In outstretched pillars. (104:1–9)

The verses begin with a divine warning, a heavenly resolve to respond with wrath
and retribution to the crime of hoarding money while being contemptuous of
the disadvantaged. This lethal combination of obsession with wealth and ridicule

of humans can only lead to hell according to the Qur’ān. The Qur’ān considers men who amass wealth and lack tolerance and compassion, men who are careless about social equality, to be a menace to society. The reference is to those who not only value and roll in riches but whose view of the world allows them to devalue their fellow humans, by backbiting them, laughing at them, whether verbally or nonverbally—that is, by cursing them, making scornful facial gestures, imitating their disabilities, or deriding them for their poverty and squalor, as if they were a completely different subclass or subspecies. Those who value money more than their fellow humans and who think money will make them eternal shall only be worthy of eternity in hell.

The Qur’ān thus brings eschatological ethics into the thick of Arabia not necessarily as a difference from Hellenism as Brown would argue, although this is always a welcome point of comparison, but as Arabia’s difference *from itself*, or to be more accurate, as taking sides in the already conflicted and entangled ethical claims of pre-Islamic Arabia. This context is key. Like Hellenism, pre-Islamic polytheistic Arabia has its versions of moral codes, including moral obligations and failures that are all too human.

Brown argues that early medieval Christian sexual ethics and monastic disciplines are better understood in the context of Greek and Roman civilizations, with the latter affording more autonomy regarding sexual practices. While sexuality in pre-Islamic Arabia is still a topic in dire need of extensive research, it is not hard to glean from Ṭarafa’s poem that there is an unchecked subjectivity to male sexuality. Yet, there are also complexities that involve race, status, and gender dynamics attached to pre-Islamic sexuality. On the one hand, one could detect an implicit principle of morality in pre-Islamic sexual ethics in al-ʿAbdī’s poem, especially in reference to honoring the rights of his neighbor (*ukrimu al-jāra wa ar ʿá ḥaqqahu*) and the implication that the wife and children of his neighbor would by default fall under that “right” of protection from emotional or physical harm. On the other hand, poetic depictions of sexual conquests present these incidents as a normal aspect of everyday life. The following lines from Imru’ al-Qays’s ode add to his strong sense of ancestral pride an enumeration of romantic exploits and sexual conquests:

فَأَلْهَيْتُهَا عَنْ ذِي تَمَائِمَ مُحْـوِلِ   فَمِثْلُكِ حُبْلَـى قَدْ طَرَقْتُ ومُرضِعٍ

بِشَق وتَحْـتِـي شِقُّـهَا لَـمْ يُحَـوَّلِ[40]   إِذَا مَـا بَكَـى مِنْ خَلْفِهَا انْصَرَفَتْ لَهُ

So I visited a woman, just like you, in the evening, who was pregnant and nursing /
    but I distracted her from her newborn, who was hung with charms.
When he cried, she leaned back to him, extending half her body / while leaving the
    other half underneath me, unstirred.

In these lines, the poetic persona is seeking to persuade his beloved to yield to his sexual advances, a dramatic monologue akin in its corporal tone to Andrew Marvell’s “To His Coy Mistress” (1681). Yet Marvell’s passionate call for sex with the woman he so fervently desires is set against the lapse of time and physical decay. In Imru's al-Qays, however, the persona demeans the "coyness" of his beloved by stating that she is no different from other women he slept with. He congratulates himself for persuading her to have sexual intercourse with him. The Arabic world *alhaytuhā* implies both agency and pleasure; he boasts how the love of a mother for her own baby is equaled by her passion for the poet, surrendering half her body to him. Imru' al-Qays's persona succeeds where Marvell's has not. The woman/beloved is not described as being forced, "coy," or even disliking the adventure. She may have enjoyed it; they may have met before; she may have instigated the encounter; she may have been recently widowed. We will never know, since *al-ma'ná fī baṭn al-shā'ir* (meaning lies in the belly of the poet), as ancient Arabs would say, and one can easily get lost in fictional speculations about fictional affairs. What we know, what the texts allows us to see, is that the poet casts himself as so irresistible that she, a pregnant and nursing mother, has no choice but to succumb to his temptation. The lines delineate how the mother lays down her baby behind her back, adorned with amulets and charms, in complete submission to the poet's sexual advances. Not only that, but even when the baby cries and is hungry for his mother's milk, she turns but with one half of her body toward him while keeping the other for her lover/poet so as not to interrupt his and her pleasure.

It is easy for a puritanical theologian such as al-Bāqillānī to interpret this formidable representation of masculinity, so graphic in its depiction of male sexual exploits, in contradistinction to the righteous tone of Qur'ān's discursive ethical authority, where matrimonially regulated sexuality becomes the mode for protecting chastity and fostering social and communal cohesions. Al-Bāqillānī sees the flamboyant tone with which the persona depicts his encounter with a female lover as a powerful manifestation of the social victory brought about by the Qur'ān. To exaggerate his sexual potency and appeal, Imru' al-Qays's persona reduces the mother/lover to a sex toy. By contrast, mothers have a supreme moral status in both the Qur'ān and the Ḥadīth. Some may deduce that a pregnant mother who is also nursing an infant may have little desire for a whimsical sexual encounter with a nightly lover. The phrase *mithluki* (the likes of you) may also be seen as loaded with gender stereotyping and the denigration of women. "Like you" or "like your kind" may sink deep into the ethical consciousness of pre-Islamic Arabia, representing a "blackening" of a woman's fame and a misdeed on the part of the poet that would run counter to the ethical turn of Islam, which embraces the virtues of virginity and chastity, and celebrates the social triumph and institutionalization of a debauchery-free community.

But to contradict the amateurish puritanism of al-Bāqillānī's theological thought, who only saw poetry as either *ḥarām* or *ḥalāl*,[41] the discourse of poetry—one cannot emphasize this enough—is not the same as religious scripture: poetry allows for fiction and for humor (Imru' al-Qays is even described as impotent in some reports). Poetry is the domain of imagination, exaggeration, linguistic play, even comedy and titillation; poets "say what they do not do," as the Qur'ān famously reminds us. There is nothing wrong with that, as I explain in the following chapter.

Unlike Christianity's adoption of celibacy as a reaction to the moral laxity of Hellenistic Rome, the Qur'ān, while aware of clerical celibacy and monastic institutions, embraces a middle ground as a reaction to the loose sexual principles of pre-Islamic Arabia. The Qur'ān does not attach to celibacy any major role. On the contrary, marital union and the raising of offspring are inalienable principles of Muslim faith. While the Qur'ān takes a firm ethical stand against human greed and self-absorption, it also does not encourage sexual abstinence. This ethical imperative is especially clear in Qur'ān 57. While the sūra advocates a continuity of acts of charity and kindness familiar to the Bible,[42] it presents us with an intriguing dialectic of discontinuity in Christian dogma. In one of its verses (57:27), the sūra presents Christian dogma as a sign of divine mercy and of God's continuous intervention in the world to offer guidance and deliverance through prophets and messengers:

ثُمَّ قَفَّيْنَا عَلَىٰ آثَارِهِم بِرُسُلِنَا وَقَفَّيْنَا بِعِيسَى ابْنِ مَرْيَمَ وَآتَيْنَاهُ الْإِنجِيلَ وَجَعَلْنَا فِي قُلُوبِ الَّذِينَ اتَّبَعُوهُ رَأْفَةً وَرَحْمَةً وَرَهْبَانِيَّةً ابْتَدَعُوهَا مَا كَتَبْنَاهَا عَلَيْهِمْ إِلَّا ابْتِغَاءَ رِضْوَانِ اللَّهِ فَمَا رَعَوْهَا حَقَّ رِعَايَتِهَا فَآتَيْنَا الَّذِينَ آمَنُوا مِنْهُمْ أَجْرَهُمْ وَكَثِيرٌ مِّنْهُمْ فَاسِقُونَ[43]

Then in their footprints we sent our messengers; we sent Jesus, son of Mary, and gave him the Gospel, and we instilled compassion and mercy in the hearts of those who followed him, and a monasticism they contrived. We did not prescribe [it] on/ to them except in order for them to seek the satisfaction of God, but they did not observe it properly, so we rewarded those among them who believed, and most of them who remained were disobedient.

This continuity serves two important functions. First, it emphasizes the decree of divine justice—that is, the claim that God is not in the habit of abandoning humanity or letting it lapse into depravity without sending periodical divine guidance. The Qur'ān states that there has not been a span of time on earth when God neglected to send a prophet to inform humanity of God's existence and to invite people to follow an ethical manual that steers them away from evil.[44] This ethical manual is often referred to in the Qur'ān as *nūr* (light) or *hudá* (guidance), in references to Judaism, Christianity, and Islam.[45] This figuration of godly guidance as "light" is crucial in Qur'ān 57[46], precisely because light connotes a dissipation of darkness in a long ethical concatenation of god-sent prophets.[47] Secondly, as verse 57:27 has it, the light always reminds us it that comes from one divine source, thus sealing the question of the oneness of God and creating an ethical continuity of Abrahamic monotheism in harmony with the context of the Qur'ān, from Noah to Abraham to Moses to Jesus to Muḥammad : a variation on the theme of calling for the one God, and an extension of the line of prophets to Muḥammad—namely, that the call of all these prophets has always been to worship one single God, and that no prophets are excepted. They are messengers and servants of God chosen at a time in human history, with various miracles suitable to the time, as al-Jāḥiẓ explains,[48] to draw people's attention to God.

On the other hand, the second half of verse 57:27 brings forth a discontinuity thesis by interrupting the Christian practice of monasticism and its associative practice of celibacy. The first half of verse 57:27 focuses on the message of Jesus, the son of Mary whom God has given the Gospel (*ātaynāhu al-Injīl*). The Qur'ān states that God instilled an ethic of compassion and mercy (*ra 'fa wa raḥma*) in the hearts of the disciples and those who followed Jesus. So far so good. But then comes the conjunctive و (*wa*, and), which initially reads like the continuity of the verse. The conjunctive *wa* is followed by the word *rahbāniyya* (monasticism) immediately after the two modifiers of "compassion" and "mercy," creating almost a double entendre. *Rāhib* literally means "fearing/someone who fears." Pious, renunciant Muslims who turned from the world could sometimes be called *rāhib*, a term that still carries strong implications of celibacy and sexual abstinence.[49] In its later development, Islam has come to strongly condemn celibacy. Recall, for instance, the well-known story about 'Uthmān ibn Maẓ'ūn, who deprived himself of sexual intercourse with women and boycotted the eating of meat. When 'Uthmān says he wants "to be a monk [*tarahhub*] in the mountains," the Prophet replies, "The 'monkhood' of my community is sitting in mosques waiting for the *ṣalā*." This story neatly shows that *rahbāniyya/tarahhub* is interpreted as an abdication of sexual desire and abandonment of society.[50] At any rate, the linguistic ambiguity in 57:27 lies specifically in the function and meaning of the conjunctive clause following *rahbāniyya*. Could the clause be read as "God has instilled compassion and mercy *and* monasticism" in the hearts of the followers of Jesus, a possible reference to the disciples but also to all guardians of Christianity in the years and centuries to come? In other words, are monasticism and its associative celibacy of the same category of love and compassion? Or is it a caesura, an interruption and therefore a *bid 'a* (, heresy)—namely, a novelty to the original Christian dogma?

Syntactically, it might be slightly confounding to read the verse as such: "God has planted in the hearts of Jesus's disciples/followers compassion, mercy, and celibacy." The way the verse reads in Arabic does not prohibit this understanding. However, *rahbāniyya* comes immediately before *ibtada 'ūhā* (they contrived it/ invented it/came up with it/designed it/imposed it on themselves), making the objectival antecedent, *-hā* (it), at the end of the verb a direct reference to that *rahbāniyya*, and thus tipping the caesura in the direction of reading the verse as follows: "and monasticism [, which] they contrived," a reading that counters another—that is to say, "and monasticism that God inspired followers of Jesus to commit themselves to in the way he inspired them to behave with compassion and mercy." One thing is clear. It is difficult, both semantically and syntactically, to read the objectival suffix *-hā* in *ibtada 'ūhā* as an antecedent to "compassion, mercy and monasticism." In other words, devising or coming up with *rahbāniyya* is of a self-imposed doctrine that God according to the Qur'ān simply did not decree, but that may have been humanly devised in the path of moral and spiritual advancement and thus deemed approved by God. Yet, just as we start to think the verse has given us a straightforward statement, we see the aporia in 57:27: "We did not dictate/prescribe [it] on/to them except in order for them to seek the satisfaction/approval/consent of God." This exception is in keeping with the main tenants of Sūra 57, which in sum is a chapter that celebrates the continuity of the light of God through the procreation of the human race. The theological aporia here lies in the implication that celibacy is an ethical practice premised on the understanding that virility is on a collision course with spiritual devotion to the very God who created the sex drive and bid humanity to multiply in the first place.

In this context, celebrating the divine will of procreation would seem to collide with *rahbāniyya*, which, in its own devotional imperative as a practice of inner freedom and spiritual growth in the service of God, is also, paradoxically, an interruption of that very divine order, and of the celestial continuity of its ethical guidance, which is manifest through the endurance of the human race. The *adab* of *rahbāniyya* in 57:27 thus serves as the extreme opposite of being an active participant of a community of believers and of having *takāthur fī al-amwāl wa al-awlād*, the boastful worldly practice of multiplying fortune and children referenced earlier in 57:20:

ٱعْلَمُوٓا۟ أَنَّمَا ٱلْحَيَوٰةُ ٱلدُّنْيَا لَعِبٌ وَلَهْوٌ وَزِينَةٌ وَتَفَاخُرٌ بَيْنَكُمْ وَتَكَاثُرٌ فِى ٱلْأَمْوَٰلِ وَٱلْأَوْلَٰدِ

Know that this lower life is but play, entertainment, adornment, boasting among yourselves, and multiplying wealth and children.

Historically, early Christianity, especially in the immediate aftermath of the crucifixion, suffered considerably. Many believers, the Qur'ān states, were persecuted, burned alive, chased across city borders, and so on. The reference to the "cave people" in Qur'ān 18 is a case in point that serves as a painful reminder of the abominable persecution of early medieval Christians, where a group of young men ran away into the mountains and hid in a cave (most likely escaping from the evil and hedonistic Roman emperor, Decius [249–51], known in Arabic sources as Diqyānūs). It is nonetheless still exegetically possible to interpret 57:27 as indicating that God has accepted the isolation—that is, the celibacy of those devout men who designed it or imposed it upon themselves, circumstantially and out of necessity—as the need to escape persecution was compelling; however, somehow in the process the practice apostatized and it may have likely become difficult for its adherents to uphold its standards. Or, as the Qur'ān says, "they failed to nurse it as properly as it should be nursed, so we rewarded those among them who believed and many of them were/are impious." In other words, celibacy demands that priests and nuns conduct themselves in proper rituals of purity and have the proper qualifications of ordination. Still, the Qur'ān neither offers a complete picture of Christian celibacy nor pronouncedly denounces it. The verse ends with deferring the whole matter to God, who would decide whom to reward based on the truth and sincerity of their faith.

The circumstances that engendered celibacy should not be overlooked, especially the revolting and unending Roman persecution against Christian minorities. Early Christianity sought to flee to the desert to avoid such brutal oppressions, and in this act to differentiate itself from pagan Greece, but also from Judaism, which, like Islam, has no interest in celibacy and puts great emphasis on marriage and family values as consecrated duties. This emphasis brings us back full circle to Brown's main argument on Islamic *adab* vis-à-vis *paideia* in relation to late antiquity and early medieval Christianity. "The novelty of the Islamic *adab*," Brown contends, "was not its religious content, but the application to men in the world, to non-monks, of a religious grooming that had been considered capable of transforming only those who had withdrawn from society to give themselves over to an alternative *paideia* in the miniature society of the celibate monastery, 'as if in another world.'"[51] Brown here is alluding to some followers of Jesus who were claimed to have deserted conjugality and family life in order to dedicate themselves to proclaiming the coming of the kingdom of God.[52] Sūra 57 takes a side in this debate. Because of the lack of upholding the standards of celibacy in the proper manner suitable for its application, Sūra 57 makes reference to a certain failing in celibacy and monasticism *writ large*, for reasons that are not mentioned in the sūra, but which one might infer could be institutional (power/authority), or personal, or both.

It is likely that Brown is not familiar with Sūra 57's take on celibacy; but, knowing that the Qur'ān makes a unique seventh-century statement on the application of celibacy, it would be injudicious to conclude that "the problem that faced the exponent of the classical concept of *adab* was a very different one from that which faced the Christian ascetic holy man," or that "unlike the Christian holy man, the Muslim exponent of *adab* could be said to stand at the 'core' of his culture, realizing at their fullest intensity the ideals to which all observant Muslims subscribed."[53] Despite the appealing testimonial from Ernst Gellner that "Islamic propriety emanates from their essence, as it were,"[54] Islamic *adab* emanates primarily from the Qur'ān *and*, as I have tried to demonstrate, from its filtered pre-Islamic culture. In the Qur'ān, the moral authority of the *homo-Islamicus* derives from the various articulations of the dos and don'ts peppered throughout its 114 sūras. But, to Brown's point, over time, celibacy did create an ascetic paradigm of moral hierarchy in early mediaeval Christianity, which chaste clergy used as a superior moral order to control the so-called "lowly" life of the uninitiated,[55] a hierarchical structure that the Qur'ān effectively nipped in the bud, but that yet somehow survived in classical Islam under a different garb of institutional hierarchy, one in which the religious elites and *'ulamā'*, *sans* sexual abstinence, became the counterparts of medieval Christianity's celibate clergy.

6

—————

The Qurʾān in Context

Monotheism and the Birth of the Unmimetic

Researching early Islamic history is a colossal task, where "the earliest extant narrative chronologies covering the first centuries of Islam," as Asad Ahmed puts it, "were compiled several decades after the events they purport to describe."[1] These chronologies, Ahmed goes on, are "raw material comprised of oral fragments, i.e., decontextualized stories that were told by semi-professional storytellers in sermons and religious gatherings," thus making it difficult for the historians of early Islam to ascertain "the reliability of sources."[2] Yet Ahmed pulls no punches in reminding us that "over the past few decades, historians of Islam [who] have tried to address the problem of the Arabo-Islamic sources," relying heavily on "criticism as developed in Old Testament and New Testament studies [,] . . . can fail at various stumbling points," especially in delivering "the details of provincial histories that are so important for reconstruing the internal contours of the larger narratives that we now possess."[3]

This "failure" to which Asad calls our attention comes as a result of a mistake superimposed on a larger error. Continuing or discontinuing certain precepts in preexisting scriptural traditions would mean that for the Qurʾān to be understood and appreciated by its first audience, the audience must have had at least some broad familiarity with this biblical background. Logic dictates that the Qurʾān would not have any appeal or leverage if this were not the case. In fact, in its response to someone who turned his back on Muḥammad's call, the Qurʾān rebukes him because he should have some knowledge about biblical prophets, especially Abraham and Moses. In this case, the Qurʾān confirms that its audience must already have had prior knowledge of what the *ṣuḥuf* (scriptures) of Moses and the faith story of Abraham entailed, thus positioning Islam in conversation with monotheistic traditions in the public pre-Islamic domain:

116

أَفَرَأَيْتَ الَّذِي تَوَلَّى. وَأَعْطَى قَلِيلًا وَأَكْدَى. أَعِندَهُ عِلْمُ الْغَيْبِ فَهُوَ يَرَى. أَمْ لَمْ يُنَبَّأْ بِمَا فِي صُحُفِ مُوسَى. وَإِبْرَاهِيمَ الَّذِي وَفَّى. أَلَّا تَزِرُ وَازِرَةٌ وِزْرَ أُخْرَى. وَأَن لَّيْسَ لِلإِنسَانِ إِلَّا مَا سَعَى

Have you seen the one who turned his back? And lent so little before he stopped?
Does he have knowledge of the unseen so that he could discern? Has he not been
informed of what is in the scriptures of Moses, and of Abraham, who fulfilled [his
covenant]: that no burdened soul shall bear the burden of another, and that humans
shall be held accountable only for what they have done? (53:33–39)

In another example, the Qur'ān specifically refers to the Torah and the Gospel as
knowable scriptures to Muḥammad's community and as an endorsement of his
own prophethood:

الَّذِينَ يَتَّبِعُونَ الرَّسُولَ النَّبِيَّ الْأُمِّيَّ الَّذِي يَجِدُونَهُ مَكْتُوبًا عِندَهُمْ فِي التَّوْرَٰةِ وَالْإِنجِيلِ يَأْمُرُهُم بِالْمَعْرُوفِ وَيَنْهَاهُمْ عَنِ الْمُنكَرِ وَيُحِلُّ لَهُمُ الطَّيِّبَٰتِ وَيُحَرِّمُ عَلَيْهِمُ الْخَبَٰئِثَ وَيَضَعُ عَنْهُمْ إِصْرَهُمْ وَالْأَغْلَٰلَ الَّتِي كَانَتْ عَلَيْهِمْ فَالَّذِينَ ءَامَنُوا بِهِ وَعَزَّرُوهُ وَنَصَرُوهُ وَاتَّبَعُوا النُّورَ الَّذِي أُنزِلَ مَعَهُ أُوْلَٰئِكَ هُمُ الْمُفْلِحُونَ

Those who follow the messenger, the *ummī* prophet, whom they find written in the
Torah and the Gospel. He instructs them to do good and forbids them from evil;
he blesses what is lawful and inhibits what is impure; he relieves them from their
burdens and the chains that restrain them. Those who believe in him, revere him,
support him, and follow the light sent down with him are the rewarded ones. (7:157)

The Qur'ān's reference to the Torah and the Gospel in the above verse confirms
its awareness of the presence of an Abrahamic theological consciousness on the
Arabian Peninsula in the seventh century. Take, for instance, the Himyaritic
Inscriptions, which make clear reference to the monotheistic presence of Judaism and Christianity in Southern Arabia (modern-day Yemen) in the sixth century.[4] This presence must have been known in some fashion to the Meccan and
Medinan communities of the early seventh-century Hijaz. It is confirmed in the
Qur'ān's heavyhearted reference to the callous murder of Christian believers who
are thrown alive into an enormous trench with burning fuel.[5] In a powerful pas-
sivation of the Arabic grammatical imperative mode *qutila*—to indicate that murderers shall pay in kind—the Qur'ān accurses the murderers as it depicts them as
callous and insensitive in perpetrating such an unforgivable deed against innocent
believers, burning them alive while sitting and watching them die:

قُتِلَ أَصْحَابُ الْأُخْدُودِ. النَّارِ ذَاتِ الْوَقُودِ. إِذْ هُمْ عَلَيْهَا قُعُودٌ. وَهُمْ عَلَى مَا يَفْعَلُونَ بِالْمُؤْمِنِينَ شُهُودٌ

Accursed are the people of the trench, [who lit] the massive fire pit, sitting around it,
and witnessing what they are doing to the believers. (85:4–7)

In addition to this acute awareness of the painful history of persecuted Christians
(in the above example and in the example of the people of the cave in 18), the
people of faith described in two separate historical events as *mu'minīn* (believers),[6] Christians are themselves some of most celebrated and finest examples of
the unwavering advocacy for God ever to be found in the Qur'ān. As such, these
exemplars of faith are not arranged chronologically, and are never mentioned for

their own sake, but are always tied to the Qur'ān's main themes of the absoluteness of God, the accountability of all humans, and the reward and punishment in the afterlife. The Qur'ān's reference to the aforementioned massacre confirms the heinous animosity that must have erupted between competing beliefs in South Arabia. It therefore matters that the Qur'ān would focus only on core and pure monotheistic values apart from the priestly classes and confessional rituals of Judaism and Christianity, embracing an autonomous median position amid irreconcilable religiosities:

وَكَذَٰلِكَ جَعَلْنَاكُمْ أُمَّةً وَسَطًا لَّتَكُونُوا شُهَدَاءَ عَلَى النَّاسِ وَيَكُونَ الرَّسُولُ عَلَيْكُمْ شَهِيدًا

> And so we have made you of a median community so that you may bear witness over people and so that the messenger may bear witness over you. (2:143)

Thematic affinities between Islam and Christianity abound, and these affinities have in turn led generations of theologians in medieval Europe to consider Islam a Christian heresy. Underlying differences lie in matters of prophecy, unicity, priesthood, confessionalism, and so on. The Qur'ān grants humans no access to God's divinity. But even when the Qur'ān categorically opposes the dogma of the Trinity, it still consecrates and details the immaculate conception as it embraces the existence of God, much like Christianity. Readers of the Qur'ān will soon realize how Jesus figures as a prophet of immense status whose confirmation of the Torah, and whose love and devotion for God make him the ideal precursor to Muḥammad.[7] Thematically, the Qur'ān simultaneously continues and discontinues both Judaism and Christianity. G. E. von Grunebaum contends that "neither untaught Christians [of Mecca] could convey scant doctrinal information, nor were the Jews of Mecca on a high enough level to transmit accurately the contents of the Torah."[8] What this means is that although Islam stands akin to both versions of Abrahamic monotheism, according to Grunebaum "it is an independent creation."[9] In fact, paganism was more thoroughly widespread in the Arabian Peninsula in the sixth century than monotheistic faiths were. It is also historically recorded that no one single monotheism in the Arabian Peninsula was ever systematized into a theology before Muḥammad, because tribal traditionalism, especially in Mecca, was the true "religion" of the land.[10] In a narrow sense, Mecca was a cosmopolitan society whose population formed a negligible but palpable minority in the vast expanse of surrounding empires, with scattered communities of faith, an overarching polytheism, and a booming trade. In fact, the Qur'ān states that seventh-century Mecca had sustained commercial ties with surrounding neighbors in Yemen, Syria, Persia, and Abyssinia through regular "winter and summer trips."[11]

This demonstrable commercial exchange is key. If it is true that vocabulary has a natural tendency to travel—to start a life of its own in other languages—then it would follow that pre-Islamic Arabic in a cross-regional trade culture must have assimilated foreign words into its own vocabulary.[12] This fact alone makes it both linguistically acceptable and expected that "where the Arabs came in contact with higher religion and higher civilization," as Arthur Jeffery puts it, "they borrowed religious and cultural terms."[13] I would add that they borrowed more than just religious and cultural terms, unless by "cultural" Jeffery also means commercial merchandize such as[14] *arā'ik* ("adorned beds" in the Yemeni dialect)[15] and[16] *al-qisṭās* ("scale/balance," believed by ancient philologists as to be derived from Greek).[17]

Moreover, while Jewish and Christian communities evidently existed in Arabia, they did so, as Hamilton A. R. Gibb notes, "independently of the organized churches."[18] They must have existed as "'heretical' offshoots," continues Gibb, "not only of Christianity, but also of Judaism or the Judeo-Christian," a conclusion that prompts Gibb to draw the reasonable analogy that "the relationship of Islam to the official Jewish and Christian churches and doctrines via these deviant groups is thus to some extent parallel to that between the early Christian church and orthodox Judaism."[19] This relationship would ultimately explain why an Arabic vocabulary of monotheism relevant to the subject matter of the Qur'ān must have existed in pre-Islamic Mecca and coalesced with the everyday language of classical Arabic. It also effectively clarifies the merging of an Arabized monotheistic vocabulary in classical Arabic, especially proper nouns such as *al-Injīl* (the Gospel) and *al-Tawrā* (Torah), as well as proper names such as *Nūḥ* (Noah), *Ibrāhīm* (Abraham), *Mūsá* (Moses), *'Īsá* (Jesus), and *Maryam* (Mary), in addition to other cognates and loanwords that have become part of the inflectional system of Arabic, and that Muslim and Arab philologists, as well as exegetes, do not fail to fully accept and recognize.[20] Not to mention the obvious fact that the Qur'ān includes important details about some prophets and prophecies that are entirely Arabian, yet still strongly tied to the theme of monotheism.[21] It is therefore farcical, to echo Gibb, to propose, even as a postulate, a Jewish or Christian foundation for Islam.[22] In sum, while monotheism was not alien to Arabia, it existed both peripherally and subsumably under a predominantly polytheistic culture. It is rather the revolutionary scale, the confrontational tone, the Abrahamic interdisciplinarity rather than the whimsical masculinity, and the counter-religiosity of the Qur'ān that, taken together, turned Muḥammad into an existential threat for polytheistic Mecca.

To understand the magnitude of this scale, it matters that we situate the Qur'ān in its immediate historical context and view it as a beginning—namely, as an oral event that took place in the life of theology itself. In this beginning, which Marshall Hodgson expertly describes as a "vision," a "culture, and a "venture,"[23] the Qur'ān starts off the seventh century with the strong capability to bring forth a radical transformation, responding to a preexisting set of theological and secular thought in a manner and style that are aesthetically and rhetorically challenging. As an oral text, the Qur'ān is cognizant of, yet breaks from and interpolates, what came before it, including the secular and individualistic ethos of pre-Islamic poetry, replacing its exemplary force by installing itself as a new beginning. Yet a beginning is not an origin, a fact that the Qur'ān also recognizes in offering itself as a complement to a historical chain of monotheistic prophethood from Noah to Abraham to Moses to Jesus to Muḥammad (42:13). This beginning, however, distinguishes itself as a discourse that discontinues certain applications of this monotheistic origin but that nonetheless intimates the same order of such higher truth, namely, that of *Lawḥ Maḥfūẓ* (a Preserved Tablet)[24] and *Umm al-Kitāb* (the Mother of all Books)[25], an origination that is wholly conscious of and answerable to itself, celebrating the absence of a mysterious divine referent.

Daniel Madigan was the first to draw attention to the status of the Qur'ān and its appositive *al-kitāb* as a process reflexive of God's all-inclusive knowledge in contradistinction to the statism imposed upon it by Western scholarship. "To say that a people has been given the *kitab*," writes Madigan, "is not to say they have been vouchsafed some great work of reference that contains all they need to know and act upon; rather it means that they have entered into a new mode of existence, where the community lives in the assurance and expectation (or perhaps even the fear) of being personally addressed by the divine authority and knowledge."[26] I will return to this connotative associations of *al-kitāb* later in this chapter, but for now it should suffice to say that Madigan's argument invites us to imagine how the audience of the Qur'ān as *kitāb* not only received it as an ever-evolving exegetical discovery, but also understood it as opening up a conversation between humanity and divinity inasmuch as it underlines an endless continuity of divine guidance and humans' interactions with and translations of such guidance.

The most ethically responsible approach toward understanding the authority of *al-kitāb*, in this Madiganian sense, is to examine it with the understanding that both pre-Islamic poetry and the Qur'ān are original and primary sources, sources that the Euro-American academy tends to view as mimetic or simulated, and whose identity is almost inevitably derivative of what was already there. There is in the Qur'ān a palpable level of sociality, coupled with an urgent intervention to remedy social inequalities and ameliorate the daily sufferings of an impoverished stratum of the Meccan and Medinan communities. This intervention is articulated through specific "lexemes" and multiple levels of ongoing conversations: between God and the angels,[27] between God and the devil, between God and the community of the believers, between God and prophets, and between prophets and their supporters as well as their detractors. Depictions of these conversations loom as potential *amthila* (exemplars/role models) as well as warnings throughout the revelation of the Qur'ān. The spirit of these multilayered conversations demand, as we showed in the previous chapter, a translation of the ethical codes of the seventh-century Arabian Peninsula from within a local context of morality where a specific understanding of *adab* is invested with a specific ethical-theological significance at a specific time in history. This is due not just to the history of the uses to which these conversations have been put, but to the narrative perspectives the Qur'ān employs to present them to its intended audience.

But all this may be lost on later generations as well as on scholarship that remains disengaged from the Arabic language or from the Arabicity of the Qur'ān and that is unaware of the meaning of such a tacitly but contextually telling text whose highly charged language directly addresses the sociopolitical valences of the first Muslim community and its complex habits. By habits, I am not just referring to pre-Islamic practices such *al-wa'd, al-nasī', al-maysir, al-anṣāb, al-azlām*, in addition to food habits and sexual customs mentioned in pre-Islamic poetry and the Qur'ān, but also to the connotative weight of quotidian vocabularies such as *dīzá, ẓann, ḥukm, tabarruj, ḥamiyya, taṭayrnā, ad'iyā'kum, tazāhrūn*, and the subtle historical-semantic differences between detractors and opponents of prophets—for example, *al-kāfirīn, al-munāfiqīn, al-fāsiqīn, al-mushrikīn, al-mulḥidīn, al-mujrimīn*, and *al-mukadhdhibīn*, and what this social division would do to a monotheistic community emerging in the midst of deep-seated polytheism.[28]

Disengaging from the Arabicity of the Qur'ān has also led to the regurgitation of obsolete issues that have beset Euro-American scholarship for decades. Take, for instance, the date and the circumstances when the Qur'ān text became "fixed," receiving an authoritative *written* form. Because Euro-American scholarship tends to view oral transmission (as well as Arabo-Islamic sources) as fluid and untrusted,[29] it matters to recall that the earliest alphabetical inscription of Arabic, which emerged from Aramaic through Nabataean and Neo-Sinaitic alphabets, is a trilingual inscription—Greek-Syriac-Arabic, dating back to 512 AD, during which the Arabian Peninsula seemed to have been predominantly non-literate.[30] Therefore, if the Qur'ān emerged between 609/10 and 632, reliance on writing would have been negligible, especially when Muḥammad was himself believed to be nonliterate. There are objections in Euro-American scholarship to this account and some scholars are even convinced that Muslim accounts of the collection and composition of the Qur'ān are contradictory and confusing.[31] This is doubtful: certainly the retentive mental capacities even of ordinary oral poets of pre-Islam, not to speak of Homeric times, continue to surprise contemporary habitual literates. However, this much can be agreed upon: that reliance on writing to preserve the Qur'ān during the life of Muḥammad was subsidiary. Muḥammad and his companions behaved in the same manner the bardic peninsulars did with their oral traditions: *al-ḥifẓ 'an ẓahr qalb* (learning by heart). The Qur'ān thus was preserved orally for the most part not inaccurately until the third caliph, 'Uthmān ibn 'Affān (576–656), ordered the compilation of a standard version of the Qur'ān in 651 AD, in what later came to be known as *Muṣḥaf 'Uthmān* (or the Samarkand Kufic Qur'ān). From there, we can affirm what Naṣr Ḥāmīd Abū Zayd has concluded: that the need to preserve the Qur'ān gradually promoted a community of literacy in the aftermath of Muḥammad's death in 632 AD; and that the emergence and development of the two main styles of Arabic writing, *Kūfī* (Iraqi script from the city of Kufa) and *naskh* (Mecca-Medina scripts) in the seventh century was coterminous with the spread of Islam in the seventh and eighth centuries.[32]

At any rate, what matters historically now is that the Qur'ān is commendably the oldest extant "book" of the Arabic language. Muslims regard it as a proclamation of its own ingenuity, an oral *tanzīl* (sending down)[33] of the direct words of God to the Meccan-born prophet Muḥammad ibn 'Abdullah,[34] who received it *munajjam* (piecemeal)[35] through the medium of *waḥy* (inner angelic communication) over a period of twenty-three years (609/10–632). In the Qur'ān, Muḥammad is also noted as *khātam al-nabiyyīn* (the last/seal) of all prophets. Following the death of Muḥammad in 632 AD, the Qur'ān was subsequently compiled into 114 sūras (chapters) varying in length and starting from longest to shortest, with the longest being 286 verses and the shortest being three verses. The Qur'ān does not bear traces of any significant modifications, alterations, or revisions over time, a fact that many Western scholars confirm.[36]

Recited in *saj'* (a rhythmic, strophic, alliterative, and assonant style), the Qur'ān contains a comprehensive message that is at once global and local, at once intergalactic and eschatological. On the one hand, it addresses the measured movement of the sun and the moon in orbit.[37] On the other, it tackles specific events in the life of the first Muslim community.[38] In all this, it has very specific themes: the world is created by one supreme being, *Allāh* (God), who has many names and who will judge all humans for their actions. In fact, half of the Qur'ān is dedicated solely to the description of this supreme being and all his attributes of divinity, his names, magnificence, awe, beauty, and power. These attributes, the Qur'ān confirms, are reminders to Muḥammad and his community to worship the one (and only) God and to obey his commands.

Even when few of its verses make reference to Prophet Muḥammad—for example, his ethics in *wa innaka la'alá khuluqin 'aẓīmin*,[39] (you are [a prophet] of exalted ethics), his status as *al-nabiyyi al-ummiyyi*[40] (the *ummī* prophet), his attributions of orphancy, lack of guidance, and poverty during his early life (*yatīman, ḍāllan, 'ā'ilan*)[41]—the Qur'ān is still strikingly a book about God and his omnipresence. Gary Wills reminds us that the Qur'ān is "haunted by something omnipresent."[42] In the local context of the seventh-century Arabian Peninsula, this omnipresent haunting bears a strong geographical affinity to the landscape of "the Arabian desert,"[43] as Wills concludes, thus making the local contextual authority of the Qur'ān even more compelling. Although varied conceptualizations of heaven and hell clearly resonated among ancient Greeks as well as Jewish and early Christian writers of late antiquity, it is still no coincidence that in the scorching heat of the Arabian Peninsula, postmortem جنة (heaven)—the eternal abode of believers who testify to the oneness of God, and who perform good deeds and administer justice on earth—would be rich in rivers, shady groves, and various kinds of drinks and fruit trees. Conversely, unimaginable punishment in the heat of جهنم (hellfire), a multiplied exponentiation of the degree of heat that customarily blazes the summers of the Arabian Peninsula, is the fate of the unjust and the nonbelievers.

In the Qur'ān, preforming justice and believing in God go hand in hand. The rhetorical eloquence of the Qur'ān's language allows the stories the audience are familiar with (e.g., those of Abraham, Joseph, and Moses) to serve the same purpose of establishing the omnipresence of God across human time. It is not hard to see why the Western academy has seldom engaged with the Qur'ān's rhetorical and aesthetic qualities. The Qur'ān addresses itself as containing both "clear" and "ambiguous" signs and verses, making it impossible to translate the latter with any degree of certainty:

هُوَ الَّذِي أنزَلَ عَلَيْكَ الْكِتَابَ مِنْهُ آيَاتٌ مُحْكَمَاتٌ هُنَّ أُمُّ الْكِتَابِ وَأُخَرُ مُتَشَابِهَاتٌ

He is the one who has sent down to you [Muḥammad] the scripture, some of whose verses are distinct—they are the mother of the Book—and others are undifferentiated. (3:7)

Because of these endless interpretive varieties, a linguistic feature akin to Umberto Eco's famous concept of infinite interpretation and unlimited semiosis, the Qur'ān remains an arduous task for translators.[44] Its *naẓm* (structural and linguistic composition), as al-Khaṭṭābī and, later, al-Jurjānī remind us, will continue to challenge even the most erudite of Arab grammarians and rhetoricians. Part of the Qur'ān's literary and linguistic distinctiveness is that it does not have a historical genre, local or foreign, to belong to, yet it still manages to become the aesthetic crown of an ancient language already complete in all its aesthetic and rhetorical dimensions—syntactically, semantically, and phonologically. It is rare to find a text that creates and becomes the only example of its own genre, a genre with its own subgenres, if we were to zoom in on Meccan as opposed to Medinan sūras. Classical philologists of the Qur'ān, including al-Khaṭṭābī, al-Rummānī, and al-Jurjānī, find this particular quality of the Qur'ān to be a key source of its inimitable power as it perpetually challenges its audience. Although my definition of genre for the purpose of this study is limited to the generic categorical differences that set the Qur'ān apart from pre-Islamic poetry and prose, researching its genres, as Devin Stewart has shown us, is a field unto itself.[45] In a recent article on the topic, Stewart offers a cumulative yet surgical analysis of the complexity of generic references in the Qur'ān. Commenting on Karim Samji's work on form in the Qur'ān,[46] Stewart calls for a treatment of both "form" and "genre" as synonymous, convincingly arguing that technically "form in this mode of interpretation does not refer merely to structure but rather to types of speech or literature that have recognizable conventions, and they both ought to refer to specific genres, such as the curse, the parable, or the fable." If adopted, Stewart's call will reshape our understandings of the Qur'ān subgenres and allow for more penetrative interrogations beyond the conventional classifications of scholars like Richard Bell, who categorized the language of the Qur'ān under the indiscriminate umbrella terms of "structure" and "style."[47]

As a literary category of artistic composition, genre itself is a social practice. We have seen this with pre-Islamic poetry—namely, that it is an accumulative mimesis, a literary and linguistic contract in which poets agree to follow certain formulaic rules in their *taqrīḍ* (making) of poetry, with all its variegated subgenres of *fakhr* (pride), *ḥamāsa* (zeal/momentum), *madīḥ* (praise/panegyric), *hijā'* (invective/scorn/satire), *rithā'* (elegy/valediction/mourning), *i'tidhār* (apology), *ghazal* (love/courting), *waṣf* (description), and so on. Yet the Qur'ān stands out, to this day, as an unparalleled textual event. This preeminence should not be overlooked. Until today, the very existence of the generic conventions of poetry, prose, and the language of soothsayers in seventh-century Hijaz fails to fully explain how the *generic* autonomy of the Qur'ān came into being, how it exhibited unmatched rhetoricity while absorbing into its formal structure a focused content conscious of the contextual elements of the very culture it addresses.

Even when cycles of a literary genre grow out of fashion and give way to new and exciting subgenres and forms of expression, as they tend to do, more often than not such a "new genre" would likely reproduce itself. The Qur'ān's linguistic distinctiveness—which students and philologists of Arabic recognize as a unique quality—invites one to ask whether a text could be autonomous, or how the Arabic language in the instance of the Qur'ān managed to soar above its immediate sociocultural contexts and free itself from the generic commonalities of the traditional Arabic *qaṣīda* and the *nathr* (prose) compositions existing before it, and finally what kind of a text the Qur'ān is in becoming autonomous and influential to this level, in which the conventional social and tribal functions of classical Arabic literature have become so arcane as to render us all oblivious to the power and influence that an artistic, fresh, and new text can exercise on its community from the seventh century to the present.

For our own purposes, the more specific questions now are how the Qur'ān is able to break out not only from the stronghold of polytheistic tribalism with its own revered social habits and establish itself as a central scripture and as the new law of the land, but also from the prison house of the linguistic familiarity of its time: from *shi'r* (poetry), *nathr* (prose), and *saj' al-kuhhān* (the rhymed prose of soothsayers); how it pays tribute to that from which it broke away, while still able to bring about a difference and make this difference last; how it jumpstarted Abrahamic monotheism at a time when the latter's heart was beating too slowly and when *al-Ḥanīfiyya* (Ḥanīfism, literary "renunciatory Abrahamism," or innate human devotion to monotheism) was itself the "other" of Meccan polytheism. In what follows, I try to answer these questions by focusing only on a few key stylistic and rhetorical aspects, to limit ourselves, which collectively thematize the Qur'ān as a discourse of difference.

THE QUR'ĀN'S DIFFERENCE

The Qur'ān achieves its difference using multiple textual modalities, but there are four simultaneous modes that especially stand out in demonstrating how it distinctively connects the moral ideal with divine authority and judgment, while suturing them all into its discourse of *I'jāz*. First, the Qur'ān implements a radically different point of view from that of poetry; secondly, it emphatically and pronouncedly declares its distinction from poetry; thirdly, it absorbs a long concatenation of prophetic tropes and narratives extant in the Old Testament, employing them differently (that is, within a multivariant reiterative structure that has the capacity to generate and interlink several prophetic episodes into a single sūra and tying them neatly to Muḥammad's prophecy); and finally, it presents itself as a unique linguistic phenomenon that cannot be equaled or surpassed.

I will expound each of these four modes and provide examples, not only in order to concretize what may otherwise appear abstract about the language of the Qur'ān, but also to show how a sample examination of Qur'ānic language *at work* may serve as a pragmatic and realistic tool for further readings and analyses of the Qur'ān text outside both the normative tradition of *tafsīr* and the blanket periodization of Eurocentrism. Before going any further, however, it is worth emphasizing that this is a literary approach, one that may have its own polemical insinuations. Examining the aesthetic dynamics of the Qur'ān with literary eyes tends to probe the text for elements of common humanism. It tends to see Qur'ānic representations of human figures, from prophets to foes to people mentioned in passing, as participants in humanism, moving across linguistic, cultural, historical, and spiritual boundaries as they find themselves caught in searching for meaning in the experiences they undergo rather than simply engaging with an omniscient voice. The cadence with which the basic "things of life" are represented has a transformative literary power, a power that readers and listeners will witness firsthand as the musical rhythm of the Qur'ān charms its audience and a new emotive pattern of divine omniscience emerges. What the Arabic language is witnessing in the Qur'ān is the birth of the unmimetic, the coming of a new kind of language confidently parting ways with both the enigmatic epigrams of soothsayers and the monosyllabic pre-Islamic *qaṣīda* with its conventional themes of departed lovers and abandoned campsites, while carrying human thought and imagination as far as it can reach.

By calling the Qur'ān unmimetic, I don't mean simply that it is inimitable, or that is not based in reality. In most cases, the Qur'ān *represents* reality, but it also delineates metaphysical concepts that do not exist in the material world. Its melody does not offer a resolution to the representational dissonance of the Arabic language. Not at all. Its rhythmical orality, though not poetic, is capable of painting an image of what does not represent or imitate reality, whereas poetry, pre-Islamic poetry that is, cannot represent things outside its material reality. The Qur'ān does not imitate. In fact, even reference to its language is in the final analysis the negation of that language. One cannot imagine that Noah, Moses, or Jesus, for instance, spoke Arabic, or that their sayings in the Qur'ān are direct Arabic quotations. Yet the Arabic language of the Qur'ān still has nonmimetic elements that are only specific to itself. Although some prophetic narratives in the Qur'ān are known to former scriptures, the Qur'ān is capable of embroidering them on a larger canvas, allowing their interior dialogic configurations to work in a new nonrepresentational manner. This reiterative narrative configuration is itself a direct result of the Qur'ān's unmimetic character, which differs remarkably from the Bible as well as from its surrounding Arabicity. At is core, the Qur'ān is a very different text from the Torah and the Gospels in its eschewal of narrative, which fundamentally complicates any accusation of borrowing. In addition, the promising perpetuation of its presence, coupled with the power of its rhetorical imagery, which reaches beyond the mere replication of human senses, reaffirms the inevitability of its own misreading: *wa mā ya'lamu ta'wīlahu illā Allāh Allāh* (only God knows its intended meaning).[48]

THE QUR'ĀN AND PRE-ISLAMIC POETRY: THE POINT OF VIEW

As we saw earlier, readings of pre-Islamic Arabic poetry and the Qur'ān demonstrate two different discursive modes of linguistic expressions. In poetry, there is a transparent secularity, a point of view that is both individualistic and tribal, embracing the ground, the ruins, the departed encampment, the rocks, and the sand. In this point of view, a whole tradition materializes in its representation of human losses and vulnerabilities against forces of nature, engendering sympathy. Poetry, freed from theological concerns, can accomplish this radical autonomy, and hence achieve its own truth. Between the two discourses in which secularization renders poetry relatable and theologization renders the Qur'ān fearful, there is always room for variation. The Qur'ān is keen on representing divine providence as truth, but as truth that takes place in the name of concrete lived realities and social conditions of the common people in the seventh-century Arabian Peninsula. Let us take as a case in point the representation of "rain" in both pre-Islamic poetry and the Qur'ān. In the Qur'ān, rain is a major sign of divine providence. There are at least fifty verses that dwell on this relationship almost compulsively,[49] both to emphasize a tangible link between heaven and earth and to present this link in theological rather than poetical terms. Representations of rain in the Qur'ān, unlike, say, in Imru' al-Qays, focus on creating and maintaining a conscious bond between divinity and humans, a phenomenology of faith, so to speak, one that comes with a deep theological presupposition, at times conditional, and at times unconditional, as in the following verses:

وَهُوَ ٱلَّذِى يُنَزِّلُ ٱلْغَيْثَ مِنْ بَعْدِ مَا قَنَطُواْ وَيَنشُرُ رَحْمَتَهُ ⁵⁰

And he is the one who sends down rain after they relinquished hope, spreading his mercy. (42:28)

وَهُوَ ٱلَّذِى يُرْسِلُ ٱلرِّيَٰحَ بُشْرًا بَيْنَ يَدَىْ رَحْمَتِهِ ۖ حَتَّىٰ إِذَآ أَقَلَّتْ سَحَابًا ثِقَالًا سُقْنَٰهُ لِبَلَدٍ مَّيِّتٍ فَأَنزَلْنَا بِهِ ٱلْمَآءَ فَأَخْرَجْنَا بِهِ مِن كُلِّ ٱلثَّمَرَٰتِ ۚ كَذَٰلِكَ نُخْرِجُ ٱلْمَوْتَىٰ لَعَلَّكُمْ تَذَكَّرُونَ

He is the one who sends the winds carrying good news in the hands of his mercy. When they are loaded with heavy clouds, we drive them to a barren land whereupon we cause the water to fall down, thus producing all kinds of fruit. This is the same manner in which we resurrect the dead, so hopefully you will remember. (7:57)

In a desert environment like the Arabian Peninsula, the belief that God won't abandon his creation to death or drought could not be more compelling. Furthermore, by making it possible for humans to contemplate and appreciate God's sacred signs in nature, the theologizing power of the Qur'ān emerges to render God, the giver of life and rain, likeable and worthy of worship. With Imru' al-Qays, "the point of view" of the poet brings forth a completely different set of emotions, such as pity, fear, and sympathy, in the face of a torrential rain storm:

أَصِنّي عَلى بَرقٍ أَراهُ وَميضِ   يُضيءُ حَبِيّاً في شَماريخَ بيضِ

وَيَهدَأُ تاراتٍ سَناهُ وَتارَةً   يَنوءُ كَتَعتابِ الكَسيرِ المَهيضِ

وَتَخرُجُ مِنهُ لامِعاتٌ كَأَنَّها   أَكُفٌّ تَلَقّى الفَوزَ عِندَ المَفيضِ

قَعَدتُ لَهُ وَصُحبَتي بَينَ ضارِجٍ   وَبَينَ تِلاعٍ يَثلُثٍ فَالعَريضِ

أَصابَ قَطاتَينِ فَسالَ لِواهُما   فَوادي البَدِيِّ فَانتَحى لِلأَريضِ ⁵¹

Help me against this lightning which I see flashing / casting light on a thick cloud on white mountain peaks.
Sometimes its flashes sit still and sometimes / they stagger forth again like a limping camel with a broken foot.
The flashes dart out shining as if they were / hands of a gambler winning a game of arrow when lots are thrown.
I had to wait it out as my fellows were stuck between Dārij / and the streams of Yathluth and al- ʿAriḍ.
It hit Qaṭātān whose sand dunes started to collapse / then the valley of al-Badiyy, then it moved toward Arīḍ.

While Imru' al-Qays's experience of torrential rain in the desert may not necessarily evoke faith, hope, or salvation as the Qur'ān does, it still makes him humanly relatable. It is the sharing of the suffering of humans that makes literature possible: a stranded traveler caught in a rainstorm that separates him from his companions, lighting up the sky and bringing down torrential rain and gushing streams of water powerful enough to force reptiles to higher grounds and shift the topography of his surroundings before his eyes. Imru' al-Qays's point of view exposes human helplessness against the awesome power of nature. In this all too human portrayal of the ravages of a rainstorm, the fearful power of nature engenders a sense of humility and prompts him to recognize his own mortality and to recall his estranged sister, making him wish the rain could reach her so she could drink from its water. This earth-to-sky point of view is the only technical choice Imru' al-Qays has, given his earthly perspective on the lightning and his physical/visual experience of the rainstorm while on the ground. Yet poetic imagination allows for an emotive disparity and scenic shift in the moving reference to his sister. Here, the poetic tableau transcends mere phenomenology and enfolds a profound empathy, woven from the threads of memory and the longing for reunion. It crafts a poignant juxtaposition between the formidable might of nature and the tender fragility of human bonds, especially the innate yearning for sibling connection. In these lines, the poet, unable to traverse the vast distance to his sister, seeks solace in the communion of their spirits through verse, channeling his wish for their reconnection into a silent prayer that his words might bridge the gap, bringing them together in the ethereal meeting place of poetry.:

أَريضَةٌ مَدافِعُ غَيثٍ في فَضاءٍ عَريضٍ   بِلادٌ عَريضَةٌ وَأرضٌ

يَحوزُ الضِبابَ في صَفاصِفَ بيضٍ   فَأَضحى يَسُحُّ الماءَ عَن كُلِّ فَيقَةٍ

وَإذ بَعُدَ المَزارُ غَيرَ القَريضِ[52]   فَأَسقي بِهِ أُختي ضَعيفَةً إذ نَأَت

Measureless land, fecund soil /channels of water bursting on an infinite space.
Water streaming from all of its udders, forcing lizards into barren plains.
May the water reach my sister, Ḍaʿīfa, who moved away / and is too far to visit, except
through poetry.

In the Qur'ān, however, the point of view is from the sky to the earth. Lightning happens and rain comes down (*anzalnā*, we have brought down), not as a result of an incalculable behavior of nature. Whereas Imru' al-Qays likens lightning to the capricious and seemingly meaningless staggering of a hurt camel, the Qur'ān depicts rain as a well-designed act of divine grace, bringing "life" down to earth in the form of water:

هُوَ الَّذِي يُرِيكُمُ الْبَرْقَ خَوْفًا وَطَمَعًا وَيُنْشِئُ السَّحَابَ الثِّقَالَ

> He is the one who makes you all see the lightning in fear and hope, and he initiates
> the heavy clouds. (13:12)

Imru' al-Qays may know that the powers that be did not cause the lightning to be viewed only by him or the rain to fall specifically for the sake of his sister, Ḍaʿīfa, but the Qur'ān makes this point pronouncedly clear. Rain is not just for one, but for all, created and brought forth and intended as an act of heavenly hospitality, which is meant to evoke gratitude among humankind. Yet, not all Qur'ānic rain is good for humans; not all rain is a wish for sharing the watery bounty with a sibling; and certainly not every low cloud brings good rain for a waste land. Some rain, like the ones brought down on the people of 'Ād, and Lot, comes as clouds (and winds) of retribution and divine vengeance:

وَأَمْطَرْنَا عَلَيْهِم مَّطَرًا ۖ فَسَآءَ مَطَرُ ٱلْمُنذَرِينَ

And we rained down on them a shower [of brimstone], and wicked was the rain on those who had been warned. (26:173)

فَلَمَّا رَأَوْهُ عَارِضًا مُّسْتَقْبِلَ أَوْدِيَتِهِمْ قَالُوا۟ هَٰذَا عَارِضٌ مُّمْطِرُنَا ۚ بَلْ هُوَ مَا ٱسْتَعْجَلْتُم بِهِ ۖ رِيحٌ فِيهَا عَذَابٌ أَلِيمٌ

And when they saw a low, dense cloud approaching their valley, they said [rejoicing], "this cloud is bringing us rain." Nay, it is what you asked [your prophet, in mockery] to hasten: a wind carrying painful punishment. (46:24)

Readers of the Qur'ān are thus brought to see these signs and the concomitant mixtures of hope and hopelessness that seem to call into question every perceivable natural phenomenon. The perspectival subjectivism that allows Imru' al-Qays to internalize his encounter with the rainstorm and insert himself and his sister into the mix of its action is transformed in the Qur'ān into a radical departure from individualism. This postindividualistic discontinuity with the first-person pronoun in favor of a syntactic plurality is paradoxical in the sense that its very plurality, while imposing a collective look at the world rather than one person's way of interpreting it, does not exonerate ethical accountability on the individual level. Natural phenomena have a way of bringing humanity together in empathy. Just like Imru' al-Qays, himself a young king who lost his father and his own kingship, prays for his absent sister, so does Shakespeare's King Lear, a stranded king in the middle of a tempestuous rainstorm, insist that his fool get into the shelter first:

> This tempest will not give me leave to ponder
> On things would hurt me more. But I'll go in.—In, boy; go first.—
> You houseless poverty—
> Nay, get thee in. I'll pray, and then I'll sleep.[53]

There are numerous examples in world literature that portray this common formulation of empathy and subjectivity, one in which human identification with suffering, without any divine plan for salvation or any expectations of it in a promised afterworld, becomes the most essential element of our common existence, as humanity continues to seek meaning in and from this world, meaning that appears in subjective, even random representations of acts of kindness, blessings, or good wishes for fellow humans.

Yet the language of the Qur'ān, intentionally or not, decenters this subjectivity altogether. Pre-Islamic poetry is known to be both individualistic and tribalist, and even to such a symbolic degree that the history of pre-Islamic Arabia it represents is tribo-centric. The Qur'ān's purpose is to dissolve this tribal centrality into a shared and diverse collectivity. In this particular sense, the Qur'ān presents itself as a solution for shattered subjectivities, one that offers a transcendence of individualism and a unification of humanity under a monotheistic ideal. This monotheistic ideal is cognizant of human commonalities and keen on administering social justice and protecting the weak, the poor, and the vulnerable, who, in the context of Muḥammad's early stages of prophethood, appear to be victims of a fallen and uncivil commerce-based society. With a view toward this ideal, the Qur'ān promotes social justice with a deep and unrelenting egalitarian spirit. It calls for a communal space committed to principles of equality, where everyone is required to perform the same duties without the elitism of religious hierarchies, where *zakā* (almsgiving) and *iḥsān* (charity) aim to close the gap of inequality between rich and poor, and where every human, in principle, should be treated equally. This ideal community derives its substance, first and foremost, from filtered communal conduct and moral character of *al-ṣāliḥūn* (good people)[54] who do *al-ṣāliḥāt* (good deeds),[55] thus making these ethics both achievable and meaningful. In the larger context, divine articulations of rain are thus overwhelmingly symptomatic of the theological itinerary of the entire Qur'ān, wherein all earthly phenomena (sky, clouds, land, wind, mountains, crops, seas, oceans, rivers, animals, humans, birds, etc.) are signs and manifestations of the same divine intentionality.

Unlike the Qur'ān, pre-Islamic poetry is mimetic, but its mimesis is honed by the complexity of its poetic technique, its multiple rhyme schemes, and its balanced verses, where the meter of each hemistich has to work in harmony with its figures and expressions. The emotional and linguistic effort exerted in the making of the pre-Islamic *qaṣīda* is the *raison d'être* of its everlasting eloquence and beauty. There are occasions when pre-Islamic poetry addresses postmortem concepts. For instance, in his panegyric of Haram ibn Sinān, the prince and master of Banū Dhubyān (d. 608), Zuhayr ibn Abī Sulmá concludes his poem with a sagacious commentary on the concept of eternity. Zuhayr reminds the prince that praiseworthy deeds do not make him eternal and that the best preparation for eternity after death lies in leaving behind a memory of good deeds that his offspring can emulate and commemorate him with. Eternity in pre-Islamic Arabic simply meant a remembrance that carries through generations. The lesson for a lasting commemoration, which Zuhayr depicts quite poetically by repeating the Arabic root *kh/l/d*, implying "eternity" twice, lies in mimesis: a compulsive emulation of the good deed delineated through a compulsive repetition of a longing for eternity, not life after death, but a legacy on the border of a lip, an enunciation that repeats, persistently, that which it aspires for:

ولكنَّ حمدَ النَّاسِ ليس بمخلدِ   فلو كان حمدٌ يخلدُ النَّاسَ لم يمت

فأورِث بنيك بعضها وتزود   ولكن منه باقياتٍ وارثةً

ولو كرهته النفس آخر موعد[56]   تزود إلى يوم الممات فإنه

> If praised deeds make people immortal, they shall not die / but people's praise does
>   not make one immortal.
> It is the good deeds that leave a lasting memory of / so bequeath them to your
>   offspring and save some for yourself.
> Save them for the day of your death, for it is, to your displeasure, your last date.

Zuhayr's view on eternity may be secular or pragmatic, but it could also be ascetic and penitent. Either way, unlike Shakespeare, who wastes no time in boasting about the immortal quality of his poetry (e.g., Sonnets 18, 55), Zuhayr uses poetry to portray a different kind of immortalization: the good deeds that live in people's hearts after death. In Shakespeare, eternity begins and ends in poetry. In Zuhayr, poetry is the space of wisdom, the reminder that if a form of eternity were ever to be granted, people have to perform good deeds and their children have to live up to and emulate them. The Qur'ān, however, presents eternity as *das Kapital* of God's monotheistic promise, where the certainty of immortality is a central motif. It is, however, an eternity that could go either way, unless God decides otherwise. In hell, there is eternal torture without break,[57] whereas paradise offers endless life and *wildānun mukhalladūn* (eternalized offspring)[58] without the corruption of the body.[59]

If anything, it is evident that pre-Islamic Arabs developed a unique taste for rhetorical brilliance and a deep appreciation for poetic genius. It is easy to convict pre-Islamic poetry of a lack of religious import and deem it irrelevant, or even antithetical to the Qur'ān, as did al-Bāqillānī. But to do so is to forget that its very poeticity decisively establishes the fate of its signification and meaning as a socio-aesthetic pretext to the Qur'ān. Pre-Islamic poetry is obviously not a derivative of theology, as Ṭāhā Ḥusayn has duly noted in his book *Fī al-Shiʿr al-Jahilī* (On Pre-Islamic poetry), nor does it have to be. But what Ḥusayn misses is that pre-Islamic poetry is relevant and significant not because of the absence of theology, but because it puts theology on trial and because theology, at least in the classical Arabic tradition, does not have a monopoly on aesthetics. Unlike the Qur'ān, *Jāhilī* poetry is not fully integrated and not fully cosmological, while remaining beautiful. *Jāhilī* poetry is not an artwork in the Kantian sense of "purposelessness," because it wholeheartedly embraces an empirical reality, serving a telos that is paramount for self-preservation. This is not the sort of poetry that loses itself to subjectivity. It neither subscribes to Wordsworth's formula of poetry as a spontaneous overflow of powerful feelings or emotions recollected in tranquility. Nor does it adhere to T. S. Eliot's understanding of poetry an escape from emotions. Nor again is the *Jāhilī* poet like the Dutch poet Willem Kloos, for whom art is "de allerindividueelste expressie van de allerindividueelste emotie" (the most individualized expression of the most individualized emotion).[60] Otherwise, one would have learned nothing from Suzanne Stetkevych's insights into the ritualistic nature of the pre-Islamic *qaṣīda*. The lyrical "I" in the poem stands for everybody, and very often the poem resembles (though Stetkevych would say "is") a rite of passage from isolation to reaggregation into the community,[61] which is no sociohistorical accident but conforms rather with the actual state of things, a literary production sensitive not only toward every element of nature and every emotion, but every tool of culture that enhances and celebrates its tradition. *Jāhilī* poetry sacrifices the metaphysical, even the historical, for the sake of the earthly, the singular, and the collective. When a poem eschews eternity or refrains from espousing any teleological meaning to life, when its expression is all too human, this expression *becomes* aesthetically meaningful precisely because it is not theological.

MUḤAMMAD AND THE POETS IN THE QUR'ĀN

Seventh-century Mecca was a booming trade center of northwestern Arabia and a hub for all kinds of business, including winemaking, craftsmanship of sacred statues, and trade in slaves.[62] Recall how Ṭarafa describes his drinking buddies in his ode: "My drinking mates are white, like the stars." This qualification is crucial for an understanding of the racist practices and ideologies of pre-Islamic Arabia. Mecca amassed its fortune by selling all kinds of slaves. Ṭarafa boasts that he is in the company of white people, who, by virtue of their skin color alone, are free—meaning not owned by any master in Mecca who would tell them what to do or where to go. Black is the color of enslavement. Just a few minutes' worth of reading 'Antara's ode would shock the reader into the racist impertinence of pre-Islamic Mecca's "white supremacy" *avant la lettre*. But in the interest of time and space, this brief reference to Ṭarafa's delineation of his "drinking buddies" as white would suffice. Ṭarafa likens the whiteness of his drinking companions to the stars, already a trope that links high power and authority with whiteness. Those white people are free to drink and free, possibly, to sleep with the "singing girl," who "comes to us late in a robe and a revealing garment." The Arabic word *mujassad*, which describes the female singer's garment, could mean a "revealing garment," or a "tight dress" that reveals her body. Her relationship to her white drinking customers is that of subservience, sexualization, and servitude. The verb *tarūḥu* is key, because it puts her in a position of servitude, whether in waiting on them, singing for them, or giving herself to them. The Arabic word *qīnatun* is rich in connotations. It varies in meaning between "female singer," "dressing servant," "a hairdresser who keeps her hair straight and well-combed," and "a slave woman." In this context, it is not hard to know what Ṭarafa had in mind with his reference *qīnatun*. In the poem *qayna* means "a singing girl, who is a slave." The original sense of *qayn* is "artisan, craftsman" and often "smith," but in this sense a *qayna* is never a smith, of course, and always a singer (often also an instrumentalist). In this narrow sense, she is a craftswoman, and possibly a *māshiṭa* (hairdresser), but it does not seem that Ṭarafa employed her to comb his and his companions' hair. In this poem, she is a singer (*idhā naḥnu qulnā asmi 'īna inbarat lanā . . .*) and she is obviously also a sex object (*bi-jassi l-nadāmā baḍḍatu l-mutajarridī*). What is also clear is that she cannot be a free woman. Ṭarafa's sexualized female singer is a slave woman serving under the mercy, power, and capricious virility of a group of intoxicated starry-white men.[63] She is not alone. Slaves who were poor and dependent on their masters for everything formed a considerable (though politically insignificant) portion of the seventh-century Meccan population. Although the Qur'ān does not categorically abolish slavery, social justice, equity, human dignity, and freedom are all embedded in its ethos, making it, at least for its own historical time, a sanctuary for the enslaved, the impoverished, and the deprived precisely because it unequivocally states that there is no difference among humans:

كَانَ النَّاسُ أُمَّةً وَاحِدَةً فَبَعَثَ اللَّهُ النَّبِيِّينَ مُبَشِّرِينَ وَمُنذِرِينَ وَأَنزَلَ مَعَهُمُ الْكِتَابَ بِالْحَقِّ لِيَحْكُمَ بَيْنَ النَّاسِ فِيمَا اخْتَلَفُوا فِيهِ

> Humankind was one sole nation then God sent prophets to bring forth good tidings and to caution them, and with them he sent down the scripture in truth to decree among humankind on the matters they disagreed on. (2:213)

Difference in color is a sign of divine grace, just like the diversity of the planet:

وَمِنْ آيَاتِهِ خَلْقُ السَّمَاوَاتِ وَالْأَرْضِ وَاخْتِلَافُ أَلْسِنَتِكُمْ وَأَلْوَانِكُمْ ۚ إِنَّ فِي ذَٰلِكَ لَآيَاتٍ لِّلْعَالِمِينَ

> And among his signs are the creation of the heavens and the earth and the difference of your tongues and your colors. In these are signs for the knowledgeable ones. (30:22)

These verses have two themes in common: difference and learning. The address is to all humankind, who have different views on life, speak different languages, and who come in different skin colors. Thus, in seventh-century Arabia, Muḥammad, whose character is always in sync with the terms and spirit of the Qur'ān, condemns in the strongest possible terms all forms of racism and racial supremacy, declaring that all humans are equal before God and responsible for their own deeds:

لا فضلَ لعربيٍّ على عجميٍّ ، ولا لعجميٍّ على عربيٍّ ، ولا لأبيضَ على أسودَ ، ولا لأسودَ على أبيضَ إلَّا بالتَّقْوَى. النَّاسُ من آدمَ ، وآدمُ من تراب.[64]

> There is no superiority of an Arab over a non-Arab, a non-Arab over an Arab, a white person over a black person, or a black person over white person . . . except in piety. You all descend from Adam and Adam comes from dust.

As the first Meccan immigrants begin to settle and comingle with inhabitants of Medina, the Qur'ān commends them as upholding the good and prohibiting evil and celebrates them as an egalitarian community set against political systems of surrounding cultures.[65] Perhaps for the first time in human history, a book prescribes the establishment of an equitable and just community, a society without racism. But to be sure, it was still a society that did not abolish slavery, which begs the question if it is at all possible for slavery to exist without racism. The Qur'ān does not answer this question. Rather, it vehemently condemns the mistreatment of women as it persistently calls for the setting free of slaves. In other words, the Qur'ān acknowledges individual distinctions among people in the status and degree of wealth, including the ownership of slaves, while holding them all equally accountable under a monotheistic banner. Historical communities of Islam did uphold the institution of slavery and for centuries treated women as a subordinate class. On balance, though, it is fair to state that the Qur'ān is the first book in history to afford women inheritance and divorce rights as well as to accept their testimonies as legally viable. While the Qur'ān neither bans slavery nor puts women on an equal footing with men, embedded in its verses is the North Star for the abolition of slavery[66] and gender equality.[67]

This social prehistory of seventh-century Mecca and Medina is crucial for the reception of the Qur'ān in the Arabian Peninsula. Still, the Qur'ān speaks of a poor and desperate population of this particular society, a population forced into labor and slavery; of families killing their offspring out of squalor, or in fear of it; of innocent female children being buried alive; and of the injustices of *Jāhiliyya* codes. Apart from the sympathetic portrayal of poverty in the Qur'ān, the other notable aspect of its metanarrative is that the rich and slave-owning class is equally portrayed as no less "impoverished" than the poor and the slaves they are oppressing. Thus, a shared ethos of empathy and compassion among all classes is advocated throughout the Qur'ān, founded on a common abomination of a faceless *Shayṭān* (Satan) who tirelessly seeks to inflict division, antagonism, hatred, and war among humans. This revolutionary subversive stratagem of what superficially appears to be a conventional struggle between the poor and the rich reflects the genuine evolution of a new form of oral authority, a call for a just society in which the working class, the middle class, and the upper class are all invited to unite and fight the temptations of a hostile and nefarious devil.

From its early sūras, the Qur'ān sides definitively with Mecca's poor and underprivileged population. To reinforce its message, the early Meccan Qur'ān, or what is known in Qur'ānic studies as Mecca I,[68] includes brief and concise sūras with a chilling eschatological and apocalyptic tone. Rich yet nebulous in their stylistic use of language to depict heaven, hell, and prophetic narratives, these embryonic sūras could be mistaken for what is already out there—that is, *qiṭaʿ shiʿrīyya* (poetic fragments of a standard pre-Islamic form) used mostly for oracular utterances. In general, Meccan sūras rely on similes and stylistic features familiar to the local color and life of pre-Islamic Arabia in order to approximate the meaning of the Qur'ān while still making it original and easy to memorize.

Thus, the terrifying destruction of the people of ʿĀd depicts them like *aʿjāzu nakhlin khāwiya* (hollow palm trees trunks),[69] evil doers who run away from the call of God are likened to *ḥumurun mustanfira farrat min qaswara* (spooked donkeys running away from a lion).[70] Most of the Qur'ān's language contains relatable and identifiable imagery of this type. This recognizable elemental imagery is consistent with the message of the Qur'ān, since the success of the call for monotheism is predicated on its appeal to the contextual linguistic and literary sensibilities of its receivers. In this case, the Qur'ān's early sūras are appealing enough to be conflated with the language or soothsayers or poets, a conflation that the Qur'ān vehemently and insistently refutes on more than one occasion. Whether the reference is to soothsayers who spoke in cryptic سجع (rhymed prose) or poets who composed short pieces or longer odes, the Qur'ān makes it clear that its content is not soothsaying or poetry and that Muḥammad is not a soothsayer or a poet. Many of Muḥammad's accusers during the first years of his prophethood sought to "contain" his message by attributing it to something familiar, something already there; some even accused him of being a literate man,[71] who writes down stories from the past:

وَقَالُوا أَسَاطِيرُ الْأَوَّلِينَ اكْتَتَبَهَا فَهِيَ تُمْلَىٰ عَلَيْهِ بُكْرَةً وَأَصِيلًا

And they said, "These are the written fables of ancient people which he wrote down and which are dictated to him day and night." (25:5)

If proven true, such accusations would immediately eliminate the seriousness of the Qur'ān as a divine scripture and would consequently demote Muḥammad's claim of prophethood to the claim of a deranged soothsayer, or even a wannabe poet who would often represent his clan, but who this time went off on an ambitious tangent, lost his mind, and would eventually perish on his own. In particular, the Qur'ān's reference to poetry and poets is pithy, but quite resolute and firm. The noun *shiʿr* (poetry) appears only once in the following verse, where the speaker is the first person honorific "we" for God. This is one of two times God speaks directly about the subject—rebuffing, in the this first instance, the possibility that Muḥammad was even taught the craft of poetry and confirming the divinity, as opposed to the "poeticity," of the Qur'ānic message:

وَمَا عَلَّمْنَاهُ ٱلشِّعْرَ وَمَا يَنۢبَغِى لَهُ ۚ إِنْ هُوَ إِلَّا ذِكْرٌ وَقُرْءَانٌ مُّبِينٌ

And we did not teach him poetry, nor is it appropriate for him. This is a scripture and a clear Qur'ān. (36:69)

The noun *shāʿir* (poet) appears four times in the following verses:

بَلْ قَالُوا أَضْغَاثُ أَحْلَامٍ بَلِ افْتَرَاهُ بَلْ هُوَ شَاعِرٌ فَلْيَأْتِنَا بِآيَةٍ كَمَا أُرْسِلَ الْأَوَّلُونَ

Rather they said "[this scripture is nothing but] dream ramblings; or rather, he has fabricated it; or rather, he is a poet. Let him [if he is truthful] then bring us a sign as did the foregoing ones." (21:5)

وَيَقُولُونَ أَئِنَّا لَتَارِكُوا آلِهَتِنَا لِشَاعِرٍ مَّجْنُونٍ

And they say, "Are we to forsake our gods for the sake of a mad poet?" (37:36)

أَمْ يَقُولُونَ شَاعِرٌ نَتَرَبَّصُ بِهِ رَيْبَ الْمَنُونِ ۚ قُلْ تَرَبَّصُوا فَإِنِّي مَعَكُم مِّنَ الْمُتَرَبِّصِينَ

Or they would say, [he is] "a poet, let us wait till he meets his fateful death." Say "then wait, I will wait with you as well." (52:30–31)

وَمَا هُوَ بِقَوْلِ شَاعِرٍ ۚ قَلِيلًا مَّا تُؤْمِنُونَ

And it is not the saying of a poet; little do you believe. (69:41)

The noun *shu'arā'* (poets) appears only once in the following verse sequence, marking the second time God speaks directly about the subject, in denunciation of the poets as untruthful:

وَالشُّعَرَاءُ يَتَّبِعُهُمُ الْغَاوُونَ. أَلَمْ تَرَ أَنَّهُمْ فِي كُلِّ وَادٍ يَهِيمُونَ. وَأَنَّهُمْ يَقُولُونَ مَا لَا يَفْعَلُونَ

And the poets, they are followed by those who are tempted. Can't you see that in every valley they roam. And that they say what they do not do? (26:224–26)

The assertion that Muḥammad is not a poet is crucial for a basic understanding of the relationship between the Qur'ān and the former's designation as a prophet. In other words, the Qur'ān advances an understanding that it includes a nonmortal sublimity. Such understanding has a compelling connection to the meaning that the Qur'ān's language seeks to achieve. We see this sublimity celebrated with vigor in apologetic discourses as well as in the Sufi tradition, where rhetorical readings are geared toward revealing not only a *ẓāhir* (surface or external meaning) but also a *bāṭin* (internal or hidden meaning). This is why the Qur'ān dissociates itself so forcefully from poetry. On its own terms, it cannot be poetry and cannot be measured against it.

In pre-Islamic poetry, the distinctive themes and tropes eventually blend into one predictable and linear gestalt. Even the structure of the *qaṣīda* follows a preordained rhetorical course of linearity. The Qur'ān's sublimity, however, consists in its very occupation with a theological aesthetic, one in which the word envelopes the world and upholds a monotheistic meaning to life in the Abrahamic tradition, for one last time. Against this verdict of sublimity, poetry stands as a reproducible art, so to speak. In this context, pre-Islamic poetry, known in Arabic literary tradition as *fann al-'Arabiyya al-awwal* (the primary art of the Arabic language), finds itself, for the first time in its history, the subject of a negative aesthetics, a subject that al-Bāqillānī carried too far. To be sure, something in the Qur'ān is incompatible with the semblance and character of pre-Islamic poetry, not necessarily because of the claims the Qur'ān has on the poets but because poetry comes into being as a subjective semblance of art, a mark of the poet's mimetic capacity to form meaningful and symmetrically balanced verses. In other words, whereas poetry is mimetic, the Qur'ān transcends mimesis altogether. Not only that, it even confronts mimesis directly:

أَمْ يَقُولُونَ افْتَرَاهُ ۖ قُلْ فَأْتُوا بِعَشْرِ سُوَرٍ مِّثْلِهِ مُفْتَرَيَاتٍ وَادْعُوا مَنِ اسْتَطَعْتُم مِّن دُونِ اللَّهِ إِن كُنتُمْ صَادِقِينَ

Or they would say he fabricated it. Say, then, bring forth ten fabricated sūras like it and call upon [for assistance] whomever could help you besides God, if you are truthful. (11:13)

Note that the verb-subject-object sentence *iftarāhu* (he fabricated it) in 11:13 is synonymous with the act of making poetry and of becoming a *shāʿir* (a poet) in 25:5. The Qur'ān says basically that poetry is *makeable* and reproducible because of its mimetic nature, whereas the Qur'ān is irreproducible. The correspondence the Qur'ān evokes between poets and the telling of lies is uncannily Platonic. In distinguishing itself from poetry, the Qur'ān states its condition as *muʿjiz* (incapacitating, inimitable, irreproducible). This distinction clashes with the Qur'ān's claims about the poets—namely, "they say what they do not do."[72]

The above condemnation brings to mind the famous Platonic dialogue about the harmful mimesis of poetry. In the Western canon, the notion of mimesis belongs to a long traditional chain that goes back to Plato and Aristotle, where the use of language for purposes other than to communicate literal truth is denigrated in the context of universal moral values.

Plato offers a critical examination of poetry, recognizing its mimetic nature while expressing concern for its potential to do more harm than good. Rather than outright scorn, he perceives it as a powerful medium that, without careful scrutiny, may lead audiences away from the pursuit of truth. Plato is a pioneering figure in linking the analysis of language to social phenomena, acknowledging the societal implications of the spoken word. He draws a significant distinction between the imitative function of poetry and the noble quest for truth, a higher moral endeavor. In the *Republic*, particularly through the allegory of the cave, and also in dialogues like the *Phaedrus*, Plato discriminates between the beneficial and detrimental uses of language. The latter dialogue, in particular, distinguishes the soul-nourishing power of eloquent rhetoric from the seductive but deceptive charm of mere sophistry:

> Socrates: when a speaker who does not know the difference between good and evil tries to convince a people as ignorant as himself—by representing evil as in fact good, and by a careful study of popular notions succeeds in persuading them to do evil instead of good, what kind of harvest do you think his rhetoric will reap from the seed he has sown?[73]

The Qur'ān's concept of language, like Plato's, is primarily an eclectic one, making it a vehicle for delivering truth and exercising justice as a communal social principle. In Islam, *al-Ḥaqq* (truth/the true one) is one of the names of God,[74] an attribute that is emphatically synonymous with the Qur'ān in contradistinction to poetry. The poets in Plato's critiques and those depicted in the Qur'ān share a certain mimetic quality that is criticized for its potential to distort reality rather than to illuminate it. For Plato, this is because poets can create imitations that stray far from the world of the forms—the ultimate realm of truth—and thus misguide their audience by appealing to emotions over reason. Similarly, the Qur'ān cautions against those whose words are at odds with their actions, reflecting a reality that is corrupted by falsehoods. In both Platonic and Qur'ānic senses, truth is seen as a divine emanation: in Platonism, it is the world of forms, accessed through philosophical inquiry, while in the Qur'ān, truth is a revelation from God, delivered by al-Rūḥ al-Amīn (the Trustworthy Spirit, Gabriel) to the Prophet Muḥammad's heart.[75]

Although both the Qur'ānic and Platonic frameworks view truth as a higher reality and differ in their conceptions of the source and means of accessing this truth, they concur on the idea that truth exists beyond the ordinary human use of language. For Plato, language is an imitative tool that grapples with the shadows of forms, where the forms themselves are the only true reality, inaccessible in their purest form by means of physical representation. Similarly, the Qur'ān views language as a construction through which divine truth is conveyed, albeit imperfectly, by human standards. The real is not fully captured by human language, as it is an imitation of a divine reality. This presents a philosophical conundrum: language is both inadequate for and yet indispensable to conveying truth. The origin of language is pivotal; the truth can be transmitted through language only when the language is divinely inspired or philosophically precise. Thus, while truth is communicable via language, it transcends the embellishments of poetry, demanding instead a form of communication that is direct and unadorned by artistic performance.

The Qur'ān proclaims itself as coming from a completely different, unearthly, celestial source, a "sending down" in Arabic but in a manner that must never be confused with the contemporary discourse of poetry, which is also composed in that very language. There is, therefore, a strong historicity at work: the Qur'ān states that it is sent down in an inimitable Arabic to a prophet who speaks Arabic, in a society whose mother tongue is Arabic. And even though Arabic is a common denominator between pre-Islamic poetry and the Qur'ān, the latter not only distinguishes itself as non-poetry; it also challenges the Arabian community of the poets to come up with something like it.

Words in the Qur'ān name objects outside themselves. God, the Qur'ān tells us, teaches Adam the names of things and grants him the gift of language, a gift he denies the angels,[76] and a gift that could easily be abused if it were not divinely inspired. The Qur'ān thus conceives itself as both the tenor and vehicle of the words of God—inerrant, inimitable, and ultimately unmimetic. But because the lexical field in the Qur'ān is the same one for poetry, one must also infer that the Qur'ān, too, functions to create an ethos of intelligibility, given the clear recognition that the phonology, morphology, and syntax of Arabic are the foundation of a fundamental reference—namely, the belief that this language *represents* the reality of a world outside its text. This "world," in its seventh-century Arabian peninsular context, would be made up of audiences who are ultimately responsible for judging the aesthetic quality of the language they live by. In other words, if the Qur'ān were to be deemed rhetorically *mu'jiz* (inimitable/paralyzing/

incapacitating/unmimetic), it would only be so because its language appeals to a lofty sense of an aesthetic judgement *already* developed in its preformative tradition, where the language of God is still sensible to the mind but in a manner that has never materialized in language before. In other words, the Qur'ān *needs* poetry in order for the former's conceptual aesthetics distinctives to make sense. This is why al-Khaṭṭabī categorically rejects the plea of his predecessors that *I'jāz* is inexplicable to humans:

ولذلك إذا سئلوا عن تحديد هذه البلاغة التي اختص بها القرآن، الفائقة في وصفها سائر البلاغات، وعن المعنى الذي يتميز به عن سائر أنواع الكلام الموصوف بالبلاغة، قالوا إنه لا يمكننا تصويره ولا تحديده بأمر ظاهر نعلم به مباينة القرآن غيره من الكلام، و إنما يعرفه العالمون به عند سماعه ضربا من المعرفة لا يمكن تحديده . . .

قلت: وهذا لا يقنع في مثل هذا العلم، ولا يشفي من داء الجهل به، وإنما هو إشكال أحيل به على إبهام.[77]

If they were asked to define this *balāgha* which distinguishes the Qur'ān, and which surpasses all others, and to explain the sense in which the Qur'ān is distinct from other expressions [in Arabic] that are described as eloquent, they would say it cannot be depicted or defined in a clear manner that tells us exactly what the difference is between the Qur'ān and those other linguistic expressions. They would add that only the well-learned have access to this knowledge when they hear it—hermetic knowledge that cannot be explained . . . I would respond by saying that this excuse is neither acceptable for knowledge nor for the lack thereof. This is nothing but confusion added to misperception.

According to al-Khaṭṭabī, then, to say that the inimitability/incapacitation of the Qur'ān is inexplicable does not help someone to understand the Qur'ān. The inimitable is not the opposite of the explicable. But isn't the explicable necessarily mimetic? Al-Khaṭṭabī answers this question by stating that the reason for the Qur'ān's unmimesis lies in a simple yet ingenious formula:

اعلم أن القرآن إنما صار معجزاً لأنه جاء بأفصح الألفاظ في أحسن نظوم التأليف مضمناً أصح المعاني[78]

Know that the Qur'ān is inimitable because it blends together the most eloquent and exact of words with the most beautiful compositions and the most accurate meaning.

Al-Jurjānī would later expand al-Khaṭṭabī's notion of *aḥsan nuẓūm al-ta'līf* and mold it into a wholistic system of *balāgha* (rhetorical brilliance), *faṣāḥa* (eloquence), and *bayān* (clarity of expression), which comes together to constitute *naẓm*, a word that does not have a single English equivalent. *Naẓm* is the stylistic superiority and signification of the Qur'ān that combines *ma'ná* (meaning, ideas), *alfāẓ* (sounds/utterances), *kalim* (words), and *i'rāb* (grammar/sentence structure and case endings; etym. enunciation) into inimitable units of composition that achieve *I'jāz*.[79] The aesthetic dimensions of the Qur'ān's *naẓm*, which, in the Islamic tradition, is the core of its linguistic miracle, is inevitably tied to its distinction from poetry. This distinction led Navid Kermani to argue that the Qur'ān is not primarily or intentionally aesthetic. "The Qur'ān," writes Kermani, "is primarily and essentially concerned with communicating a non-aesthetic message so that it is accepted, not as beautiful, but as true."[80] There is some sense to Kermani's argument, which restores the Qur'ān to pure religiosity by separating what is true from what is beautiful, or by stating that the truth does not have to be beautiful. There is, however, a further complexity to this argument. When the English Romantic poet John Keats composed his famous lines, "'Beauty is truth, truth beauty,'—that is all/ Ye know on earth, and all ye need to know,"[81] he did not see the judgment of the beautiful as inseparable from that of the true. Even if one were to dismiss this Keatsian poeticity as idealist and naïve romanticism, there is something compellingly beautiful about truth and something inherently truthful about beauty, even if this truth is death itself, at least according to D. H. Lawrence.[82] In the Qur'ān, God attributes to himself not only beauty but the uniquely superhuman ability to create things out of nothing—that is, *ex nihilo*—and to originate matter through the power of the speech act of divine language:

بَدِيعُ السَّمَاوَاتِ وَالْأَرْضِ ۖ وَإِذَا قَضَىٰ أَمْرًا فَإِنَّمَا يَقُولُ لَهُ كُن فَيَكُونُ

> He is the unique creator of heavens and earth, and when he decides a matter, he simply says "Be" and it is. (2:117)

This creation from nothing subscribes to the Arabicity of the Qur'ān both its rhetorical and aesthetic supremacy, per al-Khaṭṭābī, over all other expressions known to the language, including the poetic. There is, to be sure, a remarkable difference between the rhetorical and the aesthetic in the Qur'ān, and even when the two have a way of becoming entangled, this difference makes the rhetorical the realm of pure form and the aesthetic the domain of content, interpretation, and appreciation. In German philosophical terms, which Kermani heavily cites in his examination of the acoustic affect of the Qur'ān, it is Kant who says aesthetics *can* reconcile pure and practical reason or link a priori judgement with sensuous perceptions.[83] It is therefore hard to agree with Kermani that the Qur'ān is "poetic" despite itself, so to speak, or that accepting the Qur'ān's reference to itself as nonpoetic would be like agreeing with Tolstoy's statement that "all his later works are unpoetic."[84] By leaning on Roman Jakobson's perspective, according to which "one does not believe a poet who, in the name of truth, the real world, or anything else, renounces his past in poetry or art,"[85] Kermani inadvertently weakens his own claim about the intrinsic "truth" of aesthetic experience.

Jakobson himself acknowledges the fluid and time-bound nature of poetry's content and concept, suggesting that "poeticity" arises when language is appreciated as an entity in itself, not merely as a vehicle for representation.[86] This "poeticity" manifests itself, according to Jakobson, "when the word is felt as a word and not as a mere representation of the object being named, when words and their composition, their meaning, their external and internal form, acquire a weight and a value of their own instead of referring indifferently to reality."[87]

While the words of the Qur'ān are powerful and resonant for adherents, they still-for the most part- refer to an external reality outside them. This dualism is indispensable for the Qur'ān, which defines itself as a "message." Such communicative or delivery principal alone puts the Qur'ān outside the Jakobsonian formula of poeticity, which seems to suggest a purely structuralist and aesthetic reading, or "listening" in Kermani's case. That the Qur'ān is not "poetry" or "poetic" does not at all mean that it is not "aesthetic." In Arabic parlance, neither is the aesthetic exclusively poetic nor is the poetic the only measure of the aesthetic.

It is in this specific Arabo-literary-linguistic framework, then, that the Qur'ān stands out differently, not as poetry, poetic, or even as "poeticity," yet still unrivalled in its aesthetic qualities. For its effect on its intended audience, the Qur'ān does not want to appear to be something more closely resembling an offshoot or a byproduct of a preexisting literary discourse. It would follow that polytheistic Meccans' confusion of the Qur'ān with poetry or soothsaying has something to do with the latter's presentation of an opposing monotheistic ideal in a different yet comparably rhymed language that "resembles" the ones they are familiar with. Against the accusations of similitude and identicalness, the Qur'ān, by negating its poeticity, is also saying that it is not the account of a mortal or a language crafted in this world, but a scripture "sent down by the one who knows the secrets of the heavens and the earth" (25:6). The moment the Qur'ān states that Muḥammad is not a poet is also the moment it affirms that he is a "messenger of God,"[88] assigned the divine task of "notifying"[89] and "reminding"[90] his people that he is only a prophet "sent to all humankind, a bringer of good tidings and a warner."[91] Where it dissociates itself from poeticity, the Qur'ān affirms prophethood, all through the medium of a shockingly new style and a unique genre. And while Kermani does not go so far as to say that other types of literary and artistic production—for example, prose or prose poetry—can also be deemed "aesthetic," it would seem embedded in his description that what has passed under the name of the "poetic" is at least for the Arabic literary canon so confining (in comparison to the European canon he draws upon) to the degree that it has no bearing on the expansive category of Arabic aesthetics.

In a socially symbolic fashion, a main reason for insisting that Muḥammad is not a poet, then, is that unlike the localized tribalism mixed with capricious individualism of pre-Islamic poetry, the Qur'ān presents itself as a *sur-tribal* revolutionary message aspiring to disassemble the status quo and rebuild afresh. When the Qur'ān was first heard as short sūras, some unversed Meccans thought the sūras were poetic fragments like the ones already in oral circulation, with nothing particularly special about them. This conflation, however, is rightly dismissed in al-Jurjānī's account of Ibn al-Mughīra's acknowledgement that the Arabs knew very well what is and what is not poetry and that what Muḥammad is saying does not at all resemble poetry.[92] To be sure, then, for the layman there are some overlaps and moments where the Qurʾān is initially confused with poetry.[93] Although the Qurʾān is its own unique genre, it would make some sense, at least for its very first hearers in Muḥammad's community, to conflate it with soothsaying or with poetry, the only similar-sounding oral discourses out there. This potential for overlapping emanates from the semi-oracular tone of the Qurʾān's early Meccan sūras, which may have led to partial confusion with the common pronouncements of pre-Islamic *kuhhān* (soothsayers). However, unlike the mundane and quotidian predictions of soothsayers, the Qurʾān's predictions, with few exceptions (e.g., 30:2–4, 48:16, 27),[94] are often otherworldly. The significance of the Qurʾān's prophecy lies mostly in something akin to what Emmanuel Levinas refers to as a *triachrony* of ethical inspiration: future and anticipation encompassing "an unparalleled thought, thinking more than it can contain," one that is dedicated to "a 'future aim' beyond what is to come [*l'a-venir*]."[95]

Another thematic difference between the two discourses lies in the fact that pre-Islamic poetry offers a content that is either a social history (a tribal exploit, a proud victory) or a personal experience (a mourning lover, an outcast)—in short, an aesthetic experience that must be reevoked and stylized after the fact. In the Qurʾān, it is the overarching transhistorical themes (e.g., the creation of the world, the absoluteness of God, the unmimetic *naẓm* of its language, and the creation of things from nothing) that govern the aesthetic force that suits its occasion and context.

Still, it is reductionist to argue that the Qurʾān eclipsed the literary and cultural constructions that preceded it, especially when the Qurʾān *uses* the same morphemes, idiomatic expressions, and grammar known and practiced by the Arabs of Muḥammad's time, poets and nonpoets alike. If anything, the Qurʾān *has to* make itself understood, even though it assertedly sets itself apart from the language of the poets. Many took this assertion too Platonically, meaning that poetry is evil, immoral, and untruthful. But the reference is to a particular brand of pre-Islamic poets who composed slanderous poetry that defamed character and honor, particularly poets who made a living by promoting prejudice, praising the corrupt rich, and lampooning the innocent or the poor, as we have seen from the above examples. In pure Platonic terms, the language of these poets does not speak truth. In classical and postclassical Islam, many a poet used their talent to craft poetry for political reasons, selling their words to the highest bidders among tribes and suiting their poems to the task. In the pre-Islamic culture, as well as in the post-Islamic polity of the caliphates, poetry was weaponized in tribal politics and dynastic rivalries. Poets composed invective and panegyrics for those who paid them. The Qurʾān calls these poets out precisely because of their empty rhetoric and untruthful sayings:

وَٱلشُّعَرَآءُ يَتَّبِعُهُمُ ٱلْغَاوُۥنَ أَلَمْ تَرَ أَنَّهُمْ فِى كُلِّ وَادٍ يَهِيمُونَ

And poets are followed by the enticed. Have you not seen that in every valley they ramble, and they say what they do not do? (26:224–26)

While the Qur'ān depicts the world in terms of good and evil, it is important to remember that it does not label all poets from the pre-Islamic era as insincere or false. This is explicitly stated in the subsequent verse that comes right after the rebuke of a particular type of poet:

إلا الذين آمنوا وعملوا الصالحات وذكروا الله كثيرا وانتصروا من بعد ما ظلموا

> Except for those who have believed and performed righteous deeds and brought up God frequently and who were vindicated after they were treated unjustly. (26:227)

A good example of this "exceptional" poetics is to be found in the works of Hassān ibn Thābit, Ka'b ibn Mālik, Ka'b ibn Zuhayr, 'Abd Allāh ibn Rawāḥa, and others who composed poetry with high moral codes and ethics, advocating virtue in a spirit that is more or less symbiotic with the general ethos of the Qur'ān. Here again, the juxtaposition with Plato is remarkable. Not all poets are banishable from Plato's ideal republic. He leaves a wiggle room for dramatic poetry that represents gods, heroes, and good men. Indeed, Plato's *Republic* still admits "good poets" engaged in "hymns about the gods and praises of good men."[96] In the context of the Qur'ān, the poetry characterized by ethical responsibility and adherence to high moral virtues stands as an exception to the customary critique. The idea is far from vague, especially for the Meccans of Muḥammad's time: ethical responsibility soars above the mundane materialism of the mortal world. The Qur'ān makes it clear that its moral code of virtue is what distinguishes between truth and error, thus opening up greater possibilities not only for justice and social healing in the seventh-century Meccan community but also for poets to continue to compose poetry, provided that their work upholds a high ethical standard.

This is why the ethico-aesthetic revolution of the Qur'ān is both original and formidable. The Qur'ān's primordial orality, its aesthetic property and thematic distinctness put it on a collision course with numerous pre-Islamic values and practices. Like pre-Islamic poetry, the Qur'ān celebrates its own Arabicity. Yet, unlike pre-Islamic poetry, this celebration is attached to an eschatological rhetoric, a function Kermani aptly characterizes as "teleological, in the purist sense of the word."[97] We see this teleology in the Qur'ān's reference to its own sending down in a clear Arabic tongue,[98] a sending conditionally attached to *balāghun mubīn* (a clear communication and conveyance of the divine message) as the only job all prophets have.[99]

The message of the Qur'ān is based precisely on a steadfast conviction that this world is not the end, but a test and a passage to *al-ḥayawān* (the real everlasting life that is yet to come, as opposed to this lower world of distraction and play).[100] But unlike the Qur'ān, pre-Islamic poetry has remained grounded in the earth while showing little interest in entertaining the supernatural or what awaits humanity after death, despite occasional solemn themes such as mourning, nostalgia, dejection, unrequited love, the transience of life, melancholy, and so on. Even the notion of "eternity" simply meant for pre-Islamic poets having enough wealth to live a good life and be "immortalized" in poetry or in annals that record the deeds and history of Arabs.

With the revelation of the Qur'ān, the authority of the highly stylized pre-Islamic poetry, which had reached a pinnacle of formal and aesthetic specialization by the outset of the seventh century, began to taper off. By the time the Qur'ān emerged, pre-Islamic poetry had developed its sagas, sung its heroes, and celebrated the aesthetic intelligence of its poets. Before long, the authority of pre-Islamic poets, who were once the recipients of the highest recognition as spokesmen for their tribes, slowly began to erode, giving way to a new oral authority. Instead of professional bards and reciters carrying each newly composed ode with zeal and admiration throughout the peninsula, adherents of the new faith were committing to their hearts each new verse and each new sūra of the Qur'ān and sharing it, enthusiastically and devotionally, with the rest of the world. Yet, to this day, pre-Islamic Arabic poetry remains for the Arabic philologist, grammarian, and exegete the one and only immediate, and therefore, the one and only completely authentic source for all syntactic, semantic, and phonological significations on whose basis the text of the Qur'ān is understood and appreciated.

MUḤAMMAD AND THE PROPHETS

In a recent study that delineates the geographical contours leading to the dawn of Islam, Maria Dakake reminds us that "the story of the revelation of the Qur'ān is, above all, 'a tale of two cities,' Mecca and Medina."[101] Dakake's study penetrates the rich topography of seventh-century Mecca and Medina to investigate a deep geo-theological history which, in accordance with the Qur'ān, as well as with Ḥadīth and Sīra literatures, attaches itself to a formative narrative that relates Abraham to the *Kaaba*. In a world in which geography and theology intermingle, the story of Abraham, writes Dakake, "aligns with some aspects of the biblical narrative of Hagar and Ishmael in Genesis but fully locates the story in the con-text of ancient Arabia, with its itinerant, tribal inhabitants."[102] Dakake's statement is a sobering reminder that seventh-century Mecca was not simply a poetry salon, but a realm for the sacred with all its iterative associations. It is within this interlaced geotheology that the Qur'ān relates Muḥammad to a series of monotheistic prophets, even identifying their teachings with his.[103] All prophetic narratives and conversations in the Qur'ān are dramatized in order to invite its audience to respond to its orality and participate in the events it recounts with intentionality. The Qur'ān narrates that thousands of years of committed monotheistic faith come to a culmination in Islam, with the discovery that "Islam," in its etymological sense—a submission of one's face to the will of God—has always already been there:

شَرَعَ لَكُم مِّنَ الدِّينِ مَا وَصَّىٰ بِهِ نُوحًا وَالَّذِي أَوْحَيْنَا إِلَيْكَ وَمَا وَصَّيْنَا بِهِ إِبْرَاهِيمَ وَمُوسَىٰ وَعِيسَىٰ ۖ أَنْ أَقِيمُوا الدِّينَ وَلَا تَتَفَرَّقُوا فِيهِ

> He carved for you a path for faith, of that which he commended for Noah, and with which we have inspired you [Muḥammad], and which we commended for Abraham, and Moses, and Jesus, that you must all uphold the faith and never be divided.[104]

In the direction of this long path Muḥammad is inspired to uphold the same faith.[105] To experience the Qur'ān properly, thus, is to view it atavistically—as a flashback of faith/history—and thus to be transformed (as a result of the aesthetic orality of such transhistorical drama) from a mystified listener or reader to a potential believer, despite the obvious fact that God's authority paradoxically allows for very limited knowledge about such prophets and pious figures. Still, readers and listeners identify with the pleadings of Noah, the testing of Abraham's faith, the maladies of Job, the exploits of Moses, the sufferings of the Children of Israel, the ire of Jonah, the testament of Mary, and the suffering of Jesus. The human element of these experiences could be a cause for great agony and anguish. Readers of the Qur'ān learn that Noah lost his son when the latter refused to mount the ship.[106] In his grief, Noah asks God to forgive his drowned son only to have his request denied; God's decisions are final and irreversible.[107] To add to his pain,[108] in the middle of his arduous mission and the trials that came with his prophetic duties, Noah suffered the betrayal of his wife, adding another personal dimension to his struggles. Abraham loses the love and support of his father after the latter threatens to stone him to death for abandoning their native gods.[109] Not only this, Abraham receives divine orders to slaughter his own child and is left with no choice but to proceed.[110] Lot is ordered to leave his wife behind.[111] The elder brothers of young Joseph are determined to kill him, throwing him into a dark pit and abandoning him to a likely death.[112] The sadness of Jacob over the loss of his son Joseph "turns his eyes white" with blindness.[113] Jonah throws a fit and tries to abandon the divine assignment altogether, a regrettable act that almost costs him his life in the belly of a whale.[114] The mother of Moses has to throw him as a baby into the river while he is still breastfeeding, tearing her heart apart. Jesus, from his infancy, was compelled to protect his mother's dignity in the face of a community quick to brand her with accusations of sexual misconduct. This act of defending her honor foreshadows the enduring trials he would face leading to the ultimate expression of suffering and passion upon the cross. Muḥammad's flight from Mecca was a critical moment of peril, as he narrowly evaded an assassination attempt by forty tribesmen committed to ending his life. This harrowing escape was one among the many trials he endured, reflecting the profound adversity and suffering he faced throughout his mission.[115]

Humanistically enough, the Qur'ān tells us that even long after a candid bond is established between God and his prophets, some still ask for more signs. Abraham, the natural theologian whose early search for God is tied to the dictates of the phenomenal world, asks God to make him "see" how he raises people from the dead:

وَإِذْ قَالَ إِبْرَاهِيمُ رَبِّ أَرِنِي كَيْفَ تُحْيِي الْمَوْتَىٰ قَالَ أَوَلَمْ تُؤْمِن قَالَ بَلَىٰ وَلَٰكِن لَّيَطْمَئِنَّ قَلْبِي

And Abraham said, "my Lord, let me see how you resurrect the dead." He responds, "Have you not believed?" Abraham replies "Aye, but only so as to calm my heart." (2:260).

In Islamic faith, the heart is the center of dynamic imagination—a center that, as Henry Corbin observes, "at once produces symbols and apprehends them,"[116] not simply as an intellectual practice but as an act of spiritual exegesis capable of transforming the soul. In this particular context, the Qur'ān links the act of its own "sending down" inextricably to the heart of Muḥammad, making the *tanzīl* itself a matter of the heart.[117] It is therefore important to understand Abraham's question as a question of the heart—that is, of the secret and innate understanding that reminds us of Abraham's and Muḥammad's own humanity, a humanity without which no sense of *iṭmi'nān al-qalb* (the calming of the heart) could ever be achieved. The achievement of this calming of the heart comes from the senses, and in this case from the act of seeing. Abraham needs to "see" for himself, for his own heart, how God resurrects the dead. This is not a cliché case where "seeing is believing," since Abraham is admittedly already a believer. Seeing is where belief becomes visible to the mortal heart. This visual confirmation, which Abraham is finally granted, synchs the belief of the soul with the belief of the heart and brings both into harmony.

A similar request comes from Moses, as if the arsenal of signs he is given to combat pharaoh were not enough. Moses wants his own sign. He asks God if he could see him:

وَلَمَّا جَاءَ مُوسَىٰ لِمِيقَاتِنَا وَكَلَّمَهُ رَبُّهُ قَالَ رَبِّ أَرِنِي أَنظُرْ إِلَيْكَ

When Moses came to scheduled time and when God spoke to him, he asked, "My Lord, show me how I could see you." (7:143)

While God categorically denies Moses's desire for a "visual" of him, he is considerate enough to tell Moses to "look at the mountain; if it holds out in its place, then you will see me" (7:143). The mountain could not take it; it collapses, and that is the end of that. Some, like Zechariah, were humble enough to ask God to give them a sign, as an expression of gratitude and resignation to his will.[118] God knows that signs are not just for the communities to which prophets are sent, but also for prophets themselves, so that they too know beyond doubt that he exists. In the case of Moses, God—in line with the appeal of Abraham for signs, or what we call miracles—decides to make matters easier for Moses and show him the signs of his divinity right away (20:17–22).

In academic circles, the approach to the supernatural and miraculous within religious traditions remains strictly empirical and experiential. The distinction between myth and established religion is often not recognized, nor is the valor of mythological figures like Odysseus seen differently from that of religious figures like Abraham or Moses. All are processed through the same analytical lens of mythology. Currently, most academic institutions observe the world through a lens of positivism, acknowledging the laws of physics that prevent the parting of seas or walking on water, and the improbability of flying on a winged horse from Mecca to Jerusalem. Such empirical scrutiny leads to the conclusion that prophets could not possess knowledge that transcends the limitations of their historical context. This prevalent perspective is reinforced by the dominance of postmodernism in the humanities and social sciences, which fundamentally questions the ability to know any truth rationally, casting doubt on the very possibility of accessing absolute truths.

It is equally hard to refuse to see things from the perspective of the other. In the case of Noah and his *fulk* (vessel/ship/ark), it is easy to think that the Qur'ān's "others" are the ones who are asked to suddenly abandon the faith they have cherished and embraced all their lives until that moment when a man announcing himself as a messenger from God comes up and asks them to follow a completely different doctrine or face retribution. After all, they are the ones who find themselves unexpectedly being asked to make a choice between what they know and love and what they do not know, abandon their beliefs, renounce the tradition of their own ancestors, and adopt a new theological order. Walid Saleh rightly reminds us that "opponents of Muḥammad did not live to tell their side of the story" and that "their world and ideology have to be reconstructed from the Qur'ān."[119] This is indeed the case with all God's antagonists in the Qur'ān.

It is hard to imagine a more pressing existential choice for the opponents of prophets. First, they would have to inquire about the truth of what they are asked to believe in, as we have seen in the case of Noah and his people. Then they would have to determine whether this new call for God applies to what they already know. Ultimately, they have to make a life-defining choice: embark and possibly survive, or remain on the ground and face drowning. As the flood unfolded, those who did not board the Ark with Noah were unaware of their impending doom. It is likely they never realized that Noah and everyone aboard the Ark would ultimately survive. All the Qur'ān tells us is that those who did not embark drowned. The Qur'ān offers no voice for the disappearance of voice. Yet Noah's abandoners become the sacrifice of the text. They are a reminder of what vengeful destiny awaits those who do not heed the words of God, even though theirs was a choice dictated by their own logic, their own tribal wisdom, their own faithfulness to their local traditions and religious beliefs, however uninspiring they might be to others. Those who survived, the last remnants of humanity, did so only because they mounted the ark, which delivered them as God willed it. In a similar aquatic manner, Moses too was delivered from the Nile. Over and again, the Qur'ān reminds us that God displays his omnipotence through environmentally relatable signs.

Unlike the scattered biographical narratives of the prophets, the Qur'ān does not say much about the biography of Muḥammad; nor does it provide details of his life prior to the revelation. Itself known to be the defining miracle of his prophethood, the Qur'ān is not a book *about* Muḥammad as much as it is a book *through* Muḥammad; it constantly apostrophizes him, addressing him in the second person as it commands him to spread the word of God. Unlike Abraham in the Qur'ān, Muḥammad does not destroy the statues of his polytheistic tribe only to end up thrown into a furnace that miraculously does not burn his body before he finds God.[120] Nor does he float in a chest on the waters of the Nile River, like baby Moses, to be washed ashore and picked up by his own future enemy,[121] or split the Red Sea as an adult to free the people of Israel from a bloodthirsty pharaoh.[122] Unlike Jesus, Muḥammad is neither born miraculously,[123] nor does he, like the messiah in the Qur'ān, speak to people from the cradle, create living birds from molded clay, heal the blind and the leper, or resurrect the dead.[124]

What is generally known about Muḥammad's early biography in the Muslim tradition is that he was born in Mecca in or around the year 570 AD. The Qur'ān makes reference to him growing up as an orphan, unguided and impoverished.[125] Other references to events in Muḥammad's prophetic life, including social reform, combats, debates, and so on abound in the Qur'ān and are enmeshed throughout all its sūras.[126] But a most pronounced attribute the Qur'ān gives Muḥammad is that of an *ummī* prophet,[127] a designation that is often translated, controversially, as "illiterate," thus attributing Muḥammad's knowledge to an unsullied divine source as opposed to teachable human sources of knowledge.[128] Yet the word *ummī* and its plural forms *ummiyyīn/ ummiyyūn*, which appear six times in the Qur'ān,[129] carry variable contextual significations that make the designation more than the sum of mere "illiteracy." In fact, from a purely grammatical position, the Qur'ān ascribes to Mecca the compound noun *umm al-qurá* (mother of villages/towns), which, in classical Arabic syntax, would allow for the case ending of the nisba attribution to be attached to the first indefinite noun,[130] in which case Muḥammad from *umm al-qurá* would be appropriately called *ummī* (i.e., a Meccan) in the same manner someone from Sub-Saharan Africa is called Sub-Saharan. However, contextually within the Qur'ān, *ummī* refers either to someone who is not among *ahl al-kitāb* (the People of the Book)—that is, someone who is not a Jewish or Christian (7:175) —or someone who is ignorant of the scriptures of Jews and Christians (3:20). *Ummī* is thus quite plausibly a *nisba* (grammatical attribution) of *umma*, "nation, community," or rather of the plural *umam*, so that *ummī* is the equivalent of the Hebrew/Jewish *goy*, "gentile," making Muḥammad the prophet sent to the gentiles, with *ummī* later misinterpreted as "illiterate." In consistency with this understanding, the Qur'ān is unambiguous in stating that Muḥammad is neither a scribe nor a reader of script:

وَمَا كُنتَ تَتْلُواْ مِن قَبْلِهِ مِن كِتَٰبٍ وَلَا تَخُطُّهُ بِيَمِينِكَ ۖ إِذًا لَّارْتَابَ ٱلْمُبْطِلُونَ

You could not read any scripts before this [Qur'ān] or write with your hand, otherwise the beliers would have been suspicious. (29:48)

In the end, the crux of the matter, as Muḥammad Shahrur puts it, is that "language for Prophet Muḥammad was primarily the language of the tongue and the ear (speaking and listening) of his people and that he received the Qur'ān orally, that is, it came to him unwritten as voice and was called the scripture."[131]

MUḤAMMAD AND ABRAHAM

Retreat, contemplation, and reverence are enduring characteristics of the prophets chronicled in the Qur'ān. The scripture illustrates two paths to divine discovery: through natural theology, exemplified by intellectual and philosophical inquiry into the nature of God, and through revelation, the direct imparting of divine wisdom. Abraham, predating Judaism, is portrayed in the Qur'ān as a quintessential figure of deep reflection and seclusion, embodying the journey of understanding God through contemplation of the natural world. Abraham's quest for the divine was marked by an unwavering pursuit, seeking signs that would lead to God. The Qur'ān narrates to Muḥammad that Abraham engaged in a profound journey of discovery, withdrawing into contemplation as an act of natural theology. This pursuit was akin to searching for cosmic signs, hoping to find God's presence within them.

فَلَمَّا جَنَّ عَلَيْهِ اللَّيْلُ رَأَىٰ كَوْكَبًا ۖ قَالَ هَٰذَا رَبِّي ۖ فَلَمَّا أَفَلَ قَالَ لَا أُحِبُّ الْآفِلِينَ

فَلَمَّا رَأَى الْقَمَرَ بَازِغًا قَالَ هَٰذَا رَبِّي ۖ فَلَمَّا أَفَلَ قَالَ لَئِن لَمْ يَهْدِنِي رَبِّي لَأَكُونَنَّ مِنَ الْقَوْمِ الضَّالِّينَ

فَلَمَّا رَأَى الشَّمْسَ بَازِغَةً قَالَ هَٰذَا رَبِّي هَٰذَا أَكْبَرُ ۖ فَلَمَّا أَفَلَتْ قَالَ يَا قَوْمِ إِنِّي بَرِيءٌ مِمَّا تُشْرِكُونَ

إِنِّي وَجَّهْتُ وَجْهِيَ لِلَّذِي فَطَرَ السَّمَاوَاتِ وَالْأَرْضَ حَنِيفًا ۖ وَمَا أَنَا مِنَ الْمُشْرِكِينَ

When the night fell upon him, he saw a star; he said, "This is my God," but when it disappeared, he said, "I do not like those who disappear." / When he saw the moon shining, he said, "This is my God," but when it disappeared, he said, "unless my God guides me, I will be among the lost people." / When he saw the sun shining, he said, "this is my God; this is bigger," but when it disappeared, he said, "my people, I exonerate myself from your gods." (6:76–78)

Moving from one source of natural light to another, Abraham uses simple logic to sift through phenomenal nominees for the designation of God. In Abraham's mind, God shines and is enormous; he is high and above, but still reaches down. He is also one and only one. So it is easy to decide, among the stars, the moon and the sun, who God would likely be. It is possible Abraham did not know the names of the stars he was pointing at and conceivably looking for which one is bigger and has more light. Arabic has a clear gender distinction between the moon (he) and the sun (she), a distinction Abraham did not seem to care about in his search for God, using the nominative third person single demonstrative pronoun *hādhā* (this). Although historically masculine, *hādhā* is also used in classical Arabic to designate something that is not yet known, even if the referent is feminine as in 50:32: *hādhā mā tū'adūna li-kulli awwābin ḥafīẓ* (This is what you were promised, everyone who submitted to God and every keeper [of faith]), where the feminine referent is *al-Janna* (paradise). Thus, Abraham infers that God, being ever-present, transcends gender, and is referred to as "He" not as an indication of gender but as a convention in language. This divine presence does not wane, cease, or vanish, not even temporarily.

Abraham's phenomenal nominees, including the sun as a front-runner candidate, disappear from the sphere of his vision for a period of time. He was determined to find God that night, and his mind is settled that whatever or whoever the divine being he is looking for is, this being has to be as enormous as the sun. God would ever possibly be luminous, non-gender-specific, and ever-present. The Qur'ānic Abraham thus tries hard but eventually fails to find a matching divinity in the list of visible colossal celestial shiny bodies he designated as potential candidates for the God position. It is not clear why Abraham believed so deeply that there was a god without any material evidence. The Qur'ān depicts him as a man in search of God, whom he was certain existed, perhaps innately, but whom he still must find. When the celestial bodies of the stars, the moon, and the sun eventually fall short in Abraham's mental image of God, he does not give up. Rather, he arrives at the metaphysical conclusion that God must be mightier than what his eyes could see and greater that what his mind could grasp on that starry night:

إِنِّي وَجَّهْتُ وَجْهِيَ لِلَّذِي فَطَرَ السَّمَاوَاتِ وَالْأَرْضَ حَنِيفًا ۖ وَمَا أَنَا مِنَ الْمُشْرِكِينَ

I have turned my face to the one who created the heavens and the earth, in pure monotheism, and I am not among the polytheists. (6:79)

Because none of these phenomenal candidates qualifies, Abraham makes the mental leap from the physical to the metaphysical. God, if God is, is not from the phenomenal world, but is responsible for it. God, if there is a God, must have created this world and is now being sincerely invoked, and appealed to, for guiding Abraham in his search. This act of giving up to God is also an act of opening up for God. Praying to a God that the heart feels or hopes is there but the mind cannot materialize in the physical world, is the beginning of faith. Abraham's deductive reason from natural theology reaches beyond the limits of the physical world and offers a thought, or perhaps a trace of human thought for as far as it could possibly reach, a reason that leads to the failure of human reason and a hope for what is beyond reason. In Abraham's natural theology, God *is* beyond reason. He is the frustration of reason. He cannot make himself available to us through reason. The implication is that only the exhaustion of reason has the potential of opening up God for the seeker. This is one way of finding God, and this is definitely Abraham's way in the Qur'ān.

Unlike natural theology, the Qur'ān reminds us that the sending down of a message is much more direct. God simply finds a way to contact a human, a chosen human who has no idea, a sleeper prophet, so to speak, who, upon reaching a certain age, realizes through a divine revelation that he is chosen by God to convey his message. God relates to this prophet that He is the Creator of the world, provides him with some miraculous signs, and assigns him the task. The task of the prophet is predictable: to tell people that he bears a message from God and that they are to heed the message in order to be guided well in this world and the hereafter. The prophet enacts the assignment and carries the task, often encountering resistance, ridicule, and death threats from his own people. The confrontation is always rough and may result in divisive conflict, splitting the community into two or more opposing camps: followers of the prophet, on the one hand, and his opponents, on the other.

The Qur'ān does not tell us to what extent Muḥammad was outspoken in his rejection of his people's idolatrous practices before the revelation. However, what is related in the Qur'ān and Muslim sources is that Muḥammad's access to God, or God's access to Muḥammad, was exacted through a divinely ordained encounter with the archangel Gabriel, resulting in the revelation of a book/scripture (26:193–95) In this respect, Muḥammad is more like Moses, the prophet of Judaism, who received the sacred tablets from God after a series of divine encounters.

MUḤAMMAD AND MOSES

Although current scholarship examining the relationship between Muḥammad and Moses in the Qur'ān has begun to shift from a pattern of borrowing and imitation to a pattern of "intertextuality" and "parallelism," there remains the concern that such a shift may still represent "borrowing" under a different name, especially when little to no attention is paid to how Qur'ānic depictions of Moses figure not only in establishing a distinct but overlapping Muslim identity, but also in exploring how such depictions serve the intentionality of the Qur'ān's oral message and the prophetic authority of Muḥammad.[132] The parallels between Moses and Muḥammad in the Qur'ān are uncanny. Moses not only had to get the Israelites out of Egypt; he also had to get Egypt out of the Israelites. Likewise, Muḥammad had to get his followers out of pagan Mecca and pagan Mecca out of the hearts of his followers. If the Qur'ān rejects "appearances" and "form" and celebrates essence and substance, then the similarities between Moses and Muḥammad must always be emphasized. Remarkably, both messengers share a later-life commencement of their prophetic missions, with Moses's journey starting in his adulthood as described in scriptural narratives, mirroring Muḥammad's own prophetic call at the age of forty. Like Moses, Muḥammad's prophethood was honed and advanced in exile. What launches both of their prophetic careers is a voice. In a parallel of prophetic communication, Muḥammad's experience of the Qur'ān was characterized by listening to the divine message conveyed through an angelic voice, resonating with the notion that God's truth was imparted to both prophets through celestial speech. Moses's prophethood assignment begins with the voice of God as a vehicle of His truth:

فَلَمَّا أَتَىٰهَا نُودِىَ يَٰمُوسَىٰٓ. إِنِّىٓ أَنَا۠ رَبُّكَ فَٱخْلَعْ نَعْلَيْكَ ۖ إِنَّكَ بِٱلْوَادِ ٱلْمُقَدَّسِ طُوًى

When he arrived at it (the fire), his name was called: "O Moses. I am your God, so remove your sandals, you are in the sacred valley of *Ṭuwá*." (20:11–12)

In the Qur'ān, the story of Moses is at once the most ubiquitous and the most circumscribed of all narratives.[133] It is a story that keeps reiterating itself in numerous sūras, where the Qur'ān emphatically shows divine omnipresence through "signs" and, in Moses's case, through the miracle of the staff turning into a serpent, which Moses uses to split open the Red Sea. In particular, through the sign of *aṣá Mūsá* (the staff of Moses), the Qur'ān emphasizes once again the biblical understanding that the confrontation between Moses and pharaoh is one between essence and phenomenon, a confrontation in which *siḥr* (magic/sorcery) becomes the embarrassment of pharaoh and the turning point of liberation for the people of Israel. Of all prophets in the Qur'ān, perhaps Moses has the most complete biography.[134] Collating different verses from various sūras, it is easy to reconstruct the life of Moses from childhood to prophecy and beyond, including his birth, his killing of an Egyptian, his flight to *Madyan* (Midian), his marriage, his encounter with the voice of God in Sinai, his confrontation with pharaoh, the revealing of the Torah, the episode of the golden calf, and even tangential stories like the didactic narrative in Sūra 18, which narrates of Moses's accompaniment of the good servant of God, known in Islamic exegesis as al-Khidr.

In Sūra 20, when God speaks to Moses and instructs him to take off his shoes in reverence, he asks him about his staff. Suddenly there is a narrative shift. God, who is always commanding, now has a curious question for Moses, and the voice moves from directiveness and dominance to inclusiveness and dialogue, inviting Moses to respond to God's question:

وَمَا تِلْكَ بِيَمِينِكَ يَٰمُوسَىٰ[135]

And what is this, in your right hand, O Moses? (Q. 20:17)

Some scholars argue that the Arabic language in this particular dialogical setting is a motif familiar to both Jewish and Christian traditions, one with biblical precedents characteristic of late antiquity.[136] Yet the stories of Moses and all prophets in the Qur'ān, unlike in the biblical tradition, do not appear in a chronological setting, but are reiterated and peppered throughout the text in a number of separate verses with clear ethical lessons and psychological implications (for Muḥammad) that are related to the sūra(s) in which they appear. Comparatively at least, such a discontinuous mode of narration complicates the dialogical intentions of a chronological biblical narratives. In the Qur'ānic episodes involving Moses, for instance, this complexity suggests a remarkable difference not only in communicative exchange between him and God within fragmented storylines (e.g., 20) but also in the overall communicative reference of the Qur'ān, which often addresses Muḥammad in the second person and tells him the story of Moses as an example of divine love and a solace for his fears and cares. One level of reading this verse presents God's question for Moses as simple and straightforward. But a deeper exegetical level reveals the innocence of the exiled prophet in the making and his moral distance from Egypt's indulgence in sorcery and magic, a subtle parallel to Muḥammad's own life. This parallelism alone is evidence that the extent to which the Mosaic narrative could be a product of late antiquity is not as compelling as the insights it yields for the contemporary context of its invocation in the Qur'ān. The therapeutic projections of the stories of Moses not only reflect the sociolinguistic milieu of Muḥammad's time, but they also strengthen his psychological position during some of the most challenging times in his prophetic career:

طه. مَآ أَنزَلْنَا عَلَيْكَ الْقُرْآنَ لِتَشْقَى. إِلاَّ تَذْكِرَةً لَّمَن يَخْشَى

. . . . .

وَهَلْ أَتَاكَ حَدِيثُ مُوسَىٰ

Ṭāhā. We have not sent the Qur'ān down to you so that you would be miserable. But it is a reminder for those who are in awe (of God).

. . . . . .

Have you heard the story of Moses? (20:1–2; 9)

In the Meccan verses of Sūra 20, Muḥammad is learning to listen to, and to share, the story of a fellow prophet, who, three thousand years prior to his own time, had to undergo a daunting mission for the sake of God. It is by sharing these narratives of Moses at a crucial moment in Muḥammad's life that the latter manages not only to discover a shared humanity with Moses but also to rekindle his confidence and trust in God who chose and commanded Moses, a stuttering prophet with a temper, to deliver the Israelites from the tyranny of a murderous pharaoh. The Qur'ān reminds us of Moses's humanity, how he is frightened and unsure about whether or not he could take up the mission:

قَالَ رَبِّ إِنِّى أَخَافُ أَن يُكَذِّبُونِ. وَيَضِيقُ صَدْرِى وَلَا يَنطَلِقُ لِسَانِى

He said, "My Lord, I fear they will accuse me of lying, my chest will tighten, and my tongue will be tied." (26:12–13)

In these verses, Moses confesses his human vulnerability, his fear, anxiety, and stutter to God. But it is Moses's very humanity that makes him a role model for his people and a forerunner for Muḥammad, precisely because he has to learn to overcome and transcend his limitations. The lesson is clear and concrete: if Moses the fearful, the unsure, and the stutterer can deliver the people of Israel and convert them into God-obeying Jews by teaching them the way of God, then so too can Muḥammad teach his own community how to submit to God. Indeed, the Qur'ān establishes this thematic affinity between Moses and Muḥammad early on in the Meccan sūras, where the assignment of Muḥammad is tightly linked to that of Moses through the rhetorical use of the simile particle كما (just as/in the same manner):

إِنَّا أَرْسَلْنَا إِلَيْكُمْ رَسُولًا شَاهِدًا عَلَيْكُمْ كَمَا أَرْسَلْنَا إِلَىٰ فِرْعَوْنَ رَسُولاً

We have sent a messenger to you who is a witness on you just as we sent a messenger to pharaoh. (73:15)

Moses gives the people of Israel not only laws to follow but also the Torah, a scripture of teaching and learning whose enactment safeguards their identity and national existence throughout time. The Qur'ān, too, carves a path that guarantees Muslim identities and continued existence in time. It offers a special imagination of Arabian peninsular culture, interlinks it with the time of Moses's Egypt, and puts Muḥammad's mission in perfect synchronicity with Moses's. Arabia, like ancient Egypt, is steeped in tales of enchantments and serpents. If Moses, amid Egypt's legendary sorcery, did not adopt their methods to make ropes "seem" like snakes, can it not be argued that Muḥammad, in the middle of Arabia's celebrated poetic tradition, did not assimilate the craft of its poets or claim authorship of the Qur'ān? Or is the realm of the miraculous already outside the sphere of thought? We learn from the Qur'ān that the staff of Moses in its pre-miraculous condition is a hardened tree branch he uses as a walking stick to lean on and to round up and feed his sheep. Could it be argued that a pre-supernatural stick in the hand of Moses is as uneventful as language is for Muḥammad before the Qur'ān? If the divine decree is to match the miracle with the communal practices of a prophet's own people, then a closer examination of the associations between the Qur'ān and the classical Arabic tradition reveal Moses's staff to be a fitting wonder, not only for Judaism but also for the formative environment of early Islam.

Nevertheless, there are no human champions in the Qur'ān. Despite the centrality that both Moses and Muḥammad exhibit in the text, they are neither protagonists nor epic heroes.[137] The one and only absolute hero is God. Even though readers identify with the struggling prophets and people of faith (Nūḥ, Ibrāhīm, Yaʿqūb, Yūsif, Banū Isrā'īl, Mūsá, Hārūn, Maryam, ʿĪsá, Aṣḥāb al-Kahf, Aṣḥāb al-Ukhdūd, etc.), the rhythmic cadence of such narratives leads only to a confirmation of God's omnipresence and absoluteness. Readers encounter occasional but repetitive disavowals and affirmations, characteristic of Qur'ānic monotheism, in the context of unfailing human impulses to resist the calls of prophets and question the ulterior motive of monotheistic doctrine.[138] But in the end, all shall die, states the Qur'ān, and only the face of God shall remain:

كُلُّ مَنْ عَلَيْهَا فَانٍ. وَيَبْقَى وَجْهُ رَبِّكَ ذُو الْجَلَالِ وَالْإِكْرَامِ

All that is on it shall perish. Only the face of your God shall remain, in majesty and glory. (55:26–27)

In this world of transience, the theological unconscious in the Qur'ān is not vague: Muḥammad's prophethood is a dialectical continuity, or, if you will, a discontinuous continuity of Abrahamic monotheism. In this dialectic, the Qur'ān both preserves the older conglomeration and creates a new accumulation of the monotheistic idea, one that has rendered Muḥammad the very figure of the other, the very unacknowledged center of the medieval and modern religious history of the monotheistic West. For centuries, negative depictions of Muḥammad have been one of the key stipulations of protectionism in Christian and post-Christian Western Europe.[139] The concept commonly referred to as the Judeo-Christian tradition, as Arthur Cohen suggests, involves a transformation of Jewish principles and rituals, in which they are often reinterpreted rather than strictly conserved, or, to use Cohen's words, "sublated rather than preserved, a revisionism objectionable to believers to whom the old is the only testament."[140] This perspective, which can be seen as controversial among those who view the original Jewish teachings as definitive, raises the following question: Is it accurate to attribute this conceptual blend solely to Christianity? Such a synthesis seems less characteristic of historical Catholic doctrine and more akin to the liberal movements within Protestantism, especially those emerging in the late nineteenth and early twentieth centuries. It may even resemble a modern, secular Jewish thought pattern, aligning more closely with the philosophy of figures like Hermann Cohen than with traditional Christian theology.

Moreover, it is the historical distance and often the accumulative antipathy towards Muḥammad and the Qur'ān that have contributed to shaping a protective Judeo-Christian self-concept. This protective stand has, intentionally or not, accelerated the formation of a tradition that has increasingly omitted Islam, despite its rightful place within the Abrahamic tradition. Indeed, the "Judeo-Christian tradition" could well consider the addition of a hyphen to include Islam. After all, Islam resonates deeply with the heart of Judaism in its emphasis on laws and justice, and with the soul of Christianity in its belief in the hereafter and the resurrection of the dead. In recognizing the congruent values among these faiths, perhaps it is time to expand our understanding of this interlinked heritage.

INSIDE I'JĀZ : THE QUR'ĀN AND THE MIRACLE

Arming messengers with miraculous signs matters tremendously in prophetic traditions. The signs act as proof that a prophet seeking to persuade his people to embrace a religious truth has something of the supernatural to show them in order to convince them that what they are saying is not a figment of their own imagination. When the sorcerers of Egypt's pharaoh intimidate Moses, God inspires the latter to throw his staff in order to reveal the sign: "Throw what is in your right hand; it will devour what they have devised" (20:69). The Qur'ānic story of Moses becomes a kind of solace for Muḥammad's own story. Muḥammad is comforted in learning that God would keep him from harm and would grant him a sign, as he did with Moses, especially when the former knows full well how his people adore their gods and what they would do to protect their religious beliefs and rituals. As Muḥammad had anticipated, the people of Quraysh would not simply accept the news that there was a new prophet in town. And so, as al-Jāḥiẓ reminds us, in his own historical context, Muḥammad's need for a sign, akin to the need of Moses and Jesus, would be especially appropriate and fitting.[141]

The Qur'ān constantly reminds Muḥammad that it is not easy to be a prophet. Almost all the prophets mentioned in the Qur'ān were not believed or were persecuted by the majority of their people. All of them were met with hostility and malevolence. His fate won't be any different. The task is daunting and the mission is arduous. Immediately upon his assignment, he is asked to perform miraculous tasks to prove himself. He may have to lose the support of his own people and family members. He is charged with asking his community to stop doing what they have been doing for ages; he is asking them to abandon their sacred traditions and start worshiping a new God. He cannot fully explain this God beyond the fact that he was assigned this divine task. Muḥammad can neither abandon the mission nor resort to reason to convince his people that God exists. He cannot even verify the sincerity of his messages. But he knows in his heart that it is true. Abraham before him tried to reason with his own people. Indeed, Abraham was quite the rational rebel. The Qur'ān narrates that Abraham used common sense with his community first, hoping to convert them (21:52–56), but when he exhausted the limits of his reason, he took matters into his own hands and destroyed their sculpted gods, almost getting himself burnt alive in the process (21:57–58). Could Muḥammad go fully "Abrahamic" on his people and smite their sacred figures? Or would he seek to win them over with his integrity and good character?

At this stage, all Muḥammad has to his credit moving forward is the biographical credit of truth and honesty. But first he must himself believe in God and believe in the mission assigned to him. Then, he must muster the courage to share the news with his community:

يَا أَيُّهَا الرَّسُولُ بَلِّغْ مَا أُنْزِلَ إِلَيْكَ مِنْ رَبِّكَ وَإِنْ لَمْ تَفْعَلْ فَمَا بَلَّغْتَ رِسَالَتَهُ

> O messenger, proclaim what has been sent down to you from your God, and if you
> do not, then you have not delivered his message. (5:57).

He simply, and yet not so simply, has to tell his people what God assigned him to say: "People, I am God's messenger to all of you, who owns the heavens and the earth. There is no other God but him; he makes life and death. Believe in God and his messenger, the *ummī* prophet, who believes in God and his words, and follow him so that you might be guided" (7:158). In delivering the message publicly, Muḥammad submits fully, and without reservation, to the compelling demands of divinity—and with it, to the consequences of his actions. Eventually, when he is forced to flee Mecca with its high culture, commerce, and gods, Muḥammad chooses a path of no return. In doing so, he feels more liberation than loss. Yet it is also an exit that comes at a painful cost, recognized in the Qur'ān as a moment in which the dejected prophet mitigates the sadness of his companion in complete reliance on the will of God: *lā taḥzan inna Allāha ma'anā* (be not sad for God is with us). He flees with a deep yearning for a return confirmed by a divine promise: *la-tadkhulunna al-masjida al-ḥarāma in shā'a Allāhu āminīna ru'ūsakum wa muqaṣṣirīna lā takhāfūn* (you shall enter the holy mosque safely), a promise that shall become *fatḥan mubīnan* (a mighty opening). Muḥammad's exit from Mecca is celebrated in the Islamic tradition as *hijra* (migration/renunciation), a blessing and a new calendrical beginning equal in value to all divine beginnings in religious history.

In the Qur'ān, as in all scriptures, God wants to be known and worshipped. He wants to be known publicly, to everyone, and this promulgation is, in essence, the job of all his messengers: to announce his presence in public, to let people know about him, to believe in him, to love him, and to serve him. Once Muḥammad has gathered all his people and announced to them that he is carrying a message from God, there is no coming back. He leaves his people with two choices—either to realize that Muḥammad is telling a joke or to own up to the fact that he is telling the truth. Muḥammad was not known to monger silly jokes, or to tell lies, or to make fun of his community. In light of his own *ethos*, he must have been serious. If so, then there are only two options: to believe him or not to believe him. It is easy to guess that Muḥammad's first of kin, though not all of them, were among the first to sympathize with him and believe him because they knew his mental bearings and his moral qualities. But those who knew of his character but did not know him personally must have thought that the man had lost his mind.

It is one thing to show miracles to prove a point, and it is a completely different thing to only say that one has heard the voice of God. When Moses tells pharaoh that God speaks to him, pharaoh takes Moses to be "bewitched" (17:101). But Moses comes equipped with miraculous signs (20:20–22) and with enough God-inspired confidence, as well the presence of his eloquent brother, Hārūn (Aaron), to respond to pharaoh's insult with insult (17:102). Unlike Moses, Muḥammad's prophetic task consists mainly of receiving the *qawlan thaqīlan* (heavy saying) of God (73:5) and delivering it to his people, a delivery brought down by a "trusted spirit" to settle upon his heart and in a language and a style that he and his people could understand (26:193–94). In this heavy burden of prophethood, Muḥammad becomes the ultimate receiver of the word of God. Although his people may still need a fantastic sign to seal his prophethood, he is himself marked by the word of God, which makes the Qur'ān itself the sign for the special society to which he belongs.

In the end, Muḥammad has to make a conscious decision about how he would respond to this "mediated" voice/sign of God. The burden is to confirm, to himself first, that this is indeed a voice from God. How does he know for certain that it is God? A sense of urgency is always attached to the prophetic burden. A prophet, Gilles Deleuze and Félix Guattari remind us, is not in a position to "decline the burden God entrusts to him."[142] When God instructs Muḥammad to tell his next of kin about his divine assignment (26:214), it is Muḥammad alone who has to make the final decision that he is God's messenger. He alone has the intuition of the presence of God. He alone knows that the one and only sign there is, is the word of God itself. This is the moment when the Qur᾽ān becomes the sign and the miracle of Islam.

For all these reasons, it is absolutely crucial for a voice-inspired prophet to bring forth signs, signs that have to be both compelling and convincing in order for people to abandon the intimate and the familiar and to heed, instead, the path of God. The Qur᾽ān acknowledges the dialectical challenges of the prophetic moment coupled with God's protection of his prophets. Because so much depends on the signs of God, or the signs from God, it is perfectly normal for people to expect them and to demand them, especially if one's own life—the lives of one's family and the entire community—all depend on the decisions made after witnessing those signs. But Muḥammad did not have any of the miraculous signs of Abraham, Moses, or Jesus. With respect to Muḥammad, God's extraordinary nature-defying, super-phenomenological acts take a different shape, giving us a completely novel approach to the sign. This is an interesting discontinuity within the Abrahamic tradition. In addition to this, the sign of prophecy is traditionally different from the message being conveyed. Religious history has taught us that there is an awful temporality to supernatural signs after all; extraordinary wonders live and die with the people who encounter them. Like all supernatural phenomena, signs are subjective and terminal, and by the time the people who witness the miracles die, those miracles, even if they had been true, would themselves fade into the past and soon lapse into myths and be crushed under the wheels of skeptical and agnostic thought.

Not surprisingly, Muḥammad's community, the Qur᾽ān tells us, wondered about the signs. Just like Noah's people, they wanted signs that he was indeed a prophet, signs that related to their communal sense of judgement and corresponded to what they already knew divine signs should look like. In short, they needed a wonder to impress them, all of them, collectively:

وَقَالُواْ مَالِ هَٰذَا ٱلرَّسُولِ يَأْكُلُ ٱلطَّعَامَ وَيَمْشِى فِى ٱلْأَسْوَاقِ ۙ لَوْلَآ أُنزِلَ إِلَيْهِ مَلَكٌ فَيَكُونَ مَعَهُ نَذِيرًا. أَوْ يُلْقَىٰ إِلَيْهِ كَنْزٌ أَوْ تَكُونُ لَهُ جَنَّةٌ يَأْكُلُ مِنْهَا وَقَالَ الظَّالِمُونَ إِنْ تَتَّبِعُونَ إِلَّا رَجُلًا مَسْحُورًا.

They said "what is it with this 'messenger" who eats food and walks in the markets? Why is there no angel sent down for him to accompany him in warning? Or "why is he not given a treasure or a garden [by his God] from which he eats?" And the unjust ones said, "You are only following a possessed man." (25:7–8).

To make these demands, the culture of pre-Islamic Mecca must have known about the signs of Abraham, Moses, and Jesus. In their historical conceptual thinking, if Muḥammad were indeed God's prophet, where or what would his sign be? The lives of prophets before him were loaded with divine signs, signs that the Qur᾽ān itself triumphantly narrates. Moses enjoyed his share of the miraculous from the day he was thrown into the river in a chest until the day he turned a staff into a snake and split open the Red Sea. Jesus was a sign unto himself, from the immaculate birth to speaking in the cradle, to healing blindness and leprosy, to landing a table full of food from the sky. In Muḥammad's case, something else has happened. The scripture became the sign; the sign became the scripture, a divergence from conventional understandings of prophethood, which Ibn Khaldūn cogently characterizes as follows:

القرآن هو بنفسه الوحي المدعى، وهو الخارق المعجز، فشاهده في عينه، ولا يفتقر إلى دليل مغاير له كسائر المعجزات مع الوحي. فهو أوضح دلالة لاتحاد الدليل والمدلول فيه.[143]

> The Qur'ān is itself the claimed revelation, itself the extraordinary and incapacitating sign; its witness is itself; it needs no proof outside itself as other miracles do with revelation. It is the clearest sign of the union between the signifier and the signified.

It is impossible to know divine intentions, but this reflection by Ibn Khaldūn reminds us how Muslims believe the Qur'ān not be a book in the same way, say, the Bible is a book, a belief that does not diminish the sacredness of the latter. It is just that, in Muslim faith, the Qur'ān is a book like Jesus is the messiah, the incarnate word of God. It is the *I'jāz* (the miracle of linguistic inimitability and incapacitation, per Ibn Khaldūn) that materializes and speaks itself, the word that is at once the secret and its own *raison d'être*. But Ibn Khaldūn shies away from answering the most pressing question: what exactly is *I'jāz* and how does it present itself?

"BEFORE YOU BLINK": THE RHETORIC OF I'JĀZ IN SŪRA-T-AL-NAML (27)

Sūra-t-al-Naml (27) ties *āya/āyāt* (miracle[s]/sign[s]) and *'ilm* (knowledge) together in a dynamic interaction between extraordinary phenomena and divine knowledge. This interaction has its own semantic cycle within the verses of the sūra, at times spiraling centrifugally outside of it, thus demonstrating the need for intratextual and trans-sūra knowledge of the Qur'ān to understand the references. For instance, the sūra does not mention what the nine signs of Moses are in *fī tis'i āyātin ilá fir'awna wa qawmihi* (in nine signs to pharaoh and his people, 27:12). In monotheistic discourses, the relationship of a prophet to a miracle is like that of a bird to its feather. One simply cannot exist without the other. The Arabic word for miracle is *mu'jiza*, whose three consonants, '/j/z, correspond at some level with the Latin noun *miraculum* and the verb *mirari*, which means to "wonder at." To be sure, the Arabic word *mu'jiza* does not mean "miracle." The verb *a'jaza* means "to make incapable, incapacitated, weak, disabled." But its root suggests or rather instills "wonder" precisely because *mu'jiza* refers to "being incapable" of meeting the challenge by reproducing something similar to the Qur'ān. This "incapacity" is also an act of *I'jāz*, which connotes impossibility and inimitability—namely, that which humans can wonder at, admire with great astoundment, but that which they cannot mimic or reproduce. *Sūra-t-al-Naml* (27) enumerates the miracles of several prophets (e.g., Moses, David, Solomon, Sāliḥ), all presented as a break with the laws of nature. In the sūra, the word that describes the giving of the miracle is the di-transitive Arabic verb آتينا (we have given/provided someone with/ bestowed upon someone), as in the following verse:

وَلَقَدْ آتَيْنَا دَاوُودَ وَسُلَيْمَانَ عِلْمًا

Indeed, we have bestowed knowledge upon David and Solomon. (27:15)

Like many sūras in the Qur'ān, *Sūra-t-al-Naml* offers no exception to the rule of the miracle, except that the miracle of Muḥammad does not manifest itself in the presentation of a marvelous act, but rather in the text of the Qur'ān itself, as an extraordinary linguistic and rhetorical phenomenon. This does not prevent the Qur'ān from speaking about the miracles of bygone prophets. These supernatural acts are all performed, the Qur'ān confirms, under the knowledge and direction of God, as miraculous proofs of his existence. Yet much of the credibility of miracle narratives does depend, to use the words of David Hume, "on the truth of that religion whose credibility they were first intended to support."[144] How, then, does the credibility of the miracle narrative in the Qur'ān hold itself against the credibility of the Qur'ān *as* a miracle? What rhetorical tools does the Qur'ān employ, to use *Sūra-t-al-Naml* as an example, to allow the audience to embrace both phenomenality and textuality and to find a seamless parallelism between narratives of past miracles and linguistic brilliance, between mountains commanded to repeat prayers and a language perfected to speak that which is unsurpassable?

There are no easy answers to these questions. The root for *I'jāz* and *mu'jiza* is the same in Arabic. The root is inextricably tied to the Qur'ān as both miraculous and inimitable. The inimitability is tied to the very definition of *āya* (verse/ sign) and *sūra*, (a Qur'ānic chapter). The word *sūra* (pl. *suwar*) is Qur'ān-specific. It denotes a group of *āyāt* (verses) that constitute textual units of various lengths, such as *Sūra-t-al-Naml*, which consists of ninety-three *āyāt* (verses). But the word *āya* also has the double meaning of a "Qur'ānic verse" and "a thing of wonder." In traditional Muslim exegesis, this understanding corresponds to the concept that every *āya* is an *āya*—that is, that every verse of the Qur'ān, from the smallest to the largest self-referential verbal/textual unit or verse of a sūra, is itself a miracle. Although the word *sūra* does not appear in *Sūra-t-al-Naml*, the reference to it is common in the middle and late Meccan periods, and more prominently in the context of *Āyāt al-Taḥaddī* (Verses of Challenges), where the Qur'ān dares its receiving audience and beyond to bring forth a textual unit similar to itself:

أَمْ يَقُولُونَ افْتَرَاهُ قُلْ فَأْتُوا بِسُورَةٍ مِّثْلِهِ وَادْعُوا مَنِ اسْتَطَعْتُم مِّن دُونِ اللَّهِ إِن كُنتُمْ صَادِقِينَ

Or would they say, "he made it up," say bring forth then a *sūra* like it, and call out to whom you can other than God if you were telling the truth. (10:38).[145]

Readers of *Sūra-t-al-Naml* will notice that the word *Qur'ān* appears four times. The first reference is at the outset of the sūra, which opens with the proclamation that what is coming or what is to be witnessed and narrated are the words of God—that is, the verses/signs of the Qur'ān—thus enveloping the reader/listener within the realm of wonder:

طس ۚ تِلْكَ آيَاتُ الْقُرْآنِ وَكِتَابٍ مُبِينٍ

ṬāSīn. These are the verses/signs of the Qur'ān and a clear scripture. (27:1)

In *Sūra-t-al-Naml*, the word *Qur'ān* asserts itself both as orality, or as "that which has to be recited," and as scripture. This synonymous apposition is a common duality throughout the Qur'ān, which I address in more detail shortly. The second reference to *Qur'ān* comes in 27:6, immediately before a series of narratives on the miracles of prophets. In this particular *āya*, the Qur'ān addresses Muḥammad in the second person, a shift in the method of narration and an apostrophization that interpolates him, as a receiver of the oral Qur'ān from God, within the domain of miracles. Note that the action of receiving the Qur'ān is "passivized" in the verb *la-tulaqqá* (you are given/gifted) to confirm the divine source of the revelation and to prevent assumptions of human authorship. The same verse also repeats the divine attributes of *ḥikma* and *'ilm* (wisdom and knowledge), which are key to the thematic unity and unfolding of all miracles in the sūra:

وَإِنَّكَ لَتُلَقَّى الْقُرْآنَ مِنْ لَدُنْ حَكِيمٍ عَلِيمٍ

And indeed, you are receiving the Qur'ān from the all-wise and the all-knowing. (27:6)

From there, the Qur'ān's self-reference takes a back seat and does not resurface in the verses until the very end, specifically in 27:76, when all prophets' miraculous stories and feats are told. In so doing, 27:6 and 27:76 perform two simultaneous functions: first, they create a totalizing *enframement* of such miracle narratives not only by bracketing them but also by casting the Qur'ān within the import of their mixtures. Secondly, they recast such miraculous narratives back to the present moment of Muḥammad's recitation of the Qur'ān, already established at the beginning of the sūra in 27:1–6. This rhetorical act envelops the past of supernatural miracles within the present of the Qur'ān's linguistic moment *as a miracle* to its own audience. In this context, 27:76 refers to a certain audience, *Banī Isrā'il* (children of Israel) in the third person, presenting the Qur'ān as a clarifying narrative, one that tells a "story" to the people of Israel, so to speak, to guide them into an explanation of most of what they have disagreed on, thus casting Islam as a continuity of the Mosaic covenant of monotheism:

إِنَّ هَٰذَا الْقُرْآنَ يَقُصُّ عَلَىٰ بَنِي إِسْرَائِيلَ أَكْثَرَ الَّذِي هُمْ فِيهِ يَخْتَلِفُونَ

Indeed, this Qur'ān explains to the children of Israel most of what they disagree on. (27:76)

The shift from Moses and the children of Israel to Muḥammad and his community is neither sudden nor jarring in *Sūra-t-al-Naml*. It has been established that the Qur'ān addresses a community familiar with both Judaism and Christianity. Like Judaism, Quranic "monotheism" is antipolytheistic; it emphasizes the continuity of monotheism, as the voice of God reminds Muḥammad of his primary assignment as a prophet.[146] The apostrophization of Muḥammad in the imperative verse of 27:92 to proclaim the Qur'ān as the words of God and, by default, Muḥammad himself as a prophet, makes it clear that his job is to tell his people he is commanded to worship God, to join all Muslims, to recite the Qur'ān, and to remember that he is only a warner. In Islam, as in Judaism, to recite is to mark the divine word in the world, individually and publicly. The ritual of تلاوة (enunciating/reciting) the Qur'ān is the form of *shahāda* (witness/testimony) that individual and communal Muslims perform: it is their self-identification and the proclamation of faith. It is thus fitting for *Sūra-t-al-Naml* to conclude as it begins, with *āyāt*, thus rounding up and accentuating the divine significations of the Qur'ān as signs/recitations—that is, as an act of reading that prompts the verbal performance of the signs of God, a celebration of a miracle recognizable only to those who want to listen and seek guidance:

إِنَّمَا أُمِرْتُ أَنْ أَعْبُدَ رَبَّ هَٰذِهِ الْبَلْدَةِ الَّذِي حَرَّمَهَا وَلَهُ كُلُّ شَيْءٍ ۖ وَأُمِرْتُ أَنْ أَكُونَ مِنَ الْمُسْلِمِينَ وَأَنْ أَتْلُوَ الْقُرْآنَ ۖ فَمَنِ اهْتَدَىٰ فَإِنَّمَا يَهْتَدِي لِنَفْسِهِ ۖ وَمَنْ ضَلَّ فَقُلْ إِنَّمَا أَنَا مِنَ الْمُنْذِرِينَ. وَقُلِ الْحَمْدُ لِلَّهِ سَيُرِيكُمْ آيَاتِهِ فَتَعْرِفُونَهَا ۚ وَمَا رَبُّكَ بِغَافِلٍ عَمَّا تَعْمَلُونَ.

I have been commanded to worship the God of this town who has made it sacred, and to whom everything belongs, and I am commanded to be among Muslims and to recite the Qur'ān. Whoever elects to be guided, this guidance will be for their own benefit. Whoever goes astray, then say, "I am but a warner." And say, "Praise be to God! He will show you his signs so you would recognize them. And your God is never unmindful of what you do. (27:91–93)

The four occurrences of the word *Qur'ān* in 27:1, 6, 76, and 92 are split even as they bracket the miracle narratives of several prophets—notably Moses, David, Solomon, Sāliḥ, and Lot. The first of these narratives describes Moses with clear reference to the burning bush and the staff turning into a snake:

فَلَمَّا جَاءَهَا نُودِيَ أَنْ بُورِكَ مَنْ فِي النَّارِ وَمَنْ حَوْلَهَا وَسُبْحَانَ اللَّهِ رَبِّ الْعَالَمِينَ. يَا مُوسَىٰ إِنَّهُ أَنَا اللَّهُ الْعَزِيزُ الْحَكِيمُ. وَأَلْقِ عَصَاكَ ۚ فَلَمَّا رَآهَا تَهْتَزُّ كَأَنَّهَا جَانٌّ وَلَّىٰ مُدْبِرًا وَلَمْ يُعَقِّبْ ۚ يَا مُوسَىٰ لَا تَخَفْ إِنِّي لَا يَخَافُ لَدَيَّ الْمُرْسَلُونَ.

When he reached it, he was called "Blessed be the one at the fire and the one around it. Glory be to God, the lord of the worlds. O Moses. It is I. I am God—the almighty, the all-wise. Throw your staff." When he saw it shaking like a snake, he ran off without looking back. "O Moses, fear not. My messengers shall have no fear." (27:8–10)

In the following narrative we find similar miraculous feats. But this time, the miracle is not just given in a divine encounter, but bestowed in the form of a divine gift of knowledge. In this case, God gives the gift of علم (knowledge) to both David and Solomon:

وَلَقَدْ آتَيْنَا دَاوُودَ وَسُلَيْمَانَ عِلْمًا ۖ وَقَالَا الْحَمْدُ لِلَّهِ الَّذِي فَضَّلَنَا عَلَىٰ كَثِيرٍ مِنْ عِبَادِهِ الْمُؤْمِنِينَ

Indeed, we have given knowledge to David and Solomon. And they said, "Praise be to God who has favored us over many of his faithful servants." (27:15)

Even though the word *Qur'ān* is absent in this verse, its semantic memory is preserved in the verb *ātaynā* (we have given), which is often associated with the indication that the scripture is a gift from God, as it is the case in God's gifting of the "book" to Moses,[147] Jesus,[148] and Muḥammad.[149] In other words, the book—the scripture that contains the words of God—is a gift no less miraculous than the gift of learning how to speak to birds or to control the wind. This gift is manifest in the package of knowledge gifted to Solomon with the strong emphasis on the act of "giving" to specify that Solomon was *taught*—namely, that he was granted, from God, the knowledge of the language of birds, ants, and the knowledge to gather an army of birds, humans, and jinn:

وَوَرِثَ سُلَيْمَانُ دَاوُودَ ۖ وَقَالَ يَا أَيُّهَا النَّاسُ عُلِّمْنَا مَنْطِقَ الطَّيْرِ وَأُوتِينَا مِنْ كُلِّ شَيْءٍ ۖ إِنَّ هَٰذَا لَهُوَ الْفَضْلُ الْمُبِينُ وَحُشِرَ لِسُلَيْمَانَ جُنُودُهُ مِنَ الْجِنِّ وَالْإِنْسِ وَالطَّيْرِ فَهُمْ يُوزَعُونَ. حَتَّىٰ إِذَا أَتَوْا عَلَىٰ وَادِ النَّمْلِ قَالَتْ نَمْلَةٌ يَا أَيُّهَا النَّمْلُ ادْخُلُوا مَسَاكِنَكُمْ لَا يَحْطِمَنَّكُمْ سُلَيْمَانُ وَجُنُودُهُ وَهُمْ لَا يَشْعُرُونَ.

Then Solomon succeeded David and said, "O people! We have been taught the language of birds, and given everything. This is indeed great grace." Solomon's army of jinn, humans, and birds were rallied and perfectly organized for him. When they came across the valley of ants, an ant said, "O ants! enter your dwellings lest Solomon and his soldiers crush unaware." (27:16–18)

The relationship between miracle and knowledge/learning continues to build up in the incident of summoning the throne of the Queen of Sheba to Solomon's court:

قَالَ يَا أَيُّهَا الْمَلَأُ أَيُّكُمْ يَأْتِينِي بِعَرْشِهَا قَبْلَ أَنْ يَأْتُونِي مُسْلِمِينَ. قَالَ عِفْرِيتٌ مِنَ الْجِنِّ أَنَا آتِيكَ بِهِ قَبْلَ أَنْ تَقُومَ مِنْ مَقَامِكَ وَإِنِّي عَلَيْهِ لَقَوِيٌّ أَمِينٌ. قَالَ الَّذِي عِنْدَهُ عِلْمٌ مِنَ الْكِتَابِ أَنَا آتِيكَ بِهِ قَبْلَ أَنْ يَرْتَدَّ إِلَيْكَ طَرْفُكَ. فَلَمَّا رَآهُ مُسْتَقِرًّا عِنْدَهُ قَالَ هَٰذَا مِنْ فَضْلِ رَبِّي لِيَبْلُوَنِي أَأَشْكُرُ أَمْ أَكْفُرُ. وَمَنْ شَكَرَ فَإِنَّمَا يَشْكُرُ لِنَفْسِهِ ۖ وَمَنْ كَفَرَ فَإِنَّ رَبِّي غَنِيٌّ كَرِيمٌ.

He said, "O court! who can bring her throne to me before they come to me as Muslims. An 'ifrīt from the jinn answered, "I will bring it to you before you rise from your council, and I am strong enough and dependable for it." The one who has knowledge of the book said, "I will bring it to you before you blink." So when he saw it steady before him, he said, "This is from the grace of God to test me if I were to thank or disbelieve. Whoever thanks, he thanks for his own benefit, and whoever disbelieves, my God is indeed affluent and generous." (27:38–40)

There are various interpretations of the contest to bring forth the throne of the Queen of Sheba to Solomon. The word *'ifrīt* appears only once in the Qur'ān. It is therefore not clear if it is an adjective or a noun, though its syntactic position in the verse makes it the doer of the action. Here, the *'ifrīt* is clearly identified as a male or a masculine being from among the jinn who offered to bring the throne of the Queen of Sheba to Solomon before the latter left his council-seat. It is unclear, linguistically, if *'ifrīt* refers to a ranking member or type among the jinn or if it is a modifier referring to a specific, formidable jinn. In classical Arabic, the word *'ifrīt* denotes a cunning, vicious, and malicious creature. Furthermore, the other "being" in Solomon's council who counters the offer of the *'ifrīt* is not mentioned by name, but is referred to as "the one who has *'ilm*' (knowledge of/from) of the *kitāb* (book). In exegetical sources, interpretations of who that one is have ranged from Solomon's scribe, Āṣif ibn Barkhiyā, to a deeply knowledgeable friend of Solomon, to Gabriel, to even Solomon himself. What is clear in the sūra, however, is that because of this divinely inspired act, this "being" who "has knowledge of the book" is able to bring forth the throne of the Queen of Sheba before Solomon blinked.

But whether it takes a few hours or the blink of an eye, the act of brining the throne of the Queen of Sheba would still be a miraculous superhuman feat given that Solomon was historically positioned in modern-day Syria and the Queen of Sheba resided in Yemen, separated by hundreds of miles. Is it, then, a contest of language, of *bayān*, of the perfection of speech? Or is it about saying it more aesthetically, or is it a contest of speed and a competition in miraculous competencies? We will never know. What we do know is that the Qur'ān gives a speech-act, a supersonic actualization of thought on the spot as a manifestation of such a miracle. Interestingly enough, this miracle is tied to something else, without which it would seem that it won't be realized, and that is the *'ilm min al-kitāb* (knowledge of/from the book/scripture). There is therefore a strong affinity between *'ilm* and *kitāb* in *Sūra-t-al-Naml*, a connection that bridges the phenomenological and metaphysical and ties them together in the realm of the miracle.

Variations on the root *'ilm* appear eleven times throughout the sūra, mostly tied to *āyāt* as verses, signs, demonstrations, and miracles. The word *āyāt*, appearing ten times in the sūra with varying semantic references, has a binary interconnection with *kitāb*. An interactive semantic interlocution of the four words *āyāt*, *'ilm*, *Qur'ān* and *kitāb* is formed throughout *Sūra-t-al-Naml*, as the definition of each word is interdependent on the others. But the word that rounds it all off is *āyāt*, the keyword at the outset of the sūra, the grammatical *khabar* (predicate) of its very beginning:

طس ۚ تِلْكَ آيَاتُ الْقُرْآنِ وَكِتَابٍ مُبِينٍ

ṬāSīn. These are the verses/signs/revelations of the Qur'ān and a clear book. (27:1)

The predicate *āyāt* is modified by the genitive case of *āyāt al-kitāb* (verses/signs of the book) and the adjectival noun phrase conjunction of *kitāb mubīn* (and a clear book/script). This modification will eventually culminate in a hierarchy of complex miraculous narratives: we first have the miracles of Moses, followed by those of Solomon, then Ṣāliḥ, then Lot, as monotheistic prophets receiving the gift of extraordinariness. On a distinctly similar level, but nevertheless miraculous, we find the Qur'ān. The opening of *Sūra-t-al-Naml* thus eloquently predicts and connects its own trajectory to the miraculous. Note that *āyāt* could also be translated into English as an appositive to the Qur'ān itself, although I haven't seen it done yet, and could make the opening of the sūra read as: "These are the verses of the Qur'ān, a clear book," because in Arabic grammar the comma often replaces the و (*wa*, and) connector, thus affirming not only the semantic synonymity of the Qur'ān *as* a book and of the book *as* the Qur'ān, but more importantly its miraculous nature. In this sense, the indefinite noun phrase *kitāb mubīn* (a clear book) in 27:1 could itself be an appositive to *āyāt al-Qur'ān* (the signs/verses/revelations of the Qur'ān), a synonymous relationship that is frequent in the Qur'ān, and a good case where Arabic grammar is a prerequisite for Qur'ānic exegesis.[150]

While synonymous, *kitāb* and *Qur'ān* are not identical, especially not in *Sūra-t-al-Naml* where the referent *kitāb* assumes various semantic functions and creates effective paronomasia. For example, in 27:28–29, the *kitāb* Solomon writes and commissions the hoopoe to bring to the Queen of Sheba is a brief letter, perhaps small enough to be flown by a hoopoe, assuming that the hoopoe is of a similar size to the current species. Qur'ān 27:75 makes references to yet another *kitāb*—namely, a book that keeps the records and knowledge of everything, known and unknown, in heaven and earth, which could be a possible reference to *al-Lawḥ al-Maḥfūẓ* (the Preserved Tablet) in the realm of the divine that has record of all creation:

وَمَا مِنْ غَائِبَةٍ فِي السَّمَاء وَالأَرْضِ إلاَّ فِي كِتَابٍ مُّبِينٍ

There is nothing unseen/hidden/imperceptible in heaven or the earth without [it] being in a clear book. (27:75)

It is worth noting that a variation on the root of Islam in the word *muslimīn* (Muslims/adherents of Islam) appears five times in the sūra, three of which occur in the context of Solomon and the Queen of Sheba. Solomon's letter to the Queen of Sheba begins with: *bi-sm Allāh al-Raḥmān al-Raḥīm* (in the name of God the most merciful, the most compassionate), thus signaling the first and only time the customary Muslim *basmala* occurs inside the text of the Qur'ān.[151] The semantic effect of this occurrence serves yet as another rhetorical connector approximating the phenomenological miracles of Solomon with the linguistic miracle of the Qur'ān. Whereas some might see in the act of Sheba's "submission" to God a curious ambiguity,[152] the word *muslimīn*, which defines this very submission as the core of Islam—linguistically, semantically, and physically—is itself tied functionally to the message of the *kitāb* (Solomon's letter to the Queen of Sheba), which consists of six precise Arabic words:

أَلاَّ تَعْلُوا عَلَيَّ وَأْتُونِي مُسْلِمِينَ

Do not feel superior to me, but come to me as Muslims. (27:31)

And which he reiterates in the following verse:

قَالَ يَا أَيُّهَا الْمَلَأُ أَيُّكُمْ يَأْتِينِي بِعَرْشِهَا قَبْلَ أَن يَأْتُونِي مُسْلِمِينَ

He said, "O court! Who can bring her throne to me before they come to me as Muslims" (27:38)

And which he also emphasizes upon the Queen of Sheba's arrival to his palace, witnessing the marvel of transferring her throne:

فَلَمَّا جَاءَتْ قِيلَ أَهَكَذَا عَرْشُكِ قَالَتْ كَأَنَّهُ هُوَ وَأُوتِينَا الْعِلْمَ مِن قَبْلِهَا وَكُنَّا مُسْلِمِين

So when she came, she was asked, "Does your throne look like this?" She said, "It is as if this is my throne." We have indeed been given knowledge before this [miraculous act] and we have already been Muslims. (27:42)

And upon which she finally submits with Solomon to God:

قَالَتْ رَبِّ إِنِّي ظَلَمْتُ نَفْسِي وَأَسْلَمْتُ مَعَ سُلَيْمَانَ لِلَّهِ رَبِّ الْعَالَمِينَ

She said, "My God, I have done myself wrong, and have become Muslim with Solomon before God, lord of the worlds." (27:44)

Here the referent *aslamtu* (I have submitted to the will of God/ I have become Muslim) creates a linguistic atavism for the call for Islam—the religion of Muḥammad— by granting it historical validity. In other words, Islam is as old as this world; it has already happened, not just in the Meccan period in which Muḥammad is reciting the new textual miracle—that is, the Qur'ān or *al-kitāb*—but in the far off days of Solomon. Calling the Qur'ān *kitāb* is not just a sign that the latter is different from other texts existing in Arabia during the time of Muḥammad. To be sure, the Qur'ān is the first complete text ever to be written down in the history of the Arabic language, notwithstanding the writings of the *Mu'allaqāt* and the hanging of them on the walls of the *Kaaba* in pre-Islamic Mecca. In the Arabic-speaking world, the writing of the Qur'ān thus constitutes a decisive moment of transition from a preliterate society to a society of the book. Recall that the Qur'ān refers to Christians and Jews as *Ahl al Kitāb* (People of the Book), a term that often casts itself against *al-ummiyyīn* (nonscriptural/gentile communities), which includes Arab polytheists. The Qur'ān as *kitāb* distinguishes itself from the Arabian culture of polytheism but also from the scriptures of the People of the Book by asserting itself as *Kitāb 'Arabiyyin* or *bi-lisānin 'Arabiyyin mubīn* (an Arabic scripture/a scripture in a clear Arabic tongue). This distinction is important because it signifies the function of the Qur'ān text in the framework of its own social environment as an important marker of the transition from a preliterate to a literate society. To this effect, G. E. von Grunebaum contends that "by giving the Arabs a book, God elevated them to the rank of the other scripturaries; by giving them the final revelation of the Koran He lifted them above the others. Since the Hellenistic period the possession of a revealed book had been the mark of most new religious groups. In Muḥammad's world the primitive polytheist lacked this distinction."[153]

Furthermore, primitive polytheists, to extend von Grunebaum's point, lacked the rebuttal to the persistent and enduring rhetorical challenge that had become more prominent from the middle Meccan period onward. Verse 27:81 testifies to this challenge by stating that the words of God will only appeal to those who want to believe and embrace Islam, like Solomon, Sheba, and her people:

وَمَا أَنتَ بِهَادِي الْعُمْيِ عَن ضَلَالَتِهِمْ إِن تُسْمِعُ إِلَّا مَن يُؤْمِنُ بِآيَاتِنَا فَهُم مُّسْلِمُونَ

Nor can you guide the blind out of their misdirection. Only those who believe in our signs will hear you, for they are Muslims. (27:81)

Thus, the confirmation to Muḥammad that the signs of God are available to those who are willing to *listen* makes the act of listening to the Qur'ān a central gateway to faith. But why is this background important for the list of miracles in *Sūra-t-al-Naml*? Because whenever the word *āyāt* is mentioned, the syntax and the rhetoric of the sūra tie themselves into one single knot that captures the process of understanding the Qur'ān *as* a miracle. It also serves as a reminder of why and how these narratives are integrated in a contextual and rhetorical system of a language that asserts itself regardless of historical revisionism. In the Islamic tradition, the relationship between the text and its immediate culture is predicated on what such culture understands divinity to be. Divinity is attached to miraculous acts in a manner that surpasses the epistemological limits of such cultures. Addressing the rhetorical miracle of the Qur'ān, al-Zarkashī, perhaps guided by a hint from al-Jāḥiẓ, makes the following statement:

ونحن تتبين لنا البراعة في أكثره، ويخفى وجهها في مواضع لقصورنا عن مرتبة العرب يومئذ في سلامة الذوق وجودة القريحة وميز الكلام. وقامت الحجة على العالم بالعرب إذ كانوا أرباب الفصاحة ومظنة المعارضة، كما قامت الحجة في معجزة عيسى بالأطباء وفي موسى بالسحرة، فإن الله تعالى إنما جعل معجزات الأنبياء بالوجه الشهير أبرع ما تكون في زمن النبي الذى أراد إظهاره، فكان السحر في مدة موسى قد انتهى إلى غايته، وكذا الطب في زمان عيسى، والفصاحة في مدة محمد.[154]

We witness this linguistic brilliance in most of it [the Qur'ān], and we miss some owing to our lack of the degree of Arabicity which the bygone Arabs attained in the soundness of taste, the eminence of poetic talent, and the excellence of speech. The Qur'ān's defiance of the world thus materialized through these ancient Arabs, precisely because they were the ultimate masters of eloquence and the most qualified among all humans to produce an Arabic parody of the Qur'ān if they could, just as divine defiance targeted physicians in the time of Jesus and magicians in the time of Moses. God exacts miracles in a manner that outdoes the best of what people have in the eras of their respective prophets. Magic reached its zenith in the time of Moses, as did medicine in a time of Jesus, and linguistic eloquence in the time of Muḥammad.

Whether one agrees with al-Zarkashī's premises or with his definition of the miracle as a socially tailored act or not, *Sūra-t-al-Naml* in particular, and the Qur'ān in general, brings together, linguistically, figuratively, and rhetorically these widespread narratives in order to tie them neatly into semantic connectors with an overarching thematic unit, creating what Kermani describes as "an aesthetic proof of a religion's truth."[155] Whether or not the goal is to defy the Arabs of Muḥammad's time with an oral account that they can marvel at but not reproduce, what stands before us now is a *kitāb* seeking to persuade its audience that what granted the staff to Moses, what bestowed the special *ʿilm* on Solomon, what destroyed the people of Thamūd, and what obliterated the people of Lot, is the same spirit that sent down the Qurʾān and trusted an inimitable scripture to the heart of an *ummī* man.

This close reading of *Sūra-t-al-Naml* shows that one can find in the Qurʾān rhetorical continuities that are seamlessly consistent and articulate. Somewhere in between, at the interface of all these miracle narratives, the word *Qurʾān* comes to embody this very consistency. And even if it only occurs four times in the sūra, its carefully placed occurrences, together with the atavistic reference to "Islam" as a future in the past and a past in the future, allows for a mode of discourse to take place within a concatenation of prophetic narratives that can no longer be separated from the present time of *tanzīl*. This mode of discourse would become even more discernable if, instead of focusing on whether the Qurʾān got the biblical story of Solomon "right" or not, we delved into the intricate aesthetics and rhetorical structures that scaffold the Qurʾān's narrative, thereby revealing the text's profound depth and nuance.

Appropriately enough, European academics have always responded to linguistic and figural complexities of this kind in their respective national literatures, and, understandably in cases of disagreement, they conveyed their points in ethical and civil terms. It would be absurd to believe that one could ever fully exhaust the rhetorical or aesthetic aspects of the Qurʾān. But it would be even more absurd to think that one can avoid doing so by adopting a method insensitive to the most obvious features of the text. Even if one has to read only *Sūra-t-al-Naml* in the Qurʾān, it is easy to see that much of its investment is in building an architectural mapping of monotheism, which, if taken as a whole, would offer a way of interpreting the world. But this very mapping is produced in admirable figurations and linguistic features, which should in turn trigger curious questions: What is the meaning of this unique act of storytelling and of all such extraordinary events that are inexplicable by the laws of physics? What is the story of monotheism? What message does it convey? How did its journey begin, and why? Such questions would lead to the conclusion that *Sūra-t-al-Naml* is itself a fragment of a larger narrative, or that monotheism, or even the archetypal structuration of prophetic advocacy for the one God across human time, is itself a piece of a larger puzzle, a space between memory and history, and a charted course that somehow wants to interpolate us within its sphere. What connections do we have to such fragmented narratives that make us defend one version of monotheism against the other, or perceive them as parts of an existential puzzle, one that we feel authorized to piece together complete, or simply dismiss? It is not easy to find satisfying answers to these questions. At the very least, for the seasoned Arabist, the undeniable elegance and the commanding presence of the Qur'ān's language are far more compelling than the myriad questions its verses may invoke.

To conclude, these four modes—the cosmic point of view, the dissociation from poetry, the (dis)continuity of the monotheistic idea, and the quality of its linguistic miracle—are only parts of the larger system that constitutes the Qur'ān's unique and authoritative eloquence. Together, they reveal the existential positioning of prophets as human subjects, the experience of daily life, the social habits of the first Muslim community, the countering of the nomadic "point of view" of pre-Islamic poetry with a cosmic one, and the Qur'ān's distinct structure for the production of meaning. And even though it has now become one of the most global and most deterritorialized of all books of faith, the Qur'ān's local context will always remain the anchor of its oral character and the mark of its rhetorical singularity. A critical method seeking to place it within the grand narrative of world history will necessarily have to respect its complex Arabicity and envision new methods to do it justice. The argument for the Qur'ān's distinctiveness in what has now become the patented ideological space of late antiquity will depend largely on the future methodological enrichment of the field of Qur'ānic studies. This pursuit transcends academic curiosity; it is a critical venture with far-reaching political ramifications, as it essentially contributes to shaping the narrative and direction of a global religion within the very forums of our contemporary and future academic discourses.

Conclusion

The Future of Qur'ānic Studies

At the outset of this study, I suggested that pre-Islamic Arabic literature, rather than the category of late antiquity, is the most effective way of approaching and understanding the Qur'ān. I then tried to demonstrate that pre-Islamic Arabic thought and culture are "symbolic," both aesthetically and socially, of the foremost exception that is the Qur'ān itself, a scripture that both reflects and eclipses its own contemporary historical setting. Over the course of this book's chapters, I have taken this argument one step further. I have tried to demonstrate that whereas pre-Islamic poetry represents poetic discourse turned into a socio-aesthetic space, the Qur'ān represents aesthetic discourse turned against itself. On a pragmatic level, this distinction does not seem substantial. Both discourses, after all, end up as social-political aesthetics. However, what the transformative power of the Qur'ān has introduced to the field of aesthetics, that the transformative sovereignty of poetry into socio-aesthetics could not, is a much more profound integration of social and aesthetic categories than has ever been witnessed before in the entire history of the Arabo-Islamic world.

This is no small feat. For this reason, it has been important for me, and as I assume for all global readers alike, to redirect the course of Qur'ānic studies in the Euro-American academy. I did so by interrogating Euro-American scholarship's reliance on the historical-critical method, a method that fulfills the path of biblical criticism by treating the Qur'ān as a footnote to such history. To this day, most Euro-American scholarship on the Qur'ān operates from within an epistemological framework that presupposes such a primary biblical "intertext" (a new euphemism for "influence" or "borrowing").[1] By taking the immediate prehistory of the Qur'ān out of this equation, this predominant approach clings only to a method of interpreting the text from the theoretical end tail of extrapeninsular sources, leaving behind the story of the Qurʾānʾs Arabicity, its internal dialogues and conversations with its immediate pre-Islamic culture, and the local literary and socio-economic contexts associated with its age. Geert Jan van Gelder, whose estimable work on pre-Islamic Arabic "respects the Muslim tradition" and expresses hopes that "enlightened Muslims" would be able to address the extraordinary literariness of the Qurʾān, does not fail to underscore the necessity of a series engagement with pre-Islamic Arabic poetry.[2]

In this spirit, the guiding principle of this study has been to let the Qurʾān speak for itself, and to let it make its own statement, in its own distinct way, through its own language, images, narratives, and themes. Readers of and listeners to the Qurʾān in its original Arabic would realize how inviting the freedom and open-endedness of its figural ingenuity is. The Qurʾān proclaims its difference from poetry, and it retains within its own text the evidence of its difference. To argue that the Qurʾān reflects the context of its age is neither new nor, for the most part, contestable, but it is nonetheless an argument that continues to be understudied.

This book has engaged directly with this literariness and and has offered a rhetorical, literary, and linguistic reading of the two discourses of pre-Islamic poetry and the Qurʾān. It has focused on the aesthetic potential of the Arabic language, as well as on the autonomous possibilities of its significations in both discourses. As far as the comparison between pre-Islamic poetry and the Qurʾān is concerned, the truth that interests a literary critic is not of the order of broad categorizations or sweeping generalities. As I have sought to demonstrate, a literary reading is skeptical of the bulldozering and levelling that a historical categorization makes, and of all similarities that it must construct to justify its own status. Yet such a reading remains concerned with a specific reality, and because this reality goes as far as to question the validity of broad historical categorizations, it chooses to stand outside the comfy blanket of late antiquity, which paints everything "as a night," to recall Hegel, "in which all cows are black."[3] The method this study calls for does not yield to the historical imperative of one size that fits all.

While I steer away from hankering after origins and histories of texts, I focus on the language, aesthetics, ethics, individuals, and communities associated with the primary texts of seventh-century Arabia. My main objective is to open new horizons in the field of Qurʾānic studies. There is a definition of Islam in relationship to late antiquity that views the Qurʾān as organic, and not necessarily advocating for the abandonment of its native soil in favor of "out-sourcing." Thomas Sizgorich offers this position by stating that "the birth and early growth of the Muslim community within a late antique cultural milieu did nothing to undermine the evolution of a distinctively Islamic cultural tradition. Rather, the tradition begun within that milieu would prove so powerful as to recast ancient signs and symbols as uniquely its own."[4]

Sizgorich's statement reminds us that historical traditions cannot be reduced to texts. However, when a text becomes the main concern of a certain brand of historians, it follows that its very history will only be made available through a serious and direct engagement with its form and content. In fact, it was only two hundred years ago, in the long aftermath of Europe's scientific revolution, that the notion of discovering a truth behind the past through a "scientific method" became the preoccupation of history. In Europe, the birthplace of the historical-critical method, the end of the nineteenth and beginning of the twentieth centuries witnessed the academic rise of revisionism, with an agenda that Frederick Beiser aptly describes as "simple but ambitious: to legitimate history as a science. Its aim was to show what makes history a science. All the thinkers in the historicist tradition . . . wanted to justify the scientific status of history. They used 'science' in a broad sense of that term corresponding to the German word 'Wissenschaft,' that is, some methodical means of acquiring knowledge."[5] I address this issue elsewhere, but suffice it here to say that the move toward the "scientification" of history as a discipline is akin to the polarization we witness nowadays in the university, where the humanities are perceived as providing lesser market value than STEM research.[6]

In its Abrahamic version, a history of monotheism means for scholars of the Qur'ān and late antiquity that there is an intended execution of the original idea, a continuity thesis of Old Testament monotheism. When it comes to the Qur'ān, this continuity thesis has come to mean, or rather necessitate, the historical formation of an order of divination that is structurally identical, or at least substantially similar, to the original order of such divine history. There is truth to this claim. So, when Neuwirth states that "in its eschatological parts, the Qur'ān comes distinctively close to biblical prophet speech, although the great visions of the biblical prophets have come to be replaced by the short sura-introducing tableaux of the oath series,"[7] she advances the argument that divine history (scripted divine history, that is) is an order of calculated repetitions, not of voluntary or original spontaneity, and that the only changes are more or less technical, designed to "orient themselves stylistically to the ancient Arabic models of the seer speech."[8] Neuwirth further contends that apocalyptic visions "such as that of the 'valley of the rotting bones' in Ezekiel 37 have their Qur'ānic counterpart in the oath of Q. 100:1–5 on the suddenness of the awakening, or Q. 82:1–5 on the loosing [*sic*] of the cosmos."[9] She maintains for the Qur'ān what Daniel Weidner says of the Bible—namely, that "it is speech performance in the most eminent sense of the word, performance with apocalyptic power."[10] In this particular instance, she effectively demonstrates the parallels between the Bible and the Qur'ān and confirms, perhaps with a hint from Stefan Sperl and James Kugel, that "just as in the Bible, in the Qur'ān context the speech owes its impressing power to poetic strategies—an immanent potential for conflict—which in both cases requires a demarcation between prophecy and poetry, which in the case of the Qur'ān already occurred during the genesis of the text itself."[11]

This is how Neuwirth makes a powerful case for Islam as a "shared tradition" of late antiquity. For her intended audience, Neuwirth's argument is considered a revolutionary academic venture, coming a time when Europe has grown so scholastically accustomed to alienating and distancing itself from Islam and Muslims. Armed with her penetrative expertise in biblical criticism, Neuwirth proves that Islam has been misunderstood and treated as the *other* of Europe, whereas it is indeed part of Europe's own inherited theological history. This is perhaps the best and most sophisticated retooling of late antiquity as a bridge between a highly appreciated period that led to the very idea and foundation of Western Europe and the less historical appreciated ramifications of the period. Neuwirth's approach responds effectively to a current crisis in modern and contemporary political thought in Germany and a timely call for de-exoticizing and de-othering Islam, asking the question, "gehört der Islam zu Deutschland/Europa?" (does Islam belong to Germany/Europe?).

But to retool late antiquity this way blankets, rather than levels, the variegated histories of Judaism, Christianity, and Islam in Europe, Africa, and Asia.[12] In fact, while "sameness" implies "repetition," at least theoretically and, to some extent, monotheistically, in accord with the Abrahamic tradition, one must not, in practice, ignore the differences. Reading the Qur'ān with biblical eyes, or searching for the Bible in the Qur'ān, one is conditioned to spot only "similarities" and hence derivativeness—variations on an original theme. Academically, at least, the historical sources of this issue lie clearly in a centralized Old-Testament*ism* that has shaped Euro-American scholarship on the Qur'ān since the nineteenth century. Repetition is an attractive idea, and it insightfully facilitates Neuwirth's inclusion of the Qur'ān in the ancient cycles of biblical history. But one must also learn to see, and accept, the differences and diversities of the Qur'ānic text. The Qur'ān includes alternative themes, ideas, commentaries, references, inversions, subversions, and interpretations that must not be lost in the macrocosm of the late antique debate. In addition to its similar attachment to a monotheistic ideal, the Qur'ān remains a document of alterity with intricate microlinguistic significations and with "inside" references and subtleties that will be lost if read only as part of the complex continuum of a *terra incognita*. It certainly does include staggering fragments of language and dehistorized arrangements of sūras that may appear "illogical" to Western eyes.[13] But to "rationalize" it and reduce it to a category that makes it look like an end product of late antique biblical history repeats the same vicious circle of *othering* by a different name.

One would thus hope that future scholarship on the Qur'ān would regard it with Brechtian eyes, as a *Verfremdungseffekt*, a distancing or estrangement effect, precisely because it emerged in and engaged with a distinct linguistic tradition. This estrangement effect serves two important functions. First, it ultimately allows for more nuanced appreciations not only of the diverse literariness and language of the text—or what we might call the aesthetics of the text—but also of the text itself as different, which we might call the ethics of reading the text. Second, it will make us more aware of the extent to which a consistent and methodical ideology has dictated its conceptual limitations on ethical and aesthetic judgments of the celebrated tradition of another culture, imposing them on academic curricula, and continuing to project erroneous simulations of Islam's history—which is obviously one of the "privileges" through which Euro-American academe has access to history itself.

When we recall that the language of the Qur'ān rivaled poetry as a new discourse of aesthetic power and that conventional *tafsīr* accounts relied fundamentally on the language of pre-Islamic poetry to explicate the Qur'ān and that without it no exegesis or translation of would have been possible, it becomes difficult to ignore the fact that the absence of pre-Islamic Arabic from current academic debates betrays a deeper contradiction in terms, leaving a gaping lacuna in the Western academy of Qur'ānic studies. It is not without a valid reason that Amīn al-Khūlī, a towering Arabist, philologist, and rhetorician of the last century, would describe the Qur'ān as *kitāb al-'Arabiyya al-aqdar wa-atharuhā al-fannī al-aqdas* (the greatest book of the Arabic language and its most revered literary heritage).[14]

This testimony is not surprising given that the Qur'ān is by far the most significant literary text of the Arabic language, even more compelling than other texts centuries before or after. In part, this may explain the rush in late antique scholarship to "include" it in its periodization, with the insistence that the Qur'ān is ultimately "homiletic" in character and "belonging to" (euphemism for "derivative of") an ancient genre that flourished in the late antique world *writ large*.[15] Yet, a literary-linguistic approach to the Qur'ān from within the context of its own Arabicity reveals that this so-called "scientific" method of interpreting the Qur'ān from the lens of the historical-critical method is neither emancipatory nor inclusive, but is at best a Eurocentric orchestration of the Old Testament's avowal of origins.

Viewing late antiquity as a new avenue for escaping the entrenched hierarchy in academic discourse offers hope. It suggests that embracing Islam within this framework could offer the most timely and considerate approach yet for addressing Eurocentrism in Qur'ānic studies and the broader academic world, thanks to its potential to explore similarities and connections between Judaism, Christianity, and Islam. However, this approach is fundamentally flawed, as it merely provides a partial resolution. It not only overlooks the specific historical context and diversity of the Qur'ān; it also portrays a Judeo-Christian world that appears static and unmoved in its own textuality, disregarding the significant historical evolutions of these texts and of the Qur'ān itself. This perspective recurrently adopts a negative analogy of the Qur'ān, relying on a methodology grounded in derivative thought rather than the much needed positive analogy that would acknowledge the Qur'ān both as a product of its era and as a transformative force within the monotheistic tradition.

A positive analogy would in fact put the Qurʾān into its own immediate *mise en scène*, allowing it be the document of history that it is, noticing that it is a *commentary* on biblical history that lends itself easily to a comparison between seemingly incompatible versions of divine narratives. As a result of this comparison, the Qurʾān points out affinities, allusions, equivalences, and resemblances among preceding prophetic narratives whether recurring in the Qurʾānic text or acknowledged without inclusion;[16] more importantly, however, it also draws distinctions between narratives that are, in fact, comparable, but whose comparability subscribes to certain terms—for example, sociohistorical conditions and power relations in seventh-century Hijaz, rather than just the thin linearity of an origin and its replica.

Yet the law of Eurocentrism has always been a law of an original versus a copy, not the acknowledgement of difference as authority, but the dissolution of this authority into an "inclusive" act of hierarchical referentiality. It is not at all difficult to amass a series of passages from the Qurʾān that are analogous to biblical and para-biblical traditions.[17] The reason for this is obvious: the Qurʾān does not disavow its relationship to Judaism and Christianity. On the contrary, the Qurʾān embraces this relationship and demonstrates deep interest in and familiarity with narratives and ethical traditions of communities from which both Judaism and Christianity originated. Yet the Qurʾān unequivocally discards claims of "influence" under any name. As is evident from the academic training of numerous Euro-American scholarships on the Qurʾān over the span of the last fifty years,[18] methodological approaches to the Qurʾān and late antiquity originate primarily in the historical-critical method of Bible interpretation. However, it remains inexplicably reductionist to approach the Qurʾān as the sum of its biblical narratives and themes, especially when these narratives serve as only one component of its overall constitutive totality. Even on occasions when the Qurʾān addresses prophetic miracles, it does so in a manner that is at once relatable to *and* different from the Old Testament, focusing more on episodic interlacing of such stories (to serve a higher moral lesson and affirm a monotheistic continuum) than on presenting each story as a sequential historical plot with a beginning, middle, and end, except perhaps for the story of Joseph (12). This progressive dehistoricized consciousness embraces a condition of admonishment where historical time is set right up to the moment in which the Qurʾān answers to it. Precisely by doing so, the lesson drawn from prophetic stories across human time is itself the transforming critique of human history.[19] In other words, the Qurʾān proclaims that it neither invents nor originates monotheism, but functions, rather, as an endorsement of its existence throughout time since creation.

In every context, the Qurʾān confirms divine justice as an inalienable attribute of divinity. God, who occupies half the space of the Qurʾān, is not in the business of abandoning humanity, the Qurʾān tells us, but is keen on sending prophets and signs to every community and nation.[20] Prophetic narratives recited in the

Qur'ān are themselves symbolic of this overarching divine justice. It therefore matters significantly that we position the Qur'ān within seventh-century Arabia, among communities with a massive appetite for language and for gods. Otherwise, it would be practically impossible to envisage the Qur'ān emerging outside this backdrop of literary aesthetics and theistic ethics. It is precisely inside this local context that the Qur'ān ascertains its theistic and linguistic triumph in the face of historical determinacy.[21] What does not simply rehash older patterns and narratives is itself historically signifying, at least in accordance with Karl Marx's remark that each era completes only the tasks assigned to it.[22]

While the argument for a superhuman prophetic narrative in the Qur'ān—or for the Qur'ān itself as an extraordinary linguistic phenomenon—may fall flat in a secular postreligious world, a world in which many of us can be found on our phones rather than reading poems, studying languages with "strange" alphabets, or reading arcane poetry, one must not rush to the conclusion that the extraordinary is not part of our world, or that the fantastic does not take place in our lived reality. It is just that its impact on our shared humanity may well be too close for comfort. In this context, what must be historically recorded—and what must not get lost in translation—is that the Qur'ān remains the most reliable source of its own language. Nothing more, nothing less. In Islam, as well as in Judaism and Christianity, the core doctrine will always remain the mysterious Logos, *kalima-tu-Allāh* (the Word of God). Whether this Word of God is incarnate or remains immaterial, its (im)materiality is inherently immaculate, beautiful, and unmimetic.

Those who choose to bypass this Arabicity and view the Qur'ān as a byproduct of an extrapeninsular historical condition of late antique times are not only missing the rich open-endedness, wealth, and complexity of its distinct language; they are masking an anxiety of having their own ideological methods laid bare by the very text they seek to read and historicize. It turns out that "including" the Qur'ān under the rubric of late antiquity is, after all, nothing but a refusal to read the Qur'ān, a refusal that has reached its highpoint in the historical-critical approach of the Euro-American academy. By freeing the Qur'ān from the *'aṣabiyya* of the "derivative," one would also embolden the Abrahamic and eventually free it from the toxic opposition between origin and replica, which is itself a genetic symptom of a naïvely mimetic Eurocentric mind.

For the field of Qur'ānic studies to have a fresh beginning, it will have to emancipate itself from relying on an outmoded method to interpret the Old Testament and the reapplication of such a method to the Qur'ān, especially when this method has already garnered the discontent of eminent Bible scholars. Not only this, but its subscription to academe must rid itself of what Neuwirth herself characterizes as "an epistemic pessimism," a rash dismissal of the "vast corpora of Islamic learning as useless for Qur'ānic studies" and "little interest in the pagan, the *Jāhilī* Arab background of the Qur'ānic event . . . for the sake of a principal re-location of the Qur'ān out of Arabia into an undetermined Christian space."[23] There is nothing necessarily perverse in juxtaposing the Qur'ān with the historical contexts of Abrahamic monotheism; the Qur'ān itself welcomes this juxtaposition. But one must do so from within the ethics of the comparative, without hijacking the Qur'ān's Arabicity or colonizing its socio-linguistic context. David Damrosch makes an excellent point when he states that "appropriately so, the Qur'ān is a gift not only to humanity in general but to comparatists in particular," a gift that may not immediately be "inviting to the literary critic,"[24] but that soon opens up to "literary analysis and insights."[25] Damrosch's words remind us of this dire need for a new generation of scholars who can study the Qur'ān, comparatively, in nonessentialist terms and challenge, where appropriate, orientalist, neo-orientalist, and even Islamist forms of "conventional wisdom."

The future of Qur'ānic studies in the Euro-American academy will flourish only when its method is no longer a prisoner to ideological nonlinguistic value judgements. Academically and ethically, today we need a method that respects the Qur'ān's Arabic language, the reception of the form and meaning of such language by its intended audience at its own historical time, and the aesthetic and linguistic modalities extant both in the language of the Qur'ān and the pre-Islamic idiom that forms and informs it. In fact, the corpus of pre-Islamic literature is rich enough to require an independent discipline to further investigate its status and relationship to the Qur'ān. Euro-American scholarship on the Qur'ān will also have to come to terms with the fact that compelling instances of humanism could also lie outside the epistemic spheres of Europe.

The Qur'ān, a seminal document of seventh-century humanism with a global reach, still beckons further exploration and a wider audience. Overlooking this strand of humanism in both pre-Islamic poetry and the Qur'ān itself not only reinforces the divisive force of *'aṣabiyya*; it also amplifies its distortion. We should imagine, then, the transformative potential were the Qur'ān to be positioned in a way that decenters biblical history from its long-standing pedestal as the sole point of reference, challenging the historical-critical method's monopoly on interpreting scripture. Could this not herald a paradigm shift, prompting a reevaluation of our collective humanism and inspiring a level of critical thought more daring and profound than ever before? What could the implications of embracing such a positive analogy be?

NOTES

INTRODUCTION: PRIMUM NON NOCERE

1. Neuwirth, *The Qu'an and Late Antiquity*, 37.

2. Ibid. (emphasis mine).

3. Ibid.

4. Ibid., 2–3.

5. Ibid., 37.

6. Ibid., 16.

7. Ibid., 2.

8. Ibid., 4.

9. Ibid., 3.

10. Ibid., x.

11. Ibid.

12. Ibid.

13. Ibid., 2, 3, 4–6, 8–12.

14. See Castell, *The Rise of the Network Society*.

15. See, e.g., Haleem, "Grammatical Shift for Rhetorical Purposes"; Haleem, "Rhetorical Devices and Stylistic Features of Qurʾānic Grammar"; Afsar, "A Literary Critical Approach to Qurʾānic Parables"; Blankinship, *The Inimitable Qurʾān*; Norman O. Brown, "The Apocalypse of Islam"; El Masri, *The Semantics of Qurʾanic Language*; Flowers, "Reconsidering Qurʾanic Genre"; Hoffmann, The Poetic Qurʾān; Kermani, *God is Beautiful*; Mir, "Between Grammar and Rhetoric"; Neuwirth, "Images and Metaphors in the Introductory Sections of the Makkan Suras"; Neuwirth "Rhetoric and the Qurʾān."

16. Bronwen, "The Earliest Greek Understandings of Islam," 227.

17. Ibid., 228.

18. MacAuliffe, ed., *The Cambridge Companion to the Qurʾān*; Rippin and Mojaddedi, eds., *The Wiley Blackwell Companion to the Qurʾān*.

179

19. This is a largely Euro-American trend in Qurʾānic studies. See, for instance, Paret, *Mohammed und der Koran*; Bobzin, *Koran*; Cook, *The Koran*; and Déroche, *Le Coran*. Over the last fifty years, there have been a few commendable attempts to engage with the Qurʾān's literary and lingo-aesthetic significations; however, most of these studies are sporadic, emanating not from a disciplinary or field orientation, but rather from individual scholars and philologists with a strong training in classical Arabic, whose findings continue to be haunted by the hundred-year-old tenuous and unfounded *intiḥāl* (forgery) thesis of both D. S. Margoliouth and Ṭāhā Ḥusayn.

20. Schneidau, *Sacred Discontent: The Bible and Western Tradition*, 249.

21. Attribution of Qurʾānic diction to pre-Islamic poetry is traced back to Nāfiʿ ibn al-Azraq ibn Qays al-Ḥanafī al-Bakrī (d. 685). He was the leader of the Kharijite faction of the Azāriqa during the Umayyad dynasty. Ibn al-Azraq is reported to have asked Ibn ʿAbbās questions about specific terminologies of the Qurʾān and evidence of their existence in pre-Islamic Arabic poetry. This report is in a Q and A format and can be found in numerous postclassical and medieval *tafsīr* sources but was not gathered in one account until al-Suyūṭī collected about two hundred questions in his *Tafsīr*. See al- al-Suyūṭī, *al-Itqān fī ʿUlūm al-Qurʾān*, 105.

22. Ibn Sallām, *Lughāt al-Qabāʾil al-Wārida fī al-Qurʾān*.

23. al-Fatḥ ʿUthmān Ibn Jinnī, *Sir Ṣināʿa -t- al-Iʿrāb*.

24. See, e.g., Sperl's essay, "The Qurʾān and Arabic Poetry."

25. See Christopher Livanos and Mohammad Salama, "A Bridge Too Far?," 145–69.

26. Schimmel, *Deciphering the Signs of God*, 150.

27. 3:144

28. 42:13.

29. Earlier scholarship tracing the exchange of words and expressions between pre-Islamic Arabic and the Qurʾān could be found in works by Julius Wellhausen, Carl Brockelmann, Toshihiko Izutsu, and Susanne Krone. For a recent application of this approach, Nicolai Sinai offers a survey of what pre-Islamic poetry has to say about the occurrence of the referent *Allāh*. Sinai's survey leads him to the conclusion that there is a "significant degree of continuity between quranic theology and earlier Arabian notions of Allāh." See Sinai, *Rain-Giver, Bone-Breaker, Score-Settler*, 4.

1. REMAPPING QURʾĀNIC STUDIES: HISTORIES AND METHODS

1. Smith's work was published in India in 1943 and is still a major work in circulation today. See Smith, *Modern Islam in India*.

2. Quoted in Graham, "The Scholar's Scholar: Wilfred Cantwell Smith and a Collegial Life of the Mind," 7.

3. Quoted in Cracknell, ed., *Wilfred Cantwell Smith*, 123. For more on Wilfred Cantwell Smith's legacy, see Hick, "On Wilfred Cantwell Smith: His Place in the Study of Religion."

4. See Winder, "Four Decades of Middle Eastern Study."

5. Philip Willard Ireland, ed. *The Near East: Problems and Prospects*.

6. H.A.R. Gibb, review of *Social Forces in the Middle East*, by Sidney Nettleton Fisher, 218.

7. Ibid.

8. For a nuanced genealogy of studying Islam as a "problem" in Western Europe, especially in relation to Christian theology and secular thought, see Hourani, "Islam and the Philosophy of History."

9. Despite the largely uncritical theses Nöldeke proposes regarding the establishment of the ʿuthmānian text, his work is still the uncontested primary source in determining the validity of the sūra chronology and the division of the history of the Qurʾān into four periods, three Meccan and one Medinan, used by contemporary scholars like Neuwirth and others. The reason behind this excessive reliance on Nöldeke is simply because, to date, no other major studies on putting the Qurʾān and the Prophet's oral preaching into writing have been attempted. The publication of a new English edition of Nöldeke's work in 2013, translated by W. H. Behn (and complete with tables, bibliography, and indexes), has finally made this magnum opus available to the international English-speaking research community of Qurʾānic studies, and is expected to trigger more scholarship on the topic. See Nöldeke et al., *The History of the Qurʾān*.

10. *Historikerstreit*, or the Historians' Debate, was a public controversy triggered in mid-1980s Germany following the publication by the Frankfurt School philosopher Jürgen Habermas of an article in *Die Zeit* (July 11, 1986) in which he criticized tendencies in the historiography of the Third Reich. For more on the historical debates leading to *Historikerstreit* and the ethical crisis of the 1980s on how to write and confront Germany's own history of racism and antisemitism in the aftermath of the Holocaust, see Fischer, *Bündnis der Eliten*; Hamilton, *Who Voted for Hitler*; Moses, *German Intellectuals and the Nazi Past*. See also Salama and Langbehn, eds., *German Colonialism*.

11. On reading the first part of *Hagarism*, Wansbrough dismissed the study as "inauthentic," with material based solely on "the authors' methodological assumptions, of which the principal must be that a vocabulary of motives can be freely extrapolated from a discrete collection of literary stereotypes composed by alien and mostly hostile observers, and thereupon employed to describe, even interpret, not merely the overt behaviour but also intellectual and spiritual development of the helpless and mostly innocent actors. Where even the sociologist fears to tread, the historian ought not with impunity be permitted to go" (Wansbrough, review of *Hagarism*, by Patricia Crone).

12. Barth, *The Epistle to the Romans*.

13. For a fuller analysis of Bultmann's influence on Wansbrough, see Stewart, "Wansbrough, Bultmann, and the Theory."

14. See also Borg, *Jesus in Contemporary Scholarship*.

15. Wansbrough, *Quranic Studies*, 11, 19.

16. See Bultmann et al., *Kerygma and Myth*.

17. Wansbrough, *Quranic Studies*, xxii.

18. Ibid., xxii.

19. Ibid., xxii–xxiii.

20. Ibid., xxiii.

21. Ibid.

22. Ibid., 99, 113.

23. See Bultmann, *Kerygma and Myth*, 10.

24. Wansbrough, *Quranic Studies*, 20, 51, 54, 72.

25. Hodgson, *The Venture of Islam*, 1:160.

26. Ibid. See also J. A. C. Brown, *Hadith*. See in particular Brown's chapter, "The Authenticity Question: Western Debates over the Historical Reliability of Prophetic Traditions," 197–239. In this chapter, Brown provides a fair-minded critique of the literature of Ḥadīth criticism in the West, identifying four main stages: Orientalism, the philo-Islamic apologetics, Western revisionism, and post-revisionism. For a more recent study of the life of Muḥammad, see Sean W. Anthony, *Muhammad and the Empires of Faith*. In this well-researched and nuanced postrevisionist examination of the life of Muḥammad, Anthony combines non-Muslim with Muslim sources. He interweaves narratives from the Greek text *Doctrina Jacobi*, which is often quoted as the earliest documentary witness to the life of Muḥammad, with classical Muslim sources such as ibn Shihāb al-Zuhrī (d. 124/742) and ibn Isḥāq (d. 150/767), and accounts from late antique Christianity, most notably the story of the Byzantine emperor Heraclius's vision and Muḥammad's letter to him. More importantly for our purpose, Anthony shows that a historically reliable investigation of Muḥammad's life can be demonstrated through a patient and careful study of early Muslim sources in the *sirah-maghazi* literature, evidence in the Qurʾān, as well as early Greek and Syriac non-Islamic sources. Combined, all these sources prove that Muḥammad lived in Mecca circa 570 AD and later claimed to belong to a long line of Abrahamic prophets who received revelation; he then moved to Yathrib (Medina) and formed a community of believers who were inspired by his teachings and who continued to preserve the message of Islam until it transformed the world.

27. The Middle East would be partitioned again with the rise of area studies in the light of the Cold War.

28. Neuwirth, *The Qurʾan and Late Antiquity*, 22.

29. Levinas calls for an acknowledgement of an exterior transcendence in the other that must be accepted, a transcendence that escapes one's comprehensive knowledge. In this acknowledgment lies the core of religio-ethical responsibility towards the other. See Levinas, *Totality and Infinity*, 49.

30. Watt, *Muslim-Christian Encounters*, 133.

31. Geiger, "Was hat Mohammed aus dem Judenthume aufgenommen?" In this essay, Geiger (1810–74) argues that the Qurʾān was derivative and that Muḥammad could not have authored it without plagiarizing numerous terms from the Hebrew Bible and rabbinic literature. See also Geiger, *Judaism and Islām*, 44.

32. See Salama and Langbehn, eds., *German Colonialism*.

33. For a nuanced analysis of Germany's complex relationship to Islam, see Almond, *The History of Islam in German Thought*.

34. See Schimmel, "Islamic Studies in Germany," 401–10.

35. See, for instance, Foucault, *The Archeology of Knowledge*; Habermas, *Knowledge and Human Interests*; de Certeau, *The Writing of History*; Young, *White Mythologies*; Gilroy, *The Black Atlantic*; Spivak, *A Critique of Postcolonial Reason*.

36. "I do not exhaustively discuss the German development after the inaugural period dominated by Sacy. Any work that seeks to provide an understanding of academic Orientalism and pays little attention to scholars like Steinthal, Müller, Becker, Goldziher, Brockelmann, Nöldeke—to mention only a handful—needs to be reproached, and I freely reproach myself" (Said, *Orientalism*, 18).

37. See, for instance, Toorawa, "Seeking Refuge from Evil," 54–60; Boullata, ed., *Literary Structures of Religious Meaning in the Qurʾān*; Monroe, "Oral Composition in Pre-Islamic

Poetry," 1–53; Montgomery, "Dichotomy in Jahili Poetry," 1–20; Izutsu, *Ethico-Religious Concepts in the Qurʾān*; J. Stetkevych, *Muhammad and the Golden Bough*; S. P. Stetkevych, *The Mute Immortals Speak*; Bauer, "The Relevance of Early Arabic Poetry for Qurʾānic Studies," 699–732; el Masri, *The Semantics of Qurʾanic Language: al-Āḫira*.

38. Stewart, "A Modest Proposal for Islamic Studies," 158.

39. Ibid., 188.

40. Ibid., 187.

41. See Popper, *Open Society*, esp. chapter 23.

42. Quoted in Cracknell, ed., *Wilfred Cantwell Smith*, 123.

2. WHAT IS LATE ANTIQUITY AND WHAT DOES THE QURʾĀN HAVE TO DO WITH IT?

1. Sadeghi and Goudarzi, "Ṣanʿāʾ 1 and the Origins of the Qurʾān," 1. See also Sadeghi and Bergmann, "The Codex of a Companion of the Prophet and the Qurʾān of the Prophet," 343–436.

2. Examples of this trend include Wansbrough, *Quranic Studies*; Wansbrough, *The Sectarian Milieu*; Hawting, "The Literary Context of the Traditional Account of Pre-Islamic Arab Idolatry," 21–41; Hawting, *The Idea of Idolatry and the Emergence of Islam*; Rippin, "The Exegetical Genre *asbāb al-nuzūl*: A Bibliographical and Terminological Survey," 1–15.

3. See, e.g., Crone, "Islam, Judeo-Christianity and Byzantine Iconoclasm," 59–95; Lüling, *A Challenge to Islam for Reformation*; Luxenberg, *Die syro-aramäische Lesart des Koran*; Luxenberg, *The Syro-Aramaic Reading of the Koran*; Reynolds, *The Qurʾan and its Biblical Subtext*; Zellentin, *The Qurʾan's Legal Culture*.

4. I borrow the term "late antiquarians" from Devin Stewart, who is the first to coin it in his survey, "Reflections on the State of the Art in Western Qurʾanic Studies," 30–31.

5. See, e.g., Fowden, *From Empire to Commonwealth*; Cameron and King, eds., *The Byzantine and Early Islamic Near East II*; Cameron, ed., *The Byzantine and Early Islamic Near East III*; Griffith, *The Qurʾan in Arabic*.

6. There are many scholars whose work represents this trend, including, among others, Garth Fowden, Hugh Kennedy, Aaron Hughes, Robert Hoyland, Guy Stroumsa, Nicolai Sinai, and Holger Zellentin. See, for instance, Stroumsa, *The Making of the Abrahamic Religions in Late Antiquity*; Hoyland, "Early Islam as a Late Antique Religion," 1053–77.

7. Neuwirth, "Locating the Qurʾan in the Epistemic Space of Late Antiquity," 159–79. Neuwirth's article is also published under a slightly different title. See "Locating the Qurʾan and Early Islam in the Epistemic Space of Late Antiquity."

8. See *Studien zur Komposition der mekkanischen Suren*. See also Neuwirth, "Rezension zu Wansbrough, *Qurʾanic Studies, Die Welt des Islams*"; Neuwirth, Sinai, and Marx, eds., *The Qurʾān in Context*; Neuwirth and Sells, eds., *Quranic Studies Today*; Neuwirth, *Der Koran als Text der Spätantike*; Neuwirth, *Scripture, Poetry and the Making of a Community*.

9. See N. O. Brown, *The Challenge of Islam*, 55–59.

10. Neuwirth, *The Qurʾan and Late Antiquity*, 25.

11. See Sperl and Dedes, eds., *Faces of the Infinite*.

12. Dussel, *Beyond Philosophy*, 54.

13. Foucault, "Nietzsche, Genealogy, History," 79.

14. In the context of Islamic legal studies, Wael B. Hallaq confronts this serious issue in a number of articles. See, for instance, Hallaq, "On Orientalism, Self-Consciousness and History," 387–439; "The Quest for Origins or Doctrine?," 1–31; and "Review: The Use and Abuse of Evidence," 79–90.

15. See Anderson, *Lineages of the Absolutist State*. See in particular Anderson's chapter, "The House of Islam," 361–96. Islam was no doubt a subject of heated historical debates among many intellectuals in Europe across the centuries. See also Prideaux's *True Nature of Imposture Revealed in the Life of the Impostor Mohammad* (1697), a remarkable account of a derisive historiographic polemic rampant in seventeenth-century Europe. A work like Henry Stubbe's *An Account of the Rise and Progress of Mahometanism with the Life of Mahomet and a Vindication of Him and His Religion from the Calumnies of Christians* (1676) expresses reverence for Islam and favorably considers it a religion similar to Christianity. In his book, Stubbe describes Muḥammad as a "genius." The difference of course is in circulation. Whereas Prideaux's work circulated widely in Europe and North America, Stubbe's work remained unpublished. For more positioning of Islam as the "other" of Europe, see Hourani, "Islam and the Philosophers of History," 206–68; see also Salama, *Islam, Orientalism, and Intellectual History*, 78–145.

16. Bevir, "Why historical distance is not a problem," p. 25.

17. See Sallustius Crispus (Sallust), *De Coniuratione Catilinae* (44–40 BC); Gaius Cornelius Tacitus, *Agricola* (98 AD), and Titus Livius (Livy), *Ab Urbe Condita* (753 BC).

18. Durant, *The Story of Civilization*, vol. 3, 665.

19. P. Brown, *The World of Late Antiquity*, 7.

20. Mommsen, *The History of Rome*, vol. 3, 611.

21. H. I. Bell, *Egypt from Alexander the Great to the Arab Conquest*, 133–34.

22. Wickham, *Framing the Early Middle Ages*.

23. See Pirenne, "Mahomet et Charlemagne," 77–86.

24. Pirenne, *Mohammed and Charlemagne*.

25. E. Ashtor, "Quelques observations d'un Orientaliste sur la these de Pirenne," 188.

26. Ehrenkreutz, "Another Orientalist's Remarks concerning the Pirenne Thesis," 104.

27. P. Brown, *The World of Late Antiquity*, 189.

28. Ibid., 190.

29. Ibid., 190–93.

30. Ibid., 203.

31. See, for instance, Clover and Humphreys, "Towards a Definition of Late Antiquity," 3–26; Cameron, "The 'Long' Late Antiquity," 165–91.

32. Murray, "Peter Brown and the Shadow of Constantine," 195.

33. P. Brown, *The World of Late Antiquity*, 158.

34. Ibid., 131.

35. Ibid., 68.

36. Ibid., 169–70.

37. See Cameron, "The 'Long' Late Antiquity," 190.

38. Crone and Cook, *Hagarism*, 3.

39. Donner, review of *Hagarism*, 199.

40. Ibid.

41. There has been further elaboration of this phenomenon in in the works of Aziz al-Azmeh and Averil Cameron. See Al-Azmeh, *The Emergence of Islam in Late Antiquity*; see Cameron, "Patristic Studies and the Emergence of Islam," 249–78.

42. Hegel, *Introduction to the Philosophy of History*, 97.

43. Ibid., 98.

44. Neuwirth, *The Qur'an and Late Antiquity*, 108.

45. Kennedy, "Islam," 219.

46. Griffith, *Arabic Christianity in the Monasteries of 9th-Century Palestine*.

47. Kennedy, "Islam," 235.

48. See Jones, *The Later Roman Empire*, 284–602.

49. See H. I. Marrou, *A History of Education in Antiquity*.

50. See Elton, *Warfare in Roman Europe, AD 350–425*; Elton, *The Roman Empire in Late Antiquity*; Cameron, ed., *The Byzantine and Early Islamic Near East*.

51. See Valantasis, ed., *Religions of Late Antiquity in Practice*.

52. Hughes, "Religion without Religion: Integrating Islamic Origins into Religious Studies," 869.

53. Ibid., 869n4.

54. See, e.g., Hughes, *Abrahamic Religions*; Stroumsa, "Athens, Jerusalem and Mecca," 153–68; Stroumsa, *The Making of the Abrahamic Religions in Late Antiquity*.

55. Neuwirth, *The Qur'an and Late Antiquity*, 456–57.

56. Neuwirth, "Locating the Qur'an and Early Islam in the Epistemic Space of Late Antiquity," 167.

57. I am grateful to Dr. Christian Junge for explaining the multiple connotations of "zugang."

58. Neuwirth, *The Qur'an and Late* Antiquity, 455.

59. Ibid., 22.

60. Ibid., 420 (emphasis mine).

61. Ibid., 22.

62. Ibid.

63. See John Barton, ed., *The Cambridge Companion to Biblical Interpretation*.

64. Weil, *Mohammed der Prophet, sein Leben und seine Lehre* (1843). Quoted in Nöldeke et al., *The History of the Qur'ān*, 373.

65. Neuwirth, *The Qur'an and Late Antiquity*, 23.

66. See Berman, *Inconsistency in the Torah*. See in particular Berman's scintillating chapter 11: "A Critical Intellectual history of the Historical-Critical Paradigm in Biblical Studies," 201–26.

67. Neuwirth, *The Qur'an and Late Antiquity*, 306.

68. Ibid., 241–86.

69. Ibid., 286–90, 334–37.

70. Thomas Bauer, "The Relevance Of Early Arabic Poetry For Qur'ānic Studies Including Observations On *Kull* and on Qur'ān 22:27, 26:225 And 52:31," 700.

71. Ibid., 459.

72. Ibid., 410.

73. Von Grunebaum, "Ausbreitungs-und Anpassungsfähigkeit," 14. Quoted in Neuwirth, *The Qur'an and Late Antiquity*, 41.

74. Neuwirth, *The Qur'an and Late Antiquity*, 41–42.

75. See also 12:2; 12:2; 13:37; 16:13.

76. Montgomery, "Dichotomy is Jahili Poetry," 1–20.

77. Zwettler, *The Oral Tradition of Classical Poetry*.

78. Neuwirth, *The Qur'an and Late Antiquity*, 21.

79. Israel and Silverthorne, eds., *Spinoza*, 101–2.

80. Crone and Cook, *Hagarism*.

81. Luxenberg, *Die syro-aramäische Lesart des Korans*.

82. See, e.g., Donner's notion of the "community of Believers" in *Muhammad and the Believers*, 78.

83. Zellentin, ed., *The Qurʾan's Reformation of Judaism and Christianity*, 1.

84. Ibid., 2.

85. Ibid.

86. Zellentin, "The Rise of Monotheism in Arabia," 158.

87. Ibid.

88. Ibid., 159.

89. LaCapra, "Rethinking Intellectual History and Reading Texts," 274.

90. According to Lee Ross's theory of "attribution bias," scientists, including psychologists and scholars, often find themselves caught in ideologically biased assumptions, derived largely from predominant cultural societal factors: "The intuitive scientist's ability to master his social environment depends in large measure upon the accuracy and adequacy of his hypotheses, evidence, and methods of analysis and inference. Conversely, sources of oversight, error, or bias in his assumptions and procedures may have serious consequences, both for the lay psychologist himself and for the society that he builds and perpetuates" (Ross, "The Intuitive Psychologist and His Shortcomings," 174).

91. LaCapra, "Rethinking Intellectual History and Reading Texts," 247.

92. Ibid. (emphasis mine).

93. Fowden, *Before and After Muhammad*.

94. Gibbon, *The History of the Decline and Fall of the Roman Empire*.

95. See Jalāl al-Dīn Abd al-Raḥmān al-Suyūṭī, *Lubāb al-Nuqūl fī Asbāb al-Nuzūl*, 168–70. See also Abū al-Ḥasan ʿAlī al-Wāḥidī, *Asbāb al-Nuzūl*, 297–99.

96. Fowden, *Before and After Muhammad*, 5.

97. Ibid., 6.

98. See Stroumsa, *The Making of the Abrahamic Religions in Late Antiquity*.

99. Cameron, "Patristics and Late Antiquity: Partners or Rivals," 299.

100. See, e.g., Hoyland, "Early Islam as a Late Antique Religion," 1055.

101. Ibid., 1070.

102. Stewart, "Reflections on the State of the Art in Western Qurʾanic Studies," 6.

103. Cameron, "Patristics and Late Antiquity: Partners or Rivals," 302.

104. See, e.g., Thomas Römer, *The Invention of God*.

105. See Salama, and Langbehn, eds., *German Colonialism*, ix–xxxi.

106. Nietzsche, *Untimely Meditations*, 72.

107. Bennet, *To Reclaim a Legacy*, 4, 22, 41.

3. INTELLIGENCE VERSUS POWER: RHETORICAL DYNAMICS IN PRE-ISLAMIC POETRY AND THE QURʾĀN

1. See Monroe, "Oral Composition in Pre-Islamic Poetry," 1–53; Zwettler, *The Oral Tradition of Classical Arabic Poetry*. Monroe's and Zwettler's studies and their use of formulaic-oral theory as valid for Arabic poetry have been sharply criticized by Gregor Schoeler,

Ewald Wagner, Thomas Bauer, Suzanne Stetkevych, and others. See, more specifically, S. P. Stetkevych, "Structuralist Analyses of Pre-Islamic Poetry," 85–10. See also Agha, "Of Verse, Poetry, Great Poetry and History," 1–35; Stetkevych, *The Mute Immortals Speak*; Montgomery, *The Vagaries of the Qaṣīdah*. See also Montgomery "The Empty Hijaz," 37–97; Farrin, *Abundance from the Desert*; Beeston, "Himyarite Monotheism," 149–54; Conrad, "The Arabs," pp. 678–700.

2. Nöldeke, "Arabia, Arabians" 272–75. See also *Encyclopaedia Biblica*, pp. 272–75.

3. In *Mohammed and the Rise of Islam*, Margoliouth writes that "the language of the Koran was thought by experts to bear a striking likeness to that of the early poetry: and though for us it is difficult to pass an opinion on this point, seeing that the early poetry is largely fabrication modelled on the Koran, we may accept the opinion of the Arabs" (60).

4. Ḥusayn, *Fī al-Shiʿr al-Jāhilī*, 7.

5. Ibid., 88.

6. See, e.g., Dmitriev, "An Early Christian Arabic Account of the Creation of the World."

7. For more on Ṭāhā Ḥusayn's venture on pre-Islamic poetry, see Salama, *The Qurʾān and Modern Arabic Literary Criticism*, 17–36.

8. Arberry, *The Seven Odes*, 238.

9. Gibb, Review of *The Seven Odes* 272.

10. Stetkevych, *Muhammad and the Golden Bough*.

11. Stetkevych, *The Mute Immortals Speak*, 27.

12. Ibid., 27–28.

13. While the examination of the phonology and lexicology of the Qurʾān in light of the North Arabian inscriptions is still embryonic, Ahmad al-Jallad has taken positive steps in examining the etymological history of Arabic, especially when it comes to finding an evidentiary nexus between the Qurʾān's language and pre-Islamic Arabic poetry. In a recent study, al-Jallad makes reference to numerous Arabic Qurʾānic roots (e.g., *qsm, hdy, m(y)t, taʿa, ḏll, siḥr, nʾr*), as well as to ritualistic stems that are traceable to pre-Islamic Arabic in its historical evolution via Safaitic inscriptions, many of which appear in pre-Islamic poetry. See al-Jallad, *The Religion and Rituals of the Nomads of Pre-Islamic Arabia*, 53, 65–66, 69, 72, 97. See also al-Jallad's discussion of votive inscriptions and the literary background of the Qurʾān, in particular the structural affinities between the South Arabian *Hymn of Qāniya* and the early Meccan sūras, such as 75 and 84 (Al-Jallad, "The Linguistic Landscape of pre-Islamic Arabia," 122–25).

14. See Key, *Language between God and the Poets*.

15. Thomas Bauer, "The Relevance of Early Arabic Poetry for Qurʾānic Studies Including Observations on Kull and on Q 22:27, 26:225, and 52:31," 699–700.

16. See, in particular, Bauer's argument about the grammar *of kull*, followed by *ism mufrad nakira* versus *kull*, followed by *ism jamʿ muʿrraf*, and how such a subtle and minute difference allows (with insight from pre-Islamic poetry) for a more accurate and nuanced understanding of this construct in the Qurʾān. See Bauer, "The Relevance of Early Arabic Poetry," 706–15.

17. Wagner, *Grundzüge der klassischen arabischen Dichtung*, 12–29.

18. Von Grunebaum, "The Nature of Arabic Unity Before Islam."

19. Meinecke, *Weltbürgertum und Nationalstaat*, 1–22.

20. Von Grunebaum, "The Nature of Arabic Unity Before Islam," 6.

21. Ibid., 7. See also Watt, *Muhammad at Medina*, 142–43.

22. Von Grunebaum, "Pre-Islamic Poetry," 40.

23. Ibid., 8.

24. James Montgomery criticizes von Grunebaum's "stereotypical" depiction of nomad-Arab, but still agrees to the value of "Bedouinised" poetry in identifying the rise of the Arabs. See Montgomery "The Empty Hijaz," 37–97.

25. Ibid., 8.

26. Dmitriev, "An Early Christian Arabic Account of the Creation of the World," 349–88.

27. Ibid., 388.

28. Ibid.

29. Ibid.

30. Ibid.

31. See, e.g., J. A. C. Brown, "The Social Context of Pre-Islamic Poetry," 29–50.

32. Bauer, "The Relevance of Early Arabic Poetry for Qur'ānic Studies," 705–6.

33. Ibid., 705.

34. Serrano, *Qur'ān and the Lyric Imperative*, 125.

35. Abū al-Ḥasan 'Alī (b. 'Īsā) al-Rummānī, "al-Nukat fī I'jāz al-Qur'ān," 75.

36. Bauer, "The Relevance of Early Arabic Poetry for Qur'ānic Studies," 706.

37. See, e.g., Albert Arazi's chapter, "La nuit et le jour," 49–103. See also Pellat, "Layl and Nahār," 707–10.

38. Muḥammad ibn Makram ibn Manẓūr, *Lisān al-'Arab*, 4115.

39. To be sure, there is an instance Homer's *Iliad* (1.10–23) where Chryses begs Agamemnon for the return of his daughter Chryseis. In 1.24–32, Agamemnon harshly rejects Chryses's plea and sends him packing. Then 1.33–34 reads as follows (in Lattimore's translation): "So he spoke, and the old man in terror obeyed him /And went silently away beside the murmuring sea beach." Upon which, Chryses prays to Apollo, who sends his plague into the Achaians' camp. This is a credible example of pathetic fallacy, although Lattimore's "murmuring" is probably too weak. See Kirk, *The Iliad: A Commentary*, 56–57: "Is there an intended contrast between the priest's silence . . . and the roar [!] of the sea? Ostensibly not, since . . . the sea is roaring because that is what it typically does . . . . Yet the overtones . . . are often of tension and sadness . . . and this perhaps colours Khruses' temporary silence, making it ominous."

40. al-Qays, *Dīwān Imru' al-Qays*, 18–19.

41. al-Dhubyānī, *Dīwān al-Nābigha al-Dhubyānī*, 29–30.

42. Ibid., 56.

43. 26:61.

44. See also 4:78; 4:100.

45. 10:90.

46. al-Rummānī, "al-Nukat fī I'jāz al-Qur'ān," 81–82.

47. For a nuanced, close reading of the Qur'ān's relationship to poetry with special reference to *Sūra-t- al-Shu'arā'* (26), see the following articles by Irfan Shahid: "A Contribution to Koranic Exegesis"; "Another Contribution to Koranic Exegesis"; "The Sūra of the Poets, Qur'ān XXVI," 175–220; "The Sūra of the Poets Revisited," 398–423.

48. 'Abd al-Qāhir al-Jurjānī, "al-Risāla al-Shāfiya," 122, 124–25.

49. Ibn al-Ṭayyib al-Bāqillānī, *I'jāz al-Qur'ān*, 76–85, 162–170.

50. See al-Khaṭṭābī, "Bayān I'jāz al-Qur'ān," 22–23.

51. Burke, *A Philosophical Inquiry into the Origin of Our Ideas of the Sublime and Beautiful*, 99.

52. See also the Qur'ān's depiction of *ḥūr ʿīn*, heavenly wide-eyed women of incomparable beauty (44:54; 52:20; 55:72; 56:22) and *wildān mukhalladūn*, heavenly eternal youths (76:19).

53. See, for instance, the preamble verse of *Sūra-t-Yūsuf* (12), which states the following:

نَحْنُ نَقُصُّ عَلَيْكَ أَحْسَنَ ٱلْقَصَصِ بِمَآ أَوْحَيْنَآ إِلَيْكَ هَٰذَا ٱلْقُرْءَانَ

We relate to you the best/the most beautiful of stories through Our revelation of this Qur'ān. (12:3)

54. Ṭarafa, *Dīwān Ṭarafa ibn al-ʿAbd*, 19.

55. See Heidegger, *Being and Time*.

56. Ṭarafa, *Diwān Ṭarafa ibn al-ʿAbd*, 25.

57. The Qur'ān teems with instances of this dialogic anti-resurrection tension, as in the following examples:

(16:38) وَأَقْسَمُواْ بِٱللَّهِ جَهْدَ أَيْمَٰنِهِمْ لَا يَبْعَثُ ٱللَّهُ مَن يَمُوتُ

(17:49) وَقَالُوٓاْ أَءِذَا كُنَّا عِظَٰمًا وَرُفَٰتًا أَءِنَّا لَمَبْعُوثُونَ خَلْقًا جَدِيدًا

(64:7) زَعَمَ ٱلَّذِينَ كَفَرُوٓاْ أَن لَّن يُبْعَثُواْ

(5: 22) يَٰٓأَيُّهَا ٱلنَّاسُ إِن كُنتُمْ فِى رَيْبٍ مِّنَ ٱلْبَعْثِ فَإِنَّا خَلَقْنَٰكُم مِّن تُرَابٍ

(11:7) وَلَئِن قُلْتَ إِنَّكُم مَّبْعُوثُونَ مِنْ بَعْدِ ٱلْمَوْتِ لَيَقُولَنَّ ٱلَّذِينَ كَفَرُوٓاْ إِنْ هَٰذَآ إِلَّا سِحْرٌ مُّبِينٌ

(23:81–82) بَلْ قَالُواْ مِثْلَ مَا قَالَ ٱلْأَوَّلُونَ. قَالُوٓاْ أَءِذَا مِتْنَا وَكُنَّا تُرَابًا وَعِظَٰمًا أَءِنَّا لَمَبْعُوثُونَ

(13:5) وَإِن تَعْجَبْ فَعَجَبٌ قَوْلُهُمْ أَءِذَا كُنَّا تُرَٰبًا أَءِنَّا لَفِى خَلْقٍ جَدِيد

(23:35–36) أَيَعِدُكُمْ أَنَّكُمْ إِذَا مِتُّمْ وَكُنتُمْ تُرَابًا وَعِظَٰمًا أَنَّكُم مُّخْرَجُونَ. هَيْهَاتَ هَيْهَاتَ لِمَا تُوعَدُونَ

(23:37) إن هي إلا حياتنا الدنيا نموت ونحيا وما نحن بمبعوثين

58. ʿAlī, *al-Mufaṣṣal fī Tarīkh al-ʿArab Qabl al-Islām*, 123.

59. Murtaḍá al-Zabīdī, *Tāj al-ʿArūs min Jawāhir al-Qāmūs*, 98.

60. 34:19. For an in-depth discussion of poetry as eternalization in pre-Islamic culture, see Geert Jan van Gelder, "Persons as Texts/Texts as Persons," 237–53.

61. al-Ālūsī, *Bulūgh al-Arab fī Ma ʿarifa-t-Aḥwāl al-ʿArab.* 199.

62. The word *hām* is often a near-synonym of *aṣdāʾ*, a kind of screech owl representing the ghost of a someone killed whose death has not yet been avenged, and appearing on his grave. But it can also mean "skulls." See also Homerin, "Echoes of a Thirsty Owl," 165–84.

63. ʿAlī, *al-Mufaṣṣal fī Tarīkh al-ʿArab Qabl al-Islām*, 123.

4. POETIC PAGANISM AND THE MONOTHEISTIC AESTHETIC

1. Pre-Islamic Arabia enjoyed ritualistic forms of worship and religious customs. Many scholars of early Islam, including al-Shahrastānī, Yāqūt al-Ḥamawī, and al-Azraqī, remind us that circumambulating the *Kaaba* was a common practice among pre-Islamic Arabs as part of their belief in *Bayt Allāh* (the House of God) and cyclical pilgrimages. See al-Fatḥ Muḥammad al-Shahrastānī, *al-Milal wa al-Niḥal*, 33; al-Ḥamawī, *Muʿjam al-Buldān*, 279, 281, 619; and al-Azraqī, *Akhbār Makka*, 8–9. Ibn al-Kalbī also makes reference to other pilgrimage houses pre-Islamic Arabs traveled to, such as *Bayt Thaqīf* (the House of Thaqīf). See Ibn al-Kalbī, *Kitāb al-Aṣnām*, 44–48. Al-Hamadānī confirms that Arabs performed

various pilgrimages to sacred houses, such as *Bayt Al-lāt wa-Ka ʿba-t-Najrān wa-Ka ʿba-t-Shaddād al-Ayādī wa-Ka ʿba-t-Ghaṭfā*. See al-Hamadānī, *al-Iklīl*, 84. For more references on other kaabas and houses of gods, e.g., *Ka ʿba-t-Dhī-alshará wa-Ka ʿba-t- Dhī-Ghāba, wa-Bayt Al-lāt wa-Bayt al-U ʿzzá wa-Bayt Manāt*, see the following: ʿAlī, *al-Mufaṣṣal fī Tarīkh al- ʿArab qabl al-Islām*, 152–53, 180, 214–24; al-Zabīdī, *Tāj al- ʿArūs min Jawāhir al-Qāmūs*, 271; al-Mas ʿūdī, *Murūj al-Dhahab*, 47. The rise of Mecca as a commercial hub allowed many inhabitants of the Arabian Peninsula and beyond to flock to the Meccan *Kaaba* for blessings and worship. The Qur ʾān confirms pre-Islamic Arabs' acknowledgement of a supreme god whom they called *Allah*, while they still worshiped other deities like اللات و العزى و مناة (53:19). See Ibn al-Kalbī, *Kitāb al-Aṣnām*, 13–27.

The following are examples of verses that describe pre-Islamic Arabia's knowledge of the existence of Allah, who was worshipped in association with other deities:

(43:9) وَلَئِن سَأَلْتَهُم مَّنْ خَلَقَ ٱلسَّمَٰوَٰتِ وَٱلْأَرْضَ لَيَقُولُنَّ ٱللَّهُ

(43:87) وَلَئِن سَأَلْتَهُم مَّنْ خَلَقَهُمْ لَيَقُولُنَّ ٱللَّهُ

(23:86–87) قُلْ مَن رَّبُّ ٱلسَّمَٰوَٰتِ ٱلسَّبْعِ وَرَبُّ ٱلْعَرْشِ ٱلْعَظِيمِ. سَيَقُولُون لله

(39:3) وَالَّذِينَ اتَّخَذُوا مِن دُونِهِ أَوْلِيَاءَ مَا نَعْبُدُهُمْ إِلَّا لِيُقَرِّبُونَا إِلَى اللَّهِ زُلْفَىٰ

2. Abū Zayd, *Mafhūm al-Naṣṣ*, 61.

3. Ibn al-Athīr, *al-Nihāya fī Gharīb al-Ḥadīth wa al-Athar*, 147–48.

4. Abū Zayd, *Mafhūm al-Naṣṣ*, 160.

5. 20:114.

6. 75:16–19.

7. Hegel, *Ästhetik*, 117.

8. See Adorno, *Ästhetische Theorie*, 58.

9. Van Gelder, *Sound and Sense in Classical Arabic Poetry*.

10. Macaulay, "Minute on Education," 107–17.

11. For a comprehensive account of Macaulay's educational policies, see Naik and Nurullah, *A Students' History of Education in India (1800–1973)*, 66–146. See also Said, *Orientalism*, 152, 196.

12. Nicholson, *A Literary History of the Arabs*, 134.

13. Nicholson's bias against the Qur ʾān is evident in his truncated reference to the God of the Qur ʾān as "as a stern, unapproachable despot, requiring utter submission to His arbitrary will, but infinitely unconcerned with human feelings and aspirations. Such a Being could not satisfy the religious instinct" (Nicolson, *A Literary History*, 231).

14. Ibid., 308.

15. Ibid.

16. Ibid., 77.

17. Ibid.

18. Abū Tammām, *Dīwān Abī Tammām*, 154. "ʿAmr" in this line refers to the legendary veteran warrior ʿAmr ibn Ma ʿdiyakrib (d. 642), who converted to Islam during the early hijra years, and is also known as *Fāris al- ʿArab* (the Warrior of Arabs). "Aḥnaf" is Aḥnaf ibn Qays (d. 686), a companion of the Prophet known for his gentle nature and thoughtfulness. "Iyās" is Iyās ibn Mu ʿāwiya (d. 739), a judge who lived in Basra in the seventh and eighth centuries. He was known for his immense intelligence.

19. Abū Bakr Muḥammad Ibn Yaḥyá al-Ṣūlī, *Akhbār Abī Tammām*, 231.

20. Ibid.

21. Ibid., 232.

22. Hemingway, *A Moveable Feast*, 147.

23. Reference here is not to a particular sūra but to numerous Qur'ānic instances where prophets, in this case Ṣāliḥ and Jesus, were disbelieved, persecuted and alienated by their own people. For examples of Ṣāliḥ, see 7:73–79, 11:61–68, 26:141–59, and 27:45–53. For examples of Jesus, see 2:87, 3:52, 5:87, 43:64, and 61:14.

24. Abū al-Ṭayyib Aḥmad al-Mutanabbī, *Dīwān al-Mutanabbī*, 20–22. See also ʿAbd Allāh Ibn al-Ḥusayn al-ʿUkbarī, *al-Tibyān fī Sharḥ al-Dīwān*, 319–24.

25. 12:111.

26. For detailed analyses of the representations of Maryam in the Qur'ān, see the following: Anthony, "The Virgin Annunciate in the Meccan Qur'ān," 363–85; Toorawa, "Sūrat Maryam (Q. 19)," 25–78; Mourad, "Mary in the Qur'ān," 163–74.

27. 19:16–26; 3:47.

28. Joyce, "Drama and Life."

29. See Ibn Khaldūn, *al-Muqaddima*, 408–9. See also ʿĀbid al-Jābirī, *Naḥnu wa-al-Turāth*, 323–25; Watt, *Muhammad at Mecca*, 16–20.

30. Ibn Qutayba, *al-Shiʿr wa al-Shuʿarāʾ*, 13.

31. Abū al-Qāsim Maḥmūd al-Zamakhsharī, *Asās al-balāgha*, 502.

32. Ibn Manẓūr, *Lisān al-ʿArab*, 3590.

33. ʿAntara ibn Shaddād, "Muʿallaqa-t-ʿAntara," 147.

34. Adorno, *Aesthetic Theory*, 32.

35. Ibid.

36. Kaʿb ibn Zuhayr, quoted in Ibn ʿAbd Rabbih, *al-ʿIqd al-Farīd*, 186. See also Shawqī Ḍayf, *Tārīkh al-Adab al-ʿArabī*, 226.

37. Imruʾ al-Qays, *Dīwān Imriʾ al-Qays*, 114.

38. P. Brown, *The Body and Society*, 216.

39. Ibid.

40. Ibn Abī Sulmá, *Dīwān Zuhayr ibn Abī Sulmá*, 97.

41. Imruʾ al-Qays, *Dīwān Imriʾ al-Qays*, 25.

42. Ibn Qays al-Aʿshá, *Dīwān al-Aʿshá al-Kabīr: Maymūn ibn Qays*, 57.

43. Abū Dhuʾayb al-Hudhalī, *Dīwān Abī Dhuʾayb al-Hudhalī*, 192–93.

44. Ibn Abī Sulmá, *Dīwān Zuhayr ibn Abī Sulmá*, 110.

45. Imruʾ al-Qays, *Dīwān Imriʾ al-Qays*, 8.

46. Al-Jāḥiẓ states that pre-Islamic poetry appeared one hundred to two hundred years before Islam.

47. See Saleh, "The Preacher of the Meccan Qur'ān," 74–111.

48. Saleh, "Death and Dying in the Qur'ān," 445–55.

49. See van Ess, *Theology and Society in the Second and Third Centuries of the Hijra*, 25–26.

50. Adorno, *Aesthetic Theory*, 32.

51. 26:195.

52. Saleh, "Death and Dying in the Qur'ān," 98.

53. For an elaborate discussion of Arabic notions such as *al-baʿth, al-ḥashr, al-baliyya, al-ḥisāb, al-thawāb, al-ʿiqāb, al-janna, al-nār*, etc., in pre-Islamic poetry, see ʿAlī, *al-Mufaṣṣal fī Tārīkh al-ʿArab Qabl al-Islām*, vol. 6, 123–35.

54. The Qur'ān presents most pagans as unbelievers in life after death. However, like the Greeks and the Romans, pagan Arabs worshipped many gods for material gain or simply for avoiding misfortune in life. Numerous Arab references in pre-Islamic Arabic poetry document a firm belief not only in the day of judgement but also in a return to some sort of life after bodily death. Al-Sukkarī cites enough examples from such poets as al-A'shá, Imru' al-Qays, al-Akhnas ibn Shihāb al-Tamīmī, and Ummayya ibn Abī al-Ṣalt, among others, to make a valid argument for the spread of belief in the day of judgment among pre-Islamic Arabs. See Abū Ja'far Muḥammad ibn Ḥabīb, *Kitāb al-Muḥabbar*, 320–24. See also Jawād 'Ali's elaborate discussion of the use of Arabic notions such as *al-ba'th, al-ḥashr, al-balīyya, al-ḥisāb, al-thawāb, al-'iqāb, al-janna, al-nār*, etc., in pre-Islamic poetry ('Alī, *al-Mufaṣṣal fī Tarīkh al-'Arab Qabl al-Islām*, vol. 6, 123–35).

55. Saleh, "Death and Dying in the Qur'ān," 105.

56. Ibid., 109.

57. Ibid., 106.

58. Pre-Islamic poetry includes numerous examples of this rhetorical question mode. A famous example comes from Imru' al-Qays's lines:

ومسنونةٌ زُرقٌ كأنيابِ أغوالٍ؟   أيَقْتُلُني والمَشرَفِيُّ مُضاجِعي

Can he *really* kill me when the fine sword is by my side / with its blade shining like the teeth of ghouls?

See Abū al-Ḥasan ibn Rashīq al-Qayrawānī, *al-'Umda fī Maḥāsin al-Shi'r wa Adabih wa-Naqdih*, 288. See also the same rhetorical structure used in al-Ṣaltān al-'Abdī's response to Jarīr:

ووَدَّ أبوك الكلبُ لو كان ذا نخلٍ؟   أعيرتنا أن كانت النخل مالنا

Do you mock us when the palm trees are ours / and when your father, that dog, wishes to have palm trees?

See Ibn 'Aṭiyya, *Dīwān Jarīr bi-sharḥ Muḥammad ibn Ḥabīb*, 578.

59. 17:49.

60. 19:66.

61. 67:25

62. 'Abd al-Qāhir al-Jurjānī, *Dalā'il al-I'jāz*, 114.

63. Ibid., 8–12.

64. 2:23.

65. 11:13.

66. 17:88.

67. Saleh, "Death and Dying in the Qur'ān," 99.

68. Al-Jurjānī, *Dalā'il al-I'jāz*, 8–9.

69. See Kermani, *God is Beautiful.* In this study, Kermani examines the structure of the Qur'ān's own treatment of aesthetics. One thing is certain in Kermani's study from the start: it emphasizes "community" and "voice," where the aesthetic only makes sense in the context of the larger question of the relationship of "affect" between the proclaimer and the listeners. Kermani shows that understanding the Qur'ān belongs to a more advanced but approachable state of aesthetic thought than methodological applications. Devin Stewart aptly defines Kermani's venture as a work that "presents itself as an alternative path to the Orientalists' negative assessment of the Qur'ān as an aesthetic text, which

imply that Muslims' claims about its beauty were simply the result of bias, devotion, blind adherence to tradition, and imperfect understanding" (Stewart, Review of *God is Beautiful*, 95–96). For a recent study treating voice and the affect of Qur'ānic recitals, see Nelson, *The Art of Reciting the Qur'an*.

5. *ADAB* AND THE ETHICAL AUTHORITY OF THE QUR'ĀN

1. Heidegger, "Aus einem Gespräch von der Sprache (Zwischen einem Japaner und einem Fragenden)," 151.

2. During this conversation, Heidegger calls for bypassing Plato's good old quarrel with poetry and moving beyond the binary oppositions that have beset Western metaphysics for centuries. Yet Heidegger's call is itself an aporia, in the sense Max Statkiewicz astutely describes it—that is, as philosophy's irreconcilable debt to Plato, a debt that makes Western philosophy always inevitably "Platonic." It would therefore be better if it were confronted, or "dialogued with," than bypassed. See Statkiewicz, *Rhapsody of Philosophy*, 162–63.

3. P. Brown, "Late Antiquity and Islam: Parallels and Contrasts," 25.

4. Ibid., 24.

5. Ibid., 29 (emphasis mine).

6. Ibid., 29. Cf. Festugière, *Antioche*, 218; Anawati, "Homo Islamicus," 240.

7. Jaeger, *Paideia*.

8. See Adler, "Was Homer Acquainted with the Bible?" 70–174.

9. See al-Baghdadi, "Registers of Arabic Literary History," 437–461.

10. See, for example, Michael Cook's short study on the Qur'ān. For what is be supposed to be an informed "historical" account, Cook's study offers the most cryptic and out of context ahistorical reading to date, repeatedly subjecting the Qur'ānic text to a bizarre comparison with the tenets of European modernity. See Cook, *The Koran, a Very Short Introduction*, 23–26, 37, 160–61. See also Walid Saleh's salient deconstruction of Cook's approach, among others, in "In Search of a Comprehensive Qur'ān," 143–65.

11. von Grunebaum, *Classical Islam*, p. 33.

12. Toynbee, "Greece," 167.

13. Toynbee, *A Study of History*, 450 ff.

14. Becker, *Das Erbe der Antike im Orient und Okzident.* 12.

15. Cf. Nöldeke and Schwally, eds., *Geschichte des Qorans*, 4.

16. See Fowden, *Before and After Muhammad*; al-Azhmeh, "Rome, New Rome and Baghdad: Pathways of Late Antiquity," 55–80.

17. See Bowersock, *Hellenism in Late Antiquity*.

18. Fowden, *Empire to Commonwealth*, 10.

19. Ibn Qutayba, *al-Shiʿr wa al-Shuʿarāʾ*, 9.

20. Ibn Sallām al-Jumaḥī, *Ṭabaqāt al-Shuʿarāʾ*, 26.

21. Ibn Qutayba, *al-Shiʿr wa al-Shuʿarāʾ*, 11.

22. See, e.g., al-Jurjānī, *Dalāʾilal-Iʿjāz*, 20–23.

23. Bravmann, *The Spiritual Background of Early Islam*, 1.

24. Ibid., 2.

25. Ignác Goldziher, *Muhammedanische Studien*, vol. 1, 1–39. Over the last few decades, some important studies have broken new ground in excavating the ethical landscape of pre-Islamic and Qur'ānic Arabia, thus effectively delegitimating the late antiquity thesis

by reemphasizing indigenous Arabic influence on the Qurʾan. See, e.g., Izutsu, *Ethico-Religious Concepts in the Qurʾan*. For a more recent account, see Natij, "Murūʾa: Soucis et interrogations éthiques dans la culture arabe classique," 206–63. See also Jamil, *Ethics and Poetry in Sixth-Century Arabia*. See in particular Jamil's chapter (3–29) on *ḥilm, jahl, muruwwa*, and *dīn*, in which she discusses Goldziher, Bichr Farès, Izutsu, Bravmann, among others.

26. Ḍayf, *Tārīkh al-Adab al-ʿArabī: al-ʿAṣr al-Jāhilī*, 7.

27. Quoted in ibn Aḥmad al-Qurṭubī, *al-Jāmiʿ li-Aḥkām al-Qurʾān*, Vol.22, 304. To be sure, this verse, which al-Qurṭubī attributes to Hudhalī, is not found in *Dīwān al-Hudhaliyyīn*. It is also quoted anonymously in ibn Hishām/ibn Isḥāq, *al-Sīra al-Nabawiyya*, 539, where ibn Hishām explains *al-ḥāl* as "mud (*ṭīn*) mixed with sand." My attribution of this verse to al-Hudhalī is therefore speculative.

28. See, for instance, 2:177.

29. Lev. 9:34.

30. Romans 12:20.

31. Al-Qāḍī Nāṣir al-Dīn al-Bayḍāwī, *Tafsīr al-Bayḍāwī*, 477–78.

32. ʿAmr ibn Kulthūm, "Muʿallaqa-t-ʿAmr ibn Kulthūm," 275–77, 238–40.

33. Zuhayr ibn Abī Sulmá, *Dīwān Zuhayr ibn Abī Sulmá*, 110–11.

34. al-Muthaqqib al-ʿAbdī, *Dīwān Shiʿr al-Muthaqqib al-ʿAbdī*, 227–30.

35. Ṭarafa, *Dīwān Ṭarafa ibn al-ʿAbd*, 69.

36. There are no surviving historical records of al-Hamdānī's exact dates of birth and death. The consensus is that he lived and died shortly before Islam. See Muḥammad ibn Ḥazm al-Andalusī, *Jamhara-t-Ansāb al-ʿArab*, 395.

37. Ibn Ḥarīm al-Hamdānī, *Dīwān al-Luṣūṣ fī al-ʿAṣrayn al-Jāhilī wa al-Islāmī*, 137.

38. Ṭarafa, *Dīwān Ṭarafa ibn al-ʿAbd*, 24–27.

39. 107:2–3.

40. Imruʾ al-Qays, *Dīwān Imriʾ al-Qays*, 12.

41. See al-Bāqillānī, *Iʿjāz al-Qurʾān*, 76–85, 162–70.

42. Reference to *infāq* (spending for the sake of God) in 57:7, 10, 11, 18, and 24 directly ties charity to faith and devotion. It is important to point out that *infāq* should not be confused with *zakā*. The Qurʾan makes a clear distinction between the two. While both are acts of giving for the sake of God, *infāq* has wider implications of giving that includes money among other ethical acts of self-abnegation. See, for instance, 57:10, where the spending includes possessions and one's own life. See also 8:63; 2:215, 217, 254, and 270; 34:39; 4:39; 13:22; 28:54. *Zakā*, on the other hand, is a religious *farīḍa* (obligation) and one of the commandments of Islam. Specific verses calling for *zakā* include the following: 2:42, 83, 110, 177, 277; 5:12; 6:141; 9:11; 23:4; 73:20.

43. 57:27.

44. See, for instance, 4:164; 35:24; 13:7; 16:36. To be clear, there is no contradiction between the promise made in these verses and the meaning of 5:19. While some terms overlap, there is a subtle difference between *rasūl, nabiyy*, and *nadhīr*. In this particular verse, the noun *fatra* has been traditionally translated into English as a "break" or "interval" between messengers. The verse in full reads as follows:

يَٰأَهْلَ ٱلْكِتَٰبِ قَدْ جَآءَكُمْ رَسُولُنَا يُبَيِّنُ لَكُمْ عَلَىٰ فَتْرَةٍ مِّنَ ٱلرُّسُلِ أَن تَقُولُوا۟ مَا جَآءَنَا مِنْ بَشِيرٍ وَلَا نَذِيرٍ فَقَدْ جَآءَكُم بَشِيرٌ وَنَذِيرٌ وَٱللَّهُ عَلَىٰ كُلِّ شَىْءٍ قَدِيرٌ

A hurried reading of this verse might assume that there is a contradiction in terms, namely that the Qur'ān contradicts itself by admitting to a clear six hundred-year discontinuity between Jesus and Muḥammad. The particular reference in this verse, however, is an address to the people of the book about a messenger with a "revealed book." In addition, in classical Arabic, the root f.t.r means "to relax," "lessen," or "lose intensity, as in (43:75). It could also mean "to become tepid, indifferent, or lukewarm," as in 21:20. See al-Rāzī, *Tafsīr al-Fakhr al-Rāzī*, 198–99.

45. See, for instance, the following verses:

(5:44) إِنَّآ أَنزَلْنَا ٱلتَّوْرَىٰةَ فِيهَا هُدًى وَنُورٌ

(5:46) وَقَفَّيْنَا عَلَىٰٓ ءَاثَٰرِهِم بِعِيسَى ٱبْنِ مَرْيَمَ مُصَدِّقًا لِّمَا بَيْنَ يَدَيْهِ مِنَ ٱلتَّوْرَىٰةِ وَءَاتَيْنَٰهُ ٱلْإِنجِيلَ فِيهِ هُدًى وَنُورٌ

(4:174) يَٰٓأَيُّهَا ٱلنَّاسُ قَدْ جَآءَكُم بُرْهَٰنٌ مِّن رَّبِّكُمْ وَأَنزَلْنَآ إِلَيْكُمْ نُورًا مُّبِينًا

46. See 27:9 and 27:12.

47. See 27:12, 27:13, 27:19, and 27:28.

48. Abū 'Uthmān 'Amr ibn Baḥr al-Jāḥiẓ, *al-Bayān wa- al-Tabyīn*, 272–73.

49. See the reference to Qatāda's interpretation of 57:27 as *rafḍ al-nisā' wa ittikhādh al-ṣwāmi'* (rejection of women and resort to monasteries) in Jalāl al-Dīn al-Suyūṭī, *al-Durr al-Manthūr fī al-Tafsīr bil-Ma'thūr*, 293.

50. See al-Suyūṭī, *Lubāb al-Nuqūl fī Asbāb al-Nuzūl*, 108.

51. P. Brown, "Late Antiquity and Islam: Parallels and Contrasts," 31–32.

52. Examples of popular celibates include St. Paul (ca. 0–67 AD), who applauded celibacy, though he still acknowledged the permissibility of marriage for fellow Christians who could not uphold this higher ideal. Celibacy may indeed have been an extreme ethical response to the sexual promiscuities of the times, a step better than marriage. The Council of Elvira, the first know council of the Christian church in Spain declared (ca. 306 AD) that all priests and bishops, regardless of their current marital status, should abstain from having sex. By the fourth century, the Western church adopted the celibacy principle and the monastic tradition that accompanied it, an adoption that culminated in the celebration of celibacy in the writings of church fathers like Ambrose and Augustine. In 692, the decrees of the Eastern churches in the Council of Trullo dictated that bishops must be celibate.

53. P. Brown, "Late Antiquity and Islam: Parallels and Contrasts," 32.

54. Ibid., 32. Cf. 36. See also Gellner, *Saints of the Atlas*, 149.

55. Ibid., 34. See also Tellenbach, *Church, State and Christian Society at the Time of the Investiture Contest*; Southern, *Western Society and the Church in the Middle Ages*, 34–44, 100–133.

6. THE QUR'ĀN IN CONTEXT: MONOTHEISM AND THE BIRTH OF THE UNMIMETIC

1. Asad Q. Ahmed, *The Religious Elite of the Early Islamic Hijaz*, 1–3.

2. Ibid.

3. Ibid., 5.

4. See Col. Playfair, "On the Himyaritic Inscriptions Lately Brought to England from Southern Arabia," 174–77. See also Irfan Shahid, "Byzantium in South Arabia," 27–29. For a more recent account of the Himyaritic Inscription, see Irene Gajda, *Le royaume de Himyar à l'époque monothéiste*.

5. In postclassical Shiʿa exegetic tradition, a direct cause of the downfall of the Himyaritic dynasty is said to be the religious intolerance of *Qawm Tubbaʿ* (the people of King Tubbaʿ) (44:37; 50:14) who had embraced Judaism and who persecuted Christian converts. On the pretext of the murder of the Jews by the people of Najran, Dhū Nuwās, the sovereign of Yemen, took up arms against them, occupied their city, and gave its inhabitants a choice between a return to Judaism and death by fire in a trench. When they opted to hold onto their Christian faith, a large أخدود (pit) was dug, filled with burning fuel, and all who refused to renounce their faith, amounting to twenty thousand, were cast in the flames. See ʿAlī ibn Ibrāhīm al-Qummī, *Tafsīr al-Qummī*, vol. 2, 413.

6. 18:13; 85:7

7. 61:6.

8. Von Grunebaum, *Muḥammadan Festivals*, 5.

9. Ibid., 5.

10. Ibid.

11. 106:1–2.

12. See Ibn Fāris ibn Zakariyyā, *al-Ṣāḥibī fī Fiqh al-Lugha al-ʿArabiyya wa Masāʾilihā wa Sunan al-ʿArabiyya fī Kalāmihā*, 41–47.

13. Jeffery, *The Foreign Vocabulary of the Qurʾān*, iv.

14. 18:31.

15. Ibn Zakariyyā, *al-Ṣāḥibī*, 42.

16. 17:35.

17. Ibid., 45.

18. See Gibb, "Pre-Islamic Monotheism in Arabia," 271.

19. Ibid. In this context, Gibb acknowledges important work by scholars who successfully adopted this positive linguistic understanding of the Qurʾān. These scholars include Chaim Rabin, who makes the case that the Qurʾān evidences the existence of a nonrabbinic Jewish sect in seventh-century Arabia, and Edward Ullendorff, whose study investigates semitic languages, including Hebrew and classical Arabic and relies on the scholarship of Muslim grammarians as evidence suggesting Christianity in South Arabia and Ethiopia was founded on Judaic elements that existed in South Arabia in early post-Christian centuries. See Rabin, *Qumran Studies*, 112–30; see also Ullendorff, "What is a Semitic Language?" 216–36.

20. See al-Qurṭubī, *al-Jāmiʿ li-Aḥkām al-Qurʾān*, pp. 110–112. In this account, al-Qurṭubī responds to differing opinions on the "Arabicity" of the Qurʾān among Muslims scholars, including that of al-Ṭabarī, ibn ʿAṭiyya, and Abū ʿUbayda.

21. See J. Stetkevych, *Muḥammad and the Golden Bough*.

22. Gibb, "Pre-Islamic Monotheism in Arabia," 271.

23. Hodgson, *The Venture of Islam*, Vol. 1, 71–73.

24. 85:22.

25. 13:39.

26. Madigan, *The Qurʾānʾs Self-Image*, 77.

27. 2:30–34.

28. 39:3.

29. See, e.g., Shoemaker, *The Death of a Prophet*. See also Donner, *Narratives of Islamic Origins*.

30. See Chejne, *The Arabic Language*. See also Khayr Bik, *al-Lugha al-ʿArabiyya*.

31. See also Shoemaker, *Creating the Qur'ān*, 17–18.

32. Naṣr Ḥāmid Abū Zayd, *Mafhūm al-Naṣṣ*, 63.

33. 26:192–97.

34. 33:40.

35. 17:106; 25:32.

36. See Sadeghi and Goudarzi, "San'a'1 and the Origins of the Qur'ān," 1–129. See also Sadeghi and Bergmann, "The Codex of a Companion of the Prophet and the Qur'ān of the Prophet," 343–436. For a thorough precis on this topic, see Sinai, "When Did the Consonantal Skeleton of the Quran Reach Closure? Part I," 273–92; and "When Did the Consonantal Skeleton of the Quran Reach Closure? Part II," 509–21. See also Al-Azami, *The History of the Quranic Text*.

37. See 2:189; 36:38–40.

38. See, e.g., the reference to the Event of the *Ifk* of 626/7 AD in 24:11–26.

39. 68:4.

40. 7:157.

41. 93:6–8.

42. Wills, *What the Qur'ān Meant and Why It Matters*, 65.

43. Ibid., 65.

44. Eco, *Semiotics and the Philosophy of Language*, 117.

45. Stewart, "Speech Genres and Interpretation of the Qur'an," 5–6.

46. Samji, *The Qur'an: A Form-Critical History*.

47. Bell, *Introduction to the Koran*, 76–77.

48. 3:7.

49. See 77:27; 50:9; 7:57; 25:48; 35:9; Q. 56:68–70; 27:60,63; 11:52; 15:22; 6:99; 31:10, 34; 39:21; 40:13; 42:28; 43:11; 45:5; 16:10, 65; 71:10–11; 14:32; 78:14–15; 30:24, 46, 48; 29:63; 2:22, 164; 8:11; 13:12, 17; 24:43.

50. 42:28.

51. Imru' al-Qays, *Dīwān Imru' al-Qays*, 72.

52. Ibid., 73.

53. Shakespeare, *King Lear*, act 3, scene 4, 24–27.

54. See, e.g., 2:130; 7:168; 3:39, 46, 114; 21:105.

55. See, e.g., 2:25, 62, 82, 277; 3.57.

56. Ibn Abī Sulmá, *Dīwān Zuhayr ibn Abī Sulmá*, 41.

57. 76:19.

58. 76:19.

59. See also Rami Tannous's discussion of *ḥūr* (women of paradise) in the Qur'ān and the its local significations in the work of the pre-Islamic poet 'Abīd ibn al-Abraṣ (Tannous, "Negotiating the Nativity in Late Antiquity," 353–56).

60. I am grateful to Geert Jan van Gilder for providing me with this example.

61. S. Stetkevych, *The Mute Immortals Speak*, 42.

62. See Bamyeh, *The Social Origins of Islam*, 273–93. In this important study, Bamyeh situates the monotheistic call of the Qur'ān, especially in its break with paganism and a revamping of Ḥanīfism, within the context of booming trade practices, tribal shifts, and relocations, as well as other sociocultural transformations in seventh-century Mecca and the Arabian Peninsula.

63. Abū ʿAbd Allāh al-Ḥusayn al-Zawzanī, *Sharḥ al-Muʿallaqāt al-Sabʿ*, 58.

64. See Nāṣir al-Dīn al-Albānī, *Silsila-t- al-Aḥādīth al-Saḥīḥa wa Shayʾ min Fiqhihā wa Fawāʾidihā*, 449.

65. 3:110.

66. 4:92; 58:3; 90:13.

67. 3:195; 4: 7, 32, 124; 24: 4–9, 23; 33:35.

68. Bowering, "The Qurʾān," 190.

69. 69:7.

70. 75:50–51.

71. See Dayeh, "Prophecy and Writing in the Qurʾān, or Why Muḥammad was not a Scribe," 31–62.

72. 26:226.

73. Plato, *Phaedrus and Letters VII and VIII*, 72.

74. 10:32.

75. 26:193–94.

76. 2:31.

77. Al-Khaṭṭābī, "al-Qawl fī Bayān Iʿjāz al-Qurʾān," 24.

78. Ibid., 27.

79. Al-Jurjānī, *Dalāʾil al-Iʿjāz*, 49–65.

80. Kermani, *God is Beautiful*, 129.

81. Keats, "Ode on a Grecian Urn," 135.

82. Lawrence, *Selected Literary Criticism*, 398.

83. See Kant, *The Critique of Judgement*. See in particular §41, "Of the Empirical Interest in the Beautiful" and §42, "On the Intellectual Interest in the Beautiful," 174–83.

84. Kermani, *God is Beautiful*, 130.

85. Roman Jakobson, quoted in Kermani, *God is Beautiful*, 130.

86. Jakobson, *Language in Literature*, 378.

87. Ibid.

88. 48:29.

89. 51:50–51; 79: 45.

90. 88:21.

91. 34:28.

92. Al-Jurjānī, "al-Risāla al-Shāfiya," in *Thalāth Rasāʾil*, 122.

93. Al-Zarkashī narrates an incident of an Arabian who heard the following verse for the first time (22:1):

يَا أَيُّهَا النَّاسُ اتَّقُوا رَبَّكُمْ ۚ إِنَّ زَلْزَلَةَ السَّاعَةِ شَيْءٌ عَظِيمٌ

to which he responded by saying "you broke the meter. It should read as follows instead":

يـا أيهـا النـاس اتقوا ربكم   زلزلـة الـسـاعة شـيء عظـيم

Thinking that he was correcting someone's poetry by offering to remove the particle "إنَّ" so the verse would be in a correct conventional meter (*al-sarīʿ*). To which the response was: هذا القرآن ، وليس الشعر (This is the Qurʾān, not poetry). See Muḥammad ibn ʿAbd Allāh al-Zarkashī, *al-Burhān fī ʿUlūm al-Qurʾān*, 116.

94. In 30:2–4, the Qurʾān makes a brief reference to the Byzantine-Sasanian War of 602–28 AD, reporting the defeat of the Romans (Byzantines) by the Persians, but also predicting a victory soon to come:

غُلِبَت الرُّومُ. فِي أَدْنَى الْأَرْضِ وَهُمْ مِنْ بَعْدِ غَلَبِهِمْ سَيَغْلِبُونَ

The Romans were defeated. In the lowest of land; yet they will, after their defeat, triumph. (30:204).

95. Levinas, *Alterity and Transcendence*, 36.

96. Plato, *Republic*, xx.

97. Kermani, *God is Beautiful*, 129.

98. 2:1; 12:1; 14:4; 20:113; 26:192–95; 26:198; 44:58.

99. 16:35; 24:54; 29:18; 36:17.

100. 29:64.

101. Dakake, "Mecca and Medina," 23.

102. Ibid., 24.

103. See Tottoli, *Biblical Prophets in the Qurʾān and Muslim Literature*, pp. 3–70.

104. 42:13

105. See Donner, *Narratives of Islamic Origins*, 76–85.

106. 11:42–43.

107. 11:45–46.

108. 66:10.

109. 19:42–46.

110. 37:102.

111. 15:60; 37:135

112. 12:9.

113. 12:84.

114. 21:87; 27:142.

115. 9:40; 36:9.

116. Corbin, *Creative Imagination in the Sufism of Ibn ʿArabi*, 223.

117. 26:193–94.

118. 19:10–11.

119. Saleh, "Meccan Gods, Jesus' Divinity," 92.

120. 21:69.

121. 20:39.

122. 2:50; 10:90; 26:63; 20:77.

123. 19:19.

124. 5:110.

125. 93:6–8.

126. See, e.g., 2:214; 3:123–24, 159; 4:59, 84; 7:157–58; 8:30, 65; 9:40, 61, 73; 9:108–9; 15:94; 17:73–81, 90–93; 21:107; 24:11–12; 25:32; 26:214–16; 33:18–19, 21–23, 25–27; 42:52; 58:1; 62:2; 68:2–5; 80:1–10; 94:4; 74:1–2; 111:1–2.

127. 7:157–58.

128. See Günther, "Muḥammad, the Illiterate Prophet," 1–26.

129. See 7:157, 158; 2:78; 3:20,75; 62:2.

130. See Abū al-Wafāʾ Ibn ʿAqīl's argument on "al-Nasab ilá al-Ism al-Murakkab" (attribution to compound nouns), 501.

131. Shahrūr, *al-Kitāb wa al-Qurʾān*, 141.

132. For works that began to reflect on Mosaic references in the Qurʾān as informing a Muslim identity, see Bashear, *Arabs and Others in Early Islam*; Rubin, *Between Bible and Qurʾan*.

133. For earlier scholarship that views the Qurʾān as dependent on Jewish sources in prophetic narratives, see Obermann, "Koran and Agada," 23–48. See also Lassner, *Demonizing the Queen of Sheba.* For a practical critique of the neglect of the Arabo-Islamic contexts, see J. Stetkevych, *Muḥammad and the Golden Bough*; Stetkevych, "Sara and the Hyena," 13–41.

134. For a fuller and more penetrating account of Moses in the Qurʾān, see Wheeler, *Moses in the Qurʾān and Islamic Exegesis.*

135. For a thorough stylistic analysis of the use of vocatives in the Qurʾān, see ʿAbd al-Qādir Muḥammad Muntaṣir Dahmān, *Asālīb al-Nidāʾ fī al-Qurʾān al-Karīm.* For a focused study of the use of vocatives in the Medinan versus Meccan sūras in relationship to prophetic proclamations, see Stewart, "Vocatives in the Qurʾan and the Framing of Prophetic Proclamations," 199–248.

136. See, e.g., Brock, "From Ephrem to Romanos," 141. See also Dmitriev, "An Early Christian Arabic Account of the Creation of the World," 354.

137. Eric Auerbach makes a subtle distinction between representations of prophets in the Old Testament (e.g., Abraham, Jacob, and Moses) and depictions of heroes in the Homeric epics. To Auerbach, such biblical figures "produce a more concrete, direct, and historical impression than the figures in the Homeric world—not because they are better described in terms of sense (the contrary is the case) but because the confused, contradictory multiplicity of events, the psychological and factual cross-purposes, which true history reveals, have not disappeared in the representation but still remain clearly perceptible" (Auerbach, *Mimesis,* 17). It is not clear what Auerbach means by "true history," but the Qurʾān's representations of the same figures in fact differ dramatically in that they avoid the convention of a beginning, middle, and end common in Genesis narratives. Instead, the Qurʾān presents a diffused prophetic narrative, where the story of Moses, for instances, recurs over and again from different narrative angles, thus infusing such narrative portrayals with a new world of dramatization. In this mode of representation, the Qurʾān parts not only with the motifs of the world of mythologies and supernatural monsters, but also with the historical linearity of the Old Testament.

138. See 11:7–8; 13: 5; 16: 38–39; 17:10, 49–5, 97–99; 18: 48; 19: 66–68; 20:16, 22:5; 23: 112–115; 25:11; 29: 23; 30: 8, 16; 32:10, 28; 34: 7, 29; 36:48; 37:15–16;14:50; 45:24–25, 31–32; 46:17; 51:12; 56: 46–48.

139. Georges Bataille, for instance, reduces the early years of Muḥammad's prophethood to a "military enterprise," in an undisguised apology to Western Europe in order to justify the latter's antipathy toward Islam. See Bataille, *The Accursed Share,* 86.

140. Cohen, *The Myth of the Judeo-Christian Tradition.*

141. See Abū ʿUthmān ʿAmr ibn Baḥr al-Jāḥiẓ, "Ḥujaj al-Nubuwwa," 278–80. See also Stroumsa, "The Signs of Prophecy."

142. Deleuze and Guattari, *A Thousand Plateaus,* 124.

143. Ibn Khaldūn, *Muqaddima-t- Ibn Khaldūn,* 88.

144. Gaskin, introduction to David Hume, *Dialogues Concerning Natura Religion,* xii.

145. See also 2:23; 9:64, 86, 124, 127; 11:23; 24:1; and 47:20.

146. 27:92.

147. 2:53; 87; 136.

148. 2:136; 253.

149. 15:87; 20:99.

150. Chronologically, *Sūra-t-al-Naml* is not the first sūra in which the word *kitāb* appears as a strong reference to the Qur'ān. As an appositive to the Qur'ān, *kitāb* first appears in the Meccan sūra of Sad:

كِتَابٌ أنزَلْنَاهُ إِلَيْكَ مُبَارَكٌ لِّيَدَّبَّرُوا آيَاتِهِ وَلِيَتَذَكَّرَ أُوْلُوا الْأَلْبَابِ

A book We have descended unto you, blessed, so that they may contemplate its verses, and so that those with kernels of insight may be remember. (38:29)

151. For a brief account the occurrence of *basmallah* in the Qur'ān, see Nöldeke et al., *The History of the Qur'ān*, 277–78.

152. See, e.g., Penchansky, *Solomon and the Ant*, 111–12.

153. Von Grunebaum, *Islam, Essay on the Nature and Growth of a Cultural Tradition*, 89.

154. Badr al-Dīn Muḥammad ibn 'Abd Allāh al-Zarkashī, *Al-Burhān fī 'Ulūm al-Qur'ān*, 386–87.

155. Kermani, *God is Beautiful*, 251.

CONCLUSION: THE FUTURE OF QUR'ĀNIC STUDIES

1. Albert Hourani's introduction to *Islam in European Thought* is one of the most important critical interventions in the direction of deconstructing European thought on Islam. Although more essayistic and tailored in its examination of important scholars of Islam such as H. A. R. Gibb and Marshall Hodgson, Hourani touches on some inklings of this thought, especially in his work on the problems of historical sources in both Louis Massignon and Jacques Berque. Hourani has little to say about what may have existed in eighteenth- and nineteenth-century academic European thought on Islam or offer a critique of the deeper historical revisionism and its entombment of Islam's origins and sources. Nor does it expose the wider horizontal and vertical connections between the rise of historical revisionism and the persistence of racial ideologies in the postcolonial Europe. Overall, Hourani's study is more about specific authors and texts than it is about connecting the dots and finding epistemic connections in scholarship on Islam among European academics.

2. Van Gelder, *Sound and Sense in Classical Arabic Poetry*, 9–10.

3. Hegel, *Phenomenology*, 9.

4. Sizgorich, "Narrative and Community in Islamic late antiquity," 42.

5. Beiser, *The German Historicist Tradition*, 6.

6. See Salama, *The Qur'ān and Modern Arabic Literary Criticism*, 33–36.

7. Neuwirth, *The Qur'an and Late Antiquity*, 370.

8. Ibid.

9. Ibid.

10. Ibid.

11. Ibid.

12. In fact, this topic has occupied Neuwirth's intellectual thought for decades. Angelika Neuwirth's and Nora Schmidt's edited volume, *Denkraum Spätantike: Reflexionen von Antiken im Umfeld des Koran*, serves the same purpose, where the term "Denkraum" expresses the spatial presence and not just mere temporality. Neuwirth's book, *Koranforschung—eine politische Philologie? Bibel, Koran und Islamentstehung im Spiegel spätantiker Textpolitik und moderner Philologie*, revisits the same theme. This time, Neuwirth not only showcases the

complexities of the textual history of sacred texts, but also expertly exposes the biases and politics inherent in the field of philological theology.

13. See Bonald, *Mélanges littéraires, politiques et philosophiques*. For the specific case of Germany, see Humboldt, "On the Historian's Task," 69. In nineteenth-century Germany, historians needed to adopt skepticism in order to survive and be taken seriously as a discipline and be treated as equal to the sciences. It is no coincidence that early German historians of the Qur'ān (such as Gustav Weil's 1844 *Historisch-kritische Einleitung in den Koran*) wanted to arrange its text chronologically, even long before Nöldeke embarked on his field-defining work, *Geschichte des Qorâns*. It is worthy to note that the chronological distinction between Meccan and Medinan sūras is already achieved in the Muslim tradition, notably in Jalāl al-Dīn al-Suyūṭī's *al-Itqān fī 'Ulūm al-Qur'ān* (1505). For a criticism of the Noldeke-Schwally-Bergsträsser chronological sequencings, see Stefanidis, "The Qur'ān Made Linear," 1–22. See also Böwering, "Chronology and the Qur'ān" and Robinson, *Discovering the Qur'ān*, 95–96.

14. Amīn al-Khūlī, *Manāhij Tajdīd fī al-Naḥw wa-al-Balāgha wa-al-Tafsīr wa-al-Adab*, 304.

15. See Reynolds, ed., *The Qur'ān in Its Historical Context*; Reynolds, ed., *New Perspectives on the Qur'ān*; Neuwirth, Sinai, and Marx, eds., *The Qur'ān in Context*; Zellentin, *The Qur'ān's Legal Culture*; Neuwirth, *The Qur'an and Late Antiquity*.

16. 40:78.

17. As an example of this trend, see Reynolds, *The Qur'ān and the Bible*. The argument that the Qur'ān "borrows" from the Bible is as old as Marracci's *Prodromus*: "Ita ut'Alcoranus sit mixtura trium legum, seu religionum, Hebraicae, Christianae, et Israeliticae, additis paucis quisquillis, quae e cerebro suo Mahumetus extraxit." See also Livanos and Salama, "A Bridge Too Far?" 145–69.

18. Wansbrough, *Quranic Studies*; Crone and Cooks, *Hagarism*; Cooks, *The Koran*; Neuwirth, "Qur'ānic Studies and Historical-Critical Philology," 31–60; Shoemaker, *Creating the Qur'ān*.

19. 12:111.

20. 35:24.

21. 12:3. In this particular verse, the Qur'ān specifically raises the status of relating the narrative of the prophets, both in form and in content, to a grammatical superlative degree, as "the best/most mastered/most refined of narratives," narratives which, as the Qur'ān states, Muḥammad "could not have possibly been aware of before the Qur'ān's revelation."

22. Marx, *A Contribution to the Critique of Political Economy*, 12.

23. Neuwirth, "Locating the Qur'ān in the Epistemic Space of Late Antiquity," 193.

24. Damrosch, "Literary Criticism and the Qur'ān," 4–10.

25. Ibid., 6.

BIBLIOGRAPHY

al-ʿAbd, Muḥammad. *Ibdāʿ al-Dalāla fī al-Shiʿr al-Jāhilī*. Cairo: Dār al-Maʿārif, 1988.

Abdel Haleem, M. A. S. "Grammatical Shift for Rhetorical Purposes: Iltifāt and Related Features in the Qurʾān." *Bulletin of the School of Oriental and African Studies* 55, no. 3 (1992): 407–32.

———. "Rhetorical Devices and Stylistic Features of Qurʾanic Grammar." In *The Oxford Handbook of Qurʾanic Studies*, edited by Mustafa Shah and Muhammad Abdel Haleem, 327–45. Oxford: Oxford University Press, 2020.

al-ʿAbdī, al-Muthaqqib. *Dīwān Shiʿr al-Muthaqqib al-ʿAbdī*. Edited by Ḥasan Kāmil al-Ṣayrafī. Cairo: Jāmiʿa-t- al-Duwal al-ʿArabiyya. Maʿhad al-Makhṭūṭāt al-ʿArabiyya, 1971.

ʿAbduh, Muḥammad. *Tafsīr al-Manār*. Cairo: Dār al-Manār, 1954.

Abdul Aleem. "ʿIjazul Qurʾān." *Islamic Culture* 7 (1933): 64–82.

Abu Deeb, Kamal. *al-Jurjānī's Theory of Poetic Imagery*. Oxford: Aris & Phillips, 1979.

———. "Classification of *Istiʿāra* with Special Reference to Aristotle's Classification of Metaphor." *Journal of Arabic Literature* 2 (1971): 48–75.

Abū Dhuʾayb al-Hudhalī. *Dīwān Abī Dhuʾayb al-Hudhalī*. Edited by Anṭūnyūs Buṭrus. Beirut: Dār Ṣādir, 2003.

Abū Tammām. *Dīwān Abī Tammām*. Beirut: Maṭbaʿa-t- al-Qiddīs Jirjis, 1887.

Abū ʿUbayda, Muʿammar ibn al-Muthanná. *Majāz al-Qurʾān*. Edited by Muḥammad Fuʾād Sazkīn. Cairo: Maktaba-t- al-Khānjī, 1970.

Abū Zayd, Aḥmad. *Muqaddima fī al-Uṣūl al-Fikriyya li-l-Balāgha wa Iʿjāz al-Qurʾān*. Rabat: Dār al-Amān, 1989.

Abū Zayd, Naṣr Ḥāmid. *Al-Ittijāh al-ʿAqlī fī al-Tafsīr: Dirāsa fī Qaḍiyya-t- al-Majāz fī al-Qurʾān ʿindal-Muʿtazila*. Beirut: Dār al-Tanwīr, 1982.

———. *Al-Tajdīd wa al-Taḥrīm wa al-Taʾwīl*. Beirut: al-Markaz al-Thaqāfī al-ʿArabī, 2008.

———. *Falsafa-t- al-Taʾwīl: Dirāsa fī Taʾwīl al-Qurʾān ʿind ibn ʿArabī*. Beirut: al-Markaz al-Thaqāfī al-ʿArabī, 2011.

————. *Mafhūm al-Naṣṣ: Dirāsa fī ʿUlūm al-Qurʾān*. Cairo: al-Hayʾa al-Miṣriyya al-ʿĀmma li-l-Kitāb, 1990.

————. "Markaba-t- al-Majāz, Man Yaqūduhā wa ilà Ayn?" *Alif: Journal of Contemporary Poetics* 12 (1992): 50–74.

————. "Maʾziq al-Muqāraba al-Adabiyya li-l-Qurʾān." *Alif: Journal of Comparative Poetics* 23 (2003): 8–47.

Abū Zayd, Naṣr Ḥāmid, and Esther R. Nelson. *Voice of an Exile: Reflections on Islam*. Westport, CT: Praeger, 2004.

ʿAdī ibn Zayd al-ʿIbādī. *Dīwān ʿAdī ibn Zayd al-ʿIbādī*. Baghdad: Sharika-t- Dār al-Jumhūrīya lil-Nashr wal-Ṭibāʿa, 1965.

Adler, Michael. "Was Homer Acquainted with the Bible?" *Jewish Quarterly Review* 5, no. 1 (1892): 170–74.

Adorno, Theodor. *Aesthetic Theory*. Edited by Gretel Adorno and Rolf Tiedemann. Translated by Robert Hullot-Kentor. London: Continuum, 1997.

————. *Ästhetische Theorie*. Frankfurt: Suhrkamp, 1973.

Agha, Said Saleh. "Of Verse, Poetry, Great Poetry and History." In *Poetry and History: the Value of Poetry in Reconstructing Arab History*, edited by Ramzi Baalbeki, Saleh Said Agha, and Tarif Khalidi, 1–35. Beirut: American University of Beirut Press, 2011.

Ahmed, Asad Q. *The Religious Elite of the Early Islamic Hijaz: Five Prosopographical Case Studies*. Oxford: Oxford University Press, 2011.

al-Albānī, Muḥammad Nāṣir al-Dīn. *Silsila-t- al-Aḥādīth al-Saḥīḥa wa Shayʾ min Fiqhihā wa Fawāʾidihā*. Vol. 6, part 1, 2501–800. No. 2700. Riyadh: Maktaba-t- al-Maʿārif, 1996.

ʿAlī, Jawād. *Al-Mufaṣṣal fī Tārīkh al-ʿArab Qabl al-Islām*. Vols. 5 and 6. Baghdad: Maṭābiʿ Jāmiʿa-t- Baghdād, 1993.

Almond, Ian. *The History of Islam in German Thought from Leibniz to Nietzsche*. New York: Routledge, 2010.

Alshaar, Nuha. "The Qurʾan and the Character of Pre-Islamic Poetry: The Dāliyya of al-Aswad b. Yaʿfur al-Nahshalī." In *The Qurʾan and Adab: The Shaping of Literary Traditions in Classical Islam*, edited by Nuha Alshaar, 93–135. Oxford: Oxford University Press, 2017.

al-Ālūsī, Maḥmūd Shukrī. *Bulūgh al-Arab fī Maʿrifa-t- Aḥwāl al-ʿArab*. Vol. 2, edited by Muḥammad Bahja al-Atharī. Cairo: al-Maktaba al-Ahliyya, 1896.

Anawati, Georges A. "Homo Islamicus." In *Images of Man in Ancient and Medieval Thought*, edited by Gerard Bossier, 231–48. Studia G. Verbeke ab amicis et collegis dicata. Louvain: Publications Universitaires, 1976.

Anderson, Perry. *Lineages of the Absolutist State*. London: NLB, 1974.

ʿAntara ibn Shaddād. "Qāfiya-t- al-Mīm Muʿallaqa." In *Sharḥ Dīwān ʿAntara*, by Abū Zakariyyā al-Tibrīzī, 147–87. Edited by Mājid Ṭurād. Beirut: Dār al-Kātib al-ʿArabī, 1992.

Anthony, Sean W. *Muhammad and the Empires of Faith: The Making of the Prophet of Islam*. Oakland: University of California Press, 2020.

————. "The Virgin Annunciate in the Meccan Qurʾan: Q. Maryam 19:19 in Context." *Journal of Near Eastern Studies* 81, no. 2 (2022): 363–85.

————. "Why Does the Qurʾān Need the Meccan Sanctuary? Response to Professor Gerald Hawting's 2017 Presidential Address." *Journal of the International Qurʾanic Studies Association*, no. 3 (2018): 25–41.

Afsar, Ayaz. "A Literary Critical Approach to Qurʾanic Parables." *Islamic Studies*, no. 44 (2005): 481–501.

Arazi, Albert. *La réalité et la fiction dans la poésie arabe ancienne*. Paris: Maisonneuve et Larose, 1989.

Arberry, Arthur John. *Arabic Poetry: A Primer for Students*. Cambridge: Cambridge University Press, 1965.

———. *The Seven Odes: The First Chapter in Arabic Literature*. London: Allen & Unwin, 1957.

Aristotle, *Poetics*. Translated by S. Halliwell. Cambridge, MA: Harvard University Press, 1995.

Asad, Muhammad. *The Message of the Qurʾan: Translated and Explained by Muhammad Asad*. London: Book Foundation, 2003.

al-Aʿshá, Maymūn ibn Qays. *Dīwān al-Aʿshá al-Kabīr: Maymūn ibn Qays*. Edited by Muḥammad Ḥusayn. Cairo: Maktaba-t- al-Ādāb, 1950.

Ashtor, E. "Quelques observations d'un Orientaliste sur la these de Pirenne." *Journal of the Economic and Social History of the Orient* 13 (1970): 166–94.

al-ʿAskarī, Abū Hilāl. *Kitāb al-Ṣināʿatayn*. Edited by ʿAlī Muḥammad al-Bijāwī and Muḥammad Abū al-Faḍl Ibrāhīm. Cairo: Maṭbaʿa-t- ʿĪsá al-Bābī al-Ḥalabī, 1952.

Auerbach, Eric. *Mimesis: The Representation of Reality in Western Literature*. Princeton, NJ: Princeton University Press, 1957.

ʿAwaḍ, Ibrāhīm. *Maʿraka-t- al-Shiʿr al-Jāhilī*. Cairo: Maṭbaʿa-t- al-Fajr al-Jadīd, 1987.

Al-Azami, M. M. *The History of the Quranic Text: From Revelation to Compilation*. 2nd ed. London: Turath, 2008.

Al-Azmeh, Aziz. *The Emergence of Islam in Late Antiquity: Allah and his People*. Cambridge. Cambridge University Press, 2014.

———. "Rome, New Rome and Baghdad: Pathways of Late Antiquity." *Carl Heinrich Becker Lecture der Fritz Thyssen Stiftung* (2008): 55–80.

al-Azraqī, Abū al-Walīd ibn Aḥmad. *Akhbār Makka wa mājāʾa fīhā min al-Āthār. Al-Juzʾ al-Awwal*. Edited by Rushdī al- Ṣāliḥ Malḥas. Beirut: Dār al-Andalus, 1983.

ʿAzzām, Muḥammad. *Muṣṭalaḥāt Naqdiyya min al-Turāth al- ʿArabī*. Damascus: Manshūrāt Wizāra-t- al-Thaqāfa, 1995.

Badawī, ʿAbd al-Raḥman. *Fann al-Shiʿr*. Cairo: Maktaba-t-al-Nahḍa al-Miṣriyya, 1953.

El-Badawi, Emran. *The Qurʾān and the Aramaic Gospel Traditions*. London: Routledge, 2014.

Al-Bagdadi, Nadia. "Registers of Arabic Literary History." *New Literary History* 39, no. 3 (2008): 437–61.

Bamyeh, Mohammed. *The Social Origins of Islam: Mind, Economy, Discourse*. Minneapolis: University of Minnesota Press, 1999.

al-Bāqillānī, Muḥammad ibn al-Ṭayyib. *Iʿjāz al-Qurʾān*. Edited by al-Sayyid Aḥmad Ṣaqr. Cairo: Dār al-Maʿārif, n.d.

Barth, Karl. *The Epistle to the Romans*. Translated by E. C. Hoskyns. London: Oxford University Press, 1933.

Barton, John, ed. *The Cambridge Companion to Biblical Interpretation*. Cambridge: Cambridge University Press, 1998.

Bashear, Suliman. *Arabs and Others in Early Islam*. Princeton, NJ: Princeton University Press, 1997.

———. *Studies in Early Islamic Tradition*. Jerusalem: Hebrew University, Max Schloessinger Memorial Foundation, 2004.

al-Baṣrī, al-Ḥasan. *Al-Ibāna ʿan Uṣūl al-Diyāna*. Edited by Ḥammād al-Anṣārī. Medina: Maṭbūʾāt al-Jāmiʿa al-Islāmiyya, 1988.

Bataille, Georges. *The Accursed Share: An Essay on General Economy*. Vol. 1, *Consumption*. New York: Zone Books, 1988.

Bauer, Thomas. "The Relevance of Early Arabic Poetry for Qurʾanic Studies Including Observations on *Kull* and on 22:27, 26:225, and 52:31." In *The Qurʾan in Context: Historical and Literary Investigations into the Qurʾanic Milieu*, edited by Angelika Neuwirth, Nicolai Sinai, and Michael Marx, 699–732. Leiden: Brill, 2009.

al-Bayḍāwī, al-Qāḍī Nāṣir al-Dīn. *Tafsīr al-Bayḍāwī*. Vol. 1. Damascus: Dār al-Rashīd, 2000.

Becker, Carl Heinrich. *Das Erbe der Antike im Orient und Okzident*. Leipzig: Quelle & Meyer, 1931.

Beeston, A. F. L. "Himyarite Monotheism." In *Studies in the History of Arabia II: Pre-Islamic Arabia*, edited by ʿAbd al-Qādir Maḥmūd, 149–54. Riyadh: King Saud University, 1984.

Behrens-Abouseif, Doris. *Beauty in Arabic Culture*. Princeton Series on the Middle East. Princeton, NJ: Markus Weiner, 1999.

Beiser, Frederick C. *The German Historicist Tradition*. Oxford: Oxford University Press, 2011.

Bell, H. Idris. *Egypt From Alexander the Great to the Arab Conquest: A Study in the Diffusion and Decay of Hellenism*. Oxford: Clarendon Press, 1948.

Bell, Richard. *Introduction to the Koran*. Edinburgh: Edinburgh University Press, 1953.

Bennett, William J. *To Reclaim a Legacy: Report on the Humanities in Higher Education*. Washington, DC: National Endowment for the Humanities, 1984.

Berman, Joshua. *Inconsistency in the Torah: Ancient Literary Convention and the Limits of Source Criticism*. Oxford: Oxford University Press, 2017.

Bevir, Mark. "Why Historical Distance Is Not a Problem." *History and Theory* 50, no. 4 (2011): 24–37.

Black, Max. *Models and Metaphors: Studies in Language and Philosophy*. Ithaca: Cornell University Press, 1962.

Blankinship, Khalid Yahya. *The Inimitable Qurʾan: Some Problems in English Translations of the Qurʾan with Reference to Rhetorical Features*. Leiden: Brill, 2009.

Blatherwick, Helen. "Textual Silences and Literary Choices in al-Kisāʾī's Account of the Annunciation and the Birth of Jesus." *Arabica* 66 (2019): 1– 42.

Bobzin, Hartmut. *Der Koran: Eine Einführung*. Munich: C. H. Beck, 1999.

Borg, Marcus J. *Jesus in Contemporary Scholarship*. Valley Forge: Pennsylvania Trinity Press International, 1994.

Boullata, Issa J., ed. "Iʿjāz." In *The Encyclopedia of Religion*, edited by Mircea Eliade. Vol. 7. New York: Macmillan, 1987.

———. *Literary Structures of Religious Meaning in the Qurʾan*. London: Curzon, 2000.

———. "The Rhetorical Interpretation of the Qurʾan: *Iʿjāz* and Related Topics." In *Approaches to the Qurʾan*, edited by Andrew Rippin, 139–57. Oxford: Oxford University Press, 1988.

Bowering, Gerhard. "Chronology and the Qurʾan." In *Encyclopaedia of the Qurʾan*, edited by Jane Dammen McAuliffe, 315–35. Vol. 1. Leiden: Brill, 2006.

————. "The Qurʾan." In *Islamic Political Thought*, edited by Gerhard Bowering, 185–201. Princeton, NJ: Princeton University Press, 2015.

Bowersock, G. W. *Hellenism in Late Antiquity*. Ann Arbor: University of Michigan Press, 1996.

Bravmann, M. M. *The Spiritual Background of Early Islam*. Studies in Ancient Arab Concepts. Leiden: Brill, 2009.

Brock, Sebastian P., "From Ephrem to Romanos." *Studia Patristica* 20 (1989): 139–51.

Bronwen, Neil. "The Earliest Greek Understandings of Islam: John of Damascus and Theophanes the Confessor." In *Religious Conflict from Early Christianity to the Rise of Islam*, edited by Wendy Mayer and Bronwen Neil, 215–28. Berlin: De Gruyter, 2013.

Brown, Jonathan A. C. *Hadith: Muhammad's Legacy in the Medieval and Modern World*. Oxford: Oneworld, 2009.

————. "The Social Context of Pre-Islamic Poetry: Poetic Imagery and Social Reality in the Muʿallaqāt." *Arab Studies Quarterly* 25, no.3 (2003): 29–50.

Brown, Norman O. "The Apocalypse of Islam." *Social Text*, no. 8 (1984): 155–71.

————. *The Challenge of Islam: The Prophetic Tradition*. Berkeley: North Atlantic Books, 2009.

Brown, Peter. *The Body and Society: Men, Women, and Sexual Renunciation in Early Christianity*. New York: Columbia University Press, 1988.

————. "Late Antiquity and Islam: Parallels and Contrasts." In *Moral Conduct and Authority: The Place of Adab in South Asian Islam*, edited by Barbara Daly Metcalf, 23–37. Berkeley: University of California Press, 1984.

————. *The World of Late Antiquity: AD 150–750*. London: Thames and Hudson, 1972.

Bultmann, Rudolf, Ernst Lohmeyer, Julius Schniewind, Helmut Thielicke, and Austin Farrer. *Kerygma and Myth: A Theological Debate*. Edited by Hans Werner Bartsch. Translated by Reginald H. Fuller. New York: Harper & Row, 1961.

Burke, Edmund. *A Philosophical Inquiry into the Origin of Our Ideas of the Sublime and Beautiful*. London: George Bell and Sons, 1889.

Cachia, Pierre. "Arabic Literature." In *Encyclopedia of Islam*, edited by Kate Fleet, Gudrun Krämer, Denis Matringe, John Nawas, and Devin J. Stewart. 3rd ed. https://refe renceworks.brillonline.com/entries/encyclopaedia-of-islam-3/arabic-literature -COM_0010?s.num=0&s.f.s2_parent=s.f.book.encyclopaedia-of-islam-3&s.q=arabic +literature.

Cameron, Averil, ed. *The Byzantine and Early Islamic Near East III: States, Resources and Armies, Papers of the Third Workshop on Late Antiquity and Early Islam*. Studies in Late Antiquity and Early Islam 1, vol. 3. Princeton, NJ: Darwin Press, 1995.

————, ed. *The Cambridge Ancient History*. Vol. 14, *Late Antiquity: Empire and Successors*. Cambridge: Cambridge University Press, 2000.

————. "The 'Long' Late Antiquity: A Late Twentieth Century Model." In *Classics in Progress: Essays on Ancient Greece and Rome*, edited by T. P. Wiseman, 165–91. Oxford: Oxford University Press, 2002.

————. "Patristics and Late Antiquity: Partners or Rivals." *Journal of Early Christian Studies* 28, no. 2 (2020): 283–302.

————. "Patristic Studies and the Emergence of Islam." In *Patristic Studies in the Twenty-First Century: Proceedings of an International Conference to Mark the 50th Anniversary of the International Association of Patristic Studies*, edited by Brouria Bitton-Ashkelony, Theodore De Bruyn, and Carol Harrison, 249–78. Turnhout: Brepols, 2015.

Cameron, Averil, and G. R. D. King, eds. *The Byzantine and Early Islamic Near East II: Land Use and Settlement Patterns, Papers of the Second Workshop on Late Antiquity and Early Islam*. Princeton, NJ: Darwin Press, 1994.

Castell, Manuel. *The Rise of the Network Society*. Oxford: Wiley-Blackwell, 2010.

Chejne, Anwar G. *The Arabic Language: Its Role in History*. Minnesota: University of Minnesota Press, 1968.

Clover, Frank, and R. S. Humphreys. "Towards a Definition of Late Antiquity." In *Tradition and Innovation in Late Antiquity*, edited by Frank Clover and R. S. Humphreys, 3–26. Madison: University of Wisconsin Press, 1989.

Cohen, Arthur A. *The Myth of the Judeo-Christian Tradition*. New York: Schocken, 1969.

Conrad, Lawrence. "The Arabs." In *The Cambridge Ancient History Volume XIV: Late Antiquity: Empire and Successors*, edited by Averil Cameron, 678–700. Cambridge: Cambridge University Press, 2000.

Cook, Michael. *The Koran: A Very Short Introduction*. New York: Oxford University Press, 2000.

Corbin, Henry. *Creative Imagination in the Sufism of Ibn ʿArabi*. Translated by R. Manheim. Princeton, NJ: Princeton University Press, 1981.

Cracknell, Kenneth, ed. *Wilfred Cantwell Smith: A Reader*. Oxford: Oneworld, 2001.

Crone, Patricia, and Michael Cook. *Hagarism: The Making of the Islamic World*. Cambridge: Cambridge University Press, 1977.

———. "Islam, Judeo-Christianity and Byzantine Iconoclasm." *Jerusalem Studies in Arabic and Islam* 2 (1980): 59–95.

Dahmān, ʿAbd al-Qādir Muḥammad Muntaṣir. *Asālīb al-Nidāʾ fī al-Qurʾān al-Karīm*. Mansoura: Dār al-Luʾluʾa, 2020.

Dakake, Maria. "Mecca and Medina: The Sacred Geography of Qurʾanic Revelation." In *The Routledge Companion to the Qurʾan*, edited by George Archer, Maria Dakake, and Daniel A. Madigan, 23–42. London: Routledge, 2022.

Damrosch, David. "Literary Criticism and the Qurʾan." *Journal of Qurʾanic Studies* 16, no. 3 (2014): 4–10.

Dayeh, Islam. "Prophecy and Writing in the Qurʾan, or Why Muhammad was not a Scribe." In *The Qurʾanʾs Reformation of Judaism and Christianity: Return to the Origins*, edited by Holger M. Zellentin, 31–62. New York: Routledge, 2019.

Ḍayf, Shawqī. *al-Balāgha: Taṭawwur wa Tārīkh*. Cairo: Dār al-Maʿārif, 1995.

———. *Tārīkh al-Adab al-ʿArabī : al-ʿAṣr al-Jāhilī*. Cairo: Dār al-Maʿārif, 1971.

de Bonald, Louis. *Mélanges littéraires, politiques et philosophiques*. Vol. 3, *Œuvres complètes*. Paris: Migne, 1859.

de Certeau, Michel. *The Writing of History*. Translated by Tom Conley. New York: Columbia University Press, 1988.

Deleuze, Gilles, and Felix Guattari, *A Thousand Plateaus: Capitalism and Schizophrenia*. Translated by Brian Massumi. Minneapolis: University of Minnesota Press, 1987.

Déroche, François. *Le Coran, une histoire plurielle. Essai sur la formation du texte coranique*, Paris: Éditions du Seuil, 2019.

Dmitriev, Kirill. "An Early Christian Arabic Account of the Creation of the World." In *The Qurʾān in Context: Historical and Literary Investigations into the Qurʾānic Milieu*, edited by Angelika Neuwirth, Nicolai Sinai, and Michael Marx, 349–87. Leiden: Brill, 2010.

Donner, Fred. *Muhammad and the Believers: At the Origins of Islam*. Cambridge, MA: Harvard University Press, 2010.

———. *Narratives of Islamic Origins: The Beginnings of Islamic Historical Writing*. Princeton, NJ: Darwin Press, 1988.

———. Review of *Hagarism: The Making of the Islamic World*, by Patricia Crone and Michael Cook. *Middle East Studies Association Bulletin* 40, no. 2 (2006): 197–99.

Durant, Will. *The Story of Civilization*. Vol. 3, *Caesar and Christ: A History of Roman Civilization and Christianity from their beginnings to A.D. 325*. New York: Simon & Schuster, 1944.

Duri, A. A. *The Rise of Historical Writing among the Arabs*. Translated by L. I. Conrad. Princeton, NJ: Princeton, 1983.

Dussel, Enrique, *Beyond Philosophy: Ethics, History, Marxism, and Liberation Theology*. Edited by Eduardo Mendieta. Lanham, MD: Rowman & Littlefield, 2003.

Eco, Umberto. *Semiotics and the Philosophy of Language*. Bloomington: Indiana University Press, 1984.

Ehrenkreutz, Andrew S. "Another Orientalist's Remarks concerning the Pirenne Thesis." *Journal of the Economic and Social History of the Orient* 15, no. 12 (1972): 94–104.

Elton, Hugh. *The Roman Empire in Late Antiquity: A Political Military History*. Cambridge: Cambridge University Press, 2018.

———. *Warfare in Roman Europe, AD 350–425*. Oxford: *Clarendon Press*, 1998.

el Masrii, Ghassan. *The Semantics of Qurʾanic Language: al-Āḫira*. Leiden: Brill, 2015.

al-Farrāʾ, Yaḥyá ibn Ziyād. *Maʿānī al-Qurʾān*. Beirut: ʿĀlam al-Kutub, 1983.

Farrin, Raymond. *Abundance from the Desert*. Syracuse: Syracuse University Press, 2011.

Festugière, A. J. *Antioche païenne et chrétienne: Libanius, Chrysostome et les moines de Syrie*. Paris: de Boccard, 1959.

Fischer, Fritz. *Bündnis der Eliten: zur Kontinuität der Machtstrukturen in Deutschland 1871–1945*. Düsseldorf: Droste Verlag, 197.

Flowers, Adam. "Reconsidering Qurʾanic Genre." *Journal of Qurʾanic Studies*, no. 20 (2018): 19–46.

Foucault, Michel. *The Archeology of Knowledge*. London: Routledge, 1989.

———. "Nietzsche, Genealogy, History." In *The Foucault Reader*, edited by Paul Rabinow, 76–100. New York: Vintage, 1984.

———. *The Order of Things: An Archeology of the Human Sciences*. London: Tavistock, 1970.

Fowden, Garth. *Before and After Muhammad: The First Millennium Refocused*. Princeton, NJ: Princeton University Press, 2014.

———. *From Empire to Commonwealth: Consequences of Monotheism in Late Antiquity*. Princeton, NJ: Princeton University Press, 1993.

Gajda, Irene. *Le royaume de Himyar à l'époque monothéiste: L'histoire de l'Arabie du sud ancienne de la fin du IVe siècle de l'ère chrétienne jusqu'à l'avènement de l'Islam*. Paris: Académie des Inscriptions et Belles Lettres, 2009.

Gaskin, J. C. A. "Introduction to David Hume." *Dialogues Concerning Natural Religion* and *The Natural History of Religion*. Oxford: Oxford University Press, 1993.

Geiger, Abraham. *Judaism and Islam*. New York: Ktav, 1970.

———. "Was hat Mohammed aus dem Judenthume aufgenommen?" Bonn: F. Baaden, 1833.

Gellner, E. *Saints of the Atlas*. London: Weidenfeld, 1969.

Gibb, H. A. R. "Pre-Islamic Monotheism in Arabia." *Harvard Theological Review* 55, no. 4 (1962): 269–80.

———.Review of *Social Forces in the Middle East*, by Sidney Nettleton Fisher. *American Anthropologist* no. 58 (1956): 218–19.

———.Review of *The Seven Odes: The First Chapter in Arabic Literature*, by A. J. Arberry. *Die Welt des Islams* 5, no. 3 (1958): 272–73.

Gibbon, Edward. *The History and Fall of the Roman Empire*. 7 vols., edited by J. B. Bury. London: Methuen, November 1898–1925. Reprint New York: AMS Press, 1974.

Gilroy, Paul. *The Black Atlantic: Modernity and Double-Consciousness*. Cambridge, MA: Harvard University Press, 1995.

Goldziher, Ignác. *Muhammedanische Studien*. Vol. 1. Halle: Max Niemeyer, 1889.

Graham, William A. "The Scholar's Scholar: Wilfred Cantwell Smith and a Collegial Life of the Mind." *Harvard Divinity Bulletin* 29, no. 2 (2000): 6–7.

Griffith, Sidney H. *The Qur'an in Arabic: The Scriptures of "the People of the Book" in the Language of Islam*. Princeton, NJ: Princeton University Press, 2013.

———. *Arabic Christianity in the Monasteries of 9th-Century Palestine*. New York: Routledge, 1992.

Günther, Sebastian. "Muhammad, the Illiterate Prophet: An Islamic Creed in the Qur'an and Qur'anic Exegesis." *Journal of Qur'anic Studies* 4, no. 1 (2002): 1–26.

Habermas, Jürgen. *Knowledge and Human Interests*. Translated by Jeremey J. Shapiro. Boston: Beacon Press, 1968.

Hallaq, Wael B. "On Orientalism, Self-Consciousness and History." *Islamic Law and Society* 18, nos. 3 and 4 (2011): 387–439.

———. "The Quest for Origins or Doctrine? Islamic Legal Studies as Colonialist Discourse." *UCLA Journal of Islamic and Near Eastern Law* 2, no. 1 (2002–3): 1–31.

———. "Review: The Use and Abuse of Evidence: The Questions of Provincial and Roman Influences on Early Islamic Law." *Journal of the American Oriental Society* 110, no. 1 (1990): 79–90.

al-Ḥamawī, Muḥibb al-Dīn. *Tanzīl al-Āyāt 'alà al-Shawāhid 'an al-Abyāt*. Cairo: al-Bābī al-Ḥalabī, 1968.

al-Hamdanī, Abū Muḥammad al-Ḥasan. *al-Iklīl min Akhbār al-Yaman wa- Ansāb Ḥimyar*. Al-Juz' al-Thāmin. Edited by Nabīh Amīn Fāris. Sanaa: Dār al-Kalima, n.d.

al-Hamdānī, Mālik ibn Ḥarīm. *Dīwān al-Luṣūṣ fī al- 'Asrayn al-Jāhilī wa- al-Islāmī*. Vol. 2, edited by Muḥammad Nabīl Ṭurayfī. Beirut: Dār al-Kutub al-'Ilmiyya, 2004.

Hamilton, Richard F. *Who Voted for Hitler*. Princeton, NJ: Princeton University Press, 1982.

Ḥassān, Tammām. *al-Bayān fī Rawā'i' al-Qur'ān: Dirāsa Lughawiyya wa- 'Uslūbiyya li-l-Naṣṣ al-Qur'ānī*. Cairo: 'Ālam al-Kutub, 1993.

———. *Al-Lugha al-'Arabiyya: Ma'nāhā wa- Mabnāhā*. Cairo: al-Hay'a al-Miṣriyya al-'Āmma li-l-Kitāb, 1973.

———. Manāhij al-Baḥth fī al-Lugha. Casablanca: Dār al-Thaqāfa, 1973.

Hawting, Gerald R. *The Idea of Idolatry and the Emergence of Islam: From Polemic to History*. Cambridge: Cambridge University Press, 1999.

———. "The Literary Context of the Traditional Account of Pre-Islamic Arab Idolatry." *Jerusalem Studies in Arabic and Islam*, no. 21 (1997): 21–41.

Haykal, Aḥmad. *Fī al-Adab wa- al-Lugha*. Cairo: al-Hay'a al-'Āmma li-l-Kitāb, 1998.

Hegel, G. W. F. *Ästhetik*. Vol. 1, edited by Friedrich Bassenge. Berlin: Aufbau, 1965.

———. *Introduction to the Philosophy of History*. Translated by Leo Rauch. Indianapolis: Hackett, 1988.

———. *Phenomenology of Spirit*. Translated by A. V. Miller. Oxford: Oxford University Press, 1977.

Heidegger, Martin. *Being and Time*. Translated by John Macquarrie and Edward Robinson. San Francisco: Harper & Row, 1962.

———. "A Dialogue on Language (Between a Japanese and an Inquirer)." In *On the Way to Language*, translated by Peter D. Hertz, 1–54. New York: Harper & Row, 1971.

Heinrichs, Wolfhart. The Hand of the Northwind: *Opinions on Metaphor and the Early Meaning of Isti ʿāra in Arabic Poetics*. Wiesbaden: Steiner, 1977.

———. "Metaphor." In *Encyclopedia of Arabic Literature*, edited by Julie Scott Meisami and Paul Starkey. London: Routledge, 1998.

Hemingway, Ernest. *A Moveable Feast*. New York: Scribner Collection, 1964.

Hick, John. "On Wilfred Cantwell Smith: His Place in the Study of Religion." *Method and Theory in the Study of Religion* 4, nos. 1 and 2 (1992): 5–20.

Hodgson, Marshall G. S. *The Venture of Islam*. Vol. 1, *The Classical Age of Islam*. Chicago: University of Chicago Press, 1974.

Hoffmann, Thomas. *The Poetic Qurʾan: Studies on Qurʾanic Poeticity*. Wiesbaden: Harrassowitz, 2007.

Homerin, Th. Emil. "Echoes of a Thirsty Owl: Death and Afterlife in Pre-Islamic Arabic Poetry." *Journal of Near Eastern Studies*, 44 (1985): 165–84.

Hourani, Albert. *Islam in European Thought*. Cambridge: Cambridge University Press, 1991.

———. "Islam and the Philosophers of History." *Middle Eastern Studies* 3, no. 3 (1967): 206–68.

Hoyland, Robert. *Arabia and the Arabs: from the Bronze Age to the Coming of Islam*. New York: Routledge, 2001.

———. "Early Islam as a Late Antique Religion." In *The Oxford Handbook of Late Antiquity*, edited by Scott Fitzgerald Johnson, 1053–77. Oxford: Oxford University Press, 2012.

———. "New Documentary Texts and the History of the Early Islamic State." *Bulletin of the School of Oriental and African Studies*, no. 69 (2006): 395–416.

Hughes, Aaron W. *Abrahamic Religions: On the Uses and Abuses of History*. New York: Oxford University Press, 2012.

———. "Religion without Religion: Integrating Islamic Origins into Religious Studies." *Journal of the American Academy of Religion* 85, no. 4 (2017): 867–88.

al-Ḥumṣī, Naʿīm. "Tārīkh fikra-t- Iʿjāz al-Qurʾān mundhu al-Biʿtha al-Nabawiyya ḥattá al-ʿAṣr al-Ḥāḍir, maʿa Naqd wa Taʿlīq." In *Majalla-t- al-Majmaʿ al-ʿIlmī al-ʿArabī*. Vol. 27. Damascus: Majmaʿ al-Lugha al- ʿArabiyya bi-Dimashq, 1952.

Ḥusayn, Ṭāhā. 1927. *Fī al-Shiʿr al-Jāhilī*. Cairo: Dār al-Maʿārif, 1962.

Hussein, Mahmoud. *Understanding the Qurʾān Today*. Translated by David Bond. London: Saqi Books, 2013.

Ibn ʿAbd Rabbih. *al-ʿIqd al-Farīd*. Vol. 6., edited by Mufid Aḥmad Qumayḥa. Beirut: Dār al-Kutub al-ʿIlmiyya, 1983.

Ibn ʿAqīl, Abū al-Wafā. *Sharḥ ibn ʿAqīl*. Edited by Muḥammad Muḥyī al-Dīn ʿAbd al- Ḥamīd. Cairo: Dār al-Turāth, 1980.

Ibn al-Athīr, *al-Nihāya fī Gharīb al-Ḥadīth wa al-Athar*. Vol. 2. Cairo: al-Maṭbaʿa al-Khayriyya, n.d.

Ibn Fāris ibn Zakariyyā, Abū al-Ḥusayn Aḥmad. *al-Ṣāḥibī fī Fiqh al-Lugha al-ʿArabiyya wa Masā ʾilihā wa Sunan al-ʿArab fī Kalāmihā*. Edited by al-Sayyid Aḥmad Ṣaqr. Cairo: Maṭbaʿa-t-ʾĪsá al-Bābī al-Ḥalabī wa Shurakāh, 1977.

Ibn Ḥabīb, Muḥammad Abū Jaʿfar. *Kitāb al-Muḥabbar, Riwāya-t-Abī Saʾīd al-Ḥasan al-Sukkarī*. Edited by Ilse Lichtenstädter. Beirut: Dār al-Āfāq al-Jadīda, n.d.

Ibn Ḥazm, Abū Muḥammad ʿAlī ibn Aḥmad. *al-Faṣl fī al-Milal wa- al-Ahwāʾ wa- al-Niḥal*. Cairo: Maktaba-t- al-Salām al- ʿĀlamiyya, n.d.

———. *Jamhara-t- Ansāb al-ʿArab*. Edited by ʿAbd al-Salām Muḥammad Harūn. Dār al-Maʿārif, n.d.

Ibn Hishām/Ibn Isḥāq. *al-Sīra al-Nabawiyya*. Vol. 1. Cairo: Maṭbaʿa-t-Muṣṭafá al-Bābī al- Ḥalabī, 1955.

Ibn Jinnī, Abū al-Fatḥ ʿUthmān. *al-Khaṣā ʾiṣ*. Edited by Muḥammad ʿAlī al-Najjār. Beirut: Dār al-Hudá li-l-Ṭibāʿa wa al-Nashr, 1958.

———. *Sirr Ṣinā ʿa -t- al-I ʾrāb*. Vol.1, edited by Muṣṭafá al-Saqqā, Muḥammad al-Zifzāf, Ibrahīm Muṣṭafá, and ʿAbd Allah Amīn. Cairo: Wizāra-t- al-Maʿārif, 1954.

Ibn al-Kalbī, Hishām. *The Book of Idols or The Kitāb al-Aṣnām*. Translated by Nabih A. Faris. Princeton, NJ: Princeton University Press, 1952.

———. *Kitāb al-Aṣnām*. Edited by Aḥmad Zakī Pāshā. Cairo: Dār al-Kutub al-Miṣriyya, 1913.

Ibn Kathīr, Abū al-Fidāʾ Ismāʿīl ibn ʿUmar. *Tafsīr al-Qurʾān al- ʿAẓīm*. Edited by Sāmī ibn Muḥammad al-Salāma. Vol. 6. Cairo: Dār Ṭayba li-l-Nashr wa al-Tawzīʿ, 1999.

Ibn Khaldūn, ʿAbd al-Rahmān. *al-Muqaddima*. Vol. 2, edited by ʿAlī ʿAbd al-Wāḥid Wāfī. Cairo: Lajna-t- al-Bayān al-ʿArabī, 1960.

———. *Muqaddima-t- Ibn Khaldūn*. Edited by ʿAlī ʿAbd al-Wāḥid Wāfī. Cairo: Dār al-Shaʿb, 1950.

Ibn Kulthūm, ʾAmr. "Muʿallaqa-t-ʿAmr ibn Kulthūm." In *al-Muʿallaqāt al- ʿAshr wa Akhbār Qā ʾilīhā* by Abū Zakariyyā al-Tibrīzī. Cairo: Maṭbaʿa-t- Muḥammad ʿAlī Ṣubayḫ wa Awlādih, 1947.

Ibn Manẓūr, Muḥammad ibn Makram. *Lisān al-ʿArab*. Edited by ʿAbd Allāh ʿAlī al-Kabīr, Muḥammad Aḥmad Ḥasab Allāh, and Hāshim Muḥammad al-Shādhilī. Cairo: Dār al-Maʿārif, n.d.

Ibn Qutayba, Abū Muḥammad ʿAbd Allāh ibn Muslim. *al-Shiʿr wa al-Shuʿarāʾ*. Edited by Mufid Qumayḥa and Muḥammad Amīn al-Dannāwī. Beirut: Dār al-Kutub al-ʿIlmiyya, 2009.

———. *Ta ʾwīl Mushkil al-Qurʾān*. Edited by Al-Sayyid Aḥmad Ṣaqr. Cairo: Dār al-Turāth, 1973.

Ibn Rashīq, Abū al-Ḥasan al-Qayrawānī. *al- ʿUmda fī Maḥāsin al-Shiʿr wa-Ādābih wa-Naqdih*. Edited by Muḥammad Muḥiyī al-Dīn ʿAbd al-Ḥamīd. Cairo: Maṭbaʿa-t- Saʿāda, 1955.

Ibn Sallām, Abū ʿUbayd al-Qāsim. *Lughāt al-Qabāʾil al-Wārida fī al-Qurʾān*. Edited by ʿAbd al-Ḥamīd al-Sayyid Ṭalab. Cairo: n.p., 1984.

Ibn Sulaymān, Muqātil. *Al-Ashbāh wa al-Naẓāʾir fī al-Qurʾān al-Karīm*. Edited by ʿAbd Allāh Maḥmūd Shiḥāta. Cairo: al-Hayʾa al-Miṣriyya al-ʿĀmma li-l-Kitāb, 1975.

Imruʾ al-Qays. *Dīwān Imriʾ al-Qays*. Edited by Muḥammad Abū al-Faḍl Ibārhīm. Cairo: Dār al-Maʿārif, n.d.

Ireland, Philip Willard, ed. *The Near East: Problems and Prospects.* Chicago: University of Chicago Press, 1942.

Israel, Jonathan, and Michael Silverthorne, eds. *Spinoza: Theological Political Treatise.* Cambridge: Cambridge University Press, 2007.

Izutsu, Toshihiko. *Ethico-Religious Concepts in the Qurʾan.* Montreal: McGill-Queen's University Press, 2002.

al-Jābirī, Muḥammad ʿĀbid. *Naḥnu wa- al-Turāth.* Beirut: Dār al- Ṭalīʿa, 1980.

Jaeger, Werner. *Paideia: The Ideals of Greek Culture.* Vol. 1, *Archaic Greece, The Mind of Athens.* Oxford: Oxford University Press, 1974.

al-Jāḥiẓ, Abū ʿUthmān ʿAmr ibn Baḥr. *al-Bayān wa- al-Tabyīn.* Edited by ʿAbd al-Salām Muḥammad Hārūn. Cairo: Maktaba-t- al-Khānjī, 1998.

———. "Hujaj al-Nubuwwa." In *Rasāʾil al-Jāḥiẓ,* edited by ʿAbd al-Salām Muḥammad Hārūn, 221–82. Vol. 3. Beirut: Dār al-Jīl, 1991.

Jakobson, Roman. *Language in Literature.* Edited by Krystyna Pomorska and Stephen Rudy. Cambridge, MA: Belknap Press, 1987.

Al-Jallad, Ahmad. "The Linguistic Landscape of pre-Islamic Arabia: Context for the Qurʾan." In *The Oxford Handbook of Qurʾanic Studies,* edited by Mustafa Shah and Muhammad Abdel Haleem, 111–27. Oxford: Oxford University Press, 2020.

———. *The Religion and Rituals of the Nomads of Pre-Islamic Arabia: A Reconstruction Based on Safaitic Inscriptions.* Leiden: Brill, 2022.

Jamil, Nadia. *Ethics and Poetry in Sixth-Century Arabia.* Edinburgh: Edinburgh University Press 2017.

Jarīr ibn ʿAṭiyya. *Dīwān Jarīr bi-sharḥ Muḥammad ibn Ḥabīb.* Vol. 2, edited by Nuʿmān Muḥammad Amīn Ṭāhā. Cairo: Dār al-Maʿārif, 1986.

Jeffery, Arthur. *The Foreign Vocabulary of the Qurʾan.* Baroda: Oriental Institute, 1938.

al-Jīlī, Aḥmad al-Ḥasanī al-Ḥusayn. *Al-Bayān fī Iʿjāz al-Qurʾān.* Deoband: al-Qism al-ʿArabī, al-Jāmiʿa al-Islāmīyya, 1953.

Johns, J. "Archaeology and the History of Early Islam: The First Seventy Years." *Journal of the Economic and Social History of the Orient* 46 (2003): 411–36.

Jones, A. H. M. *The Later Roman Empire, 284–602: A Social, Economic, and Administrative Survey.* Vols. 1 and 2. Baltimore: Johns Hopkins University Press, 1986.

Joyce, James. "Drama and Life." *Fortnightly Review,* April 1, 1900.

al-Jumaḥī, ibn Sallām. *Ṭabaqāt al-Shuʿarāʾ.* Edited by Ṭāhā Aḥmad Ibrāhīm. Beirut: Dār al-Kutub al-ʿIlmiyya, 2001.

al-Jurjānī, Abū Bakr ʿAbd al-Qāhir. "al-Risāla al-Shāfiya." In *Thalāth Rasāʾil fī Iʿjāz al-Qurʾān,* edited by. Muḥammad Khalaf Allāh and Muḥammad Zaghlūl Sallām. Cairo: Dār al-Maʿārif, 1956.

———. *Asrār al-Balāgha.* Edited by Muḥammad ʿAbd al-Munʿim Khafājī and ʿAbd al-ʿAzīz Sharaf. Beirut: Dār al-Jīl, 1991.

———. *Dalāʾil al-Iʿjāz.* Edited by Maḥmud Muḥammad Shākir. Cairo: Maktaba-t- al-Khānjī, 1984.

Kadi, Wadad. "The Primordial Covenant and Human History in the Qurʾān." *Proceedings of the American Philosophical Society* 147 (2003): 332–38.

Kant, Immanuel. *The Critique of Judgement.* Translated by J. H. Bernard. London: Macmillan and Co., 1914.

Kennedy, Hugh. "Islam." In *Late Antiquity: A Guide to the Postclassical World*, edited by Glen W. Bowersock, Peter R. L. Brown and Oleg Grabar. Cambridge, MA: Harvard University Press, 1999.

Kermani, Navid. "From Revelation to Interpretation: Nasr Hamid Abu Zayd and the Literary Study of the Qurʾan." In *Modern Muslim Intellectuals and the Qurʾan*, edited by Suha Taji Farouki. Oxford: Oxford University Press, 2004.

———. *God is Beautiful: The Aesthetic Experience of the Qurʾan*. Translated by Tony Crawford. Cambridge: Polity Press, 2015.

Key, Alexander. *Language between God and the Poets: Maʿnā in the Eleventh Century*. Berkeley: University of California Press, 2018.

Khalaf Allāh, Muḥammad Aḥmad. "Ahl al-Adab li-l-Adab wa Ahl al-Dīn li-l-Dīn." *Adab wa Naqd* 74 (1991).

———. *Al-Fann al-Qaṣaṣī fī al-Qurʾān al-Karīm*. Cairo: Sināʾ li-l-Nashr, 1999.

———. *Al-Risāla*. Issues 741–52 (September–December 1947).

Khalaf Allāh, Muḥammad Aḥmad, and Muḥammad Zaghlūl Sallām. *Thalāth Rasāʾil fī Iʿjāz al-Qurʾān li-l-Rummānī wa- al-Khaṭṭābī wa-ʿAbd al-Qāhir al-Jurjānī*. Cairo: Dār al-Maʿārif, 1956.

Khalidi, T. *Arabic Historical Thought in the Classical Period*. Cambridge: Cambridge University Press, 1994.

al-Khaṭṭābī. "al-Qawl fī Bayān Iʿjāzal-Qurʾān." *Thalāth Rasāʾil fī Iʿjāz al-Qurʾān li-l-Rummānī wa- al-Khaṭṭābī wa-ʿAbd al-Qāhir al-Jurjānī*. Cairo: Dār al-Maʿārif, 1956.

al-Khaṭīb, ʿAbd al-Karīm. *Iʿjāzal-Qurʾān fī Dirāsa Kāshifa li-Khaṣāʾiṣ al-Balāgha al-ʿArabiyya wa- Maʿāyīrihā*. Cairo: Dār al-Fikr al-ʿArabī, 1964.

Khayr Bik, Mājid. *al-Lugha al-ʿArabiyya: Judhūruhā -Intishāruhā- Taʾthīruhā fī al-Sharq wa al-Gharb*. Damascus: Dār Saʿd al-Dīn, 1992.

al-Khūlī, Amīn. *Manāhij Tajdīd fī al-Naḥw wa-al-Balāgha wa-al-Tafsīr wa-al-Adab*. Cairo: Dār al-Maʿrifa, 1961.

Kirk, G. S. *The Iliad: A Commentary*. Vol. 1, *Books 1–4*. Cambridge: Cambridge University Press, 1985.

Koren, J., and Nevo, Y. D. "Methodological Approaches to Islamic Studies." *Der Islam*, no. 68 (1991): 97—107.

LaCapra, Dominick. "Rethinking Intellectual History and Reading Texts." *History and Theory* 19, no. 3 (1980): 245–76.

Lassner, Jacob. *Demonizing the Queen of Sheba: Boundaries of Gender and Culture in Postbiblical Judaism and Medieval Islam*. Chicago: University of Chicago Press, 1993.

Lawrence, D. H. *Selected Literary Criticism*, ed., Anthony Beal. London: William Heinemann, 1955.

Levinas, Emanuel. *Alterity and Transcendence*. Translated by Michael B. Smith. London: Athlone Press, 1999.

———. *Totality and Infinity: An Essay on Exteriority*. Translated by Alphonso Lingis. Pittsburgh: Duquesne University Press, 1969.

Livanos, Christopher and Mohammad Salama. "A Bridge Too Far? Ludovico Marracci's Translation of the Qurʾan and the Persistence of Medievalism." *Boundary* 2, 50, no. 3 (2023): 145–69.

Lüling, Günter. *A Challenge to Islam for Reformation: The Rediscovery and Reliable Reconstruction of a Comprehensive Pre-Islamic Christian Hymnal Hidden in the Koran under Earliest Islamic Reinterpretations*. New Delhi: Motilal Banarsidass, 2003.

Luxenberg, Christoph. *Die syro-aramäische Lesart des Koran. Ein Beitrag zur Entschlüsse-lung der Koransprache*. Berlin: Hans Schiler, 2000.

——. *The Syro-Aramaic Reading of the Koran: A Contribution to the Decoding of the Language of the Koran*. Berlin: Hans Schiler, 2007.

MacAuliffe, Jane Dammen, ed. *The Cambridge Companion to the Qurʾān*. Cambridge: Cambridge University Press, 2006.

Macaulay, Thomas Babington. "Minute on Education." *Bureau of Education. Selections from Educational Records*. Part I (1781–1839). Edited by H. Sharp Calcutta: Superintendent, Government Printing, 1920. Reprint, Delhi: National Archives of India, 1965.

Madelung, Wilferd. "The Origins of the Controversy Concerning the Creation of the Koran." *Orientalia Hispanica* 1 (1974).

Madigan, Daniel A. *The Qurʾanʾs Self-Image: Writing and Authority in Islamʾs Scripture*. Princeton, NJ: Princeton University Press, 2001.

de Man, Paul. *Aesthetic Ideology*. Minneapolis: University of Minnesota Press, 2008.

Margoliouth, David Samuel. *Mohammed and the Rise of Islam*. New York: G. P. Putnam's Sons, 1905.

——. *The Relations between the Arabs and Israelites Prior to the Rise of Islam*. London: Published for the British Academy by H. Milford, Oxford University Press, 1921.

Marracci, Ludovico. 1698. *Alcorani textus universus ex correctioribus Arabum exemplaribus summa fideatque pulcherrimis characteribus descriptus*. Padua: Typographia Seminarii, 1969. https://archive.org/details/AlcoranusTextusMaracci.

Marrou, H. I. *A History of Education in Antiquity*. Translated by George Lamb. Madison: University of Wisconsin Press, 1956.

Marx, Karl. *A Contribution to the Critique of Political Economy*. Translated by N. Stone. Chicago: C. H. Kerr, 1904.

El Masri, Ghassan. *The Semantics of Qurʾanic Language: Al-Akhira*. Leiden: Brill, 2020.

al-Masʿūdī, Abū al-Ḥasan ibn ʿAlī. *Murūj al-Dhahab wa Maʿādin al-Jawhar. Al-Juzʾ al-Rābiʿ*. Edited by Kamāl Ḥasan Marʿī. Beirut: al-Maktaba al-ʿAṣriyya, 2005.

al-Māwardī, Abū al-Ḥasan. *al-Nukat wa al-ʿUyūn*. 6 vols, edited by al-Sayyid ibn ʿAbd al-Maqṣūd ibn ʿAbd al-Raḥīm. Beirut: Dār al-Kutub al-ʿIlmiyya, 1992.

Meinecke, Friedrich. *Weltbürgertum und Nationalstaat*. Berlin: Oldenbourg Wissenschafts-verlag, 1922.

Mir, Mustansir. "Between Grammar and Rhetoric (Balaghah): A Look at Qurʾan 2:217." *Islamic Studies*, no. 29 (1990): 277–85.

Mommsen, Theodor. *The History of Rome*. Vol. 3., translated by William Purdie Dickson. New York: C. Scribner's and Sons, 1895.

Monroe, James. "Oral Composition in Pre-Islamic Poetry." *Journal of Arabic Literature*, no. 3 (1972): 1–53.

Montgomery, James, ed. *Arabic Theology, Arabic Philosophy: From the Many to the One; Essays in Celebration of Richard M. Frank*. Leuven: Peeters, 2006.

——. "Dichotomy in Jahili Poetry." *Journal of Arabic Literature* 17, no. 1 (1986): 1–20.

——. "The Empty Hijaz." In *Arabic Theology, Arabic Philosophy. From the Many to the One: Essays in Celebration of Richard M. Frank*, edited by James Montgomery, 37–97. Leuven: Peeters, 2006.

——. *The Vagaries of the Qaṣīdah: The Tradition and Practice of Early Arabic Poetry*. Cambridge: E. J. W. Gibb Memorial Trust, 1997.

Moses, Dirk. *German Intellectuals and the Nazi Past*. Cambridge: Cambridge University Press, 2007.

Mourad, Suleiman A. "Mary in the Qurʾān: A reexamination of her presentation." *The Qurʾan in its Historical Context*, edited by Gabriel Said Reynolds, 163–74. London: Routledge, 2008.

Murray, Alexander. "Peter Brown and the Shadow of Constantine." *Journal of Roman Studies* 73 (1983): 191–203.

Musurillo, Herbert, ed. *The Acts of the Christian Martyrs*. Oxford: Clarendon Press, 1972.

al-Mutanabbī, Abū al-Ṭayyib Aḥmad. *Dīwān al-Mutanabbī*. Beirut: Dār Bayrūt lil- Ṭibāʿa wa al-Nashr, 1983.

al-Nābigha al-Dhubyānī. *Dīwān al-Nābigha al-Dhubyānī*. Edited by ʿAbbās ʿAbd al-Sātir. Beirut: Dār al-Kutub al-ʿIlmiyya, 1996.

Naik, J. P., and Syed Nurullah. *A Students' History of Education in India (1800–1973)*. Delhi: Macmillan, 1974.

al-Naḥḥās, Abū Jaʿfar. *Iʿrāb al-Qurʾān*. Edited by Khālid al-ʿAlī. Beirut: Dār al-Maʿrifa, 2008.

Natij, Salah. "*Murūʾa*: Soucis et interrogations éthiques dans la culture arabe classique." *Studia Islamica* 112, no. 2 (2017): 206–63.

———. "*Murūʾa*: Soucis et interrogations éthiques dans la culture arabe classique." *Studia Islamica* 113, no. 1 (2018): 1–55.

Nelson, Kristina. *The Art of Reciting the Qurʾan*. Cairo: American University of Cairo Press, 2010.

Neuwirth, Angelika. *Der Koran als Text der Spätantike. Ein europäischer Zugang*. Berlin: Verlag der Weltreligionen, 2010.

———. "Images and Metaphors in the Introductory Sections of the Makkan Suras." In *Approaches to the Qurʾan*, edited by Gerald R. Hawting and Abdul-Kader A. Shareef. London: Routledge, 1993.

———. "Locating the Qurʾan and Early Islam in the Epistemic Space of Late Antiquity." In *Islam and its Past: Jahiliyya, Late Antiquity and the Qurʾan*, edited by Carol Bakhos and Michael Cook, 165–85. Oxford: Oxford University Press, 2017.

———. "Locating the Qurʾan in the Epistemic Space of Late Antiquity." *Ankara Üniversitesi İlahiyat Fakültesi Dergisi* 54, no. 2 (2013): 189–203.

———. "Locating the Qurʾan in the Epistemic Space of Late Antiquity." In *Books and Written Culture of the Islamic World*, edited by Andrew Rippin and Roberto Tottoli, 159–79. Leiden: Brill, 2015.

———. *The Qurʾan and Late Antiquity*. Translated by Samuel Wilder. Oxford: Oxford University Press, 2019.

———. "Qurʾanic Studies and Historical-Critical Philology." *Philological Encounters* 1, nos. 1–4. (2016): 31–60.

———. "Rezension zu Wansbrough, Qurʾanic Studies." *Die Welt des Islams* 23–24 (1984): 539–42.

———. "Rhetoric and the Qurʾan." In *Encyclopedia of the Qurʾan*. Edited by Jane Dammen McAuliffe, 461–76. Vol. 4. Leiden: Brill, 2004.

———. *Scripture, Poetry and the Making of a Community*. Oxford: Oxford University Press, 2014.

———. *Studien zur Komposition der mekkanischen Suren.* Berlin: De Gruyter, 1981.

Neuwirth, Angelika, and Michael Sells, eds. *Quranic Studies Today.* London: Routledge, 2016.

Neuwirth, Angelika, Nicolai Sinai, and Michael Marx, eds. *The Qurʾan in Context: Historical and Literary Investigations into the Qurʾānic Milieu.* Leiden: Brill, 2011.

Neuwirth, Angelika, and Nora Schmidt. Denkraum Spätantike: Reflexionen von Antiken im Umfeld des Koran. Wiesbaden: Harrassowitz Verlag, 2016.

Nicholson, Reynold A. *A Literary History of the Arabs.* New York: Charles Scriber's Sons, 1907.

Nietzsche, Friedrich. *Untimely Meditations.* Edited by Daniel Breazeale. Translated by R. J. Hollingdale. Cambridge: Cambridge University Press, 1997.

Nöldeke, Theodor, "Arabia, Arabians." *Encyclopaedia Biblica* (1899): 272–75. Qurʾan

Nöldeke, Theodor, and Friedrich Schwally, eds. *Geschichte des Qorans.* Part 1, *Über den Ursprung des Qorans.* Leipzig: T. Weicher, 1909. Reprint. Hildesheim: T. Weicher, 2005.

Nöldeke, Theodor, Friedrich Schwally, Gotthelf Bergstrasser, and Otto Pretzl. *The History of the Qurʾan.* Edited and translated by Wolfgang Behn. Leiden: Brill, 2013.

Nowottny, Winifred. *The Language Poets Use.* London: Athlone Press, 1965.

Obermann, Julian. "Koran and Agada: The Events at Mount Sinai." *American Journal of Semitic Languages and Literatures,* no. 58 (1941): 23–48.

Paret, Rudi. *Mohammed und der Koran: Geschichte und Verkündigung des Arabischen Propheten.* W. Kohlhammer Verlag, 1980.

Pellat, Ch. "Layl and Nahār." In *Encyclopaedia of Islam,* edited by P. Bearman, Th. Bianquis, C. E. Bosworth, E. van Donzel, and W. P. Heinrichs, 5:707–10. 2nd ed. https://reference works.brillonline.com/entries/encyclopaedia-of-islam-2/layl-and-nahar-SIM_4651?s .num=0&s.f.s2_parent=s.f.book.encyclopaedia-of-islam-2&s.q=%E2%80%9CLayl+and +Nah%C4%81r%22.

Penchansky, David. *Solomon and the Ant: The Qurʾan in Conversation with the Bible.* Eugene, OR: Cascade Books, 2021.

Pirenne, H. "Mahomet et Charlemagne." *Revue belge de philologie et de l'histoire* 1 (1922): 77–86.

———. *Mohammed and Charlemagne.* Translated by Bernard Miall. London: George Allen & Unwin., 1939.

Plato. *Phaedrus and Letters VII and VIII.* Translated by Walter Hamilton. London: Penguin Books, 1973.

———. *The Republic.* Translated by Desmond Lee. London: Penguin Classics, 1955.

Playfair, Col. "On the Himyaritic Inscriptions Lately Brought to England from Southern Arabia." *Transactions of the Ethnological Society of London* 5 (1867): 174–77.

Popper, Karl R. *The Open Society and Its Enemies.* Vol. 2., *The High Tide of Prophecy: Hegel, Marx, and the Aftermath.* Princeton, NJ: Princeton University Press, 1971.

Prideaux, Humphrey. *True Nature of Imposture Revealed in the Life of the Impostor Mohammad.* London: William Rogers, 1697.

al-Qummī, ʿAlī ibn Ibrahīm. *Tafsīr al-Qummī.* Vol. 2. Beirut: Maṭbaʿa-t- Muʾassasa-t- al-Wafāʾ, 1993.

al-Qurṭubī, Muḥammad ibn Aḥmad. *al-Jāmiʿ li-Aḥkām al-Qurʾān.* Edited by ʿAbd Allāh ibnʿAbd al-Muḥsin al-Turkī. Vols. 1 and 22. Beirut: Muʾassas-t- al-Risāla, 2006.

Rabin, Chaim. *Qumran Studies*. Oxford: Oxford University Press, 1957.

al-Rāzī, Fakhr al-Dīn. *Tafsīr Fakhr al-Dīn al-Rāzī*. Vol.11. Beirut: Dār al-Fikr, 1981.

Reynolds, Gabriel S. *The Qurʾan and the Bible: Text and Commentary*. New Haven, CT: Yale University Press, 2018.

———. *The Qurʾan and its Biblical Subtext*. London: Routledge, 2010.

Rippin, Andrew. "The Exegetical Genre *asbab al-nuzul*: A Bibliographical and Terminological Survey." *Bulletin of the School of Oriental and African Studies*, no. 48 (1985): 1–15.

Rippin, Andrew, and Jawid Mojaddedi, eds. *The Wiley-Blackwell Companion to the Qurʾān*. Oxford: Wiley-Blackwell, 2017.

Rippin, Andrew, and Khaleel Mohammed, eds. *Coming to Terms with the Qurʾan: A Volume in Honor of Professor Issa Boullata*. North Haledon, NJ: Islamic Publications International, 2008.

Robinson, Neal. *Discovering the Qurʾan: A Contemporary Approach to a Veiled Text*. Washington, DC: Georgetown University Press, 2004.

Römer, Thomas. The *Invention of God*. Translated by Raymond Geuss. Cambridge, MA: Harvard University Press, 2015.

Ross, Lee. "The Intuitive Psychologist and His Shortcomings: Distortions in the Attribution Process." In *Advances in Experimental Social Psychology*, edited by Leonard Berkowitz, 173–220. New York: Academic Press, 1977.

Rubin, Uri. *Between Bible and Qurʾan: The Children of Israel and the Islamic Self-Image*. Princeton, New Jersey: Princeton University Press, 1999.

al-Rummānī, Abū al-Ḥasan ʿAlī (b. ʿĪsā). "al-Nukat fī Iʿjāz al-Qurʾān." In *Thalāth Rasāʾil fī Iʿjāz al-Qurʾān li-l-Rummānī wa- al-Khaṭṭābī wa-ʿAbd al-Qāhir al-Jurjānī*, edited by Muḥammad Khalaf Allāh and Muḥammad Zaghlūl Sallām. Cairo: Dār al-Maʿārif, 1956.

Sadeghi, Behnam, and Mohsen Goudarzi. "Sanʾaı and the Origins of the Qurʾan." *Der Islam* 87, nos. 1–2 (2012): 1–129.

Sadeghi, Behnam, and Uwe Bergmann. "The Codex of a Companion of the Prophet and the Qurʾān of the Prophet." *Arabica* 57, no. 4 (2010): 343–436.

Said, Edward. *Orientalism*. New York: Vintage Books, 1978.

Salama, Mohammad. *Islam, Orientalism, and Intellectual History: Modernity and the Politics of Exclusion Since Ibn Khaldūn*. London: I. B. Tauris, 2011.

———. *The Qurʾān and Modern Arabic Literary Criticism: From Ṭāhā to Naṣr*. London: Bloomsbury, 2018.

———. "The Untranslatability of the Qurʾānic City." In *The City in Arabic Literature: Classical and Modern Perspectives*, edited by Nizar F. Hermes and Gretchen Head, 1–18. Edinburgh: Edinburgh University Press, 2018.

Salama, Mohammad, and Volker Langbehn, eds. *German Colonialism: Race, the Holocaust, and Postwar Germany*. New York: Columbia University Press, 2011.

Saleh, Walid. "Death and Dying in the Qurʾan." In *Troubling Texts, Sacred Topics: Readings in Hebrew Bible, New Testament, and Qurʾan*, edited by Roberta Sterman Sabbath, 445–55. Berlin: De Gruyter, 2021.

———. "In Search of a Comprehensive Qurʾan: A survey of Some Recent Scholarly Works." *Bulletin of the Royal Institute for Inter-Faith Studies* 5, no. 2 (2003): 143–65.

———. "Meccan Gods, Jesus' Divinity: An Analysis of Q 43 Surat al-Zukhruf." In *The Qurʾanʾs Reformation of Judaism and Christianity: Return to the Origins*, edited by Holger Zellentin, 92–111. New York: Routledge, 2019.

———. "The Preacher of the Meccan Qur'an: Deuteronomistic History and Confessionalism in Muḥammad's Early Preaching." *Journal of Qur'anic Studies* 20, no. 2 (2018): 74–111.

Samji, Karim. *The Qur'an: A Form-Critical History*. Berlin: De Gruyter, 2018.

Schimmel, Anne Marie. *Deciphering the Signs of God: A Phenomenological Approach to Islam*. Albany: State University of New York Press, 1994.

———."Islamic Studies in Germany: A Historical Overview." *Islamic Studies* 49, no. 3 (Autumn 2010): 401–10.

Schneidau, Herbert N. *Sacred Discontent: The Bible and Western Tradition*. Berkeley: University of California Press, 1976.

Serrano, Richard. *Qur'ān and the Lyric Imperative*. Lanham, MD: Lexington Books, 2016.

Shahid, Irfan. "Another Contribution to Koranic Exegesis: The Sūra of the Poets, XXVI." *Journal of Arabic Literature*, no. 14 (1983): 1–21.

———. "Byzantium in South Arabia." *Dumbarton Oaks Papers*, no. 33 (1979): 27–29.

———. "A Contribution to Koranic Exegesis." In *Arabic and Islamic Studies in Honor of Hamilton A. R. Gibb*, edited by George Makdisi, 563–80. Leiden: Brill, 1965.

———. "The Sūra of the Poets, Qur'ān XXVI: Final Conclusions." *Journal of Arabic Literature* 35, no. 2 (2004): 175–220.

———. "The Sūra of the Poets Revisited." *Journal of Arabic Literature*, no. 39 (2008): 398–423.

al-Shahrastānī, Abū al-Fatḥ Muḥammad. *al-Milal wa al-Niḥal*. Vol. 2, edited by Aḥmad Fahmī Muḥammad. Cairo: Maktaba-t- al-Ḥusayn al-Tijāriyya, 1948.

Shaḥrūr, Muḥammad. *al-Kitāb wa al-Qur'ān: Qirā'a Mu'āṣira*. Damascus: al-Ahālī, 1990.

Shakespeare, William. *King Lear*. London: Bloomsbury Arden Shakespeare. 1997.

Shoemaker, Stephen J. *Creating the Qur'an: A Historical-Critical Study*. Oakland: University of California Press, 2022.

———. *The Death of a Prophet: The End of Muhammad's Life and the Beginning of Islam*. Philadelphia: University of Pennsylvania Press, 2001.

Sinai, Nicolai. *Rain-Giver, Bone-Breaker, Score-Settler: Allāh in Pre-Quranic Poetry*. American Oriental Series, Essay 15. *American Oriental Society* (2019): ix–79.

———. "When Did the Consonantal Skeleton of the Quran Reach Closure? Part I." *Bulletin of the School of Oriental and African Studies* 77, no. 2 (2014): 273–92.

———. "When Did the Consonantal Skeleton of the Quran Reach Closure? Part II." *Bulletin of the School of Oriental and African Studies* 77, no. 3 (2017): 509–21.

Sizgorich, Thomas. "Narrative and Community in Islamic Late Antiquity." *Past & Present*, no. 185 (2004): 9–42.

Smith, Wilfred Cantwell. *Faith and Belief*. Princeton, NJ: Princeton University Press, 1987.

———. *The Meaning and End of Religion*. Minneapolis: Fortress Press, 1991.

———. *Modern Islam in India: A Social Analysis*. London: V. Gollancz, 1946.

———. *Religious Diversity: Essays*. New York: HarperCollins, 1976.

———. *What Is Scripture? A Comparative Approach*. Fortress Press. 1993.

Southern, R. W. *Western Society and the Church in the Middle Ages*. Pelican History of the Church 2. London: Penguin Books, 1971.

Sperl, Stefan. "The Qur'an and Arabic Poetry." In *The Oxford Handbook of Qur'anic Studies*, edited by Mustafa Shah and Muhammad Abdel Haleem, 401–15. Oxford: Oxford University Press, 2020.

Sperl, Stefan, and Yorgos Dedes, eds., *Faces of the Infinite: Neoplatonism and Poetry at the Confluence of Africa, Asia and Europe*. Oxford: Oxford University Press, 2022.

Spivak, Gayatri Chakravorty. *A Critique of Postcolonial Reason: Toward a History of the Vanishing Present*. Cambridge, MA: Harvard University Press, 1999.

Statkiewicz, Max. *Rhapsody of Philosophy: Dialogues with Plato in Contemporary Thought*. University Park: Penn State University Press, 2009.

Stefanidis, Emmanuelle. "The Qur'an Made Linear: A Study of the Geschichte des Qorâns' Chronological Reordering." *Journal of Qur'anic Studies* 10, no. 2 (2009): 1–22.

Stetkevych, Jaroslav. *Muhammad and the Golden Bough; Reconstructing Arabian Myth*. Bloomington: Indiana University Press, 1996.

———. *The Zephyrs of Najd*. Chicago: University of Chicago Press, 1993.

Stetkevych, Suzanne Pinckney. *The Mute Immortals Speak: Pre-Islamic Poetry and the Poetics of Rituals*. Ithaca, NY: Cornell University Press, 1993.

———. "Sara and the Hyena: Laughter, Menstruation, and the Genesis of a Double Entendre." *Journal of the History of Religion* 36, no.1 (1996): 13–41.

———. "Structuralist Analyses of Pre-Islamic Poetry: Critique and New Directions." *Journal of Near Eastern Studies*. 43 (1983): 85–10.

Stewart, Devin J. "Introductory Oaths and the Question of Composite Surahs." In *Structural Dividers in the Qur'an*, edited by M. Klar, 267–337. London: Routledge, 2021.

———. "A Modest Proposal for Islamic Studies." In *Identity, Politics, and the Study of Islam: Current Dilemmas in the Study of Religions*, edited by Matt Sheedy, 157–200. Sheffield: Equinox, 2018.

———. "Reflections on the State of the Art in Western Qur'anic Studies." In *Islam and its Past: Jahiliyya, Late Antiquity, and the Qur'an*, edited by Carol Bakhos and Michael Cook, 4–68. Oxford: Oxford University Press, 2017.

———. Review of *God is Beautiful: The Aesthetic Experience of the Qur'an*, by Navid Kermani. *American Journal of Islam and Society* 33, no. 1 (January 2016): 95–96.

———. "Speech Genres and Interpretation of the Qur'an." *Religions* 12, no. 529 (2021): 1–34.

———. "Vocatives in the Qur'an and the Framing of Prophetic Proclamations." In *Unlocking the Medinan Qur'an*, edited by Nicolai Sinai, 199–248. Brill: Leiden, 2022.

———. "Wansbrough, Bultmann, and the Theory." In *Qur'ānic Studies Today*, edited by Angelika Neuwirth and Michael A. Sells, 17–52. New York: Routledge, 2016.

Stroumsa, Guy. "Athens, Jerusalem and Mecca: The Patristic Crucible of the Abrahamic Religions." *Studia Patristica* 62, no. 10 (2013): 153–68.

———. *The Making of the Abrahamic Religions in Late Antiquity*. Oxford: Oxford University Press, 2015.

Stroumsa, Sarah. "The Signs of Prophecy: The Emergence and Early Development of a Theme in Arabic Theological Literature." *Harvard Theological Review* 78, nos. 1/2 (1985): 101–14.

Stubbe, Henry. *An Account of the Rise and Progress of Mahometanism with the Life of Mahomet and a Vindication of Him and His Religion from the Calumnies of Christians*. Edited by Hafez Mahmud Khan Shairani. London: Luzac, 1911.

al-Ṣūlī, Abū Bakr Muḥammad ibn Yaḥyá. *Akhbār Abī Tammām*. Edited by Khalīl Maḥmūd ʿAsākir, Muḥammad ʿAbduh ʿAzzām, and Naẓīr al-Islām al-Hindī. Cairo: Maṭbaʿa-t Lajna-t- al-Taʾlīf wa al-Tarjama wa-al-Nashr, 1937.

al-Suyūṭī, Jalāl al-Dīn Abd al-Raḥmān. *al-Durr al-Manthūr fī al-Tafsīr bil-Maʾthūr*. Vol. 14, edited by ʿAbd Allāh ibn ʿAbd al-Muḥsin al-Turkī. Cairo: Markaz Hajr lil-buḥūth wa al-Dirāsāt al-ʿArabiyya wa al-Islāmiyya, 2003.

———. *al-Itqān fī ʿUlūm al-Qurʾān.* Vol. 2. Edited by Muḥammad Abū al-Faḍl Ibrāhīm. Cairo: al-Hayʾa al-Miṣriyya al-ʿĀmma lil-Kitāb, 1974.

———. *Lubāb al-Nuqūl fī Asbāb al-Nuzūl.* Beirut: Muʾassasa-t- al-Kutub al-Thaqāfiyya, 2002.

al-Ṭabarī, Abū Jaʿfar. *Jāmiʿ al-bayān ʿan Taʾwīl āy al-Qurʾān.* 26 vols. Edited by ʿAbd Allāh ibn ʿAbd al-Muḥsin al-Turkī. Cairo: Dār Hajr, 2001.

Tannous, Rami. "Negotiating the Nativity in Late Antiquity: The Qurʾān's Rereading of Mary's Preparation for the Conception of Jesus." PhD diss., University of Toronto, 2019.

Ṭarafa, ibn al-ʿAbd. *Dīwān Ṭarafa ibn al-ʿAbd.* Edited by Mahdī Muḥammad Nāṣir al-Dīn. Beirut: Dār al-Kutub al-ʿIlmiyya, 2002.

Tellenbach, G. *Church, State and Christian Society at the Time of the Investiture Contest.* Translated by R. E. Bennett. Oxford: Blackwell, 1946.

al-Tibrīzī, Abū Zakariyyā. *al-Muʿallaqāt al-ʿAshr wa Akhbār Qāʾilīhā.* Cairo: Maṭbaʿa-t Muḥammad ʿAlī Ṣubayḥ wa- Awlādih, 1947.

Toorawa, Shawkat M. "Seeking Refuge from Evil: The Power and Portent of the Closing Chapters of the Qurʾan." *Journal of Qurʾanic Studies* 4 (2002): 54–60.

———. "Sūrat Maryam (Q. 19): Lexicon, Lexical Echoes, English Translation." *Journal of Qurʾanic Studies* 23 (2011): 25–78.

Tottoli, Roberto. *Biblical Prophets in the Qurʾan and Muslim Literature.* London: Routledge, 2002.

Toynbee, Arnold J. "Greece." In *The Balkans: A History of Bulgaria, Serbia, Greece, Rumania, Turkey,* edited by Nevill Forbes, Arnold J. Toynbee, D. Mitrany, and D. G. Hogarth, 163–250. Oxford: Oxford University Press, 1915.

———. *A Study of History.* Vol. 12, *Reconsiderations.* Oxford: Oxford University Press, 1961.

al-ʿUkbarī, ʿAbd Allāh ibn al-Ḥusayn. *Al-Tibyān fī Sharḥ al-Dīwān.* Edited by Muṣṭafá al-Saqqā, Ibrāhīm al-Abyārī, and ʿAbd al- Ḥafiẓ Shalabī. Vol. 1. Cairo: Maṭbaʿa-t Muṣṭafá al-Bābī al-Ḥalabī, 1971.

Ullendorff, Edward. "What is a Semitic Language? (A Problem of Linguistic Identification)." *Journal of Semitic Studies* (1956): 216–36.

Valantasis, Richard, ed. *Religions of Late Antiquity in Practice.* Princeton, NJ: Princeton University Press, 2000.

van Ess, Josef. *Theology and Society in the Second and Third Centuries of the Hijra: A History of Religious Though in Early Islam.* Vol. 1 Translated by John O'Kane. Leiden: Brill, 2017.

van Gelder, Geert Jan van. "Persons as Texts/Texts as Persons." In *Conscious Voices: Concepts of Writing in the Middle East,* edited by Stephan Guth, Priska Furrer, and Johann Christoph Bürgel, 237–53. Stuttgart: Nomos Verlagsgesellschaft, 1999.

———. *Sound and Sense in Classical Arabic Poetry.* Arabische Studien 10. Wiesbaden: Otto Harrassowitz, 2012.

von Grunebaum, Gustave E. "Ausbreitungs-und Anpassungsfähigkeit." *Studien zum Kulturbild und Selbstverständnis des Islams* (1969): 11–22.

———. *Classical Islam: A History 600–1258.* Translated by Katherine Watson. Chicago: Aldine, 1970.

———. *Islam, Essay on the Nature and Growth of a Cultural Tradition.* London: Routledge and Kegan Paul, 1955.

———. *Muhammadan Festivals.* New York: Henry Schuman, 1951.

———. "The Nature of Arabic Unity Before Islam." *Arabica,* no. 10 (1964): 5–23.

———. "Some Recent Constructions and Reconstructions of Islam." In *The Conflict of Traditionalism and Modernism in the Muslim Middle East,* edited by Carl Leiden, 141–60. Austin: University of Texas Press, 1966.

von Humboldt, Wilhelm. "On the Historian's Task." *History and Theory* 6, no. 1 (1967): 57–71.

Wagner, Ewald. *Grundzüge der klassischen arabischen Dichtung.* Vol. 1. Darmstadt: Wissenschaftliche Buchgelsellschaft, 1987.

al-Wāḥidī, Abū al- Ḥasan ʿAlī. *Asbāb al-Nuzūl.* Edited by ʿIṣām ibn ʿAbd al-Muḥsin al-Ḥumaydān. Dammam: Dār al-Iṣlāḥ, 1992.

Wansbrough, John. *Quranic Studies: Sources and Methods of Scriptural Interpretations.* Oxford: Oxford University Press, 1977.

———. Review of *Hagarism,* by Patricia Crone: *Bulletin of the School of Oriental and African Studies* 41, no. 1 (1978): 155–56.

———. *The Sectarian Milieu: Content and Composition of Islamic Salvation History.* New York: Oxford University Press, 1979.

Watt, William Montgomery. *Muhammad at Mecca.* Oxford: Clarendon Press, 1960.

———. *Muhammad at Medina.* Oxford: Oxford University Press, 1956.

———. *Muslim-Christian Encounters: Perceptions and Misperceptions.* London: Routledge, 1991.

Weil, Gustav. *Historisch-kritische Einleitung in den Koran.* Leipzig, Velhagen & Klasing, 1844.

———. *Mohammed der Prophet, sein Leben und seine Lehre.* Stuttgart: Metzler, 1843.

Wheeler, Brannon M. *Moses in the Qurʾan and Islamic Exegesis.* New York: Routledge, 2002.

Wickham, Chris. *Framing the Early Middle Ages: Europe and the Mediterranean, 400–800.* Oxford: Oxford University Press, 2007.

Wills, Garry. *What the Qurʾan Meant and Why It Matters.* New York: Penguin Books, 2018.

Winder, R. Bayly. "Four Decades of Middle Eastern Study." *Middle East Journal* 41, no. 1 (1987): 40–63.

Yāqūt al-Ḥamawī. *Muʿjam al-Buldān.* 5 vols. Beirut: Dār Ṣādir, 1977.

Young, Robert. *White Mythologies: Writing History and the West.* London: Routledge, 1990.

al-Zabīdī, Muḥammad Murtaḍá. *Tāj al-ʿArūs min Jawāhir al-Qāmūs.* Vol. 5, edited by Muṣṭafá Ḥijāzī. Kuwait: Maṭbaʿa-t Ḥukūma-t- al-Kuwait, 2004.

al-Zajjāj, Abū Isḥāq. *Maʿānī al-Qurʾān.* 5 vols. Edited by ʿAbd al-Jalīl ʿAbduh Shalabī. Beirut: ʿĀlam al-Kutub, 1988.

al-Zamakhsharī, Abū al-Qāsim Maḥmūd. *Asās al-Balāgha.* Beirut: Dār Ṣādir, n.d.

al-Zarkashī, Badr al-Dīn Muḥammad ibn ʿAbd Allāh. *Al-Burhān fī ʿUlūm al-Qurʾān.* Edited by Abū al-Faḍl al-Dumyāṭī. Cairo: Dār al-Ḥadīth, 2006.

al-Zawzanī, Abū ʿAbd Allāh al-Ḥusayn. *Sharḥ al-Muʿallaqāt al-Sabʿ.* Beirut: al-Dār al-ʿĀlamiyya, 1992.

al-Zayn, Aḥmad, ed. *Dīwān al-Hudhaliyyīn.* Cairo: Maṭbaʿa-t-Dār al-Kutub al-Miṣriyya, 1945.

Zellentin, Holger Michael. *The Qurʾan's Legal Culture: The Didascalia Apostolorum as a Point of Departure.* Tübingen: Mohr Siebeck, 2013.

———, ed. *The Qurʾan's Reformation of Judaism and Christianity: Return to the Origins.* New York: Routledge, 2019.

———. "The Rise of Monotheism in Arabia." In *A Companion to Religion in Late Antiquity,* edited by Josef Lössl and Nicholas J. Baker-Brian, 158–80. London: John Wiley & Sons, 2018.

al-Zubaydī, Abū Bakr. *Ṭabaqāt al-Naḥwiyyīn wa-l-Lughawiyyīn*. Edited by Muḥammad Abū Faḍl Ibrāhīm. Cairo, 1984.

Zuhayr ibn Abī Sulmá. *Dīwān Zuhayr ibn Abī Sulmá*. Edited by Ḥasan Fāʿūr. Beirut: Dār al-Kutub al-ʿIlmiyya, 1988.

Zwettler, Michael. *The Oral Tradition of Classical Arabic Poetry: Its Character and Implications*. Columbus: Ohio State University Press, 1978.

naẓm, 56, 123, 139, 142

Neil, Bronwen, 6–7

Neoplatonism, 10, 28. *See also* philosophy

Neuwirth, Angelika, 1–4, 201n12; *The Qur'an as a Text of Late Antiquity*, 2–4, 7, 11, 24–29, 34, 38, 41–44–45, 50, 173–74, 177

New Cambridge Ancient History, 39

Nicholson, Reynold, 79, 84, 96; *A Literary History of the Arabs*, 80–81, 190n13

Nietzsche, Friedrich, 51–52

night, Qur'ānic, 65–67. See also *layl*

nihilism, 75

Noah, 145, 147, 158

Nöldeke, Theodor, 54, 101, 181n9; "Geschichte des Qorān" (doctoral dissertation), 17

nūr, 112

orality: of Arabic aesthetics, 78, 82–83, 96; of classical Arabic poetry, 78, 82; of the Qur'ān, 77–78, 119–20, 126. *See also* aesthetics

orientalism, 29, 37–40, 44, 50, 178, 182n36, 192n69; classical, 7, 37, 46, 49, 79

paganism, 28, 31

paideia, 98–99, 101, 104, 115

panegyric, 82, 142. *See also* classical Arabic poetry

pathetic fallacy, 60–61, 64, 66–68

patristics, 50

Persia, 33

Petra, 35

philosophy: Aristotelian influence in Islamic, 48; classical Muslim, 12; pre-Islamic Arabian poetic, 92. *See also* Neoplatonism

Pickthall, Marmaduke, 10

piety, 47

Pirenne, Henri, 31–32

plagiarism, 49

Plato, 101, 138, 193n2; critical examination of poetry of, 137, 143; *Phaedrus*, 137; *Republic*, 137, 143

polytheism, 110, 119; Hellenistic, 101; Meccan, 124, 141; monotheistic community emerging in the midst of, 121, 148, 166; primitive, 166–67; and tribalism, 124

postcolonialism, 5, 13, 46

postmodernism, 1, 51, 147

poverty, 134

power: and historical inquiry, 12; of literature, 10; Qur'ānic discourse of, 68; rhetoric of, 64, 68

pre-Islamic Arabic literature, 13, 42, 45, 53, 171; poetry, 7–13, 36, 42–47, 53–75, 80–115, 120, 124–44, 169, 172, 187n13, 192n54; prose, 22, 42, 57, 124, 142. *See also* Arabic language; classical Arabic poetry; pre-Islamic Arabs

pre-Islamic Arabs, 9, 17, 57, 73–74, 89; annals that record the deeds and history of, 144; culture and religion of, 47; literary and poetic sensibility of, 9, 96, 102, 131; Northern, 57; peninsular Arabic sources for the literary traditions and social habits of, 26; social and linguistic habits of, 96; Southern, 57; spread of belief in the day of judgment among, 192n54. *See also* Arabia; pre-Islamic Arabic literature

pre-Islamic Bedouins, 57, 188n24

Pretzl, Otto, 17

Prideaux, Humphrey: *True Nature of Imposture Revealed in the Life of the Impostor Mohammad*, 184n15

prolepsis, 71

prophecies, 47; and divine justice, 176–77; of Muḥammad, 130; of Noah, 145; proof of, 56. *See also* Qur'ān

qaṣīda, 55, 61–62, 72, 74, 82, 88, 136; pre-Islamic, 100, 124–25, 130–31. *See also* classical Arabic poetry

qawlan thaqīlan, 157

qayn, 132

qīnatun, 132

qiṭaʿ shiʿrīyya, 134

Qur'ān: antimaterialistic view of the world of the, 109; Arabicity of the, 1–6, 11, 23, 38–46, 76–77, 84–85, 96, 101, 121, 126, 140, 143, 167, 169, 172, 175–78; Arabic prehistory of the, 53, 142, 144, 187n13; *Āyāt al-Taḥaddī* (Verses of Challenge) of the, 95; *balāgha* of the, 4, 9; biographical references to Muḥammad in the, 4, 132–44, 148, 151; Christians in the, 117–18; as complement to a historical chain of monotheistic prophethood, 120; death in the, 64; as dialectical text, 24; as discourse of difference, 125–26; elegance and the commanding presence of the language of the, 167, 169; ethical value and authority of the, 33, 97–115; Euro-American scholarship on the, 1–26, 38, 41, 45–46, 50–51, 79, 84, 96, 101, 120–21, 171, 174–78, 180n19; European translations of the, 10; generic autonomy of the, 123–24; inevitability in the, 63–64; as integral part of the religious history of the West, 38; Islamic linguistic and rhetorical scholarship on the, 11, 76; as key source

Founded in 1893,
UNIVERSITY OF CALIFORNIA PRESS
publishes bold, progressive books and journals
on topics in the arts, humanities, social sciences,
and natural sciences—with a focus on social
justice issues—that inspire thought and action
among readers worldwide.

The UC PRESS FOUNDATION
raises funds to uphold the press's vital role
as an independent, nonprofit publisher, and
receives philanthropic support from a wide
range of individuals and institutions—and from
committed readers like you. To learn more, visit
ucpress.edu/supportus.

www.ingramcontent.com/pod-product-compliance
Ingram Content Group UK Ltd.
Pitfield, Milton Keynes, MK11 3LW, UK
UKHW030956260625
460065UK00001B/1